Media Literacy in a Disru Media Environment

This book, part of the BEA Electronic Media Research Series, brings together top scholars researching media literacy and lays out the current state of the field in areas such as propaganda, news, participatory culture, representation, education, social/environmental justice, and civic engagement.

The field of media literacy continues to undergo changes and challenges as audiences are reconceptualized and reconfigured, media industries are transformed and replaced, and the production of media texts is available to anyone with a smartphone. The book provides an overview of these. It offers readers specific examples and recommendations to help others as they develop their own teaching and research agendas.

Media Literacy in a Disruptive Media Environment will be of great interest to scholars and graduate students studying media literacy through the lens of broadcasting, communication studies, media and cultural studies, film, and digital media studies.

William G. Christ is Professor Emeritus at Trinity University. He has been writing about media education for over forty years. He has edited or co-authored six books and over 65 articles and book chapters. His interests lie in bridging the gap between the liberal arts and professional education, and the challenges of assessing student learning.

Belinha S. De Abreu is an International Media Literacy Educator in the United States. Her research interests include media and information literacy education, educational technology, global perspectives, critical thinking, privacy, and big data. She is the author/editor of several papers/books including: *Teaching Media Literacy* (ALA: Neal-Schuman, 2019) and *The International Handbook for Media Literacy Education* (Routledge, 2017). She serves as the Vice President for the National Telemedia Council (NTC) and is the founder of the International Media Literacy Research Symposium.

Electronic Media Research Series
Sponsored by the Broadcast Education Association
Robert K. Avery and Donald G. Godfrey, Series Editors

Media Literacy in a Disruptive Media Environment

Edited by
William G. Christ and
Belinha S. De Abreu

Routledge
Taylor & Francis Group

NEW YORK AND LONDON

First published 2020
by Routledge
605 Third Avenue, New York, NY 10017

and by Routledge
2 Park Square, Milton Park, Abingdon, Oxon OX14 4RN

First issued in paperback 2022

Routledge is an imprint of the Taylor & Francis Group, an informa business

Publisher's Note
The publisher has gone to great lengths to ensure the quality of this reprint but points out that some imperfections in the original copies may be apparent.

Library of Congress Cataloging-in-Publication Data
A catalog record has been requested for this book

ISBN 13: 978-1-03-240046-4 (pbk)
ISBN 13: 978-0-367-41485-6 (hbk)
ISBN 13: 978-0-367-81476-2 (ebk)

DOI: 10.4324/9780367814762

Typeset in Sabon
by codeMantra

WGC
To all the teachers who work every day in the trenches

BSD
For my global media literacy colleagues around the world.
You have taught me so much.

Contents

Figure

Tables

Contributors

Rasha Allam is a graduate of the Department of Journalism and Mass Communication (BA-2002, MA-2005), School of Global Affairs and Public Policy at the American University in Cairo. She is an Honorary Alumni of the Annenberg School for Communication, University of Pennsylvania, and a graduate of the Oxford University program of Media Laws and Regulations. Her Doctorate, in Business Administration (DBA), is from Maastricht School of Management (2011), with specialization in media management.

Allam's research interests and publications focus on the Egyptian and Arab media management systems, Arab broadcast media laws and regulations, media monitoring, media and elections, freedom of speech, and freedom of the press in the Middle East.

For years, Allam has a weekly column on different regional newspapers, and in 2012 she introduced the Twitter debate, Engaging with your Readers on Twitter to the Egyptian media organizations. Allam acts also as a business consultant for different media organizations, where she contributes to the development of their business models and organizational restructure.

Jairo Becerra is professor and director of the Centro de Investigaciones Socio Jurídicas in the College of Law at the Universidad Católica de Colombia. He teaches public international law and air and space regulation, and researches information and communications technologies (ICT) and cyber law. He is also the former advisor to the general secretary of the Colombian Space Commission and is member of the International Institute of Space Law (IISL).

Natasha Casey is associate professor of communications at Blackburn College (Carlinville, Illinois, USA) where she teaches media and information literacy, communication theory and other courses in the English and Communications department. She holds a Ph.D. in communication studies from McGill University (Montreal, Quebec, Canada). Her research interests include critical race theory and critical media and information literacy. She currently serves on the editorial advisory board for the Journal of Media Literacy Education. Read her media and information literacy blog, "No Silos" at www. natashacasey.com.

William G. Christ, who was Chair of Trinity University's Department of Communication for 12 years and General Manager of the jazz radio station KRTU-FM for 14 years, has been writing about media education for over 40 years. He has written or edited 6 books and has published or presented over 125 book chapters, articles, essays, and papers on media representation, education, literacy, and assessment. He has held leadership positions in three national and international associations and served on the editorial boards of two prestigious journals. In 1999, he was named the International Radio and Television Society Foundation Professor of the Year. In 2006, he received Trinity University's Distinguished University and Community Service Award. In 2012, the Broadcast Education Association Distinguished Education Service Award, which is given to an individual "who has made a significant and lasting contribution to the American system of electronic media education," was awarded to Christ.

Marthinus Conradie holds a Ph.D. in inferential pragmatics from the University of the Free State (South Africa), where he is currently employed at the Department of English. His research interests emanate from Foucauldian discourse analysis and its application to everyday political argumentation, the construction of race and racism, as well as whiteness. His publications include analyses of South African students' online discussions of personal experiences of racial discrimination on university campuses, citizens' online deliberations via asynchronous news forums, as well as media depictions of Africa in print advertising. He has also dabbled in theologically rooted commentary on race-relevant issues. At present, his strongest interests center on blame attribution and political argumentation in online spaces.

Sherri Hope Culver serves as Director of the Center for Media and Information Literacy at Temple University, where she is an Associate Professor in the Klein College of Media and Communication. Sherri is a three-term past president of the National Association for Media Literacy Education.

George L. Daniels (Ph.D., University of Georgia) is an Associate Professor of journalism and creative media and Assistant Dean for Administration in the College of Communication and Information Sciences at the University of Alabama. A former local television news producer, Daniels is certified by the Journalism Education Association as a Master Journalism Educator. His research areas include diversity in media workplace and community-engaged scholarship. His work has appeared in journals such as *Journalism & Mass Communication Quarterly, Visual Communication Quarterly, Southwestern Mass Communication Journal,* and *Journal of Applied Communication Research.*

Ramin Chaboki Darzabi is a Ph.D. student in Communication at Texas A&M University. His research areas are media literacy, online activism, digital media, identity, and stereotype reduction. His master's thesis was on developing media literacy in Iran.

Belinha S. De Abreu is an international Media Literacy Educator with a Ph.D. in Curriculum and Instruction focusing on media literacy education. Her research interests include new media, visual and information literacy, global perspectives, data privacy, critical thinking, digital citizenship, youth, and teacher training. She is the author of *Teaching Media Literacy* (2019), co-author of *Mobile Learning through Digital Media Literacy* (2017), and co-editor of and contributor to the *International Handbook of Media Literacy Education* (2017) and *Global Media Literacy in a Digital Age* (2016). She serves as Vice President for the National Telemedia Council and is the founder of the International Media Literacy Research Symposium, which has been held in the United States and in Portugal. Follow @belmedia.

Aaron Delwiche (Ph.D. University of Washington) is a Professor in the Department of Communication at Trinity University in San Antonio, Texas. He teaches courses on topics such as game development, transmedia storytelling, and political propaganda. The co-editor of the *Participatory Cultures Handbook* (Routledge, 2012), Aaron's recent work includes a chapter about the history of computer bulletin board systems in the *Sage Handbook of Social Media* and an article about the rise of the "fake audience" for the *Sage Handbook of Propaganda*. In 2018, with support from the Mellon Foundation, Aaron overhauled the 25-year-old site Propaganda Critic, adding nearly two dozen articles exploring the emergence of computational propaganda, explaining common propaganda techniques, and teaching users how to identify bots, trolls, and sockpuppets in online spaces.

Salma ElGhetany currently works as Executive Assistant to director at the Kamal Adham Center for Television and Digital Journalism, School of Global Affairs and Public Policy, AUC. She received her M.A. in Journalism and Mass Communication from the American University in Cairo (AUC) in 2017. Her thesis study was on the Challenges and Policies of Media Literacy Education in Egyptian Schools. She received her B.A. summa cum laude from AUC in 2008, majoring in Journalism and Mass Communication. ElGhetany was awarded AUC's President's Cup (2008).

ElGhetany is considered among Egypt's media literacy experts, not only because of her postgraduate degree in the field but due to her participation in international platforms: she participated in the Broadcast Education Association twice, one in 2018 and again in 2019, both with presentations and papers on media literacy in Egypt. She is currently a reviewer with the *Journal of Media Literacy Education.*

Regionally, ElGhetany attended the Media and Digital Literacy Academy in Beirut (MDLAB 2017), which is a two-week intensive lecture and workshop camp that teaches media and digital literacy competencies on both theoretical and practical levels.

Locally, ElGhetany is planning a media literacy/education project in collaboration with the Ministry of Education and Dr. Tarek Shawki, Egyptian Minister of Education, who served as an external reader for ElGhetany's MA thesis. She has delivered lectures on critical media literacy skills at the Egyptian Ministry of Education and the American University in Cairo for Egyptian teachers of elementary grade levels.

She is currently manager of a project in partnership with UNICEF and the Supreme Council for Media Regulation, on media regulation for families and children.

ElGhetany is a professional certified trainer after receiving her PCT certificate in March 2018 from AUC. Before joining AUC, ElGhetany was a marketing officer at the Asset Management Department at HC Securities & Investment (2008–2010). She also worked as a freelance writer/editor for several publishing companies, including A.R. Group, Liquid, and ADLife Magazine.

Jennifer Fleming is a Professor in the Department of Journalism & Public Relations at California State University, Long Beach. Dr. Fleming's research focuses on news literacy, media literacy and journalism education. Her work is published in Journalism & Mass Communication Educator, Journal of Media Literacy Education, Journalism Education and others. She holds a doctorate in education from the University of California, Los Angeles. Before joining academe, Dr. Fleming worked at CTV National News where she contributed as a writer and producer to two of Canada's most watched news and current affairs programs, CTV National News with Lloyd Robertson and Canada AM.

Christopher Harris is an Associate Professor of Communication and Department Chair for Social Sciences & Business in the School of Liberal Arts & Sciences at Nevada State College. He hails from central New Jersey and earned his B.A. in Psychology from Rutgers University in 2001. He then attended Cornell University's Africana Studies & Research Center, achieving a Master's in Professional Studies (M.P.S.) degree in 2004. After taking several years off from school to run an innovative after-school program for inner-city middle-school children in his hometown, Dr. Harris conducted his doctoral studies at the University of Miami, graduating with a Ph.D. in Communication Studies in 2010. Dr. Harris has been an active member of the NSC community since his arrival, contributing to numerous strategic planning committees; representing the school on state-wide initiatives on diversity, ethnicity, and inclusion; serving a term as Faculty Senate Chair; and currently serving as the Department Chair for Social Sciences & Business.

Dr. Harris' research interests include fine-de-siècle rap music and neo-soul, critical pedagogy, media portrayals of ethnicity/race, and the relationship/interplay between power and discourse in contemporary society. He has won top paper awards at both the Broadcast Educator's Association and the National Communication Association (student) annual conventions; is a co-author of an article on the portrayal of women of color by reality television published in the *International Journal on Women's Studies*; and recently published an article on teaching content-analysis and critically vigilant media consumption in *Communication Teacher.*

Jennifer J. Henderson is a professor and chair of the Department of Communication at Trinity University in San Antonio, Texas. Her research addresses issues of media law, the ethics of media, and the use of participatory cultures for political and social action. Jennifer is co-editor of the 2012 Routledge *Participatory Cultures Handbook*. Her recent research includes book chapters in *The Rise of the Transtexts*, which proposes a new copyright scheme to accommodate increasingly common remixed and transmedia narratives, in *Social Media and the Law* on the new boundaries of free speech in social media, and in *The SAGE Guide to Key Issues in Mass Media Ethics & Law* on the new First Amendment, as well as a co-authored article analyzing the female protagonists in Marvel's Runaways in the *Journal of Graphic Novels and Comics*.

Mary Margaret Herring is a philosophy and communication major at Trinity University, and she expects to graduate in May 2020. Her essay titled "Rationality, Desire, and the Good Life" won second place in the Hemlock Competition sponsored by the Trinity University Department of Philosophy. Fascinated with dystopian visions and extremist politics, she values the role of authentic deliberation in sustaining the public sphere. In 2018, Mary Margaret earned a summer research grant from the Mellon Initiative.

Christopher Karadjov is an Associate Professor in the Department of Journalism & Public Relations at California State University, Long Beach. Dr. Karadjov's research has covered media effects, journalism practices, and online media. His articles have been published in *Journalism and Mass Communication Quarterly, Journalism Studies, Public Relations Research, Acta Sapienta,* and others. Before receiving his doctorate from the University of Florida, he worked as a reporter and editor in various publications in Bulgaria and the United States. Dr. Karadjov maintains an active schedule of media writing and appearances in television and radio news shows in Bulgaria, Russia, and the United States.

Michelle Ciulla Lipkin is the Executive Director of the National Association for Media Literacy Education. Under her direction, NAMLE has grown from 300 members to 5,000+, launched U.S. Media Literacy Week, and hosted four national conferences as well as countless local gatherings to promote media literacy. Michelle also teaches at Brooklyn College.

Paul Mihailidis is an associate professor of civic media and journalism in the school of communication at Emerson College in Boston, MA, where he teaches media literacy, civic media, and community activism. He is founding program director of the MA in Media Design, Senior Fellow of the Emerson Engagement Lab, and faculty chair and director of the Salzburg Academy on Media and Global Change. His research focuses on the nexus of media, education, and civic voices. His newest books, *Civic Media Literacies* (Routledge 2018) and *Civic Media: Technology, Design, Practice* (2016, MIT Press, with Eric Gordon), outline effective practices for engagement and action taking in daily civic life. His work has been featured in the *New York Times,* the *Washington Post, Slate Magazine,* the *Nieman Foundation, USA Today,* CNN, and others. Mihailidis holds a visiting professorship at Bournemouth University in England and the Catholic University of Argentina, Buenos Aires. He sits on the advisory board for iCivics. He earned his Ph.D. from the Philip Merrill College of Journalism at the University of Maryland, College Park.

Paula Pérez is an attorney at Rubiano López & Associates in Bogotá, Colombia, and a Colciencias research fellow with the College of Law at the Universidad Católica de Colombia. Her research work focuses on public law and information and communication technologies (ICT) with an emphasis on development of digital tools for media literacy.

W. James Potter is a professor in the Department of Communication at the University of California at Santa Barbara. He has produced more than 100 scholarly publications, including 27 books, and has served as the editor of the *Journal of Broadcasting & Electronic Media.* One of his areas of scholarship has been media literacy, where he has published *Introduction to Media Literacy* (2015) and *The Skills of Media Literacy* (2019). His book *Media Literacy* is now in its 9th Edition and is the bestselling book on this topic in the world. He has also done considerable work with media theory, where he has published books such as *Theory of Media Literacy: A Cognitive Approach* (2004), *Media Effects* (2012), *Arguing for a General Framework for Mass Media Scholarship* (2009), *An Analysis of Thinking and Research about Qualitative Methods* (1996), and *An Analysis and Evaluation of Major Theories of Media Effects* (2020). He holds a Ph.D. in Communication from Florida State University and a second Ph.D. in Instructional Systems Technology from Indiana University.

Srividya "Srivi" Ramasubramanian (Ph.D., Penn State University) is Professor of Communication at Texas A&M University. Her research focuses on critical media literacy, social justice, media activism, prejudice reduction, diversity, and identity. She was awarded the 2017 Outstanding Media Literacy Research Award by the National Association for Media Literacy Education.

Theresa Redmond, Associate Professor at Appalachian State University, teaches in Media Studies and Teacher Education. Her research focuses on curriculum and pedagogy in teaching and learning with, through, and about media and technology, with emphasis on cultivating students' preparation, fluency, and empowerment in through creative inquiry and expression.

Julián Rodríguez is a broadcast journalism specialist in the Department of Communication at The University of Texas at Arlington (UTA). He teaches television news with an emphasis on Hispanic-American media, researches Hispanic media in the United States and the adoption of new and emerging media technologies to develop and nurture awareness systems, and is the faculty advisor of the UTA Hispanic Media Initiative, a program focusing on the advancement of Hispanic media education, journalist, and research (more at www.utahispanicmedia.com).

Tania Cantrell Rosas-Moreno (Ph.D. University of Texas at Austin with a Portfolio in Nonprofit Studies, BA with University Honors & M.A. Top Scholar at Brigham Young University) is an interdisciplinary scholar of Communication and Latin American/ Latino Studies at Loyola University, Maryland, where she also serves as co-chair of her host Communication Department. She is the author of numerous publications, primarily about international news media with a directed interest in Brazil. Given her professional background in public relations and her commitment to social justice issues, she is the recipient of many academic and professional awards, most recently having been named a Ragan's Top Women in Communications 2020 Honoree. Rosas-Moreno also serves as an assistant editor for Brazilian Journalism Research and is a co-founding editor and current board member of *The Agenda-Setting Journal: Theory, Practice, Critique.*

Kristy Roschke is managing director of the News Co/Lab, an initiative aimed at helping people better understand how news works, at ASU's Walter Cronkite School of Journalism and Mass Communication. She has a Ph.D. in journalism with a focus on media literacy from ASU. Roschke has taught journalism, digital media production, and media literacy courses at the high-school and university level for more than 15 years. She previously served as executive director of KJZZ's SPOT 127 Youth Media Center, a community initiative of the Phoenix NPR member station that mentors and empowers the next generation of digital storytellers.

Jeff Share worked for ten years as a freelance photojournalist, documenting situations of poverty and social activism on three continents. After leaving journalism, he entered the elementary-school classroom to teach bilingual education in the Los Angeles Unified School District for seven years. Then he joined the Center for Media Literacy as the Regional Coordinator for Training funded by a federal media literacy grant. Once the grant ended, he returned to school to earn his Ph.D. in the Graduate School of Education and Information Studies at UCLA, where he has been working with new teachers ever since. His research and practice focus on the teaching of critical media literacy in K-12 education. Share is currently a faculty advisor in the Teacher Education Program at UCLA. In 2019, Brill/Sense published *The Critical Media Literacy Guide: Engaging Media and Transforming Education*, which Share co-wrote with Douglas Kellner.

Moses Shumow[†], Ph.D., is Associate Professor of Journalism and Digital Design at Emerson College, USA. His research examines the intersections between media, geography, and race, focusing on inequality and development in marginalized space. Dr. Shumow is the co-author of *News, Neoliberalism, and Miami's Fragmented Urban Space* (Lexington Books), and his work has been published in *Journalism, Journalism Studies, Media, Culture, & Society* and *Journal of Urban Affairs*, among others.

Robert N. Spicer is Assistant Professor of Digital Journalism at Millersville University. His primary area of research is in media and political culture. His dissertation, which he defended in June of 2014 at the Rutgers University School of Communication & Information, is titled The Discourses and Practices of Political Deception: From Campaigns to Cable to the Courts. Spicer's secondary area of research is in emerging media and philosophy of technology. His most recent publications are Long-Distance Caring Labor: Fatherhood, Smiles, and Affect in the Marketing of the iPhone 4 and FaceTime in the journal Techne: Research in Philosophy and Technology and his book Free Speech and False Speech: Political Deception and its Legal Limits (or lack thereof) for Palgrave (April 2018).

Federico Subervi-Vélez (Ph.D. University of Wisconsin, B.A. & M.A. University of Puerto Rico) developed during 33 years of his professional career as a professor at universities in the United States and as visiting professor at various universities in Brazil, Chile, Germany, and Spain. He is the author of numerous publications, primarily about Latinos and media in the United States. In 2018 he was the Visiting Leverhulme Professor at the School of Media and Communication at the University of Leeds, United Kingdom, where he wrote most of the manuscript for his (forthcoming) book: *The News Media in Puerto Rico: Journalism in Colonial Settings and Times of Crisis.* Subervi-Vélez is currently Co-Editor-in-Chief of The *Oxford Encyclopedia of Race, Ethnicity and Communication*, scheduled for publication in 2022. He is also Honorary Associate/Fellow of the Latin American, Caribbean and Iberian Studies Program at the University of Wisconsin-Madison. From his home in Austin, Texas, he continues his work as a media scholar and consultant dedicating time to collaborative research with colleagues in Puerto Rico and other countries while also participating in the Worlds of Journalism Study.

Kathleen Tyner was Associate Professor in the Department of Radio-Television-Film at The University of Texas at Austin (USA) from 2004 to 2019. She publishes, lectures, and works internationally with programs related to the media arts, digital literacy, and game-based learning. Tyner is author, co-author, and editor of numerous books, articles, and curricular materials, including *Play2Learn Proceedings* (Gamilearning, 2018), *Media Literacy* (Routledge, 2010), and *Literacy in a Digital World: Teaching and Learning in the Age of Information* (Erlbaum, 1998). She consults with non-profit organizations, museums, and NGOs to support community media research and development projects for education, health communication, civic participation, and the arts. Her public service and research projects include work with Mirabel Pictures and WeOwnTV in Sierra Leone, Optic Flare, the U.S. Embassy in Spain, and GamiLearning in Portugal. She is also a member of editorial boards and scientific committees for publications such as *Revista Communicar* (Spain).

Series Editor's Foreword

Since its inception in 1948, the Broadcast Education Association has fostered a serious commitment to scholarly research, though that commitment became more formalized with the publication of its first scholarly journal, *Journal of Broadcasting* (later *Journal of Broadcasting & Electronic Media*), in 1957. Over the Association's rich intellectual history, BEA's annual meetings have afforded both academics and professionals with a wide range of opportunities for the presentation of important scholarship focusing on broadcasting and the electronic media.

In 2008, BEA launched a new series of programs designed to advance original research initiatives under the direction of the Association's Research Committee. The name of this new scholarly venture within the framework of the annual conference is the BEA Research Symposium Series, and over the past twelve years it has served to advance the research agendas of our discipline and provide a forum for some of the leading scholars and latest ground-breaking research in our field. The first Research Symposium in 2008 was orchestrated by Professor Jennings Bryant with a focus on Media Effects. This was followed in 2009 with a Research Symposium on the subject of TechnoPolitics, under the direction of Professor Linda Kaid.

In response to these two highly successful symposia, discussions began in 2010 between BEA and the Taylor and Francis Group of Routledge to form a partnership to enable the publication of an annual volume resulting from the yearly BEA Research Symposium. That new scholarly publication venture is the Electronic Media Research Series, with cutting-edge seminal publications that offer an in-depth cross section of significant research topics. The 2010 Research Symposium Chair was Andrew C. Billings, and hence the first volume in the new series edited by Professor Billings was *Sports Media: Transformation, Integration, Consumption* published in 2011. The 2011 Research Symposium Chair, Ron Tamborini, edited the second volume, *Media and the Moral Mind*, released in 2012. The third volume growing out of the 2012 Research Symposium published in 2013 was edited by Alan B. Albarran and is titled, *Media Management and Economics Research in a Transmedia Environment.* The fourth volume, *Media and Social Life,* was co-edited by Arthur A. Raney and Mary Beth Oliver and was published in 2014.

The fifth volume, titled *Digital Technology and the Future of Broadcasting: Global Perspectives,* edited by Professor John V. Pavlik, Rutgers University, was released in 2015. *Race and Gender in Electronic Media: Content, Context, Culture* resulted from the 2015 Research Symposium and was published in 2016. This volume, the sixth of the symposia series, was edited by Rebecca Ann Lind, University of Illinois at Chicago. The series' seventh volume developed from a BEA Research Symposium on risk and health communication. Released in 2018 and edited by H. Dan O'Hair, University of Kentucky, the collection of essays is titled *Risk and Health Communication in an Evolving Media Environment.* The eighth volume in the BEA Research series was also released in 2018. Titled *Video Games: A Medium That Demands Our Attention,* the volume was edited by Nicholas Bowman. *The Golden Age of Data,* edited by Don A. Grady, Elon University, resulted from the 2019 Research Symposium. This volume offers a cutting-edge perspective on how big data and analytics now make it possible for researchers and industry professionals to quantify media content and audience usage.

The present volume, titled *Media Literacy in a Disruptive Media Environment,* resulted from the 2019 Research Symposium chaired by William G. Christ, Trinity University; Belinha S. De Abreu, Sacred Heart University; and Michelle Ciulla Lipkin, Executive Director, National Association for Media Literacy Education. This newest addition to the BEA Electronic Media Research Series, edited by Professors Christ and De Abreu, contains selected papers from the Symposium and essays written especially for this publication. The chapters in this book examine the current state of media literacy in a range of areas, including propaganda, news, and big data, among others. The chapters also address media literacy's relationship with social/environmental justice, civic engagement, and higher education media programs. This volume is meant to provide an overview to current applications in media literacy, while also offering recommendations to help others with their teaching and research agendas. The Broadcast Education Association and Routledge are proud to make this important volume available to scholars and teachers across the communication discipline and beyond.

Glenda Balas, October 2019
Professor and former Dean of Liberal Arts and Sciences
University of North Texas at Dallas

Foreword

The 2016 presidential election is often cited as a catalyst for the unparalleled attention paid to media literacy education, particularly in the United States but also internationally. In the subsequent three years media literacy has been depicted as both savior and nefarious cause of our "information polluted" environment, to use Claire Wardle's term (Giuliani-Hoffman, 2017). It has been heralded as a panacea for so-called "fake news" and demonized for creating overly skeptical students who question everything and believe nothing. (According to a Pew Research report (Stocking, 2019), Americans cited "fake news" as a bigger issue than violent crime, climate change, racism, illegal immigration, terrorism, and sexism.)

In the clamor to defend or belittle media literacy neither oversimplified position sheds much light on how to best understand media literacy education as a multidisciplinary area of study, a pedagogical approach and activism. Enter William G. Christ and Belinha S. De Abreu's well-timed collection that incorporates all these facets of media literacy and more.

While some believe a uniform definition of media literacy and "standards" (just typing this word sends shudders down my spine) will help move the field forward (and I realize even the use of "field" is contentious), there are competing definitions and many different, sometimes ideologically opposed, ways to approach it. And as you turn the pages, some of those competing epistemologies and ideologies will be evident. You will also see the varying ways media literacy is theoretically conceptualized and practically operationalized in the United States and around the world. It is these contradictions and differences that make media literacy education a robust, dynamic, and constantly evolving area of study.

Despite obvious differences in terms of approaches, traditions, influences, and contexts, a number of chapters in this collection are in useful conversation with one another. For example, Belinha De Abreu's call for an alliance between global awareness and media literacy dovetails nicely into case studies based in South Africa, Egypt, and Colombia. International media literacy approaches have long shaped U.S. versions, and it is important that these perspectives continue to be juxtaposed alongside emerging U.S. media literacy narratives. International perspectives can also help disrupt the dominant "Eurocentric White hegemonic aspects" of media literacy, to borrow Srivi Ramasubramanian and Ramin Chaboki Darzabi's phrase from their insightful chapter in this collection.

As I write this, connections between big data and children are making headlines as Google was fined a paltry $170 million for collecting data from youth without parental permission (*The Guardian*, 2019). Several authors discuss the challenges of "big data" (a phrase aptly complicated by Kathleen Tyner) and the ways in which it presents both challenges and opportunities for media literacy education. Children and the ways in which media corrupts them has long been a central focus particularly for the protectionist wing of media literacy in the United States, but a couple of chapters in this collection carefully consider long neglected populations, including senior citizens and adult learners outside of formal education settings. Senior citizens especially warrant closer examination as almost half in the United States use Facebook (Gramlich, 2019), and as a study recently argued, older Americans were seven times more likely to share so-called "fake news" stories in the run-up to the 2016 presidential election than 18–29-year-olds (Guess, Nagler & Tucker, 2019). This reality is often overlooked as those "dang kids today" and their social media use drives too many moral panic-infused media literacy conversations.

A distinctive feature of Christ and De Abreu's collection is the inclusion of theoretical arguments and perspectives alongside practical applications of media literacy. What can and does it look like in the classroom? Aaron Delwiche and Mary Margaret Herring discuss their work on the website *Propaganda Critic* and offer a myriad of ways in which this resource can be used in the classroom. Bill Christ convincingly demonstrates the overlap between media literacy and professional media education student-learning outcomes, highlighting their compatibility, and in doing so, he provides a powerful argument for the incorporation of media literacy into potentially hundreds, if not thousands, of communications programs around the United States and beyond.

Another standout aspect of Christ and De Abreu's collection is their incorporation of scholarship from both "mainstream" media literacy and critical media literacy camps. There are significant differences between the two as the latter draws on critical theory, cultural studies, and critical pedagogy traditions to shape their media literacy perspectives and practices. Christ and De Abreu realize the value of bringing both of these approaches to the collection. This is a timely move as arguably critical media literacy is gaining ground within U.S. media literacy more generally as evidenced by international critical media literacy conferences, journals (*International Journal of Critical Media Literacy*), and books

(Kellner & Share, 2019) dedicated to it, not to mention the sizable number of attendees with an interest in this area at NAMLE's (the National Association for Media Literacy Education) conference in 2019 in Washington, DC. In this collection, calls to draw on hooks, Freire, and DuBois to challenge and critique the skills-based assumptions of mainstream media literacy; calls to incorporate activism and anti-oppression pedagogy; and, a passionate plea to examine environmental justice issues are just some of the chapters that take this critical media literacy approach.

Bill Christ and Belinha De Abreu have more than half a century of combined teaching and writing about media literacy. That experience and wisdom is evident in this collection – the chapters will challenge, provoke, and inspire.

Few would argue with this title's premise – the media environment is changing and disruptive. Media literacy education research must necessarily follow suit.

Natasha Casey, September 2019
Associate professor of communications
Blackburn College, Carlinville, Illinois

References

Giuliani-Hoffman, F. (2017, November 3). "F*** News" should be replaced by these words, Claire Wardle says. Retrieved from https://money.cnn.com/2017/11/03/media/claire-wardle-fake-news-reliable-sources-podcast/index.html

Gramlich, J. (2019, May 16). 10 facts about Americans and Facebook. *Pew Research Center*. Retrieved from https://www.pewresearch.org/fact-tank/2019/05/16/facts-about-americans-and-facebook/

The Guardian (2019, September 4). YouTube fined $170m for collecting children's personal data. Retrieved from https://www.theguardian.com/technology/2019/sep/04/youtube-kids-fine-personal-data-collection-children-

Guess, A., Nagler, J., & Tucker, J. (2019). Less than you think: Prevalence and predictors of fake news dissemination on Facebook. *Science Advances, 5*(1). doi:10.1126/sciadv.aau4586

Kellner, D., & Share, J. (2019). *The critical media literacy guide: Engaging media and transforming education.* Leiden: Brill Press.

Stocking, G. (2019, June 5). Many Americans say made-up news is a critical problem that needs to be fixed. *Pew Research Center*. Retrieved from https://www.journalism.org/2019/06/05/many-americans-say-made-up-news-is-a-critical-problem-that-needs-to-be-fixed/

Introduction

"Like all literacy, media literacy isn't something you have or attain. Media literacy is enacted, including through critical negotiations with challenging ideas. Media literacy isn't content to be taught. It should provide space for trying out new & critical ideas. #medialiteracy" (Dezuanni, 2019). Media literacy is about critical discourse and enhanced perspectives on vital issues that exist in our mediated and unmediated worlds. In the last several years, we have seen change occur faster and faster with the growing evolution of new technologies and their use. Our language has shifted and adapted to fit these new realms as the way in which we socialize with each other has been disturbed. This book, *Media Literacy in a Disruptive Media Environment*, sets a frame for addressing some of these changes through the lens of media literacy education.

In the spring of 2019, the Broadcast Education Association (BEA) brought together a group of individuals who were from non-profits, and higher and secondary education. As a collective, they provided a context for the book that you are about to read. At the end of the meeting, there was also a round-chair group discussion, with attendees as well as presenters discussing some of the issues faced within our individual spaces as we considered the importance of media literacy education. Some of these thoughts are reflected in the actual chapters, but others were brought up separately as a further course for moving this work forward.

Media Literacy in a Disruptive Media Environment

Whether scholars, teachers, or students in higher education see themselves in broadcasting, multicasting, communication, media (including social media), film, production, virtual/augmented reality, or something else, the field continues to be challenged as

1 media industries are transformed and replaced
2 media texts morph through multiple distribution technologies
3 audiences are reconceptualized and reconfigured
4 artificial intelligence is used throughout the communication ecosystem

5   production tools are now available to anyone who can afford a phone
6   our public and private spaces are assaulted with divisive political and personal discourse

The chapters in this book lay out the current state of media literacy in areas from propaganda, news, research, participatory cultures, big data, representation, social/environmental justice, and civic engagement to its role in higher education media programs. It is meant to provide an overview while providing specific examples and recommendations to help others with their teaching and research agendas.

Audience

Though the book is geared for those in higher education who are teaching and studying (doing research) in media literacy, this work would appeal to many K-12 teachers and administrators who want to have a sense of where media literacy work is currently. The book would be appropriate for undergraduate, graduate, or doctoral students who are studying media literacy education, digital literacy, information literacy, and new literacies in the Schools of Communication, Education, Media Education, Media Studies, Administration, and Information Science. For academics in these fields, this book explores the use of media literacy in digital information societies within schools, communities, the news, and the roles of public institutions in civic life.

Marginalization of People and Ideas

We are at this point right now where our interactions are disruptive and concerning. The media reflects this behavior. The voices that speak on behalf of the whole are not actually speaking to the whole. The US 2016 election highlighted and legitimatized a problem with how people see each other. The disbelief or elation over the results of the election, the anger that came with the perception of who are our neighbors, and the conflict over the words that were being used to describe people were evident. One attendee at the BEA mentioned in our end discussion that people assumed, because of the color of her skin, that she automatically voted for former President Obama, which was not true. Several others mentioned that people believed that where they lived in this country, never mind the world, was being misperceived and even misrepresented. For example, one of the group members from New York City perceived the education that her students were receiving to be much the same everywhere else. Other educators in the group pointed out that New York City was a different educational experience than any other place in the world. Midwesterners, who were represented, indicated that their cultural competency and value was belittled or missing when people looked at them and their part of the nation based on political maps or how the media discussed or did not discuss them.

The lack and type of representation by the media has been an ongoing issue. How the news media talks about the general population is also problematic. Poll numbers tend to be representing a non-diverse group or the exact opposite, a diverse group, but not the totality. Because of these reasons, many of the attendees felt that work was needed at a grassroot level.

The BEA discussion included how language and words were used as descriptors or identifiers that were mainstreamed but not necessarily accurate, true, or correct. Describing people negatively because we do not agree with them politically has become a part of the mainstream discourse. People wondered how could we stop political strategizing, and how do we talk to people who think we are marginalizing them? The groups of people seem to be very large and span race, politics, and religion:

- minorities
- Trump supporters who would have voted for Obama
- Conservatives on college campuses

One person wondered if it was possible to name a group that does not feel stigmatized.

A wider discussion ensued of how media literacy education can help to serve as a way for difficult dialogues to occur, with ground rules established that a group would accept as norms. Suggestions were made about education, whether it was in communication, media studies, or in other courses. There was an obvious need to unpack what was being heard and seen and then historicizing the full context of it, whether it was limited to the singularity of a word, a visual image, or to a mainstream event, such as those related to the #MeToo movement or other social/societal challenges.

Classrooms, whether K-12, higher education, or in non-traditional routes, were considered good places to facilitate these conversations: conversations that become extremely important for how people can share about themselves and their world. These conversations become self-reflective, deliberate attempts where people can exchange ideas. Some in the group suggested items such as:

- potlucks for peace in order to bring together people who have different points of view
- interventions – for people to share their story

Beyond these ideas were the basics of how we get along with each other or talk to each other, understanding the impact of calling people names such as "deplorable(s)," or "racist," or any of the other terms that gets used.

As has become obvious in many media stories, we appear to be living in a culture of contempt, which has proved to be contentious, unrelenting, and impeding the process of civil discourse. This culture has created a breakdown in our society in how people chose to engage or disengage with each other. The filter bubbles of society have been enhanced by technology, whose original purpose was to grow our communities and connect societies. Instead, technology has contributed to a breakdown of societies and has been accused of being a tool for genocide, hate speech, and divisiveness.

Individual Truths

Truth itself has become contested with the arguments about fake news and other issues. The questioning of truth and facts has created a challenge for people trying to understand history, reality, and so much more. In the BEA post-discussion, many people felt that universities and colleges have been working on combatting false narratives forever but wondered how successful they were in reaching students in today's environment. In general, there was a consensus that people believe a good story if it fits their culture or background. Similarly, many felt that it was the task of educators and academics to make people in their classroom feel that each has a story to tell and then foster a community that listens and interacts with these individual truths. Yet, the challenge is dealing with individual stories or worldviews that were harmful to others. While people were still optimistic about education, there was also a push-back that our youth are naturally curious and critical.

At the end of the BEA joining, many believed that more needed to be done in the areas of building critical thinking, building and understanding empathy, connecting to people – what some deemed to call this point, ethics of care.

Now What?

We believe this book addresses some of the issues raised by media literacy scholars and teachers and presents answers from both national and international perspectives. The chapters provide a glimpse of the discussions that followed the BEA presentations as well as the ideas that help to answer where we should be going and what should be addressed.

There are four parts to this book. Part I is the *Overview*, which provides the background of media literacy, including big data literacy, as it stands globally and within the United States. At the same time, this part of the book provides the reader with some of the challenges faced by media literacy educators and researchers.

Part II is focused on *Media Literacy, News and Propaganda*. In this part, the authors look at the influence of misinformation and disinformation within various global communities whether in politics or as a means of disenfranchising communities and individuals. The chapters also further look into the growing focus on news literacy and the need for instruction on critical media literacy.

Part III looks at *Media Literacy and Education*. These chapters consider professional education, university curricula, pilot initiatives across age groups, and online learning of media literacy. These chapters provide case studies of the work as well as concrete suggestions.

The last one, Part IV, is *Media Literacy and Social Action*. The authors in this area take on the civic media/civic engagement lens. They look at this issue in relation to the participatory culture of our society with its effect on our environment culturally, situationally, and through our ecosystem.

Concluding Thoughts

Connecting the voices of researchers over the past several years has been a primary goal for media literacy educator advocates. Through the development of symposiums, books, and special issue pieces, the work has had a chance to grow – expanding to a worldwide glimpse of where research exists and continues to propagate at different times. As media technologies continue to expand in scope and reach, with little regard for physical or cultural borders, how we educate students, our communities, and ourselves about the role of media in our daily lives remains important. Thus, an essential and necessary relationship exists between the new digital technologies, global awareness, and media literacy. We hope this book, *Media Literacy in a Disruptive Media Environment*, is a contribution to this thinking.

Part One

Overview

1 Global Perspectives on Media Literacy

Belinha S. De Abreu

"Media literacy, our capacity to access, have a critical understanding of, and interact with the media has never been as important as in today's society" (European Commission, 2017). Media literacy education is a global and international focus. As media technologies continue to expand in scope and reach, with little regard for physical or cultural borders, how we educate students about the role of media in their daily lives increasingly incorporates perspectives that are more global. Thus, an essential and analogous relationship exists between the new digital technologies, global awareness, and media literacy. A global perspective, given the accessibility of the world via social networks and the Internet, is needed for our students and educators.

Introduction

We exist in a period of time where the connections we make with each other go beyond the everyday person-to-person and extend to whom we connect with through media. The media is the repository for these connections. It is the conduit and the influencer. It is the messenger, the producer, the innovator, and the creator. As people, we live within the frames of the development of the media and we have become the communicators as encoders, decoders, and even the methods of delivery. The media has become an augmentation of our person. Our human distinction, which separates us from the media as a tool, is our ability to discern and consider the media as a platform, as a vehicle, as a tool, and as a representation.

We are at a time and place where the answers for media and technology come across via the media as simple but wrong, or complex and right. The issue is whether the global public is willing in many cases to take the harder path of finding out truth and seeing it out consciously and directly. The headlines of the past few years are an indication of this struggle:

- "In France, School Lessons Ask: Which Twitter Post Should You Trust" (*The New York Times*, 2018)
- "The Guardians and the War on Truth" (*Time*, 2018).

- "Poor media literacy 'making Turks vulnerable to fake news'" (*Hurriet Daily News*, 2018).
- "How are first time votes in Nigeria navigating fake news?" (*BBC News World Service*, 2019).
- "How the BBC is tackling the growing problem of fake news in Asia and Africa" (*The Drum*, 2019).
- "Misinformation Is Endangering India's Election" (*The Atlantic*, 2019).

Whether it is journalists or journalism, there is a struggle going on in our world regarding media manipulation. As Umberto Eco stated, "Not long ago, if you wanted to seize political power in a country you had merely to control the army and the police… Today a country belongs to the person who controls communications (Eco, 1967, pp. 1–2). Moreover, the transmission of information is happening through various filter bubbles, individuals in power and our general society, as well as multiple technologies.

Being media literate today is about understanding that platforms of communication manipulate and that simplicity of a basic search does not often give the "best" or "correct" answer. As a global society, we have allowed the technology to control, influence, and direct us, and that has just happened in a very short period of time.

Historical Context

Media literacy has been looked at globally for quite some time but not necessarily under the name of "media literacy." As early as the 1920s, there was discussion of visual literacy in particular to the understanding of motion pictures and its incorporation into a contextual learning in the classroom. There was even an organization founded on this principle from the University of Chicago (Saettler, 2004). However, more often, especially in countries outside of the United States "media education" was used as the term for referencing the ideas of media literacy. The UK, Australia, Spain, and even Canada had media education as a principle of learning, and it wasn't until the second half of the twentieth century that we could see an exchange of terminology between "media literacy" and media "education" (Buckingham, 2019).

Duncan and Masterman

Debating the merits of media literacy education is not new. The work of media literacy education was highlighted in particular during the 1960s and 1970s as world events were creating turmoil in the world:

> The 60s…that was really the hotbed issues of civil rights, the war in Vietnam – all of those things were televisual and had a lot of

ideological implications...We were inspired by these situations that were being commodified by the media...and it obviously shaped what I was doing.

(Duncan, 2011, para. 4)

It is important to note that prior to that time, there was discussion of media education and that term has been exchanged with media literacy throughout the years. However, there is a debate about whether we would look at media education and media literacy in the same way and that continues to be true.

Duncan was one of the first media literacy educators and true pioneer of this work. He was the co-founder of the Alliance for Media Literacy in Toronto, Ontario, and Media Education Working Group of the Centre for Media and Culture in Education at OISE/University of Toronto. Much of the Ontario, Canada, work came from Duncan, who, in 1989, provided the Ministry from Ontario with a theoretical paper with eight key concepts for media literacy:

1 All media are constructions.
2 The media construct reality.
3 Audiences negotiate meaning in media.
4 Media have commercial implications.
5 Media contain ideological and value messages.
6 Media have social and political implications.
7 Form and content are closely related in the media.
8 Each medium has a unique aesthetic form (Duncan, 1989).

Another media literacy scholar, Len Masterman, from the United Kingdom, in 1989 came up with a series of principles used widely in UK for teaching and learning as related to media education. In particular, Masterman focused on the idea of media texts: "In the past, media teachers had asserted their interpretive authority over students. But the media, too, are teachers in this mold – because all media texts point audiences towards a specific set of emotional, social and intellectual responses" (Connections/MediaLit Moments, 2013, p. 2).

Masterman's works looked at both consumption and production, but more importantly he believed in critical practice that needed to be developed in schools and with educators in the UK. His work was foundational to the development of the Canadian's school of thought in regard to media literacy education and later to what was developed in the United States.

Media Literacy Globally Defined

The European Commission's definition of media literacy, articulated in its Communication on a European approach to media literacy in the digital environment, states: "Media literacy is generally defined as the ability to access the media, to understand and to critically evaluate different aspects of the media and media contents and to create communications in a variety of contexts" (European Commission, 2009, para. 3).

The UNESCO's Media and Information Literacy Curriculum for Teachers outlines the components of Media Literacy as:

- Understand the role and functions of media
- Understand the conditions under which media fulfill their functions
- Critically analyze and evaluate media content
- Use of media for democratic participation, intercultural dialogue and learning
- Produce user-generated content
- ICT and other media skills (UNESCO, 2011, p. 18).

From these definitions, it is easy to see that the media literacy movement has very much had an international bent, from the United Kingdom, Canada, Australia, Spain, and more. Historically, the work done internationally has long set the precedence for what is working and used in schools and curriculum whether in North America, Asia, or Australia.

In Australia, media literacy is actively promoted within the primary and secondary curriculum in all states. In some states it is dealt with under the guise of English, and, in others, it is offered within an Arts framework. In the later years of high school in some states, media studies is offered as a stand-alone option. However, the primary focus still appears to be on broadcast media rather than the newer digital media (Penman & Turnbull, 2007, p 5).

European Association for Viewer's Interests (EAVI) is an independent, not-for-profit international civil society organization registered in Brussels. EAVI was created to facilitate the "unifying process of all those who support citizens' and consumers' interests in the fields of media" (EAVI, 2005). This organization focuses on the digital citizen and represents media literacy as follows:

Media literate citizens are those who are aware of the content they use, how they found it, who is constructing and providing it. Furthermore they are wise, ethical and effective in media use. Literate citizens are able to fully participate in public life and interact with other people, benefiting from services and using the media as a resource in a safe way. They are open to learn, explore and have fun with the media. They will also be informed consumers when shopping and locate reliable sources of information. They are not passengers, but are in the driving seat deciding where to go. They are AWARE.

(EAVI, 2005, para. 1)

Fake News

As a discussion point, media literacy has been noted as the antidote for disinformation around the world, and it is considered the biggest issue of our times. Further, media literacy is discussed in a variety of ways, including the language of fake news, the filter bubble that helped to create fake news, even in terms of the gap instinct as described by Hans Rosling in *Factfulness*:

> We love to dichotomize. Good versus bad. Heroes versus villains. My country versus the rest. Dividing the world into two distinct sides is simple and intuitive, and also dramatic because it implies conflict, we do it without thinking all the time. Journalists know this. They set up their narratives as conflicts between two opposing people, views or groups. They prefer stories of extreme poverty and billionaires to stories about the vast majority of people slowing dragging themselves toward better lives. Journalists are storytellers. So are people who produce documentaries and movies. Documentaries pit the fragile individual against the big, evil corporation. Blockbuster movies usually feature good fighting evil.
>
> (2018, pp. 38–39)

Unfortunately, this claim appears to fit right into what has happened during the election of 2016 and subsequent activity where "fake news" became interpreted in a variety of different ways by different news agencies, politicians, and even the general populace. Here is a piece in *The Guardian*, which attempted to define the variations of "fake news":

Fake news means fictions deliberately fabricated and presented as non-fiction with the intent to mislead recipients into treating fiction as fact or into doubting verifiable fact.

- "Fictions" is meant to distinguish fake news from items which have a kernel of truth but are exaggerated, out of proportion, in the cliché "sensationalised".
- "Fabricated" emphasises the made-up, manufactured aspect of fake news.
- "Deliberately" and "intent" draw attention to how fake news is purposeful, and help to show it is distinct from the flawed journalism that can result from haste, carelessness, partiality, conflicts of interest or the successful spin of others.
- "Presented as non-fiction" focuses on the premeditation and calculation which often seem to characterise the originators of fake news, as distinct from the people who simply spread it unthinkingly.
- "Mislead" indicates seriousness of purpose and distinguishes fake news from, say, entertainment, pranks or satire.

- "Treating fiction as fact" and "doubting verifiable fact" look to consequences. These seem to be the two main political purposes of those who create fake news (Chadwick, 2017, para. 16).

This circular conversation in many ways leads back to the medium of transmission of fake news or intentional misleading of information. Within these categories is the discussion of screen time influences as well as fact checkers; news deserts in the world; and lastly and most importantly the technology of transmission whether it is Facebook, Snapchat, Twitter, or the search engine Google, with its algorithmic syntax.

Technology as a Worldwide Influence

Marshall McLuhan

Marshall McLuhan, a Canadian academic who during the 1960s attributed to being a founding father in the study of media literacy, commented, "The medium is the message." McLuhan (1964) had predicted that technology and media were growing at a rapid pace and that schools needed to adapt techniques for students to learn and process the information they were receiving, by, at that time, only television and radio.
    Marshall McLuhan (1962) coined the term "global village," which suggests a world in which communication technology unites people in remote parts of the world. The idea of the global village suggests a world in which communication technology unites people in remote parts of the world. The television was thought to help create a global village early on as the pace of communication information and world news was readily delivered throughout the world. The Internet has superseded that idea with its ability to share culture instantaneously, even if it is not well understood by the communicator.

Technology as a Vehicle for Communication

Technologies have influenced a great change in society and in education. As the number of hours that citizens connect with technology has increased, so has the need for educating students and the general public about the tools as well as the platforms that carry information. Information and communication technologies (ICT's) affect "working, accessing knowledge, socializing, communication, collaborating – and succeeding – in all areas of the professional, social, and personal life" (European Commission, 2013). This statement is true whether in Europe, the United States, or other parts of the world; our youth are directly impacted by the mass saturation provided by the digital world.
    Much conversation, especially in third world countries, has been segmented to accessing the tools or the lack of access to them. In the more

advanced parts of the world, access to technology is less of an issue, but that has not made the user smarter. In many educational settings, computers are used as a resource for locating information or for the basics of Word processing. The value of ICTs and any kind of standardization of educational technology will be as a point of evaluating and critically analyzing the messages that are carried via these platforms. Using the tool is an advantage to the young as they are able to maneuver through most platforms; the greater learning is in the depth in which they consider the media messages within the context of the medium provided by accessing the Internet and other web resources as well as in intentional focus on media literacy.

Helping them to understand between a good resource versus one that is biased and even correct is where the work of education must be directed. Accessing the tools will always be an issue of economics, but even at that point when the tools are available, the concern will be that most policymakers will consider it enough and that the work of critical thinking, understanding bias, or considering fact from fiction will be left behind or minimized – once again reinforcing the need for media literacy education.

Technology and Education

Education and technology have always been at odds because of the constant evolution of technological products. New forms of communicating are introduced regularly and certainly more quickly than ever before. Information and communication technologies have become a part of the global discussion, especially as the look at these technologies has been widely considered in the business industries. There is a realization that the development of the world and even a more efficient education system is dependent on knowledge dissemination. Further, the newest technologies now provide for an all-in-one depository that mix traditional media, such as radio and books, into the latest method of delivery. As stated in the ICTs and the education Millennium Development Goals (MDGs) guide:

> The swiftness of ICT developments, their increasing spread and availability, the nature of their content and their declining prices are having major implications for learning. They may tend to increase disparities, weaken social bonds and threaten cultural cohesion. Governments will therefore need to establish clearer policies in regard to science and technology, and undertake critical assessments of ICT experiences and options. These should include their resource implications in relation to the provision of basic education, emphasizing choices that bridge the 'digital divide', increase access and quality, and reduce inequity.
>
> (InfoDev, 2015, p. 70)

While the digital divide is real and exists even in the most affluent parts of the world, it is the interconnections of technology which is of most interest when discussing ICTs.

The reinforcement of ICTs to bridge the learning context with the eventual business and world context must begin in schools. As the language of ICTs has become a part of the dialogue of the world culture, a certain amount of fluidity needs to coincide with the learning and teaching that is generated with new pedagogical changes that have been initiated by various governments throughout the world. The paradigm of the singular educator in the enclosed classroom has been altered with the consideration of a global case for digitally supported students with digitally supported schools.

The growth of mobile technologies does offer a newfound flexibility within the confines of the classroom. ICT's standards consider this very point. This flexibility also exists in the form of communicating between teacher and students, student and teacher, and student to student. The line between classic written language and the syntax of text language is crossing over into the classroom. Yet, the potential for learning exists, and tapping into that area opens teachers to new teaching possibilities given the chance.

The civic component of mobile technologies in particular is a focal point for continued research and for educational consideration as we look at the idea of engaged citizenship. These types of conversations are evolving and will continue to increase as more educators, policymakers, and individuals internationally consider the possibilities of a connected classroom on a worldwide scale. As a global initiative, media literacy needs to be a core focus for all. Instead of looking at the media as the enemy, the media must be part of the public discourse, a part of participatory democracy, and the role examined to create informed citizenry.

The idea that media is a part of the culture of society is an accepted element to our general populace. Education in the understanding, evaluating, and provision of a critical stance is a necessary part of all teaching levels: primary, secondary, higher, adult, and lifelong education. As David Buckingham (2001) states:

> The media have increasingly penetrated all areas of social life: it is now impossible to understand the operations of the political process or of the economy, or to address questions about cultural and personal identity – or indeed about education – without taking account of the role of the media. Among the most significant changes are technological developments, economic developments, social developments, globalization.
>
> (p. 3)

Effective education was the ultimate goal that leads to the further globalized work in the area of media literacy education.

"The Medium Is the Message"

While the "medium is the message" may have been the dictate under Marshall McLuhan, the fact remains that worldwide the news media has been marginalized by popular culture events, which are not representative of the global voices around us. Over time, the medium of television news was limiting the exposure of the messages from around the world because of a perceived lack of interest from U.S. citizens (Mihailidis, 2012; Guthrie, 2010). The time period after the Cold War ended appeared to change the way in which news agencies invested in the dispensing of global news. Foreign affairs offices were closed. News agencies began to cut back on their overseas bureaus, and the news became less about the world, but more internalized.

Decline of Global News Coverage

In the United States, the lack of interest in world news was most noticeable before the events of September 11, 2001, as most of the news being reported had to do with popular culture events (Stanton, 2007). The events of that day transfixed the world, and the news world took on another dimension. The coverage intensified on the global aspect of the media as the question of "why" led to a review of conduct, information, and misinformation that was not being analyzed worldwide. In later reports from news anchors, the discussion relayed pointed to the fact that news agencies had been cutting back on their foreign affairs offices for years (Mihailidis, 2012; Utley, 1997). According to the Tyndall Report in 1997, total foreign coverage on network nightly news programs has declined precipitously, from 3,733 minutes in 1989 to 1,838 minutes in 1996 at ABC, the leader, and from 3,351 minutes to 1,175 minutes at third-place NBC. In a Tyndall Report from 2013, there was glaring negative response to how news was covered yet again especially in regard to ABC news coverage:

> 2013 marks the year when ABC World News finally rejected the mission of presenting a serious newscast. ABC covered all four of the major domestic policy stories least heavily: the Budget debate, the Healthcare rollout, Gun control, and National Security Agency surveillance. Same with foreign policy: ABC spent least time on the civil war in Syria and its chemical weapons disarmament, the military coup in Egypt, and on Afghanistan. Instead, ABC stepped up its coverage of Sports and Show Business, and highlighted

morning-style reporters Ginger Zee (weather) and Paula Faris (personal finance tips). Weather aside, the only major stories that ABC covered competitively were True Crime – the George Zimmerman trial and Ariel Castro's Cleveland hell house – and Celebrity: London's baby prince. ABC's newscast is now certifiably Disneyfied.

(Tyndall, 2013)

With infotainment taking over the majority of the news network on a nightly basis, the greater issues that were facing the world were going unnoticed. The issues regarding the lack of coverage of foreign affair news events were highlighted more negatively as the discussions of those days events continued, post 9/11. Countries and names which were unknown or distant became a part of the conversation amongst the general public. Worries grew of what we did not know and what we should have known. The rise of the cable networks added to this confusion as the idea of the 24-hour news network actually required news and filling those hours with information that would bring viewers to the screen. Opinion makers have become a part of the context of news, confusing the messaging of how facts are delivered to the public.

The World Wide Web offered an avenue and opportunity by which people could gather information. Initially, the charge for the individual user was for them to be able to find the information. Increasingly, information was being made present through various websites. Some created by individual users, and other information through the major networks that most people know, such as ABC News, CNN, and Fox. CNN in particular had grown in value to audiences in countries where censored and controlled news media existed. The World Wide Web has provided an access point to information, which was not obtainable before its inception.

Through communication technologies like the World Wide Web, people also have access to increasing amounts of information about what are happening in their own and other countries. This is especially important in countries where media are government controlled. For example, people in Pakistan and Afghanistan learn more about military actions in their countries by accessing CNN. com than through their local newspapers. In some ways, the Internet has democratized information, in that more people control and disseminate information than ever before. For example, there are some 32,000 Internet police in China, who frequently find and arrest people for criticizing the government online. They block search engine sites, close Internet cafés, and block e-mails; they can even can reroute Web site traffic to alternate sites maintained by 23 routers in Shanghai and Beijing. In spite of this and other governments' attempts to limit their citizens' access to computer-mediated communication (CMC), the Internet is providing information, world news, and possibilities for interpersonal communication that were not available previously.

(Martin & Nakayama, 2010, pp. 22–23)

In essence, the Internet provided people with an opening for obtaining information, but it also created a dichotomy.

Information Overload

All of a sudden, individuals across the globe had a plethora of information at their hands, but that was also the problem. Too much information and unverified information allowed for anyone/anywhere to receive the data, but not necessary to know for certain whether it was accurate. In addition, the Internet provided for grassroots news efforts such as that has taken off with social networks, such as Twitter and Facebook.

The Arab Spring, a popular uprising which began in December 2010, was most noted for taking to Twitter to move forward the issues the citizenry was facing during key periods of the 2011 Tunisian and Egyptian uprisings. News reporters who realized that these types of social networks were reaching a wider audience and influencing change faster than the regular news mediums propagated the agenda. Formats provided by social networks were considered non-elite points of entry for news content. The receivers of the content were the general public but eventually grew to reach the more elite news agencies. New agencies such as ABC News, CNN, and FOX News went to Twitter for information from sources that were on the ground as military strikes were occurring. News reporters became the brokers for news sources who were intent on getting the message out to the world on what was happening in their countries.

Each day news reports are communicated and filtered. At the forefront is the sender of the information and following is the receiver or who is judged to be the receiver. In Stanton's (2007) writings he examines the idea of whether the media should be leading or following. The shift in conversation has occurred with the changes presented by the transition of new media and new media tools for conveying information, such as Twitter and Facebook. In the case of social media, it is the group dynamics of these networks that place information in the public view. However, the more elite news media runs in another direction. As the media seeks out stories, it also creates the pace and the place for what is transmitted out to the public. In effect, they select material exemplifying a consensus view but oftentimes neglects a variety of events that fall outside of the established mold. It is perhaps for these reasons and also the immediacy of the transference of information that Twitter has become such a popular new media tool.

Moving Forward

Journalism and Critical Goals

The need to be the first to deliver the news hinders responsible journalism, whose motive should be about accuracy versus immediacy. Ultimately, the role of media is at a difficult junction where media conglomerates will need to make decisions regarding what news agencies should be covering, what needs to be reported while analyzing the value of what they do, and how it will further impact generations to come. A critical goal for media literacy education is to have an informed global public. One that does not jump on false bandwagons in order to create more news with little value, which later leads to further misinformation and a public that is kept perpetually ignorant.

Media literacy education is underscored throughout the thinking and consideration of where we should be in a globalized society. Organizations are in place to factcheck, such as *Poynter, The Trust Project*, and *Fact Check EU*, and this does seem to give people some direction. However, the most important piece is still missing – the necessity for critical media literacy education to be developed in schools all over the world. This work has been in flux for some time. In conferences, globally it is the topic of discussion, but now it is important to see it in implementation as we consider where our future citizenry is heading and how we can continue to see a democratized growth in civility, transparency, and learning despite political preference in order to create a more thoughtful and engaged society.

References

BBC News World Service. (2019, January 9). How are first time votes in Nigeria navigating fake news? Retrieved from https://www.bbc.co.uk/programmes/p06xkpw3

Buckingham, D. (2001). Media education a global strategy for development. *UNESCO*, Sector of Communication and Information, Institute of Education, University of London, England.

Buckingham, D. (2019). *The media education manifesto*. Cambridge, UK. Polity Press.

Chadwick, P. (2017, May 12). Defining fake news will help us expose it. *The Guardian*. Retrieved from https://www.theguardian.com/media/commentisfree/2017/may/12/defining-fake-news-will-help-us-expose-it

Connections/MediaLit Moments. (2013, March). "Theme: Len Masterman and the big ideas of media literacy." *Consortium for Media Literacy*. Retrieved from https://www.medialit.org/sites/default/files/connections/len%20masterman%20and%20the%20big%20ideas%20of%20media%20literacy.pdf

Dezuanni, M. (2019, August 17). #MediaLiteracy. Retrieved from https://twitter.com/dezuanni/status/1162680919108419584.

Duncan, B. (1989). Eight key concepts of media literacy. *Media literacy resource guide*. Toronto: Ontario Ministry of Education.

Duncan, B. (2011). *Voices of media literacy: Barry Duncan.* Center for Media Literacy. Retrieved from http://www.medialit.org/sites/default/files/Voices_PowerPoint_Aug.2011.pdf

Eco, U. (1967). *Towards a semiological guerrilla warfare.* Retrieved from http://www.kareneliot.de/downloads/UmbertoEco_Towards%20a%20Semiological%20Guerrilla%20Warfare.pdf, pp. 1–2.

European Association for Viewer's Interests. (2005). *EAVI's mission & background.* Brussels. Retrieved from http://www.eavi.eu/joomla/about-us/mission.

European Commission. (2009). *Study on the current trends and approaches to media literacy in Europe.* Retrieved from http://ec.europa.eu/culture/library/studies/literacy-trends-report_en.pdf

European Commission. (2013, February). *Survey of schools: ICT in education.* Retrieved from https://ec.europa.eu/digital-single-market/en/news/survey-schools-ict-education

European Commission. (2017, April 7). *Reporting on Media Literacy in Europe.* Retrieved from https://ec.europa.eu/digital-single-market/en/news/reporting-media-literacy-europe

Guthrie, M. (2010). *Pew report shows traditional media in decline: Project for Excellence in Journalism study finds cable news faring better than broadcast, no sustainable online model.* Broadcasting & Cable. Retrieved from http://www.broadcastingcable.com

InfoDev. (2015). *Harness new information and communication technologies to help achieve EFA goals. Quick guide: ICTs and the education Millennium Development Goals* (MDGs), pp. 69–72. Retrieved from http://www.infodev.org/articles/quick-guide-icts-and-education-millennium-development-goals-mdgs

Martin, J. N., & Nakayama, T. K. (2010). *Intercultural communication in contexts.* New York, NY: The McGraw-Hill Companies, Inc. Retrieved from http://www.rasaneh.org/Images/News/AtachFile/15-8-1390/FILE634561743619907963.pdf

McCarthy, J. (2019, January 28). How the BBC is tackling the 'growing' problem of fake news in Asia and Africa. *The Drum.* Retrieved from https://www.thedrum.com/news/2019/01/28/how-the-bbc-tackling-the-growing-problem-fake-news-asia-and-africa

McLuhan, M. (1964). *Understanding media: The extensions of man.* New York, NY: McGraw-Hill.

McLuhan, M. (1962). *The Gutenberg Galaxy: The making of typographic man.* Toronto: University of Toronto Press.

Mihailidis, P. (2012). *News literacy.* New York, NY: Peter Lang.

Poonam, S., & Bansal, S. (2019, April 1). Misinformation is endangering India's selection. *The Atlantic.* Retrieved from https://www.theatlantic.com/international/archive/2019/04/india-misinformation-election-fake-news/586123/

Penman, R., & Turnbull, S. (2007, July). Media literacy—Concepts, research, and regulatory issues. Australian Communications and Media Authority. Melbourne, Australia. Retrieved from http://www.acma.gov.au/webwr/_assets/main/lib310665/media_literacy_report.pdf

Rosling, H. (2018). *Factfulness.* New York, NY: Flatiron Books.

Saettler, P. (2004). *The evolution of American education.* Greenwich, CT: Information Age Publishing.

Satariano, A., & Peltier, E. (2018, December 13). In France, school lessons ask: Which twitter post should you trust. *The New York Times*, Retrieved from https://www.nytimes.com/2018/12/13/technology/france-internet-literacy-school.html

Stanton, R. C. (2007). *All news is local: The failure of the media to reflect world events in a globalized age* (Chapters 1 and 3). New York, NY: McFarland & Company.

Tyndall Report. (2013). *2013 year in review*. Retrieved from http://tyndallreport.com/yearinreview2013/

UNESCO. (2011). *MIL curriculum for teacher education*. Paris: UNESCO.

Utley, G. (1997, March/April). The shrinking of foreign news: From broadcast to narrowcast. *Foreign Affairs*. Retrieved from http://www.foreignaffairs.com/articles/52854/garrick-utley/the-shrinking-of-foreign-news-from-broadcast-to-narrowcast

Yinanç, B. (2018, December 10). Poor media literacy 'making Turks vulnerable to fake news' *Hurriet Daily News*. Retrieved from http://www.hurriyetdailynews.com/poor-media-literacy-making-turks-vulnerable-to-fake-news-139582

2 A *Snapshot*
The State of Media Literacy Education in the United States

Michelle Ciulla Lipkin, Sherri Hope Culver, and Theresa Redmond

Media literacy represents a necessary, inevitable, and realistic response to the complex, ever-changing electronic environment and communication cornucopia that surround us. To become a successful student, responsible citizen, productive worker, or competent and conscientious consumer, individuals need to develop expertise with the increasingly sophisticated information and entertainment media that address us on a multi-sensory level, affecting the way we think, feel, and behave.
– National Association for Media Literacy Education

Introduction

Decades of scholarship in the field of media literacy and numerous researchers, educators, and advocates have called for the widespread implementation of media literacy education (Considine, 1990; De Abreu, 2018; Hobbs, 2010; Thoman & Jolls, 2004). Since 2015, membership of the National Association for Media Literacy Education (NAMLE) has grown from about 300 members to over 5,000 members, signifying a remarkable expansion of interest in and demand for media literacy education. Paired with increasing concerns about misinformation, media literacy has moved to the forefront of national attention. Defined as the "ability to access, analyze, evaluate, create, and act using all forms of communication" (NAMLE, 2014), media literacy education is an interdisciplinary field of study and a way of teaching that cultivates attention to the social, political, economic, and cultural aspects of media and actively prepares students and citizens for critical and creative participation in the digital age.

Despite general awareness of the persuasive nature and pervasive inclusion of media in our lives, media literacy education has not been formally prioritized in U.S. education efforts. Yet, several recent trends indicating progress and development are important to mention:

* *Growth*: Attention and interest in media literacy education is expanding, as evidenced by the significant growth of NAMLE's membership, the increasing number of partner organizations involved in the Annual U.S. Media Literacy Week, and the expansion of collaboration and partnerships globally.

- *Inclusion in Standards*: A range of skills related to media literacy education are increasingly included in standards-based initiatives, such as the National Common Core State Standards and the National Media Arts Standards, as well as in the positional papers of numerous professional educational organizations, including, but not limited to: the American Library Association, National Council of Teachers of English, and National Council for the Social Studies.
- *Legislative Involvement*: A growing number of states, including Washington and California, have introduced or passed bills and amendments to address media literacy education and digital citizenship in school-based curricula. Moreover, discussions have started regarding the introduction of a national media literacy bill through the focused efforts of media literacy advocates across the country.
- *Awareness:* The term "fake news" has come into common parlance, opening the eyes of many to the power of a deftly constructed media message and bringing media literacy into the cultural conversation. Shifts in how politicians and elected officials use media, especially social media, as well as increasing insight related to privacy and data mining have heightened awareness about the need for citizens – meaning everyone – to be media literate.

Despite broad agreement about the need to ensure that people of all ages are equipped to understand and negotiate the influence of media in their lives, the United States does not devote any significant government effort, nor funding, for media literacy education research, training, or implementation. International communities, including Canada and the European Union, have made intentional efforts to prioritize media literacy education. In the United States, the field has grown on the backs of nonprofit organizations, university scholars, and dedicated teachers and practitioners across a range of educational contexts throughout the country who seek to prepare their students, peers, and colleagues to engage thoughtfully in literacy as a social practice increasingly enacted via information and communication technologies and media. While funding initiatives have benefits and drawbacks, decades of grassroots advocacy has not been enough to establish media literacy education as a foundation.

This *Snapshot* takes the position that students need media literacy education as a sustained, interdisciplinary component of schooling and its integration must be led by research-based, effective practices and trained practitioners. This *Snapshot* is a step toward that goal.

About This *Snapshot*

The intention of this *Snapshot* is to provide information that may be useful in facilitating the development of media literacy education across the country and helping the U.S. education system align with the media-rich world, in which students, and all citizens, are immersed today. Together, we seek to reinvigorate curricula so it is relevant to students' lives and their 21st-century education needs.

This *Snapshot* does not, nor was it meant to, fully answer the question "What is the state of media literacy education in the United States?" This *Snapshot* should not be interpreted as a representative research study. We chose the word "snapshot" intentionally to convey this report as a glimpse of the field and as a step toward the future. The purpose of this *Snapshot* is to inspire dialogue and create momentum to support research, training, practice, and policy efforts needed in order to grow the field of media literacy more fully as we enter 2020 and beyond. For a list of questions, see the Appendix.

Snapshot information was gathered through an online survey launched during the 4th Annual Media Literacy Week in the United States – beginning November 2018 and closing at the end of the year. The survey was created by a small, volunteer team of members from NAMLE and disseminated through various related networks (e.g., NAMLE Twitter, NAMLE Facebook, etc.). Respondents included NAMLE members (45%), non-members (38%), and those that were not sure (17%) (Culver & Redmond, 2019).

The survey focused on gathering information in three areas:

1   Community: Who are the people involved in media literacy education and what are their professional contexts?
2   Training: How are those involved in media literacy education developing the skills necessary to teach this topic?
3   Resources: What specific materials, curricula, or organizations are being tapped to bring this topic to life in classrooms and other environments?

Conceptualizing Media Literacy

Media literacy education is a hybrid field with roots in many areas, including but not limited to: semiotics, film studies, cultural studies, educational technology, instructional technology, information literacy, and many more. Attempts to define or label media literacy have had the tendency to create confusion and limit meaningful dialogue about practice. At the same time, stabilizing the concept of media literacy is an important dimension of growing the field. NAMLE's *Core Principles of Media Literacy Education* (2007) brings together myriad definitions by conceptualizing media literacy education broadly as active inquiry and critical thinking about the messages we receive and create so as to develop informed, reflective, and engaged participants, essential to a democratic society.

It is important to recognize that conceptualizations of media literacy drive curriculum choices, professional development, teacher training, resource material selection, and numerous other aspects. Moreover, even in schools or districts where media literacy is an established course or topic, the limits of time result in complex choices about which topics to include, or which topics deserve the most time, impacting the content of media literacy learning. Finally, external factors, such as national curriculum reform efforts, standardized testing, and district-level administrative priorities, may influence conceptualization and enactment. Survey respondents' selections reflect these complex factors, including their own interpretations of the definition of media literacy.

In considering the goals of this *Snapshot*, perhaps it is the recognition of media literacy as an "expanded concept of literacy" (CPMLE, 2007) that is most relevant to invite conversation. As Hobbs and Jensen (2009) explained a decade ago:

> There is a need to support the work of those who are formulating, creating, refining, and testing curriculum theory and instructional methods, practices, and pedagogy in ways that connect to students' experience with mass media, popular culture, and digital media, supporting the development of their critical thinking, creativity, collaboration, and communication skills.
>
> (p. 7)

This need persists and this report is movement forward.

Observations

Who Responded?

We received 331 responses to the survey representing participants from 45 states and the District of Columbia, as well as international responses. Since our focus was to offer a snapshot of the United States, we omitted the 37 responses that came from the international media literacy community. However, those responses affirm media literacy as a field that transcends national borders. The 294 respondents from the United States reflect a host of professional backgrounds, roles, and contexts, illuminating media literacy as a complex, interdisciplinary field. For instance, the organizational context included the following: 62% of respondents were from a public institution, 21% from a private institution, and 17% from the non-profit arena. The education background of respondents was varied, with 64% of respondents having completed a master's degree, 26% having completed a doctoral degree, and 9% having completed a bachelor's degree. In terms of media literacy training: 74% of respondents shared that they were self-taught, while 43% had an academic degree related to media literacy, 43% had engaged in related professional development, and approximately 7% engaged in a badging or certificate program. Regarding content area: 24% of respondents selected library, while 23% were in higher education, 12% in educational technology, and 11% in English language arts. Other content area selections in order of prevalence included: social studies, career and technical education, arts education, early childhood, English as a second language, health education, special education, world languages, and guidance. In terms of roles, 35% of respondents were university or college educators, while 18% were high school educators, and 9% were high school librarians. A variety of other roles were identified and, in order of prevalence, include: middle school educator, middle school librarian, elementary or primary school educator, university/college librarian, public librarian, and after school educators. Additional demographics related to age and gender were collected. Of those who preferred to answer: 72% of respondents identified as female, 26% as male, and 1% as other. Thirty percent of respondents were ages 45–54, 24% were ages 55–64, 23% were ages 35–44, 12% were 25–35, and 7% were 65 years old or older.

Together, this *Snapshot* of the media literacy community reflects that we are broad, cross-curricular, and intergenerational. It tells us that most practitioners are self-taught (74%), suggesting that degree program development, professional development, or other formalized training in media literacy education may be an essential requirement for growing the field. In conjunction with primary professional roles, we invited respondents to share their specific job titles. These titles further demonstrate the incredible diversity of professional identity, spanning from students to teachers, from artists to researchers. Yet, while our community snapshot indicates diversity regarding roles, identities, and contexts, we have much work to do in building a diverse community of practice. Eighty-five percent of respondents identified as White or Caucasian, with the remaining respondents comprising Black/African-American (5%), Hispanic or Latino (3%), Asian (2%), and other identities (5%). These numbers raise questions about visibility and inclusivity for practitioners of color. When we cross-reference snapshot information about race and ethnicity with data about the location of respondents, we noticed that most respondents live in U.S. cities in which a large portion of the population identifies as African-American (e.g., Philadelphia, 44% and New York City, 25%).

While more research is required to understand this unevenness in representation, government research reveals possible trends. For example, two 2016 reports sponsored by the U.S. Department of Education's Office of Planning, Evaluation and Policy Development note disparities in representation of people of color among K-12 school personnel, including administrators and teachers (The State of Racial Diversity in the Educator Workforce, p. 6), as well as underrepresentation among the faculty and leadership of institutions of higher education (Advancing Diversity and Inclusion in Higher Education, p. 37). Given the majority of survey respondents were from K-12 schools and institutions of higher education, the observed disparity may be anchored in larger social imbalances. Other possibilities include disparities in the distributive modes of the survey, comprising predominantly Twitter and Facebook.

Gap: Race/Ethnicity and Training and Professional Development

Collectively, the demographics of respondents revealed two gaps: the first relates to race/ethnicity and the second to training and professional development. The demographics for race/ethnicity of respondents reveal much work is needed regarding outreach and representation, positioning attention to diversity as a top concern in growing the field of media literacy education. Investments in media literacy education initiatives at multiple levels and serving many groups and audiences are required.

Seventy-four percent of respondents indicated that they are self-taught in media literacy education. This information confirms existing scholarship that degree program development, professional development, or other formalized training in media literacy education are lacking. Developing media literacy as a core curriculum topic and 21st-century pedagogy for inclusion across PK-20 contexts requires extensive revisioning of teacher education programs and the augmentation of professional development opportunities.

What Topics Are Included in Media Literacy Courses or Programs?

Respondents selected up to 10 topics from a list of 25 topics to provide insight regarding the scope and composition of media literacy courses and programs in 2018. As this is NAMLE's first State of Media Literacy *Snapshot*, there is no comparison data to determine if this list of topics would have been different in 2010 or 2015.

The topics most often selected were information literacy (69%), agenda/bias (67%), and news literacy (67%), while issues that have been recurring concerns in media literacy for years – such as celebrity culture (16%) and violence (13%) – were not widely selected. This shift in focus is not surprising as many media literacy educators have expressed a new or renewed interest in media and information literacy among their colleagues and administrators given the rise of "fake news" stories and misinformation in recent years. As most educators are addressing media literacy and related topics with limited instructional time, a reassessment seems to have taken place that favors issues related to information and news literacy. The impact of this shift for media literacy teaching and learning is yet to be determined and requires further exploration.

Other frequently selected topics connect heavily with skills related to determining fact from fiction, identifying persuasive strategies, or engaging in the ethics of media use and creation, including: copyright and fair use (56%), advertising/consumer culture (54%), and credibility (54%). Topics related to media construction followed, including: body image/identity (35%), representation (33%), and children's media (32%). Generally, these topics comprise attention to how media messages portray people, places, and ideas, specifically eliciting students' abilities to identify narrow conceptions or stereotypes that may have real impacts on audiences, policies, and politics.

Less frequently selected topics include: ecomedia literacy/sustainability (6%), regulatory (10%), health literacy (10%), violence (12%), celebrity culture (16%), and data mining/privacy/surveillance (24%).

Gap: Most and Least-Selected Topics

While *Snapshot* information about most and least-selected topics provides some insight into subject trends in media literacy education, advanced research into practice is missing. Qualitative information about what is actually happening in classrooms, courses, and programs is needed in order to effectively advance media literacy in PK-12, higher education, and other contexts. Practitioners, advocates, policymakers, and the public at large need a deep understanding of the complex purposes and pedagogies involved in media literacy education, in conjunction with studies that describe practitioners' experiences with media literacy and reports on effectiveness. Creating successful programs may require a holistic, integrated approach to media literacy education as part of traditional content areas to support overburdened teachers and a crowded curriculum.

In What Contexts Is Media Literacy Included?

The presence and placement of media literacy continues to be an area of debate and interest. Respondents referred to varied placements for media literacy in their organizations and institutions. Thirty-eight percent of respondents reported media literacy is part of a standard content area course, while 24% shared it is a stand-alone subject. In 16% of responses, media literacy was described as part of an informal context, such as an advisory, after school program, or community event. In about 13%, media literacy was included as part of the library curriculum, while about 9% collectively shared it is part of professional development, seminar or guest lecturing, or special events. Together, these varied placements suggest media literacy is valid and viable in a range of contexts and in addressing many purposes, from cross-curricular integration to professional development and community events. Media literacy, in turn, offers not only a subject of study but also a way of teaching and learning that is meaningful across contexts.

Gap: Contexts

The multiple contexts across and within which media literacy education is included and taught add to the challenge of scaling. Effective growth of the field requires comprehensive research and analysis of not only where media literacy education may be included but also an investigation into the decisions that impact the inclusion and positioning of media literacy across its varied contexts.

What Materials Are Being Used in Media Literacy Education?

Since a core component of media literacy education is the analysis, evaluation, and creation of media, then the resources that facilitate the screening, streaming, downloading, reading, listening to, and playing with media are central to any *Snapshot* of the field. Consider, however, that the 300+ responses to the survey generated a list of over 500 resources. Over half the respondents shared at least two resources, and some as many as ten or more! The resource mentioned most frequently was NAMLE, perhaps as NAMLE was distributing the survey. The organization Common Sense Media was almost as frequently mentioned. The statement "self created materials" was the third most listed resource, reflecting that educators and practitioners are often creating and customizing resources to fit their specific needs. Several organizations providing free, quality resources were frequently mentioned, including the Center for Media Literacy, Media Education Foundation, News Literacy Project, Newseum, and Project Look Sharp. Approximately two-thirds of all respondents mentioned at least one of these eight resources, without a pull-down menu of options or other visual to guide their selection.

A few of the scholars that frequently focus their research and publications on the field of media literacy are clearly relied upon as resources as they were mentioned often, including Renee Hobbs, Henry Jenkins, Douglas Kellner, and Sonia Livingstone.

However, after the eight online resources and four scholarly authors mentioned above, there is minimal consensus across all remaining resources. The list runs the gamut from TED Talks to YouTube to over 50 different books, 7 academic journals, several Twitter accounts, hashtags, and numerous websites. Resources may be categorized as: (1) media industry created and distributed, (2) education industry created and distributed, (3) personally created and used. This list of resources reflects a thriving field in which ample materials are available and useful, but it also reveals a lack of cohesion for accessing materials.

Gap: Curricular Materials

This *Snapshot* reflects a gap in comprehensive curricular materials. In other words, there is a lack of a central, online repository of comprehensive, quality curriculum materials and lesson plans available for free to teachers and other professional educators. While innumerable resources are accessible across many modalities, to move from scattered implementation to frequent, integrated practice requires an all-inclusive curriculum containing not only content materials but also scaffolded lesson plans with clear objectives and relevant assessments. Future initiatives or studies might solicit grade-leveled curricula for organization in a searchable database, beginning the process needed to develop a panoramic view of practice.

What Challenges Impact the State of Media Literacy?

Our *Snapshot* revealed that media literacy is not in all education environments, despite the availability of resources and the presence of people dedicated to bringing media literacy into their schools, colleges, and other educational contexts and programs. It is not included in all curriculum, and most schools do not have a trained person focused on media literacy education to support implementation and learning. The disconnect between recognition of need and demonstration of action is vast and poses multiple challenges. We sought to bring understanding to this disconnect by asking respondents to help us understand their biggest challenges. The two challenges cited most often actually have little to do with media literacy and everything to do with our education system. The top two challenges were "competing curricular requirements" (50%) and "lack of time" (45%). Competing curricular requirements may be tied to standardized, high-stakes testing, though that was not an option provided in the survey. Since the No Child Left Behind Act (2001) and its successor, Every Student Succeeds Act (2015), K-12 schools have been pressured to meet external demands. In schools across the country, curriculum decisions focus on subjects that will be tested statewide and nationally. Media literacy may be an acknowledged need, but it is not on the list of subjects tested and therefore is simply not as critical to school curriculum as other subject areas.

The next most common challenges were "lack of institutional understanding of what media literacy is" (26%), "lack of content/curricular resources" (24%), "funding" (22%), and "lack of content area curricular training" (19%). It is worth noting that each of these areas impacts the other. For example, a lack of institutional understanding of what constitutes media literacy may lead to a struggle in finding appropriate resources or securing funding for courses, programs, and community endeavors. Or, although respondents provided hundreds of snapshot examples of resources (as discussed in the section above), putting those resources together into a meaningful curriculum and course of study requires a deeper understanding of the field and is time consuming, especially if the goal is to create learning modules that combine critical analysis and creative action/agency in a measurable way.

Gap: Challenges

Overall, there is a lack of public understanding about what it means to be "media literate." Media literacy education is not simply addressing "fake news" or teaching skills in using information and communication technologies. Certainly, those areas are a part of media literacy, but media literacy education comprises a broader, critical field of study and cross-disciplinary pedagogy anchored in cultivating critical thinking and reflective habits of mind about the messages we receive and create.

The challenges mentioned above (competing curricular requirements, lack of resources, and the need for content area training) represent repeated and consistent barriers to media literacy practice and praxis. They reflect conversations between media literacy educators across a range of contexts, including with colleagues and peers in schools and institutions and at regional and national conference gatherings. These challenges are the topics of journal articles and book chapters. Several of these topics have been referenced in earlier observations throughout this *Snapshot*. They are core challenges in the field.

Many of these challenges reflect a lack of funding. However, funding is not a need unto itself. Funding is a need in service of other needs. To the extent that media literacy education has received funding, it has often focused on targeted projects, such as combating fake news or addressing cyber-bullying, and less on comprehensive media literacy education. Perhaps broad-based funding will become available once policies are implemented to support media literacy education and encourage high quality scalable media literacy programs.

Conclusion and Recommendations

The purpose of this *Snapshot* was to begin a conversation about the state of media literacy in the United States. While there has been growing interest and enthusiasm for media literacy education, a holistic, national effort is needed to advance the field.

This *Snapshot* is a first attempt to:

- Understand current practices of media literacy education across institutions, schools, organizations and communities;

- Facilitate general public awareness and discourse in media literacy education;
- Engage elected officials, tech companies, and others in the need to support efforts in media literacy education;
- Empower teachers to include media literacy in their curriculum;
- Identify new developments and challenges; and
- Aggregate syllabi, assessment tools, activities, books, and other resources.

As we learned in this *Snapshot*, there is much work to do in facilitating greater connections, visibility of practice, and voice in the community. The "gaps" discussed throughout this *Snapshot* serve as guideposts for the recommendations listed below:

1 *Expand training and professional development opportunities* for media literacy instruction, particularly teacher training for both pre-service and inservice teachers in colleges of education, as well as training for those coordinating after school or out-of-school programs;
2 *Outreach to diverse populations*, specifically communities of color, to support their participation, scholarship, and teaching or new program development;
3 *Support inquiry into practice* – such as small-scale qualitative case studies and larger, comprehensive ethnographic examinations – in order to understand structures that invite or prevent media literacy practice, and develop a clearer picture of how practices are enacted and evaluated to life in classrooms and other environments;
4 *Establish an online, central repository* for the collection, curation, and aggregation of resources, including not only content materials but also thoughtful and complete course designs and lessons for a variety of ages, grades, and contexts that include clear learning objectives, aligned assessments, and appropriate, relevant pedagogies;
5 *Disseminate an annual survey* to gauge changes, improvements, and challenges in research, practice, and assessment; and
6 *Advocacy for public understanding*, such as a visibility campaign, with goals to clarify the purpose and urgency of media literacy.

We recognize that there are already many positive initiatives, events, and actions taking place that address several of the recommendations stated above. For instance, public outreach and visibility are key aspects of U.S. Media Literacy Week, where coordinated regional events illustrate growing engagement in media literacy. Further, the biennial NAMLE Conference continues to bring together scholars and practitioners across diverse contexts in dialogue and sharing about professional development, teacher training programs, courses, and research. We look forward to supporting the promise and potential of media literacy, as well as tackling related challenges and struggles. Working with educators, organizations, media and technology companies, elected officials, and others interested in media literacy, we seek to intentionally advance the value, purpose, and pedagogies of media literacy education in order to best prepare today's students and citizens for a successful future.

Appendix: Survey Questions

1 Name
2 Organization Name/Institution
3 Organization Type
4 Job Title
5 Content Area
6 Education
7 City/State/Postal Code
8 Email
9 Age
10 Gender
11 Race/Ethnicity
12 Twitter Handle
13 Website/Blog
14 Are you a NAMLE Member?
15 What is your primary role?
16 Describe how media literacy has been or is currently included in your organization/institution?
17 What materials are you using to teach media literacy? Where did you receive media literacy educator training?
18 Which topics are covered within this course or program? Please limit your answer to no more than 10 topics.
19 What are your biggest challenges when incorporating media literacy into your classroom, institution, non-profit, or other organization?
20 Is there any other information you feel would be important to add?
21 If applicable, could you please share a link to your curriculum, syllabus, or website?
22 Would you be open to a follow-up phone call about media literacy?

References

Considine, D. (1990). Media literacy: Can we get there from here? *Educational Technology, 30*(12), 27–32.
Culver, S. H., & Redmond, T. (2019) Media literacy snapshot. National Association for Media Literacy Education. Retrieved from https://namle.net/2019/07/02/state-of-media-literacy-report/

De Abreu, B. (2018). Information and media literacy education: The role of school libraries. In D. E. Agosto (Ed.), *Information Literacy and Libraries in the Age of Fake News* (pp. 129–135). Denver, CO: Libraries Unlimited.

Hobbs, R. (2010). *Digital and media literacy: A plan of action. A white paper on the digital and media literacy recommendations of the Knight Commission on the Information Needs of Communities in a Democracy.* Washington, DC: Aspen Institute.

Hobbs, R., & Jensen, A. (2009). The past, present, and future of media literacy education. *Journal of Media Literacy Education, 1*(1), 1–11.

National Association for Media Literacy Education (NAMLE). (2014). Key questions to ask when analyzing media messages. Retrieved from https://namle.net/publications/core-principles/

National Association for Media Literacy Education. (2007). Core principles of media literacy education in the United States. Retrieved from https://namle.net/publications/core-principles/

Thoman, E., & Jolls, T. (2004). Media literacy: A national priority for a changing world. *American Behavioral Scientist, 48*(1), 18–29.

U.S. Department of Education. (2016). Advancing diversity and inclusion in higher education. Washington, D.C. Retrieved from https://www2.ed.gov/rschstat/research/pubs/advancing-diversity-inclusion.pdf

U.S. Department of Education. (2016). The state of racial diversity in the educator workforce. Washington, D.C. Retrieved from https://www2.ed.gov/rschstat/eval/highered/racial-diversity/state-racial-diversity-workforce.pdf

3 Media Literacy in the Age of Big Data

Kathleen Tyner

Introduction

Media Literacy in the Age of Big Data explores contemporary literacy practices within the context of "Big Data," an ambiguous term that refers to the collection, analysis, uses and reporting of information from massive data sets by an array of public and private actors for commercial, civic and social purposes. Emerging from the social sciences and engineering, Big Data practices cross all disciplinary boundaries. As the uses of digital media become increasingly ubiquitous, large-scale and real-time data mining supports a wide range of personal, social, economic and public policy decisions. In the process, Big Data practices provide both benefits and liabilities. On the one hand, Big Data supports efficient decision-making and predictive analysis that can be used to address problems across every sector of society. On the other hand, more transparency for Big Data research methods is required to trust the ethical collection, validity and reliability of the evidence.

Although regulation and policy related to data collection and its use by corporations has accelerated, governments have been slow to respond to public concerns about fair and ethical online data practices. In addition, governments have also begun to initiate Big Data practices for use in scientific research, education and national security, raising new concerns about information asymmetry between citizens and government agencies (Executive Office of the President, 2016). As a result, users struggle to obtain the critical and technical skills needed to create, protect and analyze information in the context of a dynamic digital transformation across all sectors of society.

Literacy is a lifelong pathway that challenges individuals to adapt to emerging communication tools and disruptive systems in order to build social capital and engage with their communities. Media educators routinely investigate these complex and interrelated shifts in literacy practices from print to electronic to digital media. The next challenge is to connect and reboot traditional principles of media literacy education to include data fluency within the context of computer-generated Big Data. When explored through its social uses, it could be argued that data and algorithms are also media. Analogous to critical reading, the collection, analysis and uses of the information generated through Big

Data practices require a cross-disciplinary approach that supports the skills and knowledge needed to understand its impact on citizens and societies. In addition to critical analysis, hands-on production projects that engage with complex Big Data concepts and contexts are a reciprocal way to make sense of a sea of information and to communicate it to others through multiple techniques, networks and platforms.

Catherine D'Ignazio, researcher, educator and software engineer, suggests a connection between traditional literacy and data fluency through "creative data literacy," projects that can engage people from non-technical fields who are "more likely to be the subjects of data than to use data for civic purposes" (2017, p. 1). Big Data opens an opportunity for media educators to design learning environments that support the data fluency skills needed to negotiate the ubiquitous and pervasive presence of digital tools, texts and practices. One example can be seen in interdisciplinary data visualization projects that connect traditional literacy practices with the digital literacies and data fluency needed to critically explore the impact of Big Data in every sector of society. Data visualization blends aesthetics, narratives and data that can be used to engage learners with emerging literacy practices.

Definitions for Purposeful Ambiguity

Definitions for both media literacy and Big Data are diverse and flexible in rapidly evolving communication ecosystems. Nonetheless, even provisional definitions can be used to explore connections between the two complex concepts.

Big Data

It is not surprising that the emerging concept of *Big Data* often results in "multiple, ambiguous and often contradictory definitions" (Ward & Baker, 2013, p. 1). In their groundbreaking book, *Big Data: A Revolution That Will Transform How We Live, Work and Think*, Viktor Mayer-Schönberger and Kenneth Cukier state that "there is no rigorous definition of Big Data" (2013, p. 6). Instead, they describe its impact: "Big Data refers to things one can do at a large scale that cannot be done at a smaller one, to extract new insights or create new forms of value, in ways that change markets, organizations, the relationships between citizens and governments, and more" (p. 6).

In an analysis that links Big Data with library science, De Mauro, Greco and Grimaldi (2016) acknowledge the confusion generated by dynamic and competing definitions for Big Data:

> The absence of a consensual definition of Big Data often brought scholars to adopt "implicit" definitions through anecdotes, success stories, characteristics, technological features, trends or its impact on society, firms and business processes. The existing definitions for

Big Data provide very different perspectives, denoting the chaotic state of the art. Big Data is considered in turn as a term describing a social phenomenon, information assets, data sets, storage technologies, analytical techniques, processes and infrastructures.

(p. 126)

Undoubtedly, definitions will continue to evolve as Big Data theory and practice become embedded across disciplines. For example, communication studies scholars are beginning to position data as a new discourse within existing media and communication theories (Neuman, 2016; Schrock, 2017). It is useful to conceptualize data as another form of mediated communication with its own codes, conventions and syntax. In this regard, data communication aligns with the critical analysis and production practices associated with media literacy.

Media Literacy

Tedious debates about definitions are familiar to media education scholars. Confusion about media literacy definitions is exacerbated by competing and intersecting terminologies such as *media and information literacy, digital literacy, data literacy, visual literacy, computer literacy* and *multiliteracies* (Guiterrez & Tyner, 2012; New London Group, 1996; Nichols & Stornaiuolo, 2019; Tyner, 1998). Nonetheless, due to decades of discourse, some consensus can be found for definitions that support the theories, research and assessment of media literacy practices in applied settings.

Definitions for media literacy in the United States build on a 1992 Aspen Institute retreat that was organized to shape a national framework for media literacy advocacy groups and educators. At that time, participants reported a provisional definition of media literacy as "the ability of a citizen to access, analyze, and produce information for specific outcomes" (Firestone, 1993, p. v). It was assumed that this working definition would be customized by media educators over time. Soon after the retreat, the broad definition often cited by participants evolved to "the ability to access, analyze, evaluate, and produce communication messages in a variety of forms" (Center for Media Literacy, 2019).

As discourse about the characteristics of media literacy moves beyond "what" to "why," media literacy advocates extend definitions to include the aims and purposes for media education. For example, the Center for Media Literacy (CML) builds on the Aspen Institute definition within the context of education for the critical analysis and expression needed to support democratic engagement and participation:

Media Literacy is a 21st century approach to education. It provides a framework to access, analyze, evaluate, create and participate with messages in a variety of forms – from print to video to the Internet. Media literacy builds an understanding of the role of media in society as well as essential skills of inquiry and self-expression necessary for citizens of a democracy.

(Center for Media Literacy, 2019; Thoman & Jolls, 2005, p. 190)

Similarly, the U.S.-based National Association for Media Literacy Education (NAMLE) broadly defines media literacy as "the ability to access, analyze, evaluate, create and act using all forms of communication" (National Association for Media Literacy Education, 2019). The organization goes on to provide detailed explanations that include media analysis and production practices to support interdisciplinary education, scholarship and active citizenship (National Association for Media Literacy Education. 2007). International scholars, especially those in the fields of library science and journalism, refer to *media and information literacy*. The definition continues to be customized and expanded by organizations around the world (Federov, 2003; Ofcom, 2004; UNESCO, 2017; Wallis & Buckingham, 2016).

Digital Literacy

As communication technologies shift from analog to electronic to digital contexts, the term *digital literacy (*or *digital literacies)* emerges in congruence with research about the tools, texts and social practices needed to connect media literacy and Big Data practices. The distinction between the terms "media literacy" and "digital literacy" invokes Marshall McLuhan's phrase "the medium is the message" (1964) and subsequent debates about technological determinism in media and communication studies. In a blog post related to educational policies for integrating digital media in the curriculum, Buckingham (2019) states that "the technological dimension (digital or analogue) is irrelevant: we should be talking about *media* literacy, not digital literacy."

In contrast, Nichols and Stornaiuolo (2019) argue that the term "digital literacy" provides a useful convergence of media, information and computer literacy concepts that can connect communication technologies with their social uses. They identify concepts that explain digital literacy practices as "the way that users (e.g. individuals, groups, communities) leverage technologies (e.g., computers, software, mobile devices) to consume or produce content (e.g., textual, visual, multimedia artifacts) in digital contexts" (p. 19). Nonetheless, in their review of definitions, the researchers recognize that conceptualizing literacy is a work in progress and call for the need for "flexible theories, pedagogies, and methodologies" (p. 21). Nichols and Stornaiuolo (2019) propose connecting digital literacy and media literacy concepts by focusing on historical, economic and technical theories with "an emphasis that aligns with social practice approaches to digital literacies" that were also "part of earlier traditions in media education" (p. 20).

Data Literacy and Data Fluency

Terms that are more specific to Big Data practices provide a subset of digital literacy definitions. "Data literacy" and "data fluency" have been proposed as a way to directly engage with Big Data analysis and practice in the classroom (Mandinach & Gummer, 2013; McAuley, Rahemtulla, Goulding, & Souch, 2012). D'Ignazio and Bhargava (2015) define *data literacy* as "the ability to read, work with, analyze and argue with data" (p. 2). They then extend the definition to: (1) identifying when and where data is being passively collected about your actions and interactions; (2) understanding the algorithmic manipulations performed on large sets of data to identify patterns; and (3) weighing the real and potential ethical impacts of data-driven decisions for individuals and for society (para. 13).

An even broader goal for digital literacy in the age of Big Data is *data fluency*, often referred to as a tool for evidence-based decision-making. As a connection to media education, data fluency implies that *data* is comparable to media information and *fluency* is comparable to literacy. In particular, fluency is analogous to code-switching discourse between language and linguistic systems, based on the context of communication.

It is important to note that data fluency does not necessarily require the skills of a data scientist. Data fluency grows from information and statistical literacy concepts that require a basic understanding of research methods, both quantitative and qualitative, as well as the ability to evaluate the validity and reliability of research evidence for logical argument and decision-making. Data fluency builds on traditional literacies and enables individuals to purposefully select and switch between multiple literacies with multiple devices in multiple contexts in order to support their own personal, social and civic goals.

Given their divergent complexity, interdisciplinary discourse between scholars and practitioners about the relationships between critical literacy and data fluency is also key. Interdisciplinary studies can be used to recontextualize theories, research, practice and policies that connect media education with complex and emerging areas of study like Big Data. Klein and Newell (1997) define *interdisciplinary studies* as:

> a process of answering a question, solving a problem, or addressing a topic that is too broad or complex to be dealt with adequately by a single discipline or profession... and draws on disciplinary perspectives and integrates their insights through construction of a more comprehensive perspective.
>
> (pp. 393–394)

Beyond Definitions: Conceptual Models in Context

In order to connect Big Data and media literacy practices, it is useful to compare models used to guide theory, research and practice in educational settings. These include conceptual, assemblage and contextual models. A toolbox of conceptual, assemblage and contextual models for literacy in the context of Big Data provides perspectives that can be used to inform the design of learning environments for emerging literacy practices.

Conceptual Models

Conceptual Models for media education, often referred to as "key concepts," provide consensus, priorities and practical frameworks for the design of the contemporary literacy learning environment. Examples of key concepts for literacy in North America include models from the Center for Media Literacy (2010), and the National Association for Media Literacy Education (2007). These frameworks build on eight key concepts created in Canada in 1987 by media educator Barrie Duncan and the Association for Media Literacy (Hoechsmann & Poyntz, 2017; Jolls & Wilson, 2014). Known as the Canadian Key Concepts and influenced by the work of British scholar Len Masterman, they state that:

1　All media are constructions.
2　The media construct reality.
3　Audiences negotiate meaning in media.
4　Media have commercial implications.
5　Media contain ideological and value messages.
6　Media have social and political implications.
7　Form and content are closely related in the media.
8　Each medium has a unique aesthetic form (Jolls & Wilson, p. 71).

The Canadian Key Concepts provided a useful framework to stimulate discourse and integration of media education into formal education. They also provide an opportunity for dialogue and reflection that can be used to investigate connections to Big Data concepts and topics.

　　Conceptual models for Big Data represent a rapidly evolving conversation. In a review of the literature, De Mauro, Greco and Grimaldi (2016) found that some scholarly consensus about the concept of Big Data originated with three characteristics referred to as *Velocity, Volume,* and *Variety* (Beyer & Laney 2012, pp. 1–9; Zaslavsky, Perera and Georgakopoulos, 2013; Zikopoulos & Eaton, 2011). Subsequent researchers added the characteristics of *Veracity* (Schroeck, Shockley, Smart, Romero-Morales & Tufano, 2012), *Value* (Dijcks, 2013), *Variability* (Gandomi & Haider, 2015) and *Visualization* (Sivarajah, Kamal, Irani & Weerakkody, 2016, p. 273). By 2016, these defining characteristics are referred to as *The 7vs of Big Data*: Velocity, Volume, Variety, Veracity, Value, Variability and Visualization (De Mauro et al., 2016).

In a subsequent literature review, De Mauro, Greco and Grimaldi (2019) explored a more detailed conceptual model for Big Data referred to as the *ITMI Model* (Information, Technology, Methods and Impact). The researchers identified 17 fundamental concepts related to the ITMI Model that can be used for Big Data research and practice: Overload, User-generated data, Cybersecurity, the Internet of Things, Storage Capabilities, Distributed Systems, Parallel Computing, Programming Paradigms, Machine Learning, Emerging Roles and Skills, Visualization, Decision-Making, Value Creation, Applications, Organizations Structure, Privacy and Datafication. Although the connections are not simple, these concepts provide a framework that can also be used to link the conceptual models, topics and practices for Big Data with media education.

Assemblage Models

Assemblage is a creative technique that refers to the use of existing texts to recontextualize and compose new texts as an iterative social practice. Building on collage and remix culture, the term was introduced by digital scholars Johndan Johnson-Eilola and Stuart Selber (2007) to address the postmodern shift in intertextual composition in social contexts. Building on models provided by Lankshear and Knoble (2008) and Gilster (1997), Nichols and Stornaiuolo (2019) argue for an "assemblage" approach to evolving literacy practices:

> digital literacy can be understood less as a bounded concept and more as an assemblage – a layering together of historical meanings and practices that have congealed, for the moment, into a useable discourse.
>
> (pp. 17–18)

Assemblage models are useful to design interdisciplinary tasks that build on students' prior experiences with the production of digital media as a pathway to critical textual analysis. For example, working with the concept of Media and Information Literacy (MIL), a term often used in journalism and library science, Frau-Meigs (2014) connects media education approaches to digital media practices in three broad categories: (1) operational skills (e.g., coding, computing and design); (2) editorial skills (e.g., multimedia writing-reading-producing and mixing); and (3) organization skills (e.g., navigating, sorting, filtering and evaluating). The components in Frau-Meigs framework reflect the composition and critical analysis qualities seen in assemblage models.

Building on the concepts from Frau-Meigs, an international team of researchers from the University of Lusafona in Portugal and The University of Texas at Austin (USA) initiated GamiLearning, a three-year research project that combined game creation with concepts related to Big Data. Using a constructivist approach, classroom tasks were designed to support the operational, editorial and organizational skills and knowledge needed for student reflection and management of their online identities, data privacy and online data security. The goal was to go beyond educational game play to explore the impact of students' digital game creation on their media and information literacy learning. Significant increases in media literacy learning were found in pre- and post-evaluations of the GamiLearning game creation activities (Costa, Tyner, Henriques & Sousa, 2018). The GamiLearning project demonstrates that assemblage models can be successfully used to connect creative digital composition related to Big Data topics with traditional media literacy concepts in the formal education environment.

Contextual Models

Finally, contextual models provide an approach that informs critical analysis about literacy practices in specific contexts. Given the complexity of Big Data practices, the analysis of literacy practices within their historical, social, cultural, legal, political and economic contexts provide focused, interdisciplinary frameworks. Numerous scholars have proposed contextual models that can be used to investigate critical literacy practices (Bulger & Davison, 2018; Livingstone, Wijnen, Papaioannou, Costa & del Grandio, 2013; New London Group, 1996; Nichols & Stornaiuolo, 2019; Tyner, 2011). Contextual models also provide rich and relational insights into Big Data practices (Hoeren & Kolany-Raiser, 2017).

Navigating the Affordances and Constraints of Big Data

Concerns and confusion about the potential harm to individuals and to society create a sense of urgency for an educational response. It is important to note that Big Data also comes with affordances, as well as constraints. For example, case studies have shown effectiveness in examples such as "data-driven farming," or "smart farming," a process that uses Big Data to manage the fluctuating human and material resources needed to respond to increasing unpredictable weather patterns and droughts (Bronson & Knezevic, 2016). Significant benefit can be seen in the increased ability to inform reliable, predictive analysis in record time with the potential to offer real-time solutions to time-sensitive problems across all sectors of society (Ajit, 2016). In spite of the beneficial uses of evidence provided by massive data collection and predictive analysis, escalating public concerns about Big Data practices raise legitimate questions about their potential to also harm society.

Big Data comes with significant constraints. Researchers point out that Big Data is not simply defined by its large data sets and complex analytical tools (boyd & Crawford, 2012). Even data research scientists struggle to situate Big Data within established research norms. Although machine learning and artificial intelligence increasingly enable algorithms to rapidly correct errors in massive data collection and analysis, the "correlation is not cause" standard for research still holds true.

A bigger problem is that Big Data practices have not yet provided the transparency needed to establish human understanding and trust in the results. For example, in 2013, Google was lauded in the media for using Big Data to provide more cost-efficient, timely and accurate information than the government's Center for Disease Control (CDC). Known as Google Flu Trends (GFT), the case study was used as a prominent example of the value of Big Data. Unfortunately, it was not. Subsequent research revealed that GTF was more accurate in predicting weather patterns than flu patterns (Lazar, Kennedy, King & Vespignani, 2014; Wilcox, 2016). The lesson learned was that although Big Data shows great promise for predictive analytics, traditional research methods are still needed to verify results, patterns and relationships between data sets over time.

Big Data and Personal Information

The scope and scale of Big Data also raise ethical concerns about the collection of personal information shared on hypertransparent social media platforms. User-created data is mined from social media, product reviews, responses on news sites and search engines (Chan, 2019). In addition to content, online user behavior is also collected from web traffic, news sites, financial transactions, credit card transactions and through public records. Data is harvested from video, voice messages, audio, facial recognition, mobile devices satellites and "smart devices" in public and private spaces (Chan, 2019).

These concerns are exacerbated by a growing awareness of the *information asymmetry* between data miners and users. Information asymmetry refers to the strategic advantage in negotiating economic transaction when one party has more information than the other party. The irony is that the value of user-created data is most likely to accrue to professional data miners and not to individual users. Brunton and Nissenbaum (2015) note the difficulty of countering the strategic advantage of Big Data samples that "are collected in circumstances we may not understand, for purposes we may not understand, and are used in ways we may not understand" (p. 3). Terms such as "Infonomics" and "Surveillance Capitalism" refer to the economic contexts for data accumulation models that leverage information asymmetry for corporate shareholders and governments (Foster & McChesney, 2014; Sadowski, 2019; Zuboff, 2019).

In addition, the pervasive and ubiquitous presence of data collection instruments also fuel concerns about surveillance and privacy rights in the context of digital security, target marketing, financial transactions and governance (Smith, 2018). The legal and ethical ownership of even the most personal information can be perplexing. In return for the conveniences of digital participation through devices, networks and applications, users are asked to interpret convoluted terms of agreement for the release of their personal information so that corporations and governments can mine data from their digital devices in ways that invoke George Orwell's *1984*. Personal data protections exist, but their clarity and transparency are confusing.

> Big Data also presents many formidable challenges to government and citizens precisely because data technologies are becoming so pervasive, intrusive and difficult to understand...how should we even define what is socially and legally acceptable when the practices enabled by Big Data are so novel and often arcane?
>
> (Bollier, 2010, p. 40)

It is important to note that even the most knowledgeable and data-fluent users sometimes understand and agree to trading their data for access. In 2019, the *New York Times* initiated *The Privacy Project*, a series of articles that explore the social conveniences and costs of complex digital practices. In an article that presents an overview of the Privacy Project's findings, editor Susan Fowler (2019) remarks:

> Privacy is a complex, nebulous and constantly evolving issue, but amid the chaos and complexity, we have discerned four main themes: the ubiquity of surveillance and the ready availability of surveillance tools; our considerable ignorance of where personal data goes and how companies and governments use that data; the tangible harm of privacy violations; and the possibility that sacrificing privacy for other values (say, convenience or security) can be a worthwhile trade-off.
>
> (para. 2)

Governments around the world are beginning to respond to citizen concerns with fines and regulations related to corporate data breaches and questionable practices for technology companies, beginning in 2018 with the *General Data Protection Regulation* (GDPR), a law that provides privacy protection for citizens in the European Union (Kozlowska, 2018).

Big Data and Regulation in the United States

Big Data is rapidly emerging as a daunting and complex backdrop to issues related to privacy, surveillance, information sourcing, reception and reporting at a time when public trust in traditional gatekeeping institutions, such as news organizations, government institutions and public schooling, is in decline (Ingram, 2018; Schneider, 2018). One utopian goal is to craft responsive law and policy, based on reliable research evidence, that builds citizens' trust in government. Unsurprisingly, digital technologies continue to outpace government regulation. The architecture of governance has responded incrementally by negotiating between the concerns of citizens and the powerful interests that have transformed the digital commons into digital real estate.

Historically, the responsibility to regulate corporate practices related to media content and personal data in the United States can generally be characterized under three broad categories: (1) *government regulation*, which includes law and policy directives from local, state and federal agencies; (2) *industry self-regulation*, usually through collective associations in the marketplace, and (3) *individual self-regulation* by media users. Regulation related to children's online data and media use is a frequent political priority for government and industry regulation practices and often one of the first targets for regulatory discussion (Montgomery, 2015).

In the United States, the responsibility for policy directives and legal regulations related to media falls under the Federal Communication Commission (FCC) and the Federal Trade Commission (FCT). As a consumer protection agency, the FCT has established legal precedent for consumer data privacy and protection through the *Privacy Act of 1974*, which protects unauthorized disclosure of personal information from the federal government. Obviously, communication practices have changed drastically since 1974. As a result, state governments in the United States have bypassed the federal government agencies to challenge social media practices in court. For example, the state of California adopted The *California Consumer Privacy Act* (CCPA) in 2018. This law enhances privacy rights and consumer protection for residents of California.

Policies that support industry self-regulation also have a long regulatory history. For example, the Entertainment Software Ratings Board (ESRB) provides the rating system to discourage the purchase of violent or sexual content in videogames by children (Richter, 2019). Notably, social networks prefer to identify as technology companies instead of media companies, in part to potentially avoid the stricter advertising and content guidelines that are in place for the traditional print and broadcast industries (Bell, 2018). Expectations for media self-regulation can also be seen as a cynical political strategy that avoids conflict with corporate interests. Despite sanctions and settlements with Facebook,

Google and Equifax for data breaches and mishandling of consumer data in 2019, governments have only begun to craft laws that protect citizens from unethical Big Data practices in the corporate sector.

As a result, individual self-regulation is still the major strategy for content and privacy protection across all media. In their article about data literacy, D'Ignazio & Bhargava (2015) note: "You can't work with data if it has been extractively collected and isn't available to you. You can't read data if there is a lack of transparency about when it is even being collected" (p. 2). An expanded view of media literacy positions data as media, and data fluency as another form of literacy. Big Data presents new challenges and opportunities to acquire the critical skills and knowledge needed to effectively navigate a digital world.

Designs for Critical Literacy Learning

Big Data practices address an intimidating range of knowledge and skill sets that challenge educators and learners to push outside their comfort zones. It is important to remember that media educators do not need to be quantitative research specialists or data software engineers to engage with Big Data topics. Data fluency can begin with conventional classroom practices that build on familiar literacy practices to connect with related Big Data concepts and contexts. An interdisciplinary link to data fluency might start with learning opportunities that ask students to record and reflect on their own online data creation, collection, analysis and use of data in their personal literacy practices. These reflections could include simple research tasks related to content analysis, survey results, scenarios, situational thinking, evidence-based narratives and data visualization.

Peer-learning and teamwork encourage students and their teachers to co-learn by sharing their prior learning experiences with digital literacy and data. In addition to awareness, analysis and user response to Big Data practices, constructivist, project-based work also leverages production design and problem-solving skills that reinforce a reciprocal relationship between critical analysis and practice with multiliteracy tools and texts (Tyner et al. 2015).

As media educators engage with Big Data practices in the classroom, it is useful to avoid a narrow focus on the practical, technical computer skills needed for digital reading, writing and coding. Instead, the goal is to position an expanded concept of critical literacy for social capital and civic engagement in response to disruptive digital transformations. Within this context, an understanding of Internet history, infrastructure, business models, government regulation and the uses of online data provides additional foundations to explore the rights and responsibilities of digital citizens.

*Bridging Analysis and Production: Data Visualization
across the Curriculum*

Project-based work leverages production design and problem-solving skills that reinforce a reciprocal relationship between critical analysis and practice with multiliteracy tools and texts. Student engagement with familiar digital tools and texts is an asset, but the integration of Big Data concepts in the learning environment does not require a sophisticated digital toolbox. One example can be seen in the analysis and production of data visualization projects. Data visualization can be accomplished with a range of analog and digital technical skills. More importantly, data visualization connects the critical analysis strategies that are familiar to media educators with the data fluency needed to understand Big Data practices. Visualization as a new media literacy has been defined "as the ability to interpret and create data representations for the purpose of expressing ideas, finding patterns, and persuading people to take action" (Reilly, 2014, p. 47).

Data visualization can be seen in the first drawings of geographic maps. With the emergence of data and statistical techniques in the late 1700s, data visualization pioneers pushed data visualization beyond geography to create and study relationships and patterns between maps, science and social phenomenon. In his classic book *The Visual Display of Quantitative Information*, Edward Tufte (1988) praised the data visualization work of Charles Joseph Minard, a data visualization pioneer from the early 1800s. Minard's graphic data analysis of Napoleon's 1812 disastrous March to Russia is a seminal example in the data visualization field.

Dr. John Snow, an early data visualization scholar who envisioned "graphic tables" and "figurative maps," created an iconic cholera map in 1854. His work has been compared to the uses of data visualization by contemporary journalists (Rogers, 2013). Pioneers also include Florence Nightingale, a nurse and prominent statistician who filled her notebooks with data visualization analysis (Rogers, 2010), and William Playfair, who is credited with introducing design techniques for line graphs, bar charts and pie charts, as early as 1786 (Berkowitz, 2018).

W.E.B Du Bois, a renowned American civil rights pioneer and intellectual, established one of the first sociology departments in the United States in 1897. His extensive scholarship gathered data from across the United States about the lives of African Americans after the lingering effects of slavery. In 1900, Du Bois was asked to contribute an exhibit for the 1900 Paris World Fair entitled *The American Negro* to *Exposition Universelle*. Working with his colleagues and a trove of empirical data about the experiences of black Americans, Du Bois innovatively designed 60 handmade, colorful data visualizations for the exhibition that convey African American advances and lingering oppression in the United States (Mansky, 2018). Stored in isolation for decades in the Library of Congress, the work was digitized and published in 2018 by the W.E.B. Du Bois Center at the University of Massachusetts Amherst (Battle-Baptiste & Rusert, 2018).

Contemporary data visualizations embrace digital literacy tools to communicate the complex results and relationships from massive data sets to a broader audience. The use of data visualizations in contemporary journalism is an example of their practical applications for innovative, interactive and visual storytelling (Coddington, 2014). For those with more technical experience, data visualization can go beyond narratives to inspire interactive, multimedia and experimental art pieces (FlowingData, 2019; Yau, 2011). For those new to creating classic data visualization projects, two-dimensional infographics are a good place to start. Free online tools provide an introduction to the process and support the integration of data visualization for project-based learning (Teachthought, 2015).

James Lytle, a product design specialist for the data visualization platform Juice Analytics, points out that although transparency and clarity are the goal, making data visible focuses on the constructed art of storytelling. He remarks:

in order to present meaningful, compelling, or personally motivating information, there either needs to be exactly the right data presented, given the context of the data and person, or enough dimensions and slices of data to be meaningful to a broader range of questions and needs. Supporting textual content always helps to tell the story, which builds the viewers mental model – thereby, making the data more understandable.

(Lytle, 2010, para. 11)

In other words, constructing data visualization projects requires many of the critical analysis skills found in conceptual models for media education.

Data visualization projects offer students a hands-on, interdisciplinary opportunity to engage with data and connect multiple literacy practices that require strategic and critical thinking. Pioneering scholar, Edward Tufte, describes the process of creating data visualizations as "analytic design." He goes on to say, "At their best, graphics are instruments for reasoning" (Zachary & Thralls, 2004, p. 448). In the process, students are introduced to quantitative research methods and data sets that are foundational for understanding the way that traditional data collection, analysis and use of research evidence are intended to stimulate argument and debate (Poe, Lerner & Craig, 2010, p. 14). Data visualization activities can also be used to support community discourse and civic engagement about complex issues that directly affect communities.

An example of data visualization for participatory civic projects can be found in the work of students in a summer youth media workshop sponsored by Open Youth Networks in 2007. Educator Mindy Faber introduced students to the Google My Map (GMM) application, a simple interactive tool that allows users to add multimedia digital content to Google Maps. Working with teens in Chicago and Barbados, one of their multimedia projects addressed immigration:

> *OurMap of Migrations*, as we named it, captivated the intellectual and creative imaginations of the youth participants who eagerly added their own photos, videos, bios, travels and research to the map, becoming equally engrossed in exploring its rich content and learning about one another. In populating the map with a data array of migration histories, including historical information on the transatlantic slave trade routes as well as personal stories of family diasporas, 95% of participants ended up reporting in the workshop exit survey that the map "significantly altered their views on immigration and forced migration."
>
> (Faber, 2009)

In addition, the use of multimedia data visualization for engagement with social issues can increasingly be seen by the public in contexts that range from traditional news stories to fine arts museums. In 2018, oceanographers An T. Nguyen and Patrick Heimbach collaborated with data visualization specialist Greg Foss at The University of Texas at Austin to produce a series of data visualizations and video animations of their research results about changes in the Arctic Ocean. The data visualizations were exhibited at the Visual Arts Center, a gallery that specializes in fine arts exhibitions, as a way to make complex research data accessible to a broader lay audience (Center for Space Research, 2018).

Data visualizations are increasingly used as project-based learning opportunities across the curriculum (Graham, 2017; Shreiner, 2018). In addition to math and science, data visualization projects provide opportunities to connect critical analysis with critical production in the arts and humanities through *cultural analytics*, "the analysis of massive cultural datasets and flows using computational and visualization techniques" (Lev Manovich, 2016, para. 1). The study of cultural patterns and trends through cultural analytics provides interdisciplinary connections for the arts, sciences and humanities.

Conclusion

The convergence of media literacy and Big Data practices provide significant challenges to media educators who must navigate school cultures that prioritize practical, computer skill acquisition for workforce development over the critical analysis skills needed for participatory, civic engagement. Debates about the aims and purposes for language and literacy learning in the curriculum constitute a familiar power dynamic that is reflected in iterative definitions for media literacy. In the cynical adage, "language is a dialect with an army and navy," often attributed to a lecture with linguist Max Weinrich, the distinction between a "proper" language and a dialect is defined by those in power (Maxwell, 2018). As critical literacy practices expand from humans to artificial intelligence, it could be argued that Big Data is a dialect with a manipulative robot. The time is right to confront the robot.

As digital media becomes a dominant and normative mode of communication, it could also be argued that terms such as *media and information literacy* and *digital literacy* are anachronisms that could simply be called literacy (Tyner, 2010). Until that time, opportunities to extend literacy to include data fluency in the context of ubiquitous and pervasive Big Data practices requires a broader conversation about the information, technology, research methods and impacts that intersect with traditional media education concepts. Experimental approaches to project-based work that combine Big Data concepts with critical analysis and creative production are a promising first step.

References

Ajit, K. R. (2016). Impact of Big Data analytics on healthcare and society. *Journal of Biometrics and Biostatistics, 7,* 300. Retrieved from https://www. omicsonline.org/open-access/impact-of-big-data-analytics-on-healthcare-and-society-2155-6180-1000300.php?aid=75499

Battle-Baptiste, W. & Rusert, B. (Eds.). (2018). *W. E. B. Du Bois's data portraits: Visualizing Black America.* Amherst, MA: Amherst, MA: The W.E.B. DuBois Center at the University of Massachusetts Amherst and Princeton Architectural Press.

Berkowitz, B. (2018). *Playfair: The true story of the British secret agent who changed how we see the world.* Fairfax, VA: George Mason University Press.

Bell, K. (2018, June 8). Facebook: We're not a media company. Also Facebook: Watch our news shows. *Mashable.* Retrieved from https://mashable. com/2018/06/08/facebook-media-company-news-shows/

Beyer, M. A., & Laney, D. (2012). *The importance of "Big Data": A definition.* Samford, CT: Gartner Publications.

boyd, D., & Crawford, K. (2012). Critical questions for Big Data: Provocations for a cultural, technological, and scholarly phenomenon. *Information, Communication & Society, 15*(5), 662–679.

Bollier, D. (2010). *The promise and peril of Big Data.* Washington, DC: Aspen Institute.

Bronson, K., & Knezevic, I. (2016). Big data in food and agriculture. *Big Data & Society,* January–June, 1–5. New York, NY: Sage Publications.

Brunton, F., & Nissenbaum, H. (2015) *Obfuscation: A user's guide for privacy and protest.* Cambridge, MA: MIT Press.

Buckingham, D. (2019, August 12). Beyond 'fake news': disinformation and digital literacy. Retrieved from https://davidbuckingham.net/2019/02/27/beyond-fake-news-disinformation-and-digital-literacy/

Bulger, M., & Davison, P. (2018). *The promises, challenges and futures of media literacy*. New York, NY: Data & Society.

Center for Media Literacy. (2010). CML's five core concepts. Los Angeles: Center for Media Literacy. Retrieved from http://www.medialit.org/cmls-basic-framework

Center for Media Literacy. (2019). *Media literacy: A definition and more*. Retrieved from https://www.medialit.org/media-literacy-definition-and-more

Center for Space Research. (2018). *Exploring the Arctic Ocean*. Cockrell School of Engineering, The University of Texas at Austin. Retrieved from https://www.csr.utexas.edu/9-21-18-exploring-the-arctic-ocean

Chan, J. (2019, August 9). Alternative data – A beginner's guide. *Data Driven Investor*. Retrieved from https://medium.com/datadriveninvestor/alternative-data-a-beginners-guide-data-driven-investor-d713e56a9ff8

Coddington, M. (2014). Clarifying journalism's quantitative turn: A typology for evaluating data journalism, computational journalism, and computer-assisted reporting. *Digital Journalism, 3*(3), 331–348.

Costa, C., Tyner, K., Henriques. S., & Sousa, C. (2018). Game creation in youth media and information literacy education. *International Journal of Game-based Learning, 8*(2), 1–13.

D'Ignazio, C. (2017). Creative data literacy: Bridging the gap between the data-haves and data-have nots. In I. Meirelles & K. Gillieson (Eds.). *Information Design Journal, 23*(1), 6–18.

D'Ignazio, C., & Bhargava, R. (2015, September 28). *Approaches to building Big Data literacy*. Paper presented at the Bloomberg Data for Good Exchange Conference. New York, NY: Bloomberg. Retrieved August 1, 2019 from http://rahul-beta.connectionlab.org/wp-content/uploads/2011/11/Edu_DIgnazio_52.pdf

Dijcks, J. (2013). *Oracle: Big Data for the enterprise. Oracle White Paper*. Redwood Shores, CA: Oracle Corporation.

De Mauro, A., Greco, M., & Grimaldi, M. (2016), A formal definition of Big Data based on its essential features. *Library Review, 65*(3), 122–135.

De Mauro, A., Greco, M., & Grimaldi, M. (2019). Understanding Big Data through a systematic literature review: The ITMI model. *International Journal of Information Technology and Decision Making, 18*(4), 1Executive Office of the President. (2016). *The federal big data research and development strategic plan*. Washington, DC: Executive Office of the President, National Science and Technology Council. Retrieved from https://obamawhitehouse.archives.gov/sites/default/files/microsites/ostp/NSTC/bigdatardstrategicplan-nitrd_final-051916.pdf

Faber, M. (2009, June 12). Google maps: A tool for the youth media field. *Youth Media Reporter*. Retrieved from http://www.youthmediareporter.org/2009/06/12/google-maps-a-tool-for-the-youth-media-field/

Federov, A. (2003). Media education and media literacy: Experts' opinions. UNESCO MENTOR: *A Media Education Curriculum for Teachers in the Mediterranean*, 1–17.

Firestone, C. M. (1993). *Forward*. In P. Aufderheide, *Media literacy. A report of the national leadership conference on media literacy* (pp. v–vii). Aspen Institute: Queenstown, MD.

FlowingData. (2019). Retrieved July 25, 2019 from https://flowingdata.com/

Foster, J. B., & McChesney, R. W. (2014, July). Surveillance capitalism: Monopoly finance capital, the military-industrial complex, and the digital age. *Monthly Review: An Independent Socialist Magazine.* Retrieved from https://monthlyreview.org/2014/07/01/surveillance-capitalism/

Fowler, S. (2019). The Privacy Project: What we've learned (so far). *New York Times.* July 16. Retrieved July 16, 2019 from https://www.nytimes.com/2019/07/16/opinion/privacy-project-nytimes.html?rref=collection%2Fseriescollection%2Fnew-york-times-privacy-project&action=click&contentCollection=opinion&region=stream&module=stream_unit&version=latest&contentPlacement=1&pgtype=collection

Frau-Meigs, D. (2014). Media and Information Literacy (MIL): How can MIL harness the affordances of digital information cultures post-2015? Geneva: *WSIS Action Line C9 Report on Media and Information Literacy.*

Gandomi, A., Haider, M. (2015). Beyond the hype: Big data concepts, methods, and analytics. *International Journal of Information Management, 35*(2), 137–144.

Gilster, P. (1997). *Digital literacy.* New York, NY: Wiley.

Graham, E. (2017). Introduction: Data visualization and the humanities. *English Studies, 98*(5), 449–458.

Guiterrez, A., & Tyner, K. (2012). Media education, Media literacy and digital competencies. In K. Tyner & A. Guiterrez (Eds.). Global perspectives on new media literacy, special international issue, Madrid: *Revista Communicar Scientific Journal of Media Education, 19*(38), 31–39.

Hoeren, T., & Kolany-Raiser, B. (2017). *Big Data in context: Legal, social and technological insights.* New York, NY: Springer International Publishing.

Ingram, M. (2018, September 18). Most Americans say they have lost trust in the media. *Columbia Journalism Review.* Retrieved July 1, 2019 from https://www.cjr.org/the_media_today/trust-in-media-down.php

Johndan-Eilola, J., & Selber, S. A. (2007). Plagiarism, originality, assemblage, computers and composition. *Computers and Composition, 24*(4), 375–403.

Jolls, T., & Wilson, C. (2014). The core concepts: Fundamental to media literacy yesterday, today and tomorrow. *Journal of Media Literacy Education 6*(2), 68–78.

Hoechsmann, M., & Poyntz, S. (2017). Learning and teaching media literacy in Canada: Embracing and transcending eclecticism. *Taboo: The Journal of Culture and Education, 12* (1). Retrieved from https://digitalcommons.lsu.edu/taboo/vol12/iss1/4/

Klein, J. T., & Newell, W. H. (1997). Advancing interdisciplinary studies. In J. G. Gaff, J. L. Ratcliff & Associates (Eds.), *Handbook of the undergraduate curriculum: A comprehensive guide to purposes, structures, practices, and change* (pp. 393–415). San Francisco, CA: Jossey-Bass.

Kozlowska, I. (2018, April 30). Facebook and data privacy in the age of Cambridge Analytica. Seattle, WA: The University of Washington. Retrieved August 1, 2019 from https://jsis.washington.edu/news/facebook-data-privacy-age-cambridge-analytica/

Lankshear, C., & Knobel, M. (2008). *Digital literacies: Concepts, policies, and practices.* New York, NY: Peter Lang.

Lazar, D., Kennedy, R., King, G., & Vespignani, A. (2014, March 14). The parable of Google flu: Traps in Big Data analysis. *Science, 343,* 1203–1205. Retrieved from http://j.mp/2ovtFps

Livingstone, S., Wijnen, C. W., Papaioannou, T., Costa, C., & del Grandio, M. (2013). Situating media literacy in the changing media environment: Critical insights from European research on audiences. In N. Carpentier, K. C. Schroder & L. Hallett (Eds.). *Audience transformations. Shifting audience positions in late* modernity (pp. 210–227). New York and London: Routledge.

Lytle, J. (2010). *Memorable or actionable or both?* Juice analytics. Retrieved July 1, 2019 from https://www.juiceanalytics.com/writing/writing/memorable-or-actionable-or-both

Manovich, L. (2016, May 23). The science of culture? Social computing, digital humanities and cultural analytics. *Journal of Cultural Analytics.* Retrieved from https://culturalanalytics.org/2016/05/the-science-of-culture-social-computing-digital-humanities-and-cultural-analytics/

Mansky, J. (2018, November 15). W.E.B. Du Bois' visionary infographics come together for the first time in full color. Washington, DC: Smithsonian Institute. Retrieved from https://www.smithsonianmag.com/history/first-time-together-and-color-book-displays-web-du-bois-visionary-infographics-180970826/

Mayer-Schönberger, V., & Cukier, K. (2013). *Big Data: A revolution that will transform how we live, work, and think.* New York: Houghton Mifflin.

McAuley, D., Rahemtulla, H., Goulding, J., & Souch, C. (2012). How open data, data literacy and linked data will revolutionise higher education. In L. Coiait & J. Hill (Eds.). *Blue skies: New thinking about the future of higher education in the Asia Pacific region* (pp. 52–57). Hong Kong: Pearson.

McLuhan, M. (1964). *Understanding media: The extensions of man.* New York, NY: Signet Books.

Mandinach, E. B., & Gummer, E. S. (2013). A systemic view of implementing data literacy in educator preparation. *Educational Researcher, 42*(1), 30–37.

Maxwell, A. (2018). When theory is a joke: The Weinreich witticism in linguistics. *Beitrage zur Geschichte der Sprachwissenschaft, 28*(2), 263–292. Retrieved from https://www.researchgate.net/publication/329772713_When_Theory_is_a_Joke_The_Weinreich_Witticism_in_Linguistics

Montgomery, K. C. (2015). Youth and surveillance in the Facebook era: Policy interventions and social implications. *Telecommunications Policy, 39*(9), 771–786.

National Association for Media Literacy Education. (2007, November). Core principles of media literacy education in the United States. Retrieved July 15, 2019 from http://namle.net/publications/core-principles

National Association for Media Literacy Education. (2019). Media literacy defined. Retrieved July 22, 2019 from https://namle.net/publications/media-literacy-definitions/Neuman, W. R. (2016). The digital difference: Media technology and the theory of communication effects. Cambridge, MA: Harvard University Press.

New London Group. (1996). A pedagogy of multiliteracies: Designing social futures. *Harvard Educational Review* (Spring); 66(1), 60.

Nichols, T. P., & Stornaiuolo, A. (2019). Assembling "digital literacies": Contingent pasts, possible futures. *Media and Communication, 7*(2), 14–24.

Ofcom. (2004, June 1). *Ofcom's strategy and priorities for the promotion of media literacy: Consultation Document.* London: Author.

Ontario Association for Media Literacy. (1987). *Media literacy resource guide.* Ontario: Ontario Ministry of Education.

Poe, M., Lerner, N., & Craig, J. (2010). *Learning to communicate in science and engineering: Case studies from MIT.* Cambridge, MA: MIT Press.

Reilly, E. (2014). Visualization as a new media literacy. In B. S. Abreu & P. Milhailidis (Eds.). *Media literacy education in action: Theoretical and pedagogical perspectives* (pp. 45–51.). New York, NY: Routledge.

Richter, B. K. (2019). *The entertainment software ratings board: Success after 20 years?* Chicago, IL: Stigler Center for the Economy and State. Retrieved from https://research.chicagobooth.edu/-/media/research/stigler/pdfs/casestudies/cases/esrb_vf.pdf?la=en&hash=2A2E74657108E6C666A055F188CC963DE041E2EC

Rogers, S. (2010, August 13). Florence Nightingale, data journalist: Information has always been beautiful. *The Guardian.* Retrieved July 15, 2019 from https://www.theguardian.com/news/datablog/2010/aug/13/florence-nightingale-graphics

Rogers, S. (2013, March 15). John Snow's data journalism: The cholera map that changed the world. *The Guardian.* Retrieved July 15, 2019 from https://www.theguardian.com/news/datablog/2013/mar/15/john-snow-cholera-mapSadowski, J. (2019). When data is capital: Datafication, accumulation, and extraction. *Big Data & Society, 6*(1), 1–12.

Schneider, J. (2018, October 15). How are America's public schools really doing? *Washington Post.* Retrieved July 1, 2019 from https://www.washingtonpost.com/education/2018/10/15/how-are-americas-public-schools-really-doing/?noredirect=on&utm_term=.a17a3f02b18b

Shreiner, T. L. (2018) Data literacy for social studies: Examining the role of data visualizations in K-12 textbooks. *Theory & Research in Social Education, 46*(2), 194–231.

Schroeck, M., Shockley, R., Smart, J., Romero-Morales, D., & Tufano, P. (2012). *Analytics: The real world use of big data.* New York, NY: IBM Institute for Business Value, Said Business School.

Schrock, A. (2017). What communication can contribute to data studies: Three lenses on communication and data. *International Journal of Communication, 11,* 701–709.

Sivarajah, U., Kamal, M. M., Irani, Z., & Weerakkody, V. (2016). Critical analysis of Big Data challenges and analytical methods. *Journal of Business Research, 70,* 263–286.

Smith, E. (Ed.). (2018). *Big Data surveillance.* Kingston, Ontario: Surveillance Studies Center. Retrieved from https://www.sscqueens.org/sites/sscqueens.org/files/bds_booklet_spring_2018.pdf

Teachthought. (2015, November 21). 7 data visualization tools you can use in the classroom. *Teachthought.* Retrieved from: https://www.teachthought.com/technology/5-free-data-visualization-tools-you-can-use-in-the-classroom/

Thoman, E., & Jolls, T. (2005). Media literacy education: Lessons from the Center for Media Literacy. In G. Schwartz & P. U. Brown (Eds.), *Media literacy: Transforming curriculum and teaching,* (pp. 104, 180–205). Malden, MA: National Society for the Study of Education.

Tufte, E. R. (1988). *The visual display of quantitative information.* Cheshire, CT: Graphics Press.

Tyner, K., Gutiérrez Martín, A., & Torrego González, A. (2015). Literacy without walls in the age of convergence: Digital competency and maker culture as incentives for ubiquitous education. *Revista Profesorado: Journal of Curriculum and Teacher Education, 19*(2). Granada, Spain. Retrieved from http://recyt.fecyt.es/index.php/profesorado/article/view/41515/23610

Tyner, K. (1998). *Literacy in a digital world: Teaching and learning in the age of information.* New York: Routledge.

Tyner, K. (2011). New agendas for media literacy: A multiliteracy mandala. *A manifesto for media literacy.* Retrieved January 15, 2019 from http://www.manifestoformediaeducation.co.uk/category/kathleen-tyner/

Tyner, K. (2010). *Voices of media literacy: International pioneers speak out: Kathleen Tyner interview transcript.* Los Angeles, Center for Media Literacy. Retrieved July 15, 2019 from http://www.medialit.org/reading-room/voices-media-literacy-international-pioneers-speak-kathleen-tyner-interview-transcript

UNESCO. (2017). Media and information literacy, a critical approach to literacy in the digital world. Paris, France: UNESCO. Retrieved from https://en.unesco.org/news/media-and-information-literacy-critical-approach-literacy-digital-world

Wallis, R., & Buckingham, D. (2016). Media literacy: the UK's undead cultural policy. *International Journal of Cultural Policy, 25*(2), 188–203.

Ward, J.S. & Barker, A. (2013). *Undefined by data: A survey of big data definitions.* School of Computer Science. University of St Andrews, UK. Retrieved July 1, 2018 from https://arxiv.org/pdf/1309.5821.pdf

Wilcox, M. (2016, March 4). The real reason why Google flu trends got big data analytics so wrong. *Forbes.* Retrieved July 15, 2019 from https://www.forbes.com/sites/teradata/2016/03/04/the-real-reason-why-google-flu-trends-got-big-data-analytics-so-wrong/#e61fd1237c0c

Yau, N. (2011). *Visualize this.* New York, NY: Wiley.

Zachary, M., & Thralls, C. (2004). An interview with Edward Tufte. *Technical, Communication Quarterly, 13*(4), 447–462. Mahwah, NJ: Lawrence, Erlbaum Associates, Inc.

Zaslavsky, A., Perera, C., & Georgakopoulos, D. (2013, June 12). Sensing as a service and big data. *Proceedings of the International Conference on Advances in Cloud Computing (ACC),* Bangalore, India. Retrieved from https://arxiv.org/abs/1301.0159

Zikopoulos, P., & Eaton, C. (2011). *Understanding big data: Analytics for enterprise class Hadoop and streaming data.* McGraw-Hill: Osborne Media.

Zuboff, S. (2019). *The age of surveillance capitalism: The fight for human future at the new frontier.* New York, NY: Public Affairs Press.

4 Four Fundamental Challenges in Designing Media Literacy Interventions

W. James Potter

Introduction

This chapter, highlights four challenges that designers of any media literacy intervention study will face: (1) clarifying the purpose of the intervention, (2) dealing with skills, (3) dealing with knowledge, and (4) thinking about independence. Before beginning, key terms will be defined: media literacy, intervention, targets, and agents.

Definitions

Media Literacy

Media literacy is a naturally occurring set of beliefs, knowledge, skills, and motivations that people draw from when making sense of media messages in their everyday lives. It is a continuum rather than a category such that everyone has some level of media literacy and there is a wide variation in levels across people. A person's level of media literacy can be increased in many ways, and the purpose of such increases is to give people more power to make better selections of media messages, to enable them to avoid unwanted effects, and to enhance their appreciation of the positive effects (Potter, 2019a).

Intervention

An intervention is an instructional lesson that is designed to increase the levels of media literacy in targets. These lessons can be of any length from a few minutes to many hours, and they can be one-shot lessons or a series of lessons delivered over a long period of time. Designers of media literacy interventions have used a wide range of elements in their treatments. These elements can be organized into three categories: target passive elements, target active elements, and delivery elements. The target passive elements are typically media messages that are presented to targets who are expected to do nothing more than experience the message, such as listening to some kind of lesson (e.g., Nathanson, 2002; Nathanson & Yang, 2003). Target active elements involve targets in some kind of activity that is designed to get targets to internalize the lesson by engaging in exercises where they need to apply the information from the lesson (e.g., Austin, Pinkleton, & Funabiki, 2007; Byrne, 2009). Delivery elements are all those characteristics that shape the context of the treatment and guide targets in the way they interpret the meaning and value of the intervention. These delivery elements include things like the tone of the delivery (e.g., serious, authoritarian, humorous, comforting, engaging, condescending, etc.); the relationship of the targets with the agents (degree of familiarity, trust, credibility); and the environment (classroom vs. lab; experience of receiving the intervention either alone or in a group).

Treatments

Treatments that are described in the media literacy intervention literature all have at their core the presentation of a media message along with the agent delivering some kind of a lesson to targets. Some of these intervention studies add an active target element, such as stimulating targets to critique video stories, write an essay, practice empathy (Nathanson & Cantor, 2000), discuss one's feelings in a group setting, engage in cognitive activities (Byrne, 2009), or produce a media message (Banerjee & Greene, 2006). While all these studies have a cluster of delivery elements, authors of published work typically are sparse in their description of these intervention delivery elements. This sparseness is a problem because it prevents readers from using the published literature as guides with enough detail to help them design their own media literacy studies.

Target

The targets of the intervention are the people for whom the intervention is designed. The most common targets of media literacy intervention studies are children, but some scholars also argue for the need to target special groups of adults, such as parents, teachers, and doctors.

It is useful to make a distinction between two types of targets: primary and intermediary. Primary targets are those people for whom the intervention is designed to benefit ultimately. This type of target in the literature is overwhelmingly children and adolescents (Potter & Thai, 2019). Intermediary targets – typically public school teachers, health care workers, and parents – are those people who are given training in using the intervention so that they can deliver the intervention to the primary targets.

Agent

The agent is the person who designs and delivers the intervention. Usually, this is a researcher, teacher, or parent (e.g., Nathanson, 2002; Valkenberg, Krcmar, Peeters, & Marseille, 1999). These agents are typically motivated by a concern that someone they care about is vulnerable to a negative effect from media exposures, although they also could be motivated by a desire to help their targets increase the positive effects from media exposures.

Agents are arrayed across a wide range of ability to help their targets. At one end of this range are agents who have little more than a caring for their targets and an amorphous fear that particular media content may be harming their targets. At the other end of the range are agents who have a high degree of knowledge about media literacy as well as the constellation of factors involved in the complex process of media influence.

Purpose of the Intervention

The first challenge that all designers of a media literacy intervention study encounter is to clarify the purpose of their study. This challenge is addressed in two ways. First, designers must decide whether to construct an evaluation study or a basic research study. Then, second, they must decide what the role of media literacy is in the design.

Evaluation Study or Basic Research Study?

Evaluation

The evaluation method, traditionally, meets eight conditions (see Table 4.1). First, the intervention is designed by a sponsoring agency, such as a public school system, a health agency, a consumer activist group, or a philanthropic institution. Second, the intervention is typically a complex of many presentation elements (such as lectures, print materials, videos, and websites) that involve targets in many activities (watching, reading, critiquing, discussing, and producing) that presumably work together in a system as the intervention is delivered in a series of lessons spread out over time. Third, the intervention is administered to intact groups, so random assignment of targets to conditions is not possible. Fourth, the study is conducted in the field (such as elementary school classrooms) where random assignment of intact groups to conditions is typically limited. Fifth, the people who deliver the intervention are typically part of the naturalistic environment (elementary school teachers, parents, etc.) who are given some training to administer the intervention but who are *not* expected to be perfectly matched on all instructional criteria that could account for the intervention's outcomes. Sixth, the agency has created standards for success of the intervention before its administration. Seventh, there are typically several rounds of pilot testing to help improve the success of the intervention where improvements focus on increasing clarity of materials. And eighth, the ultimate goal of this process is to develop a product that can be disseminated to other groups in the hope of overcoming some widespread problem or trying to make society better in some way.

Table 4.1 Comparing Evaluation with Basic Research Designs

	Evaluation	Basic Research
Designed by	Sponsoring agency	Researchers
Intervention	Complex of factors	Focus on one factor
Place	In field (natural setting)	In laboratory
Groups	In-tact groups	Randomly assigned participants
Agents	Teachers or parents	Researchers
Success	Meeting standards	Differences between treatment and control groups
Pilot testing	Increasing instructional value	Increasing distinctiveness of treatments on one factor
Goal	To develop a product	To make claims for influence

Basic Research

The basic research path meets the eight conditions differently (see Table 4.1). First, the intervention is designed by the researchers – not a sponsoring agency – who also design and execute the test. Second, while the intervention may consist of a complex of presentation elements that involve targets in several activities, the intervention is constructed to focus attention on only one factor of influence (or a small set of variables) while holding all other possible factors of influence constant so as to maximize the integrity of experimental design. Third, the intervention is administered to volunteers who usually come to a laboratory setting. Fourth, the participants are randomly assigned to treatment conditions. Fifth, the intervention is administered by the researchers or their confederates in a controlled situation so that uniformity is maintained across all treatment conditions with the exception of one of the factors of influence that is varied across each treatment conditions. Sixth, there are no *a priori* standards of success that can be used to determine whether the intervention was successful or not; instead, researchers are interested in assessing the degree to which treatment factors are associated with outcome measures, so they use inferential statistical tests to tell them if their findings are robust enough to have not occurred by chance alone. Seventh, when pilot testing is conducted, it focuses on *increasing the distinctiveness* of the factors of influence that are varied across treatments, rather than on *increasing the overall instructional power* of all treatments. And eight, the ultimate goal of this process is to make claims about the relative strength of different factors of influence on achieving a particular effect.

In practice, it is rare to find a pure evaluation or basic research study within the published literature of media literacy intervention; instead, almost all designs are a hybrid mix. In Potter and Thai's (2019) analysis of 88 studies of media literacy interventions, 51 (58%) studies followed the basic research characteristics more, and the other 37 followed the evaluation study characteristics more. For example, the 37 studies classified as evaluation-type studies met almost all of the criteria with the exception of the standard for effectiveness. None of the studies in the analysis presented any benchmarks to be used as criteria for effectiveness. Instead, all 37 studies defaulted to looking for statistical differences across treatment and control groups. Because none of these evaluation studies compared performance to a standard, none were able to make meaningful claims about the effectiveness of their tested interventions; instead, they were limited to making statements about whether there was a statistical difference in group means between groups of targets who experienced an intervention and control groups that had not experienced an intervention. By largely following many, but not all, of the conventions of evaluation studies, these studies were hybrids.

The argument is not that hybrid designs are always weaker than pure types of studies; in fact, hybrid studies can be stronger than traditional designs if scholars take the strongest elements from each type and synthesize those strong elements into a workable system that amplifies all the additional strengths. In contrast, if the hybrid design arises from designers taking shortcuts (e.g., it is easier to test for group means than to develop adequate performance criteria), the hybrid design can end up displaying more weaknesses than had the researchers designed a pure type. The pattern of design decisions with evaluation hybrid studies indicates that those designers have been eliminating a strength (use of standards for success) and replacing it with a weakness (comparison of means).

So what does this mean for designing a study? Ideally, if all eight characteristics suggest one design path – either evaluation or basic research – then there is a strong rationale for that type of study. However, if a given situation has characteristics from both paths, then it makes sense to look at the balance and proceed down the path that meets the majority of characteristics. Then, if possible, researchers can change their situation so that all characteristics line up. For example, if a design meets seven of the eight characteristics for an evaluation study but the eighth characteristic does not fit the pattern because the sponsoring agency has not provided any standards for success, the agency could be asked to provide those standards; or, a review of the evaluation literature could be used to identify standards used in similar instructional lessons that could then be used to construct reasonable standards.

In the case where researchers cannot change enough characteristics to meet a pure type, then they would design a hybrid study. Hybrid designs are more challenging to design well. A researcher needs to spend more time thinking through each design decision to make sure that the design options will increase the value of the findings and that each selection will work together well in a system with the other design features. If this can be done, then the resulting hybrid design will likely be as strong as a pure design and possibly even stronger.

Role of Media Literacy in the Design

The idea of media literacy can be regarded in one of three ways in designing a media literacy intervention study: as an outcome variable, as a process variable, and as an antecedent variable.

Outcome Variable

The simplest design for a media literacy intervention study is to treat media literacy as the outcome variable. The purpose of the intervention is to increase targets' levels of media literacy. In order to determine if an increase occurs, there needs to be a pre-test as well as a post-test of targets' levels of media literacy. Thus, the design is:

Media Literacy ➔ Intervention ➔ Media Literacy

When media literacy is regarded as an outcome, researchers measure targets' levels of media literacy prior to delivering the intervention; then they measure it after delivering the intervention. The greater the degree of change, the more successful the intervention.

Process Variable

When media literacy is regarded not as an end to itself but as a tool to achieve something else, the purpose of the intervention is to use it as a means to change something in targets. Thus, the simplest design is:

Intervention ➔ Media Literacy ➔ Outcome Variable

In this design, the intervention is intended to increase target's levels of media literacy, which in turn is expected to insure better scores on the outcome variable. For example, if, from years of exposure to media messages, targets have acquired some antisocial beliefs (such as, the belief that the use of alcohol and illegal drugs is exciting and not harmful), a researcher might want to design an intervention to help them increase their media literacy so they can change these beliefs and then protect them from making such false attributions in future media exposures. In this case, the intervention is designed to increase targets' levels of media literacy with the expectation that higher levels of media literacy will then lead to a reduction of antisocial beliefs that otherwise would be constantly reinforced by typical media portrayals.

Antecedent Variable

Sometimes creators of intervention studies will design a persuasion type of study where media literacy is not the focus of the intervention nor is it the outcome variable. Instead media literacy is treated as a contributing factor, along with the intervention (and perhaps some other explanatory variables) for explaining scores on the outcome variable. Thus, the design is:

> Media Literacy |
> Persuasive intervention | →   Outcome variable
> Other explanatory variables |

This is a popular design in persuasion-type research, where the focus is most strongly on some outcome variable that is usually assumed to be influenced in part by the way targets' have been processing the meaning of media messages in the everyday lives.

Skills Interventions

Frequently scholars will conceptualize media literacy as being composed in part by skills, so the design of their media literacy interventions must teach skills of some kind. This raises four issues: (1) domains of skills, (2) performance, (3) distinguishing between skills and competencies, and (4) distinguishing between broad and specialized skills.

Domains of Skills

Designers of media literacy interventions will often rely on a conceptualization of media literacy that calls for skills but then does not define those skills, leaving researchers to assume the meaning of those skills for themselves. An illustration of this is with the use of the term "critical thinking." While many scholars use this term, few define it. It is difficult to infer what those scholars who do not define it mean, but it appears that they exhibit a range of meanings. Some of these scholars seem to mean the ability to perceive more elements in media messages, which is really the skill of analysis, while other scholars seem to mean the ability to make accurate judgments about the faulty or exploitative nature of some media messages, which is the skill of evaluation. Some scholars seem to mean the ability to construct one's own meaning even when it is counter to the intention of the message designers, while others mean the ability to argue against intended meanings, and still others mean achieving a habit of being mindful during media exposures rather than allowing one's mind to continue on automatic pilot. The term "critical analysis" is used to refer to so many different configurations of types of

Table 4.2 The Seven Skills of Media Literacy

---

1 Analyzing – the breaking down of a message into meaningful elements
2 Evaluating – the making of judgments about the value of an element; the judgment is made by comparing the element to some standard
3 Grouping – determining which elements are alike in some way, and determining which elements are different in some way
4 Inducing – the inferring of general patterns from the observation of particulars, generalizing those patterns to larger aggregates, and the continual testing of those patterns
5 Deducing – the using of general principles to explain particulars in a process of logical reasoning
6 Synthesizing – the assembling of elements into a novel structure to solve some problem or complete some partially specified task
7 Abstracting – the assembling of elements into a brief, clear, and accurate description of a message

---

skills that it is meaningless unless researchers specify their definitions (Potter, 2004).

This author argues that there are seven skills in a set that are central to media literacy: skills of analysis, evaluation, grouping, induction, deduction, synthesis, and abstraction (see Table 4.2). For more on these skills, see Potter (2019b).

Performance

The current state of ambiguity over defining critical thinking has led researchers to operationalize it in a variety of ways, many of which fall outside the boundaries of what could be considered a measurement of a skill. For example, operationalizing a skill by posing a question that asks respondents how confident they are in their ability to critically analyze media messages is more a measure of belief than of skill level. Operationalizing a skill with a question that asks respondents how important is it that they critically analyze media messages is more a measure of motivation than of skill level. And asking respondents how often do they critically analyze media messages is more a measure of recall of behavior than it is a measure of skill level.

Perhaps the most significant problem with defining media literacy as critical thinking arises when researchers measure it as an attitude. For example, consider a study where researchers design an intervention that attempts to persuade teenage participants to avoid using alcohol by teaching them about the health risks and the criminal penalties. They design attitude items to measure the degree to which their participants are persuaded that alcohol use is not an acceptable behavior while they are teenagers. If the authors frame their research as a persuasion study, then the attitude outcome measures could be judged as valid.

Then when researchers look for changes in the direction and magnitude of attitude scores between pre-intervention and post-intervention, they can assess the degree of persuasiveness of the intervention. However, if the authors' intention is to teach their participants to think for themselves and not accept claims made by authorities, then thinking for one's self is not evidenced by participants' converging toward a shared attitude that demonstrates widespread acceptance of the authority position taught in the intervention. If "critical thinking" implies that people need to think for themselves instead of simply accepting what they are told, then accepting the attitudes that the media literacy intervention is teaching respondents represents uncritical persuasion rather than critical thinking.

The one thing that all skills have in common is that they require performance to learn and to assess. That is, scholars need to think of skills in terms of performance, and researchers need to measure skills by observing the actual performance of their participants. In the athletic realm, basketball coaches do not ask prospective players: How well do you shoot free throws? (very good, good, average, below average). Instead, they observe the level of their performance. While determining the level of basketball players' free-throw skill is relatively easy, determining the level of media literacy skills is much more challenging. However, researchers can begin working on this challenge by using a three-step procedure. First, they need to clarify as much as possible what the skill is. Second, they need to think about what the various levels of performance are on the skill and then determine what observables would indicate performance at each level. And third, they need to think about the skill as requiring a sequence of sub-tasks and then design measures to track participants through the process of applying that skill in order to identify how far each participant has moved through that process. For examples of how to do this with each of the seven skills of media literacy, see Potter (2019b).

Skills or Competencies

It is useful to make a distinction between skills and competencies. Competencies are relatively dichotomous; that is, either people are able to do something or they are not able. For example, people either know how to use a remote control device (RCD) to turn on their TV or they do not; they either know how to send someone a text message on a smartphone or they do not; and they either know how to recognize a particular word and match its meaning to a memorized denoted meaning or they do not. Competencies are relatively easy to learn; then once learned, they are applied automatically over and over again. Once a person has a competency, further practice makes almost no difference in the quality of their performance.

Skills, in contrast, are tools that people develop through practice. Skill ability is not dichotomous; instead, skills exist along a wide continuum from novice to expert. People's level of performance on skills is highly variable, and there is always room for more improvement through practice. Without continual practice, skills will atrophy and a person's level of skill will slide to lower levels on the skill continuum.

Skills and competencies require very different measures. Competencies present a relatively easy challenge because they are binary, and researchers can trust self-report measures. For example, researchers could simply ask something like "Do you use your smartphone to send text messages?" and provide two choices (yes or no). They do not need any more detail in the question, and they do not need to provide additional answer choices, unless they want to know how often participants send messages; but, then, this frequency may reflect things beyond simple competency.

Skills, in contrast, are much more challenging to measure. The task of assessing skill levels requires researchers to stimulate the performance of the skill so that the level of that performance can be observed in a way that participants can be placed on a continuum according to their levels of performance. It is faulty to assume that participants can rate the level of their own skills because most participants do not have an accurate idea of what skill performance means at levels above their own ability, so they do not have access to an understanding of the full continuum when rating their own skill level.

The challenge of measuring participants' skill levels lies in developing a template of indicators for each of those levels. Meeting this challenge requires researchers to be clear about what the function of a skill is and how that function can be performed at different levels of ability.

Broad or Specialized

Next, a researcher needs to decide whether the intervention skills are broad ones or specific to media literacy. Broad skills are cognitive processes that people use throughout their lives in a wide range of situations. In contrast, there are skills that are only applicable to interacting with the media in literate ways. Examples of this kind of skill are things like writing computer code for a laptop, troubleshooting problems with smartphones, lighting a scene to make a photograph that conveys a particular emotion, and so on.

If skills are regarded as broad, then it is likely that there is a wide range of ability on each of these skills. Some of this range may be accounted for in varying degrees by age and educational level, but a large part of the variation is more likely traceable to IQ, motivation, need to achieve, and reward history. No one of these factors can serve as a good predictor of skill level, so none can serve as an adequate surrogate for the skill level.

The measurement of skills believed to be special to media literacy would seem to be a bit easier challenge, because it is not likely that many people would possess these skills prior to a training-type intervention. Also, researchers are not likely to want to know the level of a participant's proficiency on these skills, so they can be treated more like competencies in the measurement. For example, we should *not* expect a high percentage of the population to have message production skills, such as designing a website, running an audio mixing board, writing a computer program for a video game, or editing raw video footage. Of course within the video production industries, making fine distinctions across skill levels is essential for employers and professional organizations, but when conducting media literacy skills assessments on general populations, it would be sufficient to distinguish between those with no skill and those with any skill. If skills are regarded as specialized to media literacy, then researchers need to think about what makes them so special to media literacy. They also need to think about whether it is really skill or competency.

In summary, scholars who present definitions of media literacy that include a skills component need to think through the four issues presented in this section. They need to provide more detail in the form of specifying domains of skills and be more clear about defining what those skills are. When specifying the skills, designers need to remember that skills require performance; without monitoring performance, the skills cannot be adequately taught or measured. Designers also need to articulate their vision about whether they are dealing with skills or competencies, and if skills, then are those skills broad or specialized to media literacy. Scholars who clearly lay out their positions on these four issues when publishing their studies will be providing a great deal more guidance to designers of future media literacy intervention studies.

Knowledge Interventions

Almost every conceptualization of media literacy suggests a knowledge component. Thus, it's difficult to conceptualize a media literacy intervention study that is not concerned with imparting knowledge of some kind. The challenge lies in determining what counts as knowledge and what knowledge should be taught in a media literacy intervention.

This section presents information on three issues about dealing with knowledge in media literacy interventions: (1) distinguishing between facts and beliefs, (2) distinguishing between information and knowledge, and (3) specifying domains of knowledge.

Facts vs. Beliefs

There are two types of information that media literacy studies typically measure in the knowledge component, and each of these types has

68   W. James Potter

different implications for measurement. One type of information has a factual basis. Factual-type information includes things like (1) FBI statistics say that 12% of all crimes are violent, (2) the National Television Violence Study found that 61% of all shows in American television contained at least one act of violence, and (3) it is illegal for teenagers to purchase and consume alcoholic beverages in the United States. The factual basis gives these statements a truth value; that is, it can be determined whether the claims in the statements are accurate or not.

In contrast, a second type of information arises through inferences derived from observing actions in the world and exists in a person's mind as beliefs. This belief-type information includes things like the world is a mean and violent place, and the high rate of violence presented in the media is harmful to society. Beliefs are typically based on social information; that is, people observe human behavior, infer patterns, and treat those patterns as social norms.

Designers of media literacy intervention studies need to make this distinction because it has implications for how information is taught in the intervention and how the success of the intervention will be measured. Factual information can be measured in a dichotomous manner, because a person either knows a fact or does not. Thus true-false response choices are appropriate. In contrast, beliefs typically vary in intensity as reflected by how important they are to people or the degree to which they believe that something exists. Therefore, beliefs should be measured on Likert-type intensity scales.

Information vs. Knowledge

In everyday language we use the terms "information" and "knowledge" interchangeably. But in the scholarly realm of media literacy, we need to make a distinction. Information is piecemeal and transitory; while knowledge is structured, organized, and is of more enduring significance. Information resides in the messages, while knowledge resides in a person's mind (see Table 4.3).

Table 4.3 Contrasting Information with Knowledge

Information	Knowledge
Piecemeal	Structured and organized
Transitory	Enduring
Resides in messages	Resides in a person's mind
Raw material	Constructed from raw material
Value lies in accuracy	Value lies in context and meaning
Focused on individual facts	Focused on meaning arising from connections

Information-Based Interventions

If the purpose of a media literacy intervention study is to give targets a few facts that are expected to shape their belief about something, then providing information may be sufficient. For example, let's say researchers fear that their targets have acquired a belief that using alcohol and illegal drugs is part of an exciting lifestyle from watching years of Hollywood movies and television programs. So they design a persuasion-type study to alter this belief in targets. In this case they can select perhaps a dozen facts that show all sorts of negative consequences of consuming such substances. The intervention would then be the conveyance of these 12 bits of information, either through a lecture, a video, or a printed list. In order to measure how successful the intervention was, designers would need to construct a 12-question post-test to determine how many of these facts their targets learned. Because each of the 12 items would have a factual basis, researchers can easily determine what the correct answers are and compute a score for each target on an information-accuracy scale by summing all the items a target answered correctly. Researchers could then conclude that targets with higher scores on the information-accuracy scale demonstrate that they have acquired a larger amount of information about the harmful effects of alcohol compared to other respondents with lower scores. But in order for these scale scores to have meaning within the context of a media literacy intervention study, researchers must make two assumptions. First, designers must assume that each item on the scale measures a bit of factual information that is equally important; that is, knowing one bit of information is no more important than knowing any other single bit of information. Second, researchers must assume that their selected 12 bits of information constitute a sufficient amount of factual learning that will make a difference to their level of media literacy, which will then make a difference on the eventual outcome variable of their intervention study.

Knowledge-Based Interventions

In contrast, if researchers conceptualize their intervention as imparting knowledge rather than information, then design decisions become more challenging, because designers need to consider structure. Recall that the idea of information treats all facts and beliefs as equally important, whereas knowledge is focused on how facts and beliefs are structured to create meaning.

Where can researchers get this structure? Either they can find knowledge structures in the media literacy literature or they must develop their own structures. Media literacy structures are rare in the literature, but several do exist. One such structure was provided by Silverblatt (1995), who suggested that people need knowledge in four areas in order to interpret media messages – process, context, structure, and production values. Silverblatt then published the *Dictionary of Media Literacy*, which included more than 300 entries (Silverblatt & Eliceiri, 1997). However, those entries were presented alphabetically, which indicated that all 300 entries were equally important to media literacy.

Researchers who care about knowledge more than information need to find – or construct – outlines to guide the design of their intervention as well as their measurement instruments. The value of an outline is that it specifies components as well as their composition. Thus an outline serves as a valuable guide for deciding how many items to write (i.e., the number of sub-components) and how those items should be clustered together into scales. For examples of such media literacy structures of knowledge exhibited in outlines, look at the beginning of chapters in *Media Literacy* (Potter, 2019a).

Domains of Knowledge

Many media literacy scholars believe that knowledge is an essential component of media literacy, but few scholars have specified what information is essential, and fewer still have outlined the structure of essential knowledge (Potter & Thai, 2019). Thus scholars who are committed to designing a media literacy intervention to teach knowledge in a structured manner have few resources upon which to draw.

Scholars who attempt to create their own knowledge structures need to consider whether their domains of knowledge are regarded as containers or as labels in a hierarchy. If the domains are containers, then all the information within each container can be regarded as equally important and existing on the same level of generality. Designers of measures for each container need simply to make a list of all relevant items and sample from among them. It doesn't matter which items are selected because all are regarded as being equally important.

If instead, the names of the knowledge domains are used more as labels for levels in a hierarchy, then it is important to think about how the information is organized within the hierarchy. If knowledge domains are regarded as being structured hierarchically, then we have multiple levels of generality to consider. For example, let's say researchers want to measure participants' knowledge about the media industries. Of course, they cannot write one item that would measure the degree to which participants vary in their knowledge of the media industries. Let's also say their conceptual base suggests that there are three key ideas about the media industries as follows: (1) an understanding of the industries' motivation to maximize profits, (2) an understanding of how the media industries have developed over time, and (3) an understanding about how the industries attract niche audiences and condition them for repeated exposures. It is possible to write a simple true-false question to measure the first of these sub-domains (i.e., the media industries have a strong motivation to maximize their profits) although such an item could be argued to measure awareness of a motive which is much more superficial than what the sub-domain calls for by way of "understanding" their motivations. But let's set that issue aside for now. The more serious challenge lies in designing a single item to measure the other two sub-domains. For the second sub-domain it is not possible to design a simple question that can make a meaningful assessment of the level of a participant's knowledge.

There are advantages and disadvantages of regarding knowledge domains as hierarchies. The major advantages are that hierarchies provide more structured guidance for designing an intervention and a measurement scheme to assess the success of the intervention. Also, using hierarchies to design media literacy studies will allow the study to achieve greater ecological validity. Cognitive psychologists have repeatedly shown that humans organize their learning into nested categories, which makes it easier for them to store and retrieve information as well as providing context for meaning (Fiske & Taylor, 1991; Lamberts & Goldstone, 2005).

In order to achieve the advantages of treating knowledge in a structured, hierarchical manner, designers of media literacy intervention studies need to invest more scholarly work into their designs. Knowledge hierarchies are more complex and typically require more items to measure well, especially if the domains are not independent (see next section for more on this point).

Independence

Perhaps the most challenging conceptual issue to think about when designing a media literacy intervention study is independence. The issue of independence forces us to think about whether the different elements, especially the components of skills and knowledge, are related to each other or whether each can stand alone. That is, can people really acquire much knowledge relevant to media literacy unless they have a certain level of skill? And can media literacy skills develop without exposure to certain kinds of information?

When thinking about this issue of conceptualizing media literacy as a basis for design decisions, it is not sufficient to lay out various elements (components and domains) in the definition; researchers must also consider whether those elements are independent from one another or whether they work together in a system. There is very little guidance in the literature on this important point.

When authors do not address this issue, readers must assume the authors are defaulting to independence; that is, the authors believe that all the elements are independent from one another and that each makes an equal contribution to a person's level of media literacy. This default option allows designers to be much more efficient in their analysis. For example, when researchers assume independence among elements, they can avoid the complex challenges involved when deciding what to put into their media literacy intervention and how to structure the presentation of those elements to make sure that certain types of skills and knowledge are developed first so as to insure the success of other skills and knowledge that are presented later.

Independence is an especially important issue to think about when dealing with skills. When we think in more depth conceptually, we are likely to conclude that skills are not independent from one another; instead, they are likely to be interlinked such that people cannot be well developed on skill Y without being highly developed first on skill X. For example, among the seven skills of media literacy (Table 4.2), the skill of analysis is the most primary because analysis is necessary to generate the raw material used in the other six skills. Therefore an intervention that concentrates on helping targets develop their skill of evaluation, for example, will have limited success if designers do not first insure that targets have an adequate level of skill on analysis. To illustrate, let's say you want to develop a media literacy intervention study that helps targets spot fake news, which focuses on the use of the skill of evaluation. You design the intervention to give targets news standards to use as criteria in making evaluative judgments about what is real news and what is fake news; then you ask them to read a selection of news stories and identify which ones are real news and which are fake news. If targets have a poor level of skill on analysis, they will not be able to identify the elements in a news story that *need to be* evaluated; they may have learned in the intervention *how* to conduct the evaluation itself, but they struggle to figure out *what* to evaluate (i.e., their skill of analysis is faulty). This is a problem of assuming independence across skills when the situation calls for designers of the intervention to realize that the skill of evaluation depends on the skill of analysis as a pre-condition.

Considering the issue of independence is also important when making design decisions about the role of knowledge in an intervention. It is typically likely that facts are interlinked in hierarchical ways in knowledge structures such that people cannot fully understand a superordinate concept X, until they understand the supporting ideas of Y and Z. Within the knowledge component, scholars need to specify whether their domains of knowledge are regarded as being linked together or whether they are independent from one another. For example, let's say that a conceptualization lays out four domains of knowledge – media industries, content, audiences, and effects. And you plan to measure participants' knowledge on only effects. If the four areas of knowledge are regarded as independent from one another, then limiting measures to one domain is not a problem. Each domain is believed to be composed of a stand-alone set of information that is not influenced by any of the other three, and people can be highly media literate if they have a lot of knowledge in any one area. However, let's say the conceptual foundation used in a study suggests that all domains areas are linked together into a system of knowledge such that the knowledge within the domain of effects cannot be understood without also understanding the knowledge within the domain of content patterns, which in turn cannot be understood without understanding industry motives and economics. With this non-independence conceptualization, designers of measures need to include measures across all linked domains of knowledge in order to arrive at a valid assessment of participants' knowledge structures.

And it is much more likely that clusters of skills work together to enhance the understanding of clusters of knowledge. If we do not consider patterns of non-independence and instead default to a belief that every element is independent and equally important, then we end up constructing interventions that have a low ceiling of effectiveness.

Implications for Measurement

If researchers assume that skills can be treated in an independent manner, then the measurement task becomes considerably simpler. Researchers need only to develop a performance task for each skill and then observe how well participants perform on each. Later in the analysis, they can test to see which skills are related; but, such *a posteriori* tests are focused more on seeing how levels of skills are related, which is not the same as believing *a priori* that certain skills are antecedents or otherwise intertwined with other skills.

When designers of measures of skills reject the assumption that skills are independent, they create a much more challenging measurement task because they must articulate the pattern of inter-dependency, and this raises a series of questions. Are there threshold levels? That is, unless a person reaches a certain level of expertise on a skill, can it be observed? Which skills are antecedents for other skills? That is, can skill #2 be performed well until a person performs skill #1 adequately? Are skills substitutable? That is, in order for people to use skill #3 well, do they need to have a high level of either skill #1 or skill #2, but not necessarily both?

Summary

This chapter has been organized around four areas of considerable challenge when designing a media literacy intervention study. The first of these challenges is clarifying the purpose of the intervention by deciding whether to design an evaluation type study or a basic research type study. The second challenge deals with skills by separating skills from competencies then committing to designing an intervention that truly teaches skills by providing a procedure for performance that provides continuous feedback to learners to help shape the development of their skills. The third challenge is dealing with knowledge in a way that separates facts from beliefs as well as information from knowledge. And the fourth challenge requires thinking about independence to determine how bits of information fit together into knowledge structures and how skills work together to create those knowledge structures.

Designing media literacy interventions that can make a meaningful difference is not a simple task. In this chapter, I have tried to organize that task for you by focusing your attention on the most important decisions you will need to make. The more you think about these decisions in the planning phase, the stronger your design will be and this will translate directly into more valuable findings.

References

Austin, E. W., Pinkleton, B. E., & Funabiki, R. P. (2007). The desirability paradox in the effects of media literacy training. *Communication Research, 34*(5), 483–506.

Banerjee, S. C., & Greene, K. (2006). Analysis versus production: Adolescent cognitive and attitudinal responses to antismoking interventions. *Journal of Communication, 56,* 773–794.

Byrne, S. (2009). Media literacy interventions: What makes them boom or boomerang? *Communication Education, 58,* 1–14.

Fiske, S. T., & Taylor, S. E. (1991). *Social cognition* (2nd ed.). New York: McGraw-Hill.

Lamberts, K., & Goldstone, R. L. (Eds.) (2005). *Handbook of cognition.* Thousand Oaks, CA: Sage.

Nathanson, A. I. (2002). The unintended effects of parental mediation of television on adolescents. *Media Psychology, 4,* 207–230.

Nathanson, A. I., & Cantor, J. (2000). Reducing the aggression-promoting effect of violent cartoons by increasing children's fictional involvement with the victim: A study of active mediation. *Journal of Broadcasting & Electronic Media, 44,* 94–109.

Nathanson, A. I., & Yang, M.-S. (2003). The effects of mediation content and form on children's responses to violent television. *Human Communication Research, 29*(1), 111–134.

Potter, W. J. (2004). *Theory of media literacy: A cognitive approach.* Thousand Oaks, CA: Sage.

Potter, W. J. (2019a). *Media literacy* (9th ed.). Thousand Oaks, CA: Sage.

Potter, W. J. (2019b). *The seven skills of media literacy.* Los Angeles, CA: Sage.

Potter, W. J., & Thai, C. (2019). Examining validity in the media literacy intervention studies. *Review of Communication Research, 7.* doi: 10.12840/issn.2255-4165.018

Silverblatt, A. (1995). *Media literacy: Keys to interpreting media messages.* Westport, CN: Praeger.

Silverblatt, A., & Eliceiri, E. M. E. (1997). *Dictionary of media literacy.* Westport, CT: Greenwood Press.

Valkenburg, P. M., Krcmar, M., Peeters, A. L., & Marseille, N. M. (1999). "Instructive mediation," "restrictive mediation," and "social coviewing." *Journal of Broadcasting & Electronic Media, 43,* 52–66.

Part Two

Media Literacy, News, and Propaganda

5   Focusing on Facts

Media and News Literacy Education in the Age of Misinformation

Jennifer Fleming and Christopher Karadjov

Introduction

At the turn of the 21st century, it would be hard to imagine how much the media ecosystem and U.S. presidential elections would change in less than a generation. In 1999, when Google celebrated its first anniversary, the first mass-market smartphone was almost a decade away from landing on store shelves. The Dow Jones Industrial Average hit 10,000 about the same time as President Bill Clinton barely survived an impeachment trial in the Senate. His predicament commenced in no small part because a news aggregation website called *Drudge Report* had made public an extramarital affair with an intern in the White House in early 1998, thus signaling the beginning of the end of mainstream press gatekeeping (Williams & Delli Carpini, 2000). Today, Google generates more than one trillion searches and $30 billion in revenues per year, while about 80% of American adults own a smartphone, catapulting iPhone's maker Apple Inc. to a market capitalization of almost $1 trillion (Pew Research Center, 2018). Another U.S. commander-in-chief is surpassing his own 10,000 mark of notoriety: according to the *Washington Post*, in barely over two years after assuming the office, President Donald Trump has clocked in more than 10,000 false or misleading claims following an unprecedented 2016 campaign riddled with exaggerations, lies, and insults to various groups and individuals (Kessler, Rizzo, & Kelly, 2019).

The complex, convoluted, and confusing media environment in 2016 signaled a dark turn in mass communication. The promises of peaceful participatory cultures made possible by affordable digital devices and widely accessible Internet access collided with the realities of individual filter bubbles and political, ideological, and commercial forces, ushering in what some have labeled the *misinformation age* (Benkler, Faris, & Roberts, 2018; Gaufman, 2018; O'Connor & Weatherall, 2018). Characteristics of the misinformation age include lack of trust, lack of context, and lack of depth in fast-moving digital cultures where individuals can surf and snack on information and images that they can also create and share at whim (Friedman, 2018; Knight Commission, 2019;

Mitchell, Simmons, Matsa, & Silver, 2018; Turkle, 2015). Simply put, *misinformation is information that is incomplete, incorrect, or unknowingly inaccurate* (Fox, 1983), while *disinformation is carefully planned false information or manipulated narrative or facts meant to mislead* (Ireton & Posetti, 2018).

Conspiracy theories, half-truths, and misleading memes often go viral and spread faster and wider than well-sourced, accurate, and in-depth reports in the misinformation age, especially during high interest news stories, such as important elections, natural disasters, terrorist attacks, and mass shootings (Carey, 2017; Grinberg, Joseph, Friedland, Swire-Thompson, & Lazer, 2019; Lazer et al., 2018; Vosoughi, Roy, & Aral, 2018). Not to mention, individuals can select what they expose themselves to and whom they engage and share information with online. Many tend to utilize only sites and groups that distribute and amplify similar viewpoints and interests, thereby avoiding information that could challenge, change, or correct dangerous, damaging, or derogatory beliefs (Manjoo, 2008; Pariser, 2011). Meanwhile, a national survey of close to 6,000 college-age students suggests that young adults get news from at least five different sources every week, and they often feel distrustful of the information they encounter (Head, Wihbey, Metaxas, MacMillan, & Cohen, 2018). Recommendations to mitigate the effects of what can be labeled a "state of information disorder" have included rebuilding local news organizations and audience trust, censoring problematic content on aggregators and social media channels, and supporting media literacy education (Wardle & Derakhshan, 2017).

In this chapter, we argue there is value in news literacy programs and fact-checking resources created by journalists to further media literacy education, even though these projects are guided mostly by journalistic instincts, and therefore they are not grounded in any identifiable body of scholarly literature. Nevertheless, journalists bring real-time fact-finding principles and practices to media literacy education. We propose one way to bridge the gap between journalistic mindsets and media literacy education theory, practice, and research is through a *factual truth framework* introduced in the 1960s. We first explore relevant research and ideas from media literacy and news literacy. Next, we define factual analysis instruction and explore factual truth theory. We then discuss selected fact-finding and fact-checking resources available to media literacy educators looking for tools, techniques, and supplemental materials to assist in teaching citizens how to identify, examine, and analyze the veracity of information and images they encounter in the multimodal misinformation age. We also suggest that the public should assume increasing responsibility for its own media diet, acquiring fact-checking skills and using the growing number of available tools.

Media Literacy

The thinking behind media literacy education, or MLE, as an antidote to the chaos of content in the 21st century is that people of all ages – middle, high school, and college-age students in particular – will become more informed, engaged, and empowered citizens when taught how to evaluate and analyze information and images critically. It seems that modern MLE suffers from many of the same ills as the broader misinformation culture, though. A "media literacy" Google search in 2010 generated 765,000 hits, and a similar Google Scholar search revealed 18,700 articles, prompting Potter (2010) to warn of more confusion ahead as the number of voices and disciplines contributing to MLE increases. The same keyword searches a decade later in 2019 yields roughly 3.7 million hits and 108,000 Google Scholar references.

MLE in the United States has always been multifaceted, multimodal, and multidisciplinary. Starting in the 1970s, educators and activists began to organize efforts to design and assess instructional interventions to mitigate the perceived ill effects of media, most notably television, given its prevalence in culture through most of the second half of the 20th century (Hobbs, 1998b; RobbGrieco, 2014). Tyner (1991) describes media literacy educators in the early days as a "fractious bunch" because of the varying approaches and intentions informing the field. Even though this emergent area of research and instruction lacked consensus, a dominant definition materialized: media literacy is the ability to access, analyze, evaluate, and create mediated messages for a variety of contexts (Aufderheide & Firestone, 1993). This four-component conceptualization of media literacy remains the most widely cited definition, and critical thinking skill development is at the core of lesson plans.

Proponents have long argued that one reason for MLE is to help *protect* young people against the media. The protectionist paradigm has been consistent throughout the history of MLE. The types of media to guard against have been changing, however. From comic books, to film to television and now social media – media literacy foci vary along with new media technologies, cultures and habits (Hobbs, 1998b; Masterman, 2003; Potter, 2013; Tyner, 1998). Another impetus for MLE is to raise *awareness* about oppressive social, political, and economic structures and systems embedded in media content. Critical theorists are the most fervent advocates of instructional programs aimed at identifying, analyzing, and challenging ideological and hegemonic messages in media (Alvermann, Moon, & Hagood, 1999; Kellner & Share, 2005, 2007). A third MLE motivation connects critical thinking competencies with civic knowledge and engagement. The idea behind the *civics* approach is that citizens are empowered when they are knowledgeable and skeptical about media messages focused on public affairs (Hobbs, 1998a; Lewis & Jhally, 1998; Martens & Hobbs, 2015; Mihailidis,

2012; Mihailidis & Thevenin, 2013; RobbGrieco, 2014; Tyner, 1998). Potter (2004) puts forth a *cognitive* theory of media literacy so as to better reflect the choices people make in the selection and interpretation of media. Potter asserts that most media literacy paradigms implicitly or explicitly suggest media exposure as a negative and/or something to guard against, which is a position he believes takes power away from individuals and leaves little room for the enjoyment and appreciation of media messages.

Potter's cognitive approach is among the most valuable and adaptable to the ever-shifting and highly personalized media technologies and habits in the misinformation age because it allows for flexible and nuanced examination of media choices, content, organizations, and effects. Another advantage of the approach is that it grounds MLE in individual awareness of consumption, interpretation, and creating/sharing. This injects the "me" into *me*dia literacy at a time when few people will experience the same media message at the same time in the same way. The individual is the only certain variable in 21st-century media ecosystems, and personal digital media are often extensions of identity (McLuhan, 1994; Messaris & Humphreys, 2006; Turkle, 2005, 2011). Individuals create personas and content, and thereby their messages and motivations should be the focus of MLE. The individual is also often the only and final arbiter of accuracy in the constant stream of digital content flashing or scrolling across screens. Understanding this is key to developing media consumer/producer responsibility and agency in the misinformation age.

News Literacy

News literacy is one of a growing number of MLE specialty areas that include but are not limited to advertising literacy, information literacy, and entertainment literacy. The thinking behind multiliteracies is that content is created with different tools and techniques; hence, different pedagogies are needed to engage with different media (Potter, 2016; Silverblatt, Ferry, & Finan, 1999; Silverblatt, Miller, Smith, & Brown, 2014). Analysis of news messages has long been inherent in MLE given the fact that news organizations have traditionally been the primary sources of public affairs information in democracies (Buckingham, 2013; Masterman, 2003). The moniker *news literacy*, however, only became popular after journalists-turned-educators at Stony Brook University and the News Literacy Project created programs aimed at teaching information-processing skills about news based on the principles and practices of journalists.

Stony Brook University became a leader in news literacy education when the John S. and James L. Knight Foundation earmarked nearly $2 million in 2006 to assist in the development, instruction, and expansion of a college-level course designed to teach students how to judge the reliability and credibility of information (Schneider, 2007). Founded in 2008 by former *Los Angeles Times* reporter Alan C. Miller, the News Literacy Project (NLP) targets middle- and high-school students with various approaches, including modules, digital platforms, and personal interactions with journalists. The key tenets of these journalist-inspired news literacy programs include an unshakeable belief in the importance of an independent press in democracies and an emphasis on the veracity of information (Fleming, 2014, 2015; Loth, 2012). A case study of the Stony Brook curriculum further confirms the instructional emphasis on teaching students how to think and analyze information like seasoned reporters.

In the study, a matrix combining Potter's (2016) four domains of media literacy learning (cognitive, emotional, aesthetic, and moral) with Silverblatt, Ferry, and Finan's (1999) approaches to media analysis instruction (ideological, autobiographical, production element, nonverbal, and mythic) is used to situate news literacy pedagogies within established media literacy frameworks. During the coding of artifacts and interviews, it was determined that none of the five MLE approaches adequately captured the essence of news literacy instruction, so a factual category was created and added. The journalists turned news literacy educators' focus intently on facts – how to find them and how to assess them. This emphasis intersects the most with the cognitive domain, given the examination of the quality and veracity information denotes analysis, evaluation, and synthesis skills. Weaknesses of journalism-inspired and journalism-informed news literacy programs include lack of instruction in the ideological, structural, and commercial forces that lead to biases, mistakes, distortions, and distractions in news media (Fleming, 2015).

Scholars in Asia adopting and adapting the Stony Brook news literacy curriculum have shied away from the term "news literacy," preferring "verification education" instead. They have argued that the latter is a more accurate term given the vague meaning of news in the 21st-century media contexts and the prominence of social media in news consumption, particularly among young people (Fleming & Kajimoto, 2016; Kruger, 2017). The verification education construct is important because it highlights how professional journalists and news organizations are no longer the sole purveyors of accurate information. We maintain that verification alone is not a strong-enough construct in the misinformation age, however, given that one can authenticate a statement's origin and it can still turn out to be untrue or misleading.

Ashley, Maksl, and Craft (2013) develop a News Media Literacy, or NML, scale to assess knowledge about news and awareness of personal news interpretation habits. These scholars prefer *news media literacy* to news literacy because of the need to specify aptitudes, attitudes, and skills associated with the consumption and interpretation of messages created by journalists and distributed by established news organizations. The distinction between news media literacy and news literacy becomes more pronounced when the source and intention of the message creator is increasingly difficult to disentangle. The findings of the NML scale survey research suggest that news media literate individuals are likely more selective and proactive in choosing what news to consume (Maksl, Ashley, & Craft, 2015). The researchers also compare the level of news media literacy of a sample of students who completed the Stony Brook news literacy course with a sample of students who did not. The results revealed that the effects of news literacy instruction are significant and long lasting (Maksl, Craft, Ashley, & Miller, 2016). The scale was later used to determine the connection between current events knowledge and high levels of news media literacy (Ashley, Maksl, & Craft, 2017) and conversely if there is a relationship between low levels of news media literacy and a person's tendency to believe conspiracy theories circulating online (Craft, Ashley, & Maksl, 2017). Taken together, the NML scale studies represent the most significant and sustained social scientific research programs in MLE, and they confirm the efficacy of such instruction.

Future Directions: Factual Truth, Unlovable Press, and Responsible Citizenry

Calls for the widespread adoption of media literacy programs emphasizing accuracy and high quality journalism have only grown louder since the first media reports suggested that Russia's Internet operatives and bots might be polluting the American media ecosystem with "active measures" spreading disinformation and fostering misinformation, as laid out most succinctly in *The Mueller Report* (U.S. Department of Justice, 2019). These calls have been at a fever pitch in no small part because of President Trump's incessant attempts at discrediting and demonizing journalists from prominent commercial media outlets starting with his election campaign and continuing into his office term (Vernon, 2018). Foundations and high-profile tech corporations such as Facebook, Google, and Apple have been pouring millions of dollars into programs designed to thwart the spread of problematic content. They have also been funding select MLE outfits that promise to educate young people about the importance of fact-based journalism (Apple, 2019; Bell, 2016; Doctor, 2016; Knight Foundation, 2019; Shahani, 2018; Strauss, 2018; Sullivan & Bajarin, 2018). Even with significant attention and investment, most of these discussions lack solid theoretical and academic grounding that could connect well-funded news literacy programs with the established MLE community. We propose revisiting and utilizing factual truth theory to bridge this gap as we move deeper into the misinformation age.

Arendt (1968) argues that truth and politics have historically been on bad terms because those who seek political power are neither altruistic in their motivations nor honest in their communications. In light of the inherent dishonest nature of political rhetoric, Arendt posits that there needs to be a way to reveal the most relevant truths in public discourse, that is, *factual truth*. To Arendt, factual truth is a concept more easily understood by what it is not: "The hallmark of factual truth is that its opposite is neither error nor illusion nor opinion ... but deliberate falsehood, or lie" (p. 249). Factual truth is distinct from philosophical truth because philosophical truth becomes opinion and argument when shared, whereas factual truth relates to events and circumstances determined by witnesses and testimony; it can be proven, often first by journalists. According to Arendt, cultures would struggle to function without factual truth because "facts inform opinions, and opinions, inspired by different interests and passions, can differ widely and still be legitimate as long they respect factual truth" (p. 238).

Media literacy programs designed before 2016 offered little in the way of a framework to uncover or analyze factual truth, which we believe is the key in recognizing and curbing misinformation. Instead, MLE educators and theorists have been most concerned with the degree a message represents or misrepresents reality; how individuals negotiate media meaning; and the commercial, ideological, and political implications of media (Aufderheide & Firestone, 1993; Livingstone, 2004). Even so, there is some evidence that factual analysis has been encouraged in select MLE programs. The Center for Media Literacy, founded in 1989, includes identifying fallacies in its definition of media literacy. However, in-depth instruction on how to determine fallacies and differentiate them from facts is not addressed in any meaningful way (Thoman & Jolls, 2004).

In college-level media literacy classes, Potter (2016) prompts students to judge the *factuality* of entertainment media by assessing the degree of how much (or little) the message shows what actually happened. For news media, Potter is more explicit about facts: one of the markers of high-quality news reports is that they are accurate and include a full set of facts, which means the story includes enough accurate information, balance, and context to facilitate a nuanced and fair understanding of the topic or event covered. *Factual information* is defined as "discrete bits of information that can be confirmed by objective sources; examples include names (of people, places, characters, etc.), dates, titles, definitions of terms, formulae, lists and the like" (p. 495). This characterization of factual information is key because 21st-century media consumption is scattered. People often ingest media content in bits – a Tweet here, a Facebook, or Instagram post there, while listening to a podcast or skimming other open tabs and watching television, instead of reading closely a full news story from start to finish or viewing complete television news reports and programs. It is also important to note that Potter associates facts with journalism, not entertainment or other types of media. There is a social and professional expectation that news sources are accurate, independent, and accountable and that an institution dedicated to telling truthful stories about public affairs and society as a whole is essential for democracy to function well. Schudson (2008) argues that self-governing societies need an "unlovable press," even as the number of information sources rises. An unlovable press is made up of journalists who "get in the face of power – and are enabled to do so because both their doggedness and their irreverence is protected by law, by a conducive political culture, and by a historical record of having served self-government well when they hunt down elusive or hidden facts" (p. 10). He adds that an independent press committed to producing factual knowledge may be "as good as we get" in democracy, and therefore such as press should be preserved and promoted (p. 2). He reinforces the same ideas a decade later, appending a caution that "journalists can and often do wear multiple hats," which does not negate the concepts of objectivity or professionalism but certainly contributes to the complexity to the media milieu (Schudson, 2018, p. 150). This is another reason for MLE to cultivate the understanding that a vibrant journalistic culture goes hand in hand with an engaged and responsible citizenry.

Journalistic independence and pursuit of facts were front and center to the journalists who created the most prominent news literacy pedagogies: Howard Schneider of Stony Brook University and Alan Miller of the News Literacy Project (NLP). Both started their respective programs around the same time in response to similar technological and commercial forces that were shrinking newsrooms, displacing journalists and blurring the lines between journalism and everything else. Fleming (2015) finds factual analysis instruction is at the core of Stony Brook curricula, given the aim of the pedagogy is to assist students in identifying, judging, and utilizing reliable and credible information. Meanwhile, the NLP's post 2016 election battle cry is to "give facts a fighting chance" (Strauss, 2018; Sullivan & Bajarin, 2018). Funding for the Stony Brook program dwindled within the decade following the Knight Foundation's initial investment in 2006. Meanwhile, the News Literacy Project has expanded its reach and attracted additional financing from multiple foundations and formed partnerships with the tech giants Facebook and Apple, making it the clear leader in news literacy education in the misinformation age.

Arendt (1968) shares similar views on the function and purpose of the press as the journalists who created the aforementioned news literacy programs. She classifies journalism as one of the outstanding "modes of truth telling" in modern societies and elevates journalists to a place of distinction because of their ethical commitment to staying outside of the power struggle of politics. Again, let us juxtapose this with Schudson's

(2018) caution that journalism practice may be more multifaceted unlike its common self-representation in the media; as long as we realize that, we can set realistic expectations that, for instance, we will not treat every journalist and media outlet as completely equivalent to the others. Moreover, President Trump has tapped into an intrinsic distrust many Americans have for journalists and the enterprises that employ them to an absurd extreme that nevertheless remains widely persuasive (Knight Foundation, 2018). This same survey that reported Americans' appallingly low trust in journalists also found that some 70% of them are willing to improve their opinion of news media upon a track record of factual reporting, thus supporting Arendt's (1968) high-mindedness about the role of the press; the difference is that nowadays press trust is not granted by default but has to be earned by journalists and learned through MLE.

U.S. journalists have been looking for and verifying facts for more than a century. They also take pride in their watchdog role, which is echoed in *The Washington Post*'s "Democracy Dies in Darkness" motto unveiled in 2017 (Farhi, 2017). It reflects the understanding of the interconnectedness between democracy; a free, accurate, and investigative press; and an informed citizenry. The role of the press in a democracy is to shine the light on those in power to ensure representative government is indeed of the people, by the people, and for the people – a role embedded in freedom of expression and press constitutional guarantees. We can all agree that without the robust journalism, democracy will suffer. But in the age of misinformation, journalists cannot be the only party shouldering the responsibility for seeking factual truth, even though they are certainly the best positioned to be the leading force. Democracy is everyone's responsibility. Below are numerous resources that subscribe to journalistic methods and mindsets that can be used by media literacy educators to build factual awareness lessons and encourage civic responsibility and agency in individuals.

One resource is the Stony Brook Center for News Literacy. It offers a deconstruction guide and other tools free (Center for News Literacy, 2017); another is the News Literacy Project (NLP). The NLP has a more robust digital menu of programs and includes journalist classroom visits in some cities. The most accessible and applicable to misinformation NLP tool available is the *Don't Get Fooled: 7 Simple Steps* guide to avoid rumors, misleading memes, and misinformation (News Literacy Project, 2019). The first three prompts encourage students to monitor their emotions, reactions, and motivations when accessing or sharing information, a stance reminiscent of Potter's (2016) cognitive approach to MLE. Other *Don't Get Fooled* steps reflect traditional MLE skills, including evaluating and analyzing information and sources, and it adds searching for more information from reputable news sources and fact-checking outlets. The checklist reflects a nuanced, complex media environment that puts personal and factual awareness front and center; however, sourcing is nonexistent. There are no references to research, even though numerous concepts appear to echo the work of others, especially that of another misinformation age funder favorite, First Draft News (Wardle & Derakhshan, 2017).

First Draft News is a global verification and collaborative investigation network housed at Harvard University. It supports journalists, academic, and technologists concerned with trust and truth in the digital age with research and training programs (First Draft News, 2019; Wardle, 2018). There is also a multitude of online-only enterprises debunking urban legends, outing liars, and filling in half-truths propagated by politicians and other information agents. Snopes, founded in 1994, claims to be the oldest; it is a commercial operation (Snopes, 2019). Others include Factcheck.org, which started in 2003 and is positioned as a consumer advocate that aims to reduce deception and confusion in U.S. politics. Foundations and donations fund FactCheck.org (FactCheck.org, 2019). PolitiFact is another nonprofit that uses "fact-checking" journalism to "give citizens information they need to govern themselves in a democracy." It was awarded the Pulitzer Prize for National Reporting for its coverage of the 2008 election. It is associated with the Poynter Institute, a nonprofit journalism training organization based in Florida. PolitiFact is funded with grants, online advertisements, donations, memberships, and content sales, and it produces the "Truth-O-Meter," which is a tool that rates stories and assertions on their degree of accuracy as determined by journalistic verification methods (Drobnic Holin, 2018). The Poynter Institute also hosts the International Fact-Checking Network; it promotes fact checking worldwide with policy support, fellowships, grants, and special events, such as International Fact-Checking Day (Poynter Institute, 2019).

The *Washington Post*'s Fact Checker newsletter is a popular resource aimed at correcting the public record with information tested and vetted by journalists. It started in 2007 during the 2008 presidential campaign and became a permanent column in 2011. The purpose is to examine the veracity of comments made by political figures, explain complex issues, and provide analysis on phrases often used by political operatives to mask truth (Kessler, 2017). The National Association for Media Literacy Education (NAMLE) awarded Fact Checker editor and chief writer Glenn Kessler its Media Literate Media award in 2015. In late April 2019, *Washington Post* Fact Checker journalists determined that President Trump had surpassed 10,000 false or misleading claims since becoming president, sometimes averaging more than 20 erroneous claims a day often during campaign-like rallies (Kessler et al., 2019). In response to doctored videos going viral and being passed on as real, the most notable being a video depicting House Speaker Nancy Pelosi as drunk, the *Washington Post* launched "The Fact Checker's Guide to Manipulated

Video." The guide helps people identify, label, and analyze different types of online video manipulation, including missing context, deceptive editing, and malicious transformation (WashPostPR, 2019).

An interesting non-U.S. approach is EU vs. Disinformation, which is a fact-checking site started in 2015. The EU vs. Disinformation project was driven by a somewhat belated response of European Union bureaucracy to forestall the long-documented attempts at news manipulation from external players, mostly Russia. The European Council made a recommendation in March 2015, a year after the annexation of Crimea by Russia, which also represented a significant step-up in the propaganda war (Daalder, 2017). The EU East StratCom Task Force was subsequently created, and the *EU vs. Disinfo* website started, accompanied by social media accounts and a weekly *Disinformation Review* newsletter (European Union, 2018). The website selects stories to be fact-checked and then provides detailed analysis based on its staff's research. Users can also search by keyword from the database of collected disinformation stories, which total close to 4,000 from fall 2015 to spring 2018.

As a part of these continuing efforts, the European Commission convened an independent working group and published a prescriptive document that was released in March 2018, under the title *A Multidimensional Approach to Disinformation: Report of the Independent High Level Group on Fake News and Online Disinformation.* The second and third prescribed responses read, correspondingly: "2. promote media and information literacy to counter disinformation and help users navigate the digital media environment; 3. develop tools for empowering users and journalists to tackle disinformation and foster a positive engagement with fast-evolving information technologies" (European Commission, 2018, p. 5). Projects such as these demonstrate that factual analysis efforts are global in scale and share the philosophy that the solution to misinformation and disinformation is partly the responsibility of individual citizens to be informed, as opposed to relying merely on the efforts of professional media.

Another useful tool that may be of great utility to individuals and educators is Indiana University's Hoaxy project, which tracks the spread of information in online stories or on Twitter. Hoaxy gives priority to low-credibility and fact-checking sources using proprietary data-sorting software (Indiana University Network Science Institute and the Center for Complex Networks and Systems Research, 2018). Thus, users can put in keywords (say, "vaccines") and visualize the spread of information from one node (grouping) to another. Larger nodes represent visually more stories originating from a certain online location that are being linked to other websites. It is important to note that Hoaxy also does not distinguish between websites that traffic in unverified or inaccurate information – deliberately or otherwise – and those whose business model is based on satire, which for all intents and purposes is often mimicking "fake news." As one of the co-authors of the project explained, the Indiana University team deliberately gave up on distinguishing between misinformation or disinformation and satire or comical exaggeration because it found this role should be left to an educated user (Valentin Penchev, personal communication, May 26, 2018).

Taken together, these resources are excellent in finding, cross check-ing, and understanding information in the pursuit of factual truth and assessing reliable and credible information in specific topic areas, but none represents thoughtful, sustained pedagogy. From modules to mini lessons to President Trump's misinformation counts, they are comple-ments to media literacy instruction, not fully developed lesson plans. In addition, most come with journalistic or other institutional biases. Such blind spots have been long studied and criticized by scholars, critical/ cultural, and MLE intellectuals. Criticism includes that news entities focus too much on profits, and journalists often emphasize scandalous stories and angles over reasoned, more nuanced pieces on substantive issues. One final weakness is the veracity of the fact checkers themselves. Researchers find that professional fact-checking outlets perform well with correcting outright falsehoods and obvious lies, but the truth is more difficult to decipher when political rhetoric is ambiguous (Young, Jamieson, Poulsen, & Goldring, 2017).

Conclusion

In this chapter, we argued that the instructional answer to critical and factual awareness lies at the intersection of media literacy, news literacy, and civic responsibility with solid theoretical grounding in factual truth. It would be foolhardy to suggest a one size-fits-all analytical approach to the factually fluid digital media ecosystem. At a time of unlimited choices in media and a seemingly endless number of voices attracted to MLE, specificity is needed now more than ever, and factual truth theory and fac-tual analysis instruction are specific solutions to guide MLE practice and research moving ahead. The fact-checking resources we discussed do not represent a comprehensive list but rather should serve as a sampling of the available materials that can be used as supplemental tools for programs designed to teach students how to become more informed, engaged, and responsible citizens by identifying, evaluating, and analyzing facts in the struggle for authenticity and accuracy in the misinformation age.

References

Alvermann, D. E., Moon, J. S., & Hagood, M. C. (1999). *Popular culture in the classroom: Teaching and researching critical media literacy*. New York: Routledge.

Apple. (2019). Apple teams with media literacy programs in the US and Europe [Press release]. Retrieved from https://www.apple.com/newsroom/2019/03/apple-teams-with-media-literacy-programs-in-the-us-and-europe/

Arendt, H. (1968). *Between past and future: Eight exercises in political thought.* New York: Viking Press.

Ashley, S., Maksl, A., & Craft, S. (2013). Developing a news media literacy scale. *Journalism & Mass Communication Educator,* 68(1), 7–21. doi:10.1177/1077695812469802

Ashley, S., Maksl, A., & Craft, S. (2017). News media literacy and political engagement: What's the connection? *Journal of Media Literacy Education,* 9(1), 79–98.

Aufderheide, P., & Firestone, C. M. (1993). *Media literacy: A report of the national leadership conference on media literacy.* Retrieved from https://files.eric.ed.gov/fulltext/ED365294.pdf

Bell, E. (2016). Facebook drains the fake news swamp with new, experimental partnerships. *Columbia Journalism Review.* Retrieved from https://www.cjr.org/tow_center/facebook_drains_fake_news_swamp_new_experimental_partnerships.php

Benkler, Y., Faris, R., & Roberts, H. (2018). *Network propaganda: Manipulation, disinformation, and radicalization in American politics.* Oxford, UK: Oxford University Press.

Buckingham, D. (2013). *Media education: Literacy, learning and contemporary culture.* Hoboken, NJ: John Wiley & Sons.

Carey, B. (2017). How fiction becomes fact on social media. *The New York Times.* Retrieved from https://www.nytimes.com/2017/10/20/health/social-media-fake-news.html

Center for News Literacy. (2017). Digital Resource Center. *Stony Brook University.* Retrieved from http://drc.centerfornewsliteracy.org/

Craft, S., Ashley, S., & Maksl, A. (2017). News media literacy and conspiracy theory endorsement. *Communication and the Public,* 2(4), 388–401. doi:10.1177/2057047317725539

Daalder, I. H. (2017). Responding to Russia's resurgence. *Foreign Affairs.* Retrieved from https://www.foreignaffairs.com/articles/russia-fsu/2017-10-16/responding-russias-resurgence

Doctor, K. (2016). Newsonomics: Fake-news fury forces Google and Facebook to change policy. *NiemanLab.* Retrieved from http://www.niemanlab.org/2016/11/newsonomics-fake-news-fury-forces-google-and-facebook-to-change-policy/

Drobnic Holin, A. (2018). The principles of the Truth-O-Meter: PolitiFact's methodology for independent fact-checking. *PolitiFact.* Retrieved from https://www.politifact.com/truth-o-meter/article/2018/feb/12/principles-truth-o-meter-politifacts-methodology-i/

European Commission. (2018). *A multi-dimensional approach to disinformation: Report of the independent high level group on fake news and online disinformation.* Retrieved from https://op.europa.eu/en/publication-detail/-/publication/6ef4df8b-4cea-11e8-be1d-01aa75ed71a1

European Union. (2018). Questions and answers about the East StratCom Task Force. *European Union External Action.* Retrieved from https://eeas.europa.

eu/headquarters/headquarters-homepage/2116/-questions-and-answers-about-the-east-stratcom-task-force_en

FactCheck.org. (2019). FactCheck.org about us: Our process; Our funding. Retrieved from https://www.factcheck.org/our-process/

Farhi, P. (2017). The Washington Post's new slogan turns out to be an old saying. *The Washington Post.* Retrieved from https://www.washingtonpost.com/lifestyle/style/the-washington-posts-new-slogan-turns-out-to-be-an-old-saying/2017/02/23/cb199cda-fa02-11e6-be05-1a3817ac21a5_story.html?utm_term=.971243cad54b

First Draft News. (2019). First Draft News: About. Retrieved from https://firstdraftnews.org/about/

Fleming, J. (2014). Media literacy, news literacy, or news appreciation? A case study of the news literacy program at Stony Brook University. *Journalism & Mass Communication Educator, 69*(2), 146–165. doi:10.1177/1077695813517885

Fleming, J. (2015). What do facts have to do with it? Exploring instructional emphasis in the Stony Brook news literacy curriculum. *Journal of Media Literacy Education, 7*(3), 73–92.

Fleming, J., & Kajimoto, M. (2016). The freedom of critical thinking: Examining efforts to teach American news literacy principles in Hong Kong, Vietnam, and Malaysia. In *Handbook of research on media literacy in the digital age* (pp. 208–235). Hershey, PA: IGI Global.

Fox, C. (1983). *Information and misinformation. An investigation of the notions of information, misinformation, informing, and misinforming.* Westport, CT: Greenwood Publishing Group.

Friedman, U. (2018). Trust is collapsing in America: When truth itself feels uncertain, how can a democracy be sustained? *The Atlantic.* Retrieved from https://www.theatlantic.com/international/archive/2018/01/trust-trump-america-world/550964/

Gaufman, E. (2018). The Trump carnival: Popular appeal in the age of misinformation. *International Relations, 32*(4), 410–429. doi:10.1177/0047117818773130

Grinberg, N., Joseph, K., Friedland, L., Swire-Thompson, B., & Lazer, D. (2019). Fake news on Twitter during the 2016 U.S. presidential election. *Science, 363*(6425), 374–378. doi:10.1126/science.aau2706

Head, A., J., Wihbey, J. P., Metaxas, T., MacMillan, M., & Cohen, D. (2018). *How students engage with news: Five takeaways for educators, journalists, and librarians.* Retrieved from http://www.projectinfolit.org/news_study.html

Hobbs, R. (1998a). Building citizenship skills through media literacy education. *The public voice in a democracy at risk* (pp. 57–76). Westport, CT: Praeger Press.

Hobbs, R. (1998b). The seven great debates in the media literacy movement. *Journal of Communication, 48*(1), 16–32. doi:10.1111/j.1460-2466.1998.tb02734.x

Indiana University Network Science Institute and the Center for Complex Networks and Systems Research. (2018). Hoaxy FAQ. Retrieved from https://hoaxy.iuni.iu.edu/faq.php

Ireton, C., & Posetti, J. (2018). Journalism & disinformation: Handbook for journalism education and training. *UNESCO series on journalism education.*

Retrieved from https://en.unesco.org/sites/default/files/journalism_fake_news_disinformation_print_friendly_0_0.pdf

Kellner, D., & Share, J. (2005). Toward critical media literacy: Core concepts, debates, organizations, and policy. *Discourse: Studies in the cultural politics of education, 26*(3), 369–386.

Kellner, D., & Share, J. (2007). Critical media literacy is not an option. *Learning Inquiry, 1*(1), 59–69.

Kessler, G. (2017). About the fact checker. *The Washington Post.* Retrieved from https://www.washingtonpost.com/politics/2019/01/07/about-fact-checker/?utm_term=.c5baa06dfc3e

Kessler, G., Rizzo, S., & Kelly, M. (2019, April 29). President Trump has made more than 10,000 false or misleading claims. *The Washington Post.* Retrieved from https://www.washingtonpost.com/politics/2019/04/29/president-trump-has-made-more-than-false-or-misleading-claims/?utm_term=.1504dea741b7&wpisrc=nl_fact&wpmm=1

Knight Commission. (2019). *Crisis in democracy: Renewing trust in America.* Retrieved from https://knightfoundation.org/reports/crisis-in-democracy-renewing-trust-in-america?ct=t%28EMAIL_CAMPAIGN_9_26_2018_17_15_COPY_01%29

Knight Foundation. (2018). *Indicators of news media trust.* Retrieved from https://kf-site-production.s3.amazonaws.com/media_elements/files/000/000/216/original/KnightFoundation_Panel4_Trust_Indicators_FINAL.pdf

Knight Foundation. (2019). Knight Foundation focuses on building the future of local news in $300 million five-year commitment [press release]. Retrieved from https://www.knightfoundation.org/press/releases/knight-foundation-focuses-on-building-the-future-of-local-news-in-300-million-five-year-commitment

Kruger, A. (2017). Ahead of the e-curve in fact checking and verification education: The University of Hong Kong's cyber news verification lab leads verification education in Asia. *Asia Pacific Media Educator, 27*(2), 264–281. doi:10.1177/1326365X17736579

Lazer, D. M. J., Baum, M. A., Benkler, Y., Berinsky, A. J., Greenhill, K. M., Menczer, F., & Zittrain, J. L. (2018). The science of fake news. *Science, 359*(6380), 1094–1096. doi:10.1126/science.aao2998

Lewis, J., & Jhally, S. (1998). The struggle over media literacy. *Journal of Communication, 48*(1), 109–120.

Livingstone, S. (2004). Media literacy and the challenge of new information and communication technologies. *The Communication Review, 7*(1), 3–14.

Loth, R. (2012). What's black and white and re-tweeted all over? Teaching news literacy in the digital age. *Chronicle of Higher Education.* Retrieved from https://www.chronicle.com/article/Teaching-News-Literacy-in-the/130613

Maksl, A., Ashley, S., & Craft, S. (2015). Measuring news media literacy. *Journal of Media Literacy Education, 6*(3), 29–45.

Maksl, A., Craft, S., Ashley, S., & Miller, D. (2016). The usefulness of a news media literacy measure in evaluating a news literacy curriculum. *Journalism & Mass Communication Educator, 72*(2), 228–241. doi:10.1177/1077695816651970

Manjoo, F. (2008). *True enough: Learning to live in a post-fact society.* Hoboken, NJ: Wiley.

Martens, H., & Hobbs, R. (2015). How media literacy supports civic engagement in a digital age. *Atlantic Journal of Communication, 23*(2), 120–137. doi:10.1080/15456870.2014.961636

Masterman, L. (2003). *Teaching the media.* London, UK: Routledge.

McLuhan, M. (1994). *Understanding media: The extensions of man.* Boston: MIT Press.

Messaris, P., & Humphreys, L. (2006). *Digital media: transformations in human communication.* New York: Peter Lang.

Mihailidis, P. (Ed.) (2012). *News literacy: Global perspectives for the newsroom and the classroom.* New York: Peter Lang.

Mihailidis, P., & Thevenin, B. (2013). Media literacy as a core competency for engaged citizenship in participatory democracy. *American Behavioral Scientist, 57*(11), 1611–1622.

Mitchell, A., Simmons, K., Matsa, K. E., & Silver, L. (2018). *Publics globally want unbiased news coverage, but are divided on whether their news media deliver.* Retrieved from http://www.pewglobal.org/2018/01/11/publics-globally-want-unbiased-news-coverage-but-are-divided-on-whether-their-news-media-deliver/#maps

News Literacy Project. (2019). Don't get fooled: 7 simple steps. Retrieved from https://newslit.org/7-steps/

O'Connor, C., & Weatherall, J. O. (2018). *The misinformation age: How false beliefs spread.* New Haven, CT: Yale University Press.

Pariser, E. (2011). *The filter bubble: How the new personalized web is changing what we read and how we think.* New York: Penguin.

Pew Research Center. (2018). *Mobile fact sheet.* Retrieved from https://www.pewinternet.org/fact-sheet/mobile/

Potter, W. J. (2004). *Theory of media literacy: A cognitive approach:* Thousand Oaks, CA: Sage.

Potter, W. J. (2010). The state of media literacy. *Journal of Broadcasting & Electronic Media, 54*(4), 675–696.

Potter, W. J. (2013). Review of literature on media literacy. *Sociology Compass, 7*(6), 417–435. doi:10.1111/soc4.12041

Potter, W. J. (2016). *Media literacy* (8th ed.). Thousand Oaks, CA: Sage.

Poynter Institute. (2019). The international fact-checking network. Retrieved from https://www.poynter.org/ifcn/

RobbGrieco, M. (2014). Why history matters for media literacy education. *Journal of Media Literacy Education, 6*(2), 3–22.

Schneider, H. (2007). It's the audience, stupid! *Nieman Reports, 61*(3), 65–68.

Schudson, M. (2008). *Why democracies need an unlovable press.* Cambridge, UK: Polity.

Schudson, M. (2018). *Why journalism still matters.* Medford, MA: Polity.

Shahani, A. (2018). Facebook moves to decide what is real news. *National Public Radio.* Retrieved from https://www.npr.org/sections/thetwo-way/2018/01/19/579285094/facebook-moves-to-decide-what-is-real-news

Silverblatt, A., Ferry, J., & Finan, B. (1999). *Approaches to media literacy: A handbook.* Armonk, NY: M. E. Sharpe.

Silverblatt, A., Miller, D. C., Smith, J., & Brown, N. (2014). *Media literacy: Keys to interpreting Media Messages.* Santa Barbara, CA: ABC-CLIO.

Snopes. (2019). About us: Snopes. Retrieved from https://www.snopes.com/about-snopes/

Strauss, V. (2018). The News Literacy Project takes on 'fake' news – and business is better than ever. *The Washington Post*. Retrieved from https://www.washingtonpost.com/news/answer-sheet/wp/2018/03/27/not-sure-whats-real-or-fake-anymore-the-news-literacy-project-teaches-kids-how-to-tell-the-difference-and-its-growing-faster-than-ever/?utm_term=.027c42ab13e2

Sullivan, M., & Bajarin, T. (2018). Can you spot fake news before hitting "share"? Kids are learning and so can you. *Fast Company*.

Thoman, E., & Jolls, T. (2004). Media literacy—A national priority for a changing world. *American Behavioral Scientist, 48*(1), 18–29. doi:10.1177/0002764204267246

Turkle, S. (2005). *The second self: Computers and the human spirit.* Cambridge: MIT Press.

Turkle, S. (2011). *Alone together: Why we expect more from technology and less from each other.* New York: Basic Books.

Turkle, S. (2015). *Reclaiming conversation: The power of talk in a digital age.* New York: Penguin.

Tyner, K. (1991). The media education elephant. *Strategies Quarterly*, 5–10. Retrieved from https://www.medialit.org/reading-room/media-education-elephant

Tyner, K. (1998). *Literacy in a digital world: Teaching and learning in the age of information.* Abingdon-on-Thames: Routledge.

U.S. Department of Justice. (2019). *Report on the investigation into Russian interference in the 2016 presidential election (the Mueller report).* Retrieved from https://www.nytimes.com/interactive/2019/04/18/us/politics/mueller-report-document.html

Vernon, P. (2018). Trump's press bashing reaches a critical mass. *Columbia Journalism Review*. Retrieved from https://www.cjr.org/the_media_today/trump-press-violence.php

Vosoughi, S., Roy, D., & Aral, S. (2018). The spread of true and false news online. *Science, 359*(6380), 1146–1151. doi:10.1126/science.aap9559

Wardle, C. (2018). 5 lessons for reporting in an age of disinformation. *First Draft News*. Retrieved from https://firstdraftnews.org/5-lessons-for-reporting-in-an-age-of-disinformation/

Wardle, C., & Derakhshan, H. (2017). *Information disorder: Toward an interdisciplinary framework for research and policy making.* Retrieved from https://rm.coe.int/information-disorder-toward-an-interdisciplinary-framework-for-researc/168076277c

WashPostPR. (2019). The Washington Post launches "The Fact Checkers Guide to Manipulated Video." *WashPost PR Blog*. Retrieved from https://www.washingtonpost.com/pr/2019/06/25/washington-post-launches-fact-checkers-guide-manipulated-video/?noredirect=on&utm_term=.10537210abce

Williams, B. A., & Delli Carpini, M. X. (2000). Unchained reaction: The collapse of media gatekeeping and the Clinton–Lewinsky scandal. *Journalism, 1*(1), 61–85. doi:10.1177/146488490000100113

Young, D. G., Jamieson, K. H., Poulsen, S., & Goldring, A. (2017). Fact-checking effectiveness as a function of format and tone: Evaluating FactCheck.org and FlackCheck.org. *Journalism & Mass Communication Quarterly, 95*(1), 49–75. doi:10.1177/1077699017710453

6 *Propaganda Critic*, Russian Disinformation, and Media Literacy

A Case Study

Aaron Delwiche and Mary Margaret Herring

Introduction

The need for widespread media literacy has never been greater. For one thing, the ubiquity of networked digital media has accelerated the flow of all types of messages, intensifying the cognitive load that we all must deal with on a daily basis. With more than 2.5 quintillion bytes of data created every single day, the number of demands on our attention has grown exponentially, contributing to information overload (Marr, 2018).

Emerging information technologies have transformed the distribution of persuasive messages in ways that were once unthinkable. Deceptive influencers use computer-controlled accounts called bots to affect the flow of information in online spaces, they amplify the reach of these bots with the help of fake user profiles called sockpuppets, and they harvest users' behavioral data to fine-tune their messages.

Researchers use the term "computational propaganda" to describe these developments (Bradshaw & Howard, 2018; Sanovich, 2017; Woolley & Howard, 2017). In this chapter, computational propaganda is defined as the attempt to influence public opinion and behavior via strategic synthesis of autonomous agents (bots), phony user accounts (sockpuppets), data mining, and active participation from targeted individuals who unwittingly spread deceptive or misleading information. This form of propaganda flourishes in the soil of social media platforms that were once heralded as enabling authentic, many-to-many communication among citizens of the world.

Since 2012, computational propaganda has been used to create the illusion of false consensus (Hofileña, 2016), demoralize political opponents (Ressa, 2016), marginalize dissidents by isolating them within a wall of noise (King, Pan, & Roberts, 2017), polarize political discussions and propagate disinformation (Bessi & Ferrara, 2016), and to elevate certain topics as "top trends" across social media platforms (Agarwal, Al-khateeb, Galeano, & Goolsby, 2017).

The existence of such technologies was thrust into public awareness in the wake of the 2016 U.S. presidential election. As researchers dug deeper into the so-called "fake news," they realized that much of this material had been distributed by networks of bots, sockpuppets, and authentic human users who unknowingly fueled the spread of disinformation.

In hindsight, we can acknowledge that scholars and communication practitioners were taken by surprise by the sophistication, extent, and effectiveness of computational propaganda. We cannot afford to repeat the same mistake during the coming years. Media literacy educators can play a vital role in explaining how computational propaganda works and in helping people develop an arsenal of critical tools that can be used to mitigate the harmful effects of disinformation. The site *Propaganda Critic* is one resource that can be used to accomplish this objective.

Created almost 25 years ago, when the web was in its infancy, *Propaganda Critic* (https://www.propagandacritic.com) promotes the lost art of propaganda analysis among critically minded individuals. The site was inspired by the pioneering work of the Institute for Propaganda Analysis (IPA). From 1937 to 1942, journalists, social scientists, and educators affiliated with the IPA published a series of books and pamphlets that offered accessible explanations of common propaganda techniques (Lee & Lee, 1939; Sproule, 1989). *Propaganda Critic* aims to bring the IPA's work into the digital age by sharing these invaluable lessons with an online audience.

In its first incarnation, *Propaganda Critic* drew heavily on the IPA's seven basic propaganda devices: name-calling, glittering generalities, the transfer technique, testimonials, plain folks, card stacking, and the bandwagon technique. Although these devices can still be useful when analyzing messages, they alone are insufficient for making sense out of the contemporary crises that threaten democracies around the world. In 2018, recognizing that global citizens urgently need resources that can help them seek the truth in an era of bots, sockpuppets, and "deep fakes," the authors of this chapter completely overhauled the site.

Featuring approximately two dozen new articles and commissioned artwork from the cartoonist Carol Lay, the updated site includes six major sections, and each section contains multiple articles. *Core Concepts* highlights the ubiquity of propaganda, documents the rise of computational propaganda, and explains how social media sites provide a fertile ground for disinformation. *Everybody Is Biased* explains that we are all inhibited by cognitive biases or "faulty ways of thinking" that are hardwired into the human brain, documenting some of the most relevant biases. *Decoding Propaganda* is focused on message analysis, discussing the seven original IPA devices and incorporating additional articles about emotional appeals and logical manipulation. *Case Studies* documents the use of persuasive techniques and technologies in real-world situations, and *Examples* invites users to test their critical thinking skills by scrutinizing examples of propaganda from all sides of the political spectrum. *Tools for Fighting Back* explains how to spot fake news, suggests strategies for detecting media bias, highlights tell-tale characteristics of bots and sockpuppets, and profiles resources that can be used to debunk rumors and to fact-check claims.

This chapter uses a case study in order to demonstrate the potential value of *Propaganda Critic* to media literacy educators. After elaborating the jaw-dropping details of Russian disinformation efforts that targeted the United States from 2014 through 2019, we excerpt content from salient pages that can help students and educators grapple with this new form of propaganda.

Computational Propaganda and the Internet Research Agency

On the morning of September 11, 2014, Twitter users woke up to frantic reports of an explosion in Centerville, Louisiana. Pictures and videos of the explosion of the Columbian Chemicals plant were circulated, and #ColumbianChemicals was soon trending on Twitter. Jon Merritt tweeted "A powerful explosion heard from miles away happened at a chemical plant in Centerville, Louisiana #ColumbianChemicals." Because the explosion occurred on the anniversary of 9/11, many users were concerned that this was another terrorist attack. Some users reached out to their senators asking if terrorists were involved in this attack. Subsequent Twitter posts implied that ISIS had taken responsibility for the explosion.

One user posted a video of an Arabic news clip that appeared to show masked members of ISIS taking credit for the explosion. *CNN seemingly* reported on the event according to a screenshot of their homepage that was posted on Twitter. The screenshot displayed headlines like "Plant Explosion in Centerville Caused Panic" and "Obama: 'We Will Destroy and Ultimately Degrade Isis,'" suggesting that the United States was preparing a military response to a terrorist attack. Public fear grew as this news spread.

But the explosion never actually happened. The supposed crisis was an elaborate hoax propagated by programmers and multimedia producers. Content producers created the pictures and videos of the fictitious smoke and fire that blazed through Centerville. Others doctored a screenshot of the *CNN* home screen to give viewers the illusion that a credible news source was reporting on it. The video clip of ISIS taking responsibility for the explosion was made specifically for this hoax. Programmers also launched an army of bots that retweeted posts containing the #ColumbianChemicals hashtag. Hoping to attract the attention of influential Twitter users, these bots tweeted about the explosion for hours. The propagandists also cloned websites of local Louisiana news outlets to display news about the fake explosion. As a final touch, they sent local residents phony text message alerts, which announced, "toxic fumes, hazard warning," warning people to "take shelter [and] check local media."

Luckily, local authorities managed to stop the rumors from spreading too far; most Americans never even knew that such a hoax had taken place. According to data scientist Gilad Lotan (Borthwick & Lotan, 2015), the hoax "did not gain enough user trust" to trigger network effects that would have accelerated the distribution of the rumor. However, for those who were paying attention, the false attack was a mystery. Who would go to such lengths to frighten people? The mystery deepened during the next several months when some of the same social media accounts that had propagated this hoax began spreading other rumors, such as false claims about an Ebola outbreak in Atlanta and a fabricated-but-believable story about Atlanta police shooting an unarmed Black woman (Brown, 2015). These rumors were clearly designed to provoke fear and to polarize Americans, but why would someone want to do such a thing?

The investigative journalist Adrian Chen (2015) continued digging, tracking these bogus accounts back to a St. Petersburg-based company called the Internet Research Agency (IRA). Directed by Yevgeny Prigozhin – a Russian businessman with close links to Vladimir Putin – the IRA paid more than 1,000 "professional trolls" to propagate pro-government messages in online forums. These employees worked 12-hour shifts, commenting on social media platforms, news sites, and tourist sites. Using proxy servers to cloak their network address, IRA workers created fully rounded online personas, embedding propaganda messages into "what appeared to be the nonpolitical musings of an everyday person." In an interview with Radio Free Europe and Radio Liberty, a former IRA puppetmaster named Marat Burkhard detailed his experience writing pro-Russian comments on municipality websites. Burkhard says that organizations are run like real factories (Volcheck & Sindelar, 2015). Employees work 12-hour shifts and must post at least 135 comments during each shift.

According to Burkhard, he and his colleagues followed a familiar pattern when attempting to discredit critics of the Russian government. First, a "villain troll" would disagree with a pro-Russia post, challenging authority figures. Second, a "link troll" would enter into debate with the villain linking to a supposedly relevant pro-government video or website. Finally, a "picture troll" would chime in by posting an easily shared image. By staging an online "discussion" between sockpuppets, these trolls gave other users the impression that the original pro-Russia post was correct.

Initially focused on domestic politics, the IRA ramped up their global disinformation efforts as part of a coordinated attempt to influence the outcome of the U.S. presidential elections (Office of the Director of National Intelligence, 2017). On February 16, 2018, the Department of Justice indicted 13 Russians and the Internet Research Agency for waging "information war against the United States of America." According to the 37-page indictment, two of the Russian propagandists

(Aleksandra Yuryevna Krylova and Anna Vladislavovna Bogacheva) had visited Louisiana in June 2014, three months before the Columbia Chemicals Plant hoax.

This large-scale, carefully coordinated hoax demonstrated that malicious individuals could disseminate disinformation quickly and efficiently across multiple media platforms, risking mass panic in the United States or any other targeted location. Why this particular hoax? Was this a dress rehearsal for future acts of information warfare? Data analyst John Kelly speculates that Russian propagandists were experimenting with the potential effectiveness of computational propaganda tools, "trying to freak people out, trying to figure out how much mileage they could get from a gallon of gas" (Foster, 2019). At the very least, we know that the incidents were part of a larger disinformation effort that, in the words of former deputy attorney general Rod Rosenstein, were intended to "promote discord in the United States and undermine public confidence in democracy" (Decker, 2017).

At approximately the same time as the Columbia chemicals plant hoax, the IRA intensified efforts aimed at influencing public opinion in the United States. According to Special Counsel Robert Mueller's *Report on the Investigation into Russian Interference in the 2016 Presidential Election*, the IRA consolidated all elements of their U.S. operations into "a single general department, known internally as the 'Translator' department." Much like a scrappy start-up company, the department was subdivided into different segments, "ranging from operations on different social media platforms to analytics to graphics and IT" (Mueller, 2019a, p. 19). In 2015, the IRA began creating phony social media profiles, such as fake Twitter account (@TEN_GOP), which pretended to represent the Tennessee Republican Party. "More commonly," notes Mueller, "the IRA created accounts in the names of fictitious U.S. organizations and grassroots groups and used these accounts to pose as anti-immigration groups, Tea Party activists, Black Lives Matter protesters, and other U.S. social and political activists" (p. 22).

These fake accounts appear to have found an audience (Shane & Frenkel, 2018). According to Oxford University's Computational Propaganda Research Project, between 2013 and 2018, more than 30 million Americans shared IRA-sponsored Facebook and Instagram posts with others in their social networks (Howard, Ganesh, Liotsiou, Kelly, and François, 2018). Regardless of the social media platform, the messages were intended to divide and polarize American voters while undermining faith in the integrity of electoral politics (Howard et al., 2018). Even after this massive campaign was exposed and publicized in 2017, Russian propagandists intensified their operations and significantly increased their activity on Instagram. Researchers found that "engagement rates increased and covered a widening range of public policy issues, national security issues, and issues pertinent to younger voters" (p. 3).

Russian propaganda efforts accelerated during the 2018 midterm elections in the United States. For example, in a database of Russian propaganda tweets compiled by communication researchers Darren Linvill and Patrick Warren, scholars found that Russian propagandists attempted to influence the outcome of the Senate race between Ted Cruz and Beto O'Rourke (Conger, 2018). One month after the elections, Defense Secretary James Mattis publicly criticized Russian president Vladimir Putin for "mucking around" in the midterm elections (Segers & Gazis, 2018). As recently as July 2019, Special Counsel Robert Mueller testified in Congress that Russian attempts to influence the outcome of U.S. elections have increased in both frequency and intensity. "It wasn't a single attempt," explained Mueller. "They are doing it as we sit here, and they expect to do it during the next campaign," he added (Mueller, 2019b).

Propaganda Critic (https://propagandacritic.com)

At the outset, we should note that Russia does not have a monopoly on computational propaganda. The People's Republic of China operates an enormous domestic propaganda unit that is believed to be the largest sockpuppet operation in existence (Gallagher, 2017; Lau, 2016). The government's "50-cent army" fabricates nearly 450 million social media comments each year in an attempt to push the party line. The United States has used fictional online identities as part of a psychological warfare operation in Iraq called Operation Earnest Voice and in the United Kingdom, the Joint Threats Research Intelligence Group (JTRIG) – a unit of the Government Communications Headquarters – has developed a number of tools that can be used to "manipulate and control online discourse" (Greenwald, 2014). Similar tools were deployed in the 2017 Alabama elections by Democratic researchers "experimenting" with disinformation tactics (Timberg, Romm, Davis, & Dwoskin, 2019), and by progressive Democrats who created fake Facebook pages in the same election in order to make it appear that some GOP voters wanted to abolish alcohol sales in Alabama (Shane & Blinder, 2019).

Whether it emerges from the right or the left, the scale and sophistication of computational propaganda poses serious risks for functioning democracies around the world. Media literacy experts have a vital role to play in fighting back and reactivating critical thinking antibodies in our democratic system. In order to truly understand this new persuasive landscape, people need to understand that bots and sockpuppets are attempting to shape their opinions, they need to understand a bit about how these technologies work, and they need access to tools and strategies for identifying phony actors online.

A growing body of academic work digs into these questions, but most of this scholarship is aimed at other academics. The following sections include lightly adapted excerpts from *Propaganda Critic*, which explain each these concepts in more colloquial language. Three pages are reproduced below: *Bots*, *Sockpuppets*, and *How to Spot Bots and Sockpuppets*. In order to improve readability, the site relies on footnotes, rather than parenthetical citations.

Bots (https://propagandacritic.com/index.php/core-concepts/bots/)

In general terms, bots are bits of automated software that are designed to perform tasks that would be tedious for a human being. Because they do not typically identify themselves to human beings, Helper bots are said to work "under the hood." They are barely noticeable. Even if you have never heard of them, you have most likely benefited from these friendly workers. They labor behind the scenes on Facebook to update your news feed, find a good match on Tinder, provide relevant search engine suggestions, and even play your favorite song. By automating mundane informational tasks, they improve the overall user experience. However, other types of bots are far from helpful.

Deceptive bots also perform tedious tasks, but with one crucial difference: they pretend to be legitimate human users in order to convince the rest of us that they are authentic human beings who are simply making their way through the digital world like the rest of us. These bots have emerged as highly effective tools for disseminating propaganda, inflating popularity metrics, and influencing the flow of online conversations.

These bots can disrupt the spread of information, manipulate public discussion, and create the illusion of false consensus. Actors, chefs, reality stars, musicians, and public influencers purchase bots to promote their brand and increase the number of followers. Unethical advertisers infect forums and social media feeds with computer-generated messages praising certain products. Politicians use bots to appear more popular, to spread political slogans, and to contain the spread of unflattering news.

In the contemporary era, budding on YouTube who are struggling to be noticed will purchase fake followers and fake "page views" to boost their popularity. Similarly, celebrities on Twitter, Facebook, and Instagram have purchased fake followers in order to amplify their brand and to earn advertising revenue. In a fascinating expose of the fake-follower industry, *The New York Times* explained that "an influencer with 100,000 followers might earn an average of $2,000 for a promotional tweet, while an influencer with a million followers might earn $20,000" (Confessore, Dance, Harris, & Hansen, 2018).

According to the Pew Research Center, approximately 2/3 of all links shared on Twitter each year are generated by bots (Romano, 2018). In the weeks leading up to the 2018 midterm elections, more than 200,000 bots posted election-related news on Twitter (Higgins, 2019). And these bots are active on other social media platforms. The research firm Ghost Data estimates that 9.5% of Instagram's users are actually bots; this works out to approximately 95 million bots (Albergotti & Kuranda, 2018).

In all of these instances, the fact that bots appear to be real human beings creates the illusion that a large number of people feel the same way about something. Bots give the illusion that there are many people riding on the bandwagon at the same time. When certain topics or tags are trending online, audiences assume that many people are interested in those issues.

Sockpuppets (https://propagandacritic.com/index.php/core-concepts/sockpuppets/)

Sometimes referred to as "trolls," sockpuppets are fake identities that malicious individuals use to deceive other people online. Just as a physical sockpuppet disguises the hand of the person who makes it speak, a digital sockpuppet conceals the real-world identity of the human being controlling the fake account. These controllers are sometimes referred to as "puppet masters." Depending upon their motivation, skill, and technical resources, a single puppet master can control five, ten, or even twenty different identities at one time.

Fake online identities controlled by human beings with the goal of deceiving other people are not a new phenomenon. Ever since the earliest days of the Internet, individuals have adopted fake online identities for personal or political reasons. However, due to the "primitive" nature of older computer networks, it was much easier for users and moderators to figure out when someone was trying to guide multiple fake identities.

Sockpuppets are sometimes referred to as trolls, but the word "troll" actually has a different meaning. Trolls provoke anger and fuel discord because they enjoy watching other people feel bad (Craker & March, 2016), but this is just one of many possible motivations driving sockpuppets. The word "troll" has become the most widely used term to describe this phenomenon in the popular press, but it is simply inaccurate. Not all trolls use sockuppets, and not all sockpuppets are wielded by trolls.

Sockpuppets are useful when someone wants to participate in an online community and needs to look like other members to fit in. These entities prey on the human tendency to favor people who are the most like us. Social psychologists refer to this as in-group bias. Even though most of us strive to be impartial, it makes sense that we would place more weight on the opinions of people whom we view as similar to us in some way.

In grassroots online communities, people ask their peers what type of car they should buy, discuss political candidates, or recommend restaurants, tennis shoes, and dentists. We tend to assume that those with whom we interact online do not have a hidden agenda. They aren't trying to sell us a certain car so they can make money; they're just sharing their opinion. Sockpuppets imitate other community members to earn our trust. If we believe that someone is a real person, we are more likely to trust their recommendations.

Sockpuppets can be used to generate money and popularity for their controllers. Just as some celebrities buy followers to bolster their brand, some corporations purchase positive reviews of their products from unscrupulous marketers (Flood, 2012). In fact, one data mining expert from the University of Illinois estimates that one-third of consumer reviews on the Internet are fake (Streitfeld, 2012). Of course, sockpuppets are used for more than book reviews. They are a powerful tool in the world of politics. Propagandists use sockpuppets to discredit and demoralize their political opponents, to guide the direction of political conversations online, and to create the illusion of false consensus. They can also use sockuppets to influence online polls, to introduce new memes and political hashtags, and to subvert collaborative projects such as Wikipedia.

How to Spot Bots and Sockpuppets (https://propagandacritic. com/index.php/tools-for-fighting-back/spotting-bots/)

After reading about the sneaky tactics used by bots to spread messages and influence online conversations, you might wonder how to distinguish fake accounts from authentic, human users. There is no single identifying characteristic of a fake account, but researchers have identified multiple characteristics that can help you recognize a bot or sockpuppet. There are even some tools that predict the authenticity of a user. The following paragraphs identify a few tell-tell signs of both bots and sockpuppets, highlighting helpful resources for the savvy social media user.

While these sophisticated bots are becoming more advanced by the minute, there are also many simple bots that are quite easy to identify. Being aware of the function that a specific bot might serve can be helpful when determining the authenticity of the account. Similarly, sockpuppets can be easy to detect if you are aware of their function or underlying motivations.

Most fake accounts have the following characteristics:

1 *Stock image profile picture.* This may be a picture of nature, a cartoon, a political image, a celebrity or a provocative picture. Always run a reverse Google search of the image if you are unsure. You can do this by dragging an image from the web into the Google search box.

2 *Missing profile picture.* Because it can be tricky to find an original profile picture, many accounts just have the default Twitter egg or silhouette of a person on Facebook.

3 *Longer usernames.* Fake accounts often have usernames that a human user would not choose. For example, they might have a lot of numbers in them or make little sense. This is particularly common in the case of bots. The puppetmasters who control sockpuppets usually try to come with a name that sounds human.

4 *Overly simple or repetitive Tweets or Posts.* The job of many bots is to make a certain topic (or hashtag) trend. Bots accomplish this by posting the same message repetitively. Sockpuppets tend to be more subtle, posting photos of kittens and lifestyle memes along with their persuasive messages. However, if you skim their timeline and look specifically for political messages, the repetitive nature of their posts will quickly become obvious.

5 *Accounts lack personality.* While humans can have bright personalities, bots cannot. This is reflected in their profiles. Bot profiles may lack bio information or give generic responses to the "about" section on Facebook. Sockpuppets put more energy into creating a convincing personality, but the façade is difficult to maintain. If your spider sense is tingling and something just feels "off" about a particular account, you should trust this feeling and do some further research.

6 *Bots follow many more people than they are followed by.* Because many people want to build the number of followers that they have, if a bot requests to follow them, they might allow it. However, because the user does not know the bot, it is unlikely that they will follow them back. So, many bots are following many more people than they are followed by. This pattern is less evident in fake accounts created for sockpuppets.

7 *Bots post more than a human would.* Bots don't have a bed-time! As software, bots are able to run non-stop. Therefore, they never need to take breaks to eat or sleep. Some bots are set on timers to make it appear that they are taking breaks from online accounts; however, if an account posts a ton of content or never takes any breaks, it is likely a bot. Sockpuppets also post regularly, but not nearly as often as bots.

8 *Fake account shares the most radical messages.* Bots and sockpuppets tend to identify with the furthest extremes of the political system. Whether they display militaristic nationalism or urge socialist revolution, these fake accounts commonly disseminate extreme viewpoints because they are attempting to pit people against one another. Of course, this doesn't mean that everyone who expresses extreme ideas is necessarily a bot or a sockpuppet. This is just one of many possible indicators.

9 *Account feeds includes an unusual amount of filler posts.* To conceal their political agenda, fake accounts often post filler content, like animal videos or inspirational quotes, in between elections or important events.

10 *Account features stolen content.* To attract a large audience to their site, some websites will repost content that originally appeared on a different news site. Bots and sockuppets often spread links to sites that feature this stolen news.

All of this information can be overwhelming. Most people do not hop on Twitter or Facebook with the intention of finding fake accounts. So, like many things, the items in this checklist may fade to the back of your memory. The most helpful tip that can help you detect fake accounts is this: Think critically about the messages the account is spreading and the source of these messages. By taking a few minutes to reflect on the account's apparent motivations and to identify any underlying biases, you will be better able to spot a fake account. The tips provided in the checklist above can be very useful when trying to find quality information, but there is no substitute for doing some serious thinking about the message and its source.

All of this information can be overwhelming. Most people do not hop on Twitter or Facebook with the intention of finding fake accounts. So, like many things, the items in this checklist may fade to the back of your memory. The most helpful tip that can help you detect fake accounts is this: think critically about the messages the account is spreading and the source of these messages. By taking a few minutes to reflect on the account's apparent motivations and to identify any underlying biases, you will be better able to spot a fake account. The tips provided in the checklist above can be very useful when trying to find quality information, but there is no substitute for doing some serious thinking about the message and its source.

Conclusion

For those of us who hoped that the Internet would play a vital role in promoting media literacy and reinvigorating participatory culture, the past five years have been a mixed bag. On the one hand, our students, colleagues, family members, and fellow citizens are now viewed by propagandists as "ideal vectors for information attack" simply because they use the global Internet (Waltzman, 2017). Considering that more than 30 million users recirculated IRA propaganda between 2015 and 2017 (Howard, Ganesh, Liotsiou, Kelly, & François, 2018), one might wonder if democracy is destined to survive this brave new world of deception.

However, these same tools that have been used to manipulate citizens have also made it possible for media literacy educators and activists to fight back. From videogames that explain how disinformation works by encouraging players to roleplay as propagandists to web-based tools like Botometer and the Junk News aggregator, creative responses to disinformation are emerging in all corners of the world. When we remind ourselves of the existence of so many excellent resources promoting critical thinking and media literacy, from *Snopes* and *Your Logical Fallacy Is* to the *Mind over Media* project of the Media Education Lab, we have grounds for optimism.

During the past 18 months since *Propaganda Critic* was rebooted, the scale and complexity of propaganda efforts has grown at a staggering rate, fueled by exponential growth in computer power and new technological developments such as "deep fake" technologies for fabricating convincing images and videos. We hope to continue updating the site by including new examples, but one of the project's key contributors will soon be heading off to graduate school. We need help from other media literacy educators in order to keep the site up to date. If you are interested in developing new modules and case studies for the site, please contact Aaron Delwiche (adelwich@trinity.edu) to discuss ways that you can contribute to this project.

References

Agarwal, N., Al-khateeb, S., Galeano, R., & Goolsby, R. (2017). Examining the use of botnets and their evolution in propaganda dissemination. *Defence Strategic Communications: The Official Journal of the NATO Strategic Communications Centre of Excellence, 2*(1), 87–112.

Albergotti, R., & Kuranda, S. (2018, July 18). Instagram's growing bot problem. *The Information.* Retrieved from https://www.theinformation.com/articles/instagrams-growing-bot-problem

Bessi, A., & Ferrara, E. (2016). Social bots distort the 2016 U.S. Presidential election online discussion. *First Monday, 21*(11). Retrieved from http://firstmonday.org/ojs/index.php/fm/article/view/7090/5653a

Borthwick, J., & Lotan, G. (2015, March 7). Media hacking. *Render—Medium.* Retrieved from https://render.betaworks.com/media-hacking-3b1e350d619c

Bradshaw, S., & Howard, P. (2018). *Challenging truth and trust: A global inventory of organized social media manipulation.* Oxford: Oxford Internet Institute.

Brown, D. (2015, June 8). Why are Russian trolls spreading online hoaxes in the United States? *PBS News Hour.* Retrieved from https://www.pbs.org/newshour/show/why-are-russian-trolls-spreading-online-hoaxes-in-the-u-s

Chen, A. (2015, June 7). The agency. *New York Times.* Retrieved from https://www.nytimes.com/2015/06/07/magazine/the-agency.html

Confessore, N., Dance, G., Harris, R., & Hansen, M. (2018, January 27). The follower factory. *The New York Times.* Retrieved from https://www.nytimes.com/interactive/2018/01/27/technology/social-media-bots.html

Conger, J. (2018, October 2). Russian hackers target Beto, Cruz, and Manu. *News 4 San Antonio.* Retrieved from https://news4sanantonio.com/news/trouble-shooters/russian-hackers-target-beto-cruz-and-manu-ginobili

Craker, N., & March, E. (2016). The dark side of Facebook: The dark tetrad, negative social potency, and trolling behaviours. *Personality and Individual Differences, 102,* 79–84.

Decker, B. (2017, February 17). Organizations in Russia indictments was linked to 2014 St. Mary alert hoax. *St. Mary Now.* Retrieved from https://www.stmarynow.com/news-local/organization-russia-indictments-was-linked-2014-st-mary-alert-hoax

Flood, A. (2012, September 4). Sockpuppetry and fake reviews: publish and be damned. *The Guardian.* Retrieved from https://www.theguardian.com/books/2012/sep/04/sock-puppetry-publish-be-damned

Foster, T. (2019, May). How Russian trolls are using American businesses as their weapons. *Inc.* Retrieved from https://www.inc.com/magazine/201905/tom-foster/russian-trolls-facebook-social-media-attacks-brands-hoax-fake-disinformation.html

Gallagher, E. (2017, January 1). Propaganda botnets on social media. *Medium.* Retrieved from https://medium.com/@erin_gallagher/propaganda-botnets-on-social-media-5afd35e94725

Greenwald, G. (2014, February 24). How covert agents infiltrate the Internet to manipulate, deceive, and destroy reputations. *The Intercept.* Retrieved from https://theintercept.com/2014/02/24/jtrig-manipulation/

Hofileña, C. (2016, October 15). Fake accounts, manufactured reality on social media. *Rappler.* Retrieved from http://www.rappler.com/newsbreak/investigative/148347-fake-accounts-manufactured-reality-social-media

Higgins, T. (2019, February 4). Twitter bots were more active than previously known during the 2018 midterms. *CNBC.* Retrieved from https://www.msn.com/en-us/money/markets/twitter-bots-were-more-active-than-previously-known-during-the-2018-midterms/ar-BBTb4nb

Howard, P., Ganesh, B., Liotsiou, D., Kelly, J., & François, C. (2018). *The IRA, social media, and political polarization in the United States: 2012–2018.* Oxford: Oxford Internet Institute.

King, G., Pan, J., & Roberts, M. (2017). How the Chinese government fabricates social media posts for strategic distraction, not engaged argument. *American Political Science Review, 111*(3), 484–501.

Lau, J. (2016, October 7). Who are the Chinese trolls of the '50 Cent Army'? *Voice of America.* Retrieved from https://www.voanews.com/a/who-is-that-chinese-troll/3540663.html

Lee, A., & Lee, E. (1939). *The fine art of propaganda: A study of Father Cough-lin's speeches.* New York, NY: Harcourt, Brace, and Company.

Marr, B. (2018, May 21). How much data do we create each day? *Forbes.* Retrieved from https://www.cnn.com/2019/06/27/politics/census-supreme-court/index.html

Mueller, R. (2019a, March). *Report on the investigation into Russian interference in the 2016 presidential election: Volume 1.* U.S. Department of Justice.

Mueller, R. (2019b, July 25) Full transcript: Mueller testimony before House Judiciary, Intelligence committees. *NBC News.* ASC Services. Retrieved from https://www.nbcnews.com/politics/congress/full-transcript-robert-mueller-house-committee-testimony-n1033216

Office of the Director of National Intelligence (2017, January 6). *Intelligence community assessment: Assessing Russian activities and intentions in recent US elections. ICA 2017-01D.* Retrieved from https://www.dni.gov/files/documents/ICA_2017_01.pdf

Pew Research Center. 2018. News use across social media platforms 2018. *Pew Research Center.* Retrieved January 3, 2019 from http://www.journalism.org/wp-content/uploads/sites/8/2018/09/PJ_2018.09.10_social-media-news_FINAL.pdf

Ressa, M. (2016, October 3). Propaganda war: Weaponizing the Internet. *Rappler.* Retrieved from http://www.rappler.com/nation/148007-propaganda-war-weaponizing-internet

Romano, A. (2018, April 9). Two-thirds of links on Twitter come from bots: The good news? They're mostly bland. *Vox.* Retrieved from https://www.vox.com/technology/2018/4/9/17214720/pew-study-bots-generate-two-thirds-of-twitter-links

Sanovich, S. (2017). *Computational propaganda in Russia: The origins of digital misinformation.* Oxford: Oxford Internet Institute.

Segers, G., & Gazis, O. (2018, December 1). Mattis says Putin tried to 'muck around' in November's midterm elections. *CBS News.* Retrieved from https://www.cbsnews.com/news/defense-secretary-mattis-says-putin-tried-to-muck-around-in-novembers-midterm-elections/

Shane, S., & Blinder, A. (2019, January 7). Democrats faked online push to outlaw alcohol in Alabama race. *New York Times.* Retrieved from https://www.nytimes.com/2019/01/07/us/politics/alabama-senate-facebook-roy-moore.html

Shane, S., & Frenkel, S. (2018, December 17). Russian 2016 influence operation targeted African-Americans on social media. *New York Times.* Retrieved from https://www.nytimes.com/2018/12/17/us/politics/russia-2016-influence-campaign.html

Sproule, J. M. (1989). Progressive propaganda critics and the magic bullet myth. *Critical Studies in Mass Communication, 6*(3), 225–246. doi: 10.1080/15295038909366750

Streitfeld, D. (2012, August 26). The best book review money can buy. *The New York Times.* Retrieved from https://www.nytimes.com/2012/08/26/business/book-reviewers-for-hire-meet-a-demand-for-online-raves.html

Timberg, T., Romm, T., Davis, A., & Dwoskin, E. (2019, January 6). Secret campaign to use Russian-inspired tactics in 2017 Alabama election stirs anxiety for Democrats. *Washington Post.* Retrieved from https://www.washingtonpost.com/business/technology/secret-campaign-to-use-russian-inspired-tactics-in-2017-alabama-election-stirs-anxiety-for-democrats/2019/01/06/58803f26-0400-11e9-8186-4ec26a485713_story. html

Volcheck, D., & Sindelar, D. (2015, March 25). One professional Russian troll tells all. *Radio Free Europe/Radio Liberty.* Retrieved from https://www.rferl. org/a/how-to-guide-russian-trolling-trolls/26919999.html

Woolley, S., & Howard, P. (2017). *Computational propaganda worldwide: Executive summary.* Oxford Internet Institute. Retrieved from http:// comprop.oii.ox.ac.uk/wp-content/uploads/sites/89/2017/06/Casestudies-ExecutiveSummary.pdf

Waltzman, R. (2017). The weaponization of information: The need for cognitive security. Testimony presented before the Senate Armed Services Committee, Subcommittee on Cybersecurity on April 27, 2017. *Rand Corporation.* Retrieved from https://www.rand.org/content/dam/rand/pubs/testimonies/ CT400/CT473/RAND_CT473.pdf

7 The Imperative of Latino-Oriented Media and News Literacy

Federico Subervi-Vélez and Tania Cantrell Rosas-Moreno

Introduction

As is made abundantly clear in other chapters of this volume, media literacy is dynamic and thriving across the United States and other parts of the globe. While empirical evidence of the outcomes of such efforts is still being gathered, there should be no doubt that millions of children and adults are benefiting from the multiple efforts to develop critical awareness and thinking about a wide range of media messages be those about entertainment, news, advertising, politics, culture, or propaganda. That public is also learning how to create new capacities for creative action and dissemination related to traditional and alternative media be these print, broadcast, or digital outlets.

What is broadly missing in practically all U.S. media (and news) literacy education programs is concerted, consistent, and robust efforts directed to Latino populations and about Latino-oriented media be these in Spanish-language, in English-language, or bilingual. The goal of this chapter is to make as evident as possible the imperative for developing an action plan for media and news literacy oriented to Latino populations and about Latino-oriented media. To that end, this chapter makes the case for such action by first pointing to the lacuna of writing on this particular topic. That is followed with demographic realities across the country and language trends. It then points to the vastness and complexity of Latino-oriented media, which are not disappearing but instead growing and adapting to the particular Latino demographics. The urgency for better incorporating Latinos in the governance and other democratic processes round out the key arguments for Latino-oriented media and news literacy education.

Brief Literature Review

The literature reviewed for this manuscript revealed a major lacuna of media or news literacy education programs directed at Latino populations or that include as a norm the assessments of Latino-oriented media. For example, a search of the EBSCO Host database with keywords such as Latino, Hispanic, and news media literacy produced only 14 results, of which not one was relevant to this study. Absent were social science-based studies of media or news literacy that included Latino populations or Latino-oriented media. Even the annual conferences of NAMLE and other organizations centered on media or news literacy have not consistently devoted sessions to Latinos or Latino-oriented media. Latino-oriented news literacy workshops were offered in Chicago in the summers of 2014 and 2015, thanks to funds from the McCormick Foundation and the auspices of Stony Brook University's News Literacy Program. Those workshops ended in 2015 and have not been replicated anywhere since. One of the partial exceptions is the recent creation by Newslit.org of a Spanish-language lesson (Adams, 2018). Another partial exception is the Spanish-language (translations) of some of CyberWise's parental guide and other documents (CyberWise, 2019). While serving on the Board of Directors of NAMLE, the first author translated some of the documents for the website. But this does not mean that NAMLE (or any other national or local organization) has ongoing Latino-oriented media or news literacy education programs.

Demographics

As of mid-June 2019, population of the United States numbered 329 million (Census.gov), of which approximately 58.9 million – more than 18 percent – were of Hispanic heritage (data based on 2017 estimates; Census.gov, 2018). As also documented by the U.S. Census Bureau, the Latino population "has been the principal driver of U.S. demographic growth, accounting for half of the national population growth since 2000" (Flores, 2017, para. 1). Latinos have also been major generators of economic growth, driving more than $700 billion into the U.S. economy (Arora, 2018), and now have an annual purchasing power that by the time this book is published in 2020 will surpass $1.72 trillion (Statista, nd).

Of the 58.9 million Latinos, about 37 percent are under the age of 21, potentially still in their educational formative years in school or undergraduate college. For non-Hispanics, the comparable age group statistic is 25 percent. These numbers show that nation-wide there is a *proportionately* larger cohort of Hispanic youth than is the case for non-Hispanics (Child Trends, 2018; Lopez, Krogstad, & Flores, 2018).

In terms of national origin, the Hispanic population is certainly not monolithic. More than 63 percent of the nation's Latinos are of Mexican heritage, 9 percent are Puerto Rican, 3.7 percent Cuban, and the other 25 percent stemming from the other regions of Latin America. These percentages vary across states and cities in which people from different countries have settled and to which they have brought their family members. States and cities in the Southwest have predominantly

Mexican-heritage Latinos. In Florida, it is Cubans in many cities, including Miami, but Puerto Ricans in Orlando and surrounding communities. In New York, Dominican-heritage Latinos have now outnumbered Puerto Ricans. However, after Hurricane María devastated Puerto Rico on September 20, 2017, more than 300,000 residents from the island have relocated to Florida and other mainland states. The actual percentage of Puerto Ricans in the United States is most probably above 10 percent of the total Latino population.

All these national origin groups differ in terms of educational attainment, employment, and income, for which some segments of each national origin have achieved more than the others. As the Census.gov data show, they share a common denominator in the large percentages of the youth cohorts (see, for example, Tables 1, 2, and 6 of The Hispanic Population of the United States: 2016, United States Census Bureau, 2016). This again attests to the significant number of all Latinos as still being in their educational formative years.

For sure, the proportion of Latinos across the country is dissimilar. While in some states they register below a small fraction of the total population, in the two largest states – California and Texas, where respectively 39 million and 28 million people live – they constitute close to 40 percent of those totals. The young profile of that population is most evident by the fact that by the year 2014, more than 50 percent of all K-12 students in California were Hispanic (Pew Research Center: Hispanic Trends 2014a, para. 7). In Texas, it was 48 percent that same year (Pew Research Center: Hispanic Trends 2014b, para. 7). By now, those numbers are certain to have increased.

In three other populous states – Florida (21.1 million), New York (19.5 million), and Illinois (12.7 million) – Hispanics respectively constitute approximately 26 percent, 19 percent, and 17 percent of those states' residents. While these percentages are lower than the case in California, they nevertheless entail a large number of people of that heritage. Meanwhile, in four other southwestern states with relatively smaller total populations – Arizona (7.2 million), Colorado (5.7 million), Nevada (3 million), and New Mexico (2 million) – the Hispanic presence is also undeniably notable as well at, respectively, 32 percent, 22 percent, 29 percent, and 49 percent. Evidently, in New Mexico almost half of that state's residents are of Hispanic heritage (Census.gov QuickFacts, based on 2018 estimates). In each of these seven states, too, the percentage of Latino K-12 students is higher than the statewide Latino population figures. Just in New Mexico, it is 60 percent. These K-12 numbers, from Pew Research Center Hispanic Trends files, have for sure changed as in each state the percentages of Latinos in those grade levels have most probably increased since 2014.

These nine states are home to more than half of the nation's total Latino population. The percentages are impressive but still do not constitute the majority for any state except pertaining to the children in K-12. However, in some major metropolitan areas, Latinos of diverse national origins are already the majority and, in some cases, the super majorities.

Building on the 2014 American Community Survey, the Pew Research Center Hispanic Trends (2016, para. 1) constructed a table showing the "Top 60 metropolitan areas, by Hispanic population." The populations of those areas, based on 2014 data, ranged from 5.979 million in Los Angeles-Long Beach-Anaheim to 125,000 in Yuma, Arizona. In 25 percent of those 60 metro areas, more than 50 percent of the residents are Latino. In another 25 percent, Latinos are one of every four residents. As with the statewide data, the Latinos in K-12 grades are even proportionately more present.

Aside from the percentages, the sheer numbers are telling of how integral Hispanics are across the country, but more so in major cities. For example, the 6.03 million Latinos in the Los Angeles-Long Beach-Anaheim metro are more numerous than the number of people who respectively live in 30 U.S. states and the District of Columbia. And the 5.08 million Latinos in the New York-Newark-Jersey City metro outnumber the respective residents of 26 states and the District of Columbia (Census Reporter, nd). Just the Latino school-aged children of those two metro areas are more numerous than all the residents of more than a dozen states, too.

Summarizing these basic demographic data, it can be affirmed that the Latino population is very large numerically and percentage-wise in the nation, in major states, and in metropolitan areas, too. They have been the main driver in the population growth of the nation, as well as in numerous states and cities, and have made enormous contributions to the economy. They hail from many Latin American countries, and while Mexican-heritage Latinos remain the vast majority of this population group, the distribution varies by states and cities. Their presence is undoubtedly noticed in many school systems, especially those in which Latinos are in fact the majority of students.

To date, those demographics have yet been precursors for systematic Latino-focused media or news literacy efforts. And while it could be argued that Latinos could and many do benefit from ongoing programs aimed at the general public, there are two factors of this population that merit distinct and special programs: language and Latino-oriented media.

Language

Not all Latinos speak Spanish, nor do all of them speak English; the majority of Latinos, regardless of their age, are to some extent bilingual, which is not the same as equally proficient in speaking, reading, writing, or comprehending either language. The language abilities of an individual or a group from any particular national heritage depend on numerous factors, of which educational attainment is just one. For Latinos, other factors include place of birth (outside or inside the United States); if he or she is an immigrant, then age of immigration and proportion of years in this country (a 15-year-old child who has also lived 5 years in the United States will not have had the same socialization experiences as a 7-year-old child who has lived in the United States that same number of years). Quality of education and whether or not any of that was in English also influences language abilities as does exposure to English-language popular culture be that in the United States, prior to, and/or after migration. The proportion of Spanish-language vis-à-vis English-language speakers in the home and neighborhood further impacts an individual or group's language acculturation, even for Latinos born in the United States.

Given these multiple conditions, and the diversity of experiences of each of the national origin Latino groups, the language patterns of this population are also not monolithic and vary by city as well as neighborhoods. While much more could be stated about this topic, the following paragraph summarizes the current reality:

> Younger generations of Hispanics (under age 55) are predominantly bilingual, and with each new generation, more English-dominant. Currently, 40.6 million Hispanics over the age of 5 speak English well, and 96% of Hispanics under 18 are either bilingual or English-dominant. In total, 55% of Hispanics are bilingual, while 27% are English-dominant and 19% are Spanish-dominant. Spanish is still spoken by many of the English-dominant speakers, however, and the growing importance of Spanish makes dual-language competence a benefit for marketers in mainstream America.
> (Nielsen, 2016, para. 5)

The same source adds: "Despite increasing proficiency in English, messaging in Spanish and in-culture is still very relevant to younger generations" (Nielsen, 2016, para. 6).

These assertions from a marketing perspective are applicable for media and news literacy programs as well. For Latinos to be included in the most relevant and significant ways, the lessons should be prepared and presented in Spanish *and/or* in English – depending on the particular language patterns of the targeted groups.

Latino-oriented media and news literacy in English must be conscientious of and take into consideration the specific lessons that would be best understood, which will be contingent on the targeted Latinos' level of education and also their particular language-learning experiences. A monolingual English-speaking Latino who has learned English since birth but primarily in informal or non-school settings will not have the same ability as a Latino English-speaker who has had formal education at increasingly higher educational settings.

Latino-oriented media and news literacy in Spanish must also pay attention to the Spanish language-learning mode and level mentioned in the previous paragraph. Most importantly, for media and news literacy efforts in Spanish, attention is indispensable to the diverse Latin American national or regional patterns and idioms. The lessons learned from the numerous errors made by advertising and marketing campaigns directed to Hispanics should certainly be applied to Latino-oriented media and news literacy programs.

For sure there are many writings on Hispanic marketing and campaigns. One recent and excellent source that addresses the language considerations is chapter four of *Hispanic Marketing: The Power of the New Latino Consumer* (Korzenny, Chapa, & Korzenny, 2017). While it is possible that the majority of Spanish speakers will understand each other (be it speaking or in writing) most of the time, it is well known that some common words in a particular country or region are not acceptable – and even offensive – in another country or region.

Thus, just as a good mainstream English-language media literacy effort would pay very close attention to the use of appropriate words in that language, the same holds for Spanish-language media literacy curricula for which instructors knowledgeable of the different idioms are recruited or at least consulted in advance. A teacher who has Latino/a students from different national origins could easily consult in advance with a knowledgeable colleague or maybe even the parents of those children – lest an offensive word (for some) be used in a lesson that could provoke the ire of parents who hear from their child about the gaff or perceived insult. Yet, given the bilingual skills of the majority of Latinos, it might even be best to have media and news literacy programs and lessons that incorporate both languages – again, depending on the particular targeted group.

Regardless of which language or languages are used for media and news literacy efforts directed to Latinos, what those efforts must not be are translations of English-language versions that do not incorporate the particular in-culture particularities that would enhance the success of such efforts. Moreover, it is also indispensable that they purposely focus on and incorporate analyses of the vast and still growing Latino-oriented media, which are available in varying formats and numbers in Spanish as well as in English.

Latino-Oriented Media

Latino-oriented media (LOM) encompass traditional as well as alternative print, broadcast, and electronic entertainment and news outlets and venues for which the main audiences (readers, viewers, listeners) are people of one or more Latino heritage. Because of the diverse language skills and preferences of this population, LOM are produced in Spanish, in English, and some even in both languages in the same outlet.

One of the most easily available LOM are the Spanish-language television networks – primarily Telemundo and Univision – along with their local stations, which via broadcast, cable, satellite, or the Internet have been delivering for decades entertainment and news content to almost every corner of the United States (Wilkinson, 2016). Some of the newer entries to the LOM television market are English-language or bilingual outlets, for example, Fusion, Mitú, and LATV. And while the national programming of those networks seeks common language and cultural denominators to attract the largest possible audiences, some stations or particular content is directed to particular national origin groups, as is the case with Mexican-American-oriented El Rey Network. Thanks to satellite and Internet connections, television stations or programs from many Latin American countries are also accessible in the United States. Excluded from the category of LOM (because they are not produced with U.S. Latinos as the primary audience) but certainly available to all Latino audiences (who are secondary albeit also profitable audiences) are the Spanish-language versions of HBO, Showtime, National Geographic, and dozens of other outlets, including Netflix Latin America, which has a broad range of content for Spanish-speaking populations.

The most abundant of the LOM are the more than 500 Spanish-language and bilingual Latino-oriented radio stations across the United States delivering content in more than 20 formats (Stroud, 2018). Many of these stations are now accessible online, and the music and other programs these stations offer reflect the national origins and culture of the audiences that are targeted in a particular city or region. Thanks to the Internet, LO radio stations from anywhere in the world are also accessible to U.S. Latinos. One particularity and shortcoming of the LO radio outlets is that very, very few offer news programs (Riismadel, 2015). Thus, Latinos who wish to be informed about the political and economic events – be these local, national, or international – must rely on the limited news offerings via television or in newspapers, if available in their communities.

Although daily *print* Latino-oriented newspapers are available in only three cities (Los Angeles, Miami, and New York), they can be accessed anywhere online. Weekly and monthly Latino-oriented newspapers and other publications are more abundant both in print and as online versions. While most are published in Spanish, many are also available in either English or in bilingual formats.

Meanwhile, via mail subscriptions and magazine racks, dozens of magazines from Latin America and Spain can also be purchased in the United States, thus enriching the diversity of Latino as well as Latin

American and Iberian-themed media options for the Hispanic population. To date, no weekly Latino-oriented *news* and current affairs magazine is available in the United States.

Aside from all of the above, during the last few years, digital and social media in Spanish, English, and in bilingual format but aimed at U.S. Latinos have been growing exponentially. These are so many and so diverse in content that inventories of such outlets and options are impossible to accurately establish. In the digital domain, however, some outlets are focused on news and current affairs.

Given such vast and diverse LOM options in the United States, when added to those in English that are available for bilingual Latinos, the media landscape and opportunities are broader for bilingual audience members than is the case for monolingual speakers. Regardless of the dominant language of any Latino individual or Latino national origin group, it is reasonable to expect that they will have a large probability to be exposed to LOM be it directly because they chose to do so or indirectly via family and/or friends.

What all this implies is that media and news literacy efforts that aim to focus on or be directed to Latinos should certainly incorporate and use examples of Spanish-language and even some English-language Latino-oriented media. For this population, media literacy should not be based only on examples from general market English-language media. Critical thinking skills about the characteristics – be these positive or negative – of particular entertainment and news content disseminated via LOM can be as beneficial as the critical thinking skills stemming from traditional media and news literacy programs. For large segments of the Latino population, however, the need for media and news literacy is even greater, given the importance of this population in the future governance and democracy of the United States.

Governance and Democracy

For the nation as a whole, but particularly for major states and dozens of cities, the future of their governance will be significantly influenced by how much and how well their growing Latino populations participate in the electoral and other democratic processes. And while there are many factors that contribute to civic and political engagement, "the mass media do and can play major roles in the political life of Latinos in the United States" (Subervi-Vélez, 2008, p. 377). Media and news literacy education can be essential tools for enhancing this population's understanding and critical thinking about governance, democracy, and participation. Deriving from what was presented above, it follows that any such media and news literacy education for Latinos must also include lessons about the content and other characteristics of Latino-oriented media.

Further, in an era of fake news, when audience confidence and trust in the mainstream media are at all-time lows, the importance of ethnic media is at all-time highs. Unlike mainstream media, which are expected to serve the interests of a general audience, including a mix of majority and minority populations, ethnic news media mainly promote the issues and concerns of a specific community through storytelling practices that resonate with their respective audiences. Ethnic groups, such as Latinos, are therefore turning to their own media outlets here in the United States, allowing them to expand – generally speaking and focusing on Internet outlets – in an era when mainstream news media are diminishing (Schmidt, 2019) as noted earlier. How messages are communicated from (both general market media and) ethnic media to their respective audiences must be understood. Even more critical to governance, democracy, and participation is unpacking (ethnic) news media message meaning. This, since it is forecast that in the upcoming 2020 presidential election the Latino vote could be the second most important, with 32 million Hispanics eligible to vote, surpassing the African American vote, with 30 million black voters (Habib, 2018).

That stated, the Latino-oriented media and news literacy education cannot be exclusively for Latino populations. Traditional media and news literacy education programs should incorporate lessons and examples that include pertinent issues about the growing and diverse Latino populations as well as about their economic, political, social, and cultural contributions. Lessons that include examples of the errors and limitations of general market media content would do well to highlight the predominance of Latino stereotypes and the effects of such content on Latinos and society at large. Moreover, efforts should be made to include the errors and limitations, as well as stereotypes that are commonly disseminated in Latino-oriented media. Those, too, influence not just the Latino audiences but also the non-Latinos with whom they interact.

What all this leads to is the imperative for media and news literacy education programs and even short-term efforts to take major steps to include a broader spectrum of the targeted populations as well as the media outlets that are addressed in the efforts to enhance critical thinking and action. Proper, informed governance, democracy, and participation depend on it.

References

Adams, P. (2018, October 5). 'Practicing quality journalism': ¡Ahora en español! *News Literacy Project*. Retrieved August 22, 2019 from https://newslit.org/updates/practicing-quality-journalism-ahora-en-espanol/

Arora, R. (2018, September 25). Latinos: A powerful force turbocharging small-business growth and driving $700 billion into the US economy. *CNBC*.

com. Retrieved August 22, 2019 from https://www.cnbc.com/2018/09/25/latinos-are-a-powerful-force-fueling-small-business-growth-in-the-us.html

Census.gov. (2018, September 13). Newsroom: Hispanic heritage month 2018. Retrieved August 22, 2019 from https://www.census.gov/newsroom/facts-for-features/2018/hispanic-heritage-month.html

Census Reporter. (nd). New York-Newark-Jersey City, NY-NJ-PA Metro Area. Retrieved August 22, 2019 from https://censusreporter.org/profiles/31000 US35620-new-york-newark-jersey-city-ny-nj-pa-metro-area/

Child Trends. (2018, December 13). Racial and ethnic composition of the child population: Key facts about the racial and ethnic composition of the U.S. child population. Retrieved August 22, 2019 from https://www.childtrends. org/indicators/racial-and-ethnic-composition-of-the-child-population

CyberWise. (2019). Conéctate con confianza. Retrieved August 22, 2019 from http://www.cyberwise.org/in-spanish

Flores, A. (2017, September 18). How the U.S. Hispanic population is changing. *Pew Research Center.* Retrieved August 22, 2019 from https://www.pewresearch. org/fact-tank/2017/09/18/how-the-u-s-hispanic-population-is-changing/

Habib, Y. (2018, February 4). Latinos could be the second most important bloc in 2020. *AL DÍA.* Retrieved August 22, 2019 from https://aldianews. com/articles/politics/elections/latinos-could-be-second-most-important-voter-bloc-2020/54957

Korzenny, F., Chapa, S., & Korzenny, B. A. (2017). *Hispanic marketing: The power of the new Latino consumer* (3rd ed.). New York, NY: Routledge.

Lopez, M. H., Krogstad, J. M., & Flores, A. (2018, September 13). Key facts about young Latinos, one of the nation's fastest-growing populations. *Pew Research Center.* Retrieved August 22, 2019 from https://www.pewresearch. org/fact-tank/2018/09/13/key-facts-about-young-latinos/

Pew Research Center: Hispanic Trends. (2014a). Demographic and economic profiles of Hispanics by state and county, 2014: California. Retrieved August 22, 2019 from https://www.pewhispanic.org/states/state/ca/

Pew Research Center: Hispanic Trends. (2014b). Demographic and economic profiles of Hispanics by state and county, 2014: Texas. Retrieved August 22, 2019 from https://www.pewhispanic.org/states/state/tx/

Pew Research Center: Hispanic Trends. (2016, September 6). Hispanic population and origin in select U.S. metropolitan areas, 2014. Retrieved August 22, 2019 from https://www.pewhispanic.org/interactives/hispanic-population-in-select-u-s-metropolitan-areas/

Nielsen. (2016, August 23). Hispanic influence reaches new heights in the U.S. Retrieved August 22, 2019 from https://www.nielsen.com/us/en/insights/article/2016/hispanic-influence-reaches-new-heights-in-the-us/

Schmidt, C. (2019, May 13). Here's the state of Hispanic media today—and where it goes from here. *Nieman Lab.* Retrieved August 22, 2019 from https://www.niemanlab.org/2019/05/heres-the-state-of-hispanic-media-today-and-where-it-goes-from-here/

Stroud, C. (2018, May 18). Everything you need to know about Hispanic radio. *Forbes.* Retrieved August 22, 2019 from https://www.forbes.com/sites/courtstroud/2018/05/18/everything-you-need-to-know-about-hispanic-radio/#58900cba7442

Riismadel, P. (2015, May 4). There are surprisingly few Spanish-language news stations. *Radio Survivor.* Retrieved August 22, 2019 from http://www. radiosurvivor.com/2015/05/04/there-are-surprisingly-few-spanish-language-news-stations/

Statista (nd). Buying power of Hispanic consumers in the United States from 1990 to 2020 (in trillion U.S. dollars). Retrieved August 22, 2019 from https:// www.statista.com/statistics/251438/hispanics-buying-power-in-the-us/

Subervi-Vélez, F. A. (Ed.). (2008). *The mass media and Latino politics: Studies of U.S. mass media content, campaign strategies and survey research: 1984–2004.* New York, NY: Routledge.

United States Census Bureau. (2016). The Hispanic population in the United States: 2016. Retrieved August 22, 2019 from https://www.census.gov/data/tables/2016/demo/hispanic-origin/2016-cps.html

Wilkinson, K. T. (2016). *Spanish-language television in the United States: Fifty years of development.* New York, NY: Routledge.

8 Blame Attribution, Warrants and Critical Thinking

South Africa's Overvaal Debacle as a Case Study

Marthinus Conradie

Introduction

Using a South African case study, this chapter participates in two lines of research on the relationship between media literacy and opinion pieces, as a subgenre of news discourse. Centred on the 2018 Overvaal High School controversy (described below), the investigation examines online opinion pieces published in reaction to this polarising event. Particular attention is devoted to analysing the arguments that cast blame on different stakeholders for aggravating racial antagonism around the incident. Two strands of scholarship anchor the analysis.

The first strand stems from the recognition that contemporary democracies are hallmarked by attempts to attach or deflect blame. To clarify, following a harmful event, different stakeholders within and outside government search for blameworthy individuals or groups and argue over the justifiability of blaming one target over others for whatever harm was suffered. When the process plays out in mass media, competing arguments about the most appropriate criteria for determining blameworthiness carry the potential to affect the knowledge democratic citizens can access about an issue. Mindful of this situation, Boukala (2016) and Hansson (2018a, 2018b) encourage research into blame attribution, based on the longstanding proposition that media discourses simultaneously reflect existing norms, assumptions, values and worldviews, while retaining the power to perpetuate and/or change these in unpredictable ways.

The second line of inquiry flows from the observation that opinion pieces, as a subcategory of news media, show a penchant for evidence-based argumentation. Arguments can be conceived of as collections of claims or statements, backed by various types of evidence. In opinion pieces, claim-evidence patterns can be articulated in numerous ways, depending on factors including culture, communicative medium and whatever an author considers most effective for persuading her/his audiences. Crucially, however, the validity of any kind of evidence remains debatable.

Moreover, two authors could use similar evidence to support mutually incompatible claims. Boukala (2016) and Hansson (2018a, 2018b) acknowledge this observation in their attempts to investigate blame attribution in democratic politics. They propose that the audiences of opinion pieces should be encouraged to pay attention to the assumptions authors rely on to link their argumentative claims with corroborating evidence. The unwritten nature of these linking assumptions make them especially important for understanding how a text can rationalise leaps from evidence to claims and ultimately normalise assumptions around the standards used to determine who can be blamed for creating or compounding social problems. To serve this research agenda, Toulmin (2003) offers a model designed to capture these assumptions in *if-A-then-B* expressions that explain the conditions under which evidence can reasonably be said to support claims.

Taken together, these two terrains of study drive this investigation into media reactions to Overvaal, especially the *if-A-then-B* assumptions that rationalise blame attribution by linking evidence and claims in the arguments formulated in online opinion pieces. To achieve this, Toulmin's (2003) framework for analysing argumentation is combined with Hansson's (2018a) refinements of this model for opinion pieces. This analysis foregrounds a tendency to blame an individual politician for intensifying racial tensions. Moreover, to rationalise blame, the authors of the opinion pieces work with an assumption about racism that might impede critical thinking, in terms of Toulmin (2003) and Hansson's (2018a) position that media discourses both reflect and shape public understandings of an issue. This position on the influence of media discourses undergirds the approach to media literacy adopted in this study. To clarify, media literacy is treated here as both an educational and a critical-cultural issue that foregrounds the urgency of analysing power dynamics, as enacted in discursive constructions of complex and historically shaped media events, as well as associated identities and assumptions about relationships between identity categories. In this respect, this chapter draws from Steyn (2015) as well as Hobbs (2007), Hobbs and Frost's (2003) proposals for expanding understandings of media literacy. In particular, it works with these authors' contention that media literacy should include critical attention to representational strategies through various means (including technologically mediated audio-visuals), as well as unpacking discourse-based argumentation strategies that enable audiences to "situate themselves in a sociopolitical context" (Hobbs & Frost, 2003, p. 351). The latter stream is especially vital to this chapter.

The next section summarises the Overvaal incident. Before doing so, it should be noted that this chapter is not advocating for the guilt or innocence of any person or group. Instead, its aim is to proffer suggestions regarding the urgency of critically evaluating discursive features such as the warrants that pervade journalistic reactions to politically divisive events, using Overvaal as a case study. Additionally, it should be noted that the event and its bearing on media literacy raise many more questions than those attended to here, both within South Africa and beyond. The theoretical and analytic approaches adopted in this chapter represent one option among many and was selected to highlight dimensions that relate to the catalogue of research on news media's potential influence on public knowledge.

Overvaal: A South African Furore

Overvaal High School is located in South Africa's Gauteng province, in the predominantly agricultural town of Vereeniging. In December 2017, the Gauteng Department of Education urged the school enrol fifty-five new learners into Grade Eight, the most junior level of high school in South Africa. A shortage of space in other schools within reasonable travelling distance had prompted the department's request for the learners to be added to Overvaal's existing intake for the 2018 academic year, starting in February. The school's governing body exercised its legal right to decline the request, insisting that its maximum capacity had already been reached. Since the fifty-five learners in question would require education in English, the SBG also cited its policy to offer instruction exclusively in Afrikaans.

Afrikaans is one of South Africa's eleven official languages. It is closely associated with the apartheid regime, during which the white minority government attempted to force other racial and ethnic groups to undergo education in Afrikaans, including the country's Black/African population. Apartheid racial categories still feature in government documentation and census data. Within the boundaries of these classifications, the fifty-five learners are grouped as Black/African, while most of Overvaal's existing learners, as well as its governing body, are classified as white. This dynamic became a bedrock for insisting that the school's claims about capacity and language concealed racial prejudice. The possibility that racial bias informed the governing body's claims took further impetus from the fact that the town in question (Vereeniging) still resembles features from its apartheid history, as many rural, agricultural communities do. Specifically, although rural communities are not officially zoned into race-specific areas, many citizens categorised as Black/African still inhabit the outskirts of towns, forcing them to travel comparatively long distances to access quality education. Travelling distances are increased if the nearest schools are too small to adequately accommodate its local population.

During subsequent media reportage of these events, Panyaza Lesufi (member of the Executive Council for Education in Gauteng) took centre stage in condemning Overvaal's governing body as racist, calling upon his extensive Twitter following to join his denunciation. The opinion pieces sampled for this study primarily engage with Lesufi's role in the controversy, charging him with fuelling racial conflict by dint of publicly airing the question of racism in the first place.

The dispute between the Gauteng department and Overvaal's governing body was legally settled when the Pretoria High Court upheld the school's refusal. Nevertheless, family members of the fifty-five learners staged protests outside the school gates, where they were joined by members of two political parties, the African National Congress and the Economic Freedom Fighters. Police forces intervened when violence erupted between the protestors and other members of the community. The racial composition of the protestors (Black/African) and the parents of children already enrolled at Overvaal (white) magnified media scrutiny and produced the opinion pieces under study.

To contextualise journalistic reactions to Overvaal in more detail, it should be noted that one of the most recurring features of blame attribution in race-relevant issues across post-1994 South Africa revolves around disagreements as to when an event, policy, public utterance or even private speech act should be considered racist (Steyn, 2015). Settling on universal criteria for identifying racism continues to provoke heated debates, including questions such as whether those South Africans who are racialised as Black/African are capable of racism and whether those racialised as white can be counted upon to promote anti-racism. Unsurprisingly, therefore, most of the authors of the opinion pieces under study combined the warrants that underpinned their claim-evidence chains with a peculiar understanding of what racism entails. This framing or construction of how racism might be defined became a bedrock for arguments aimed at rejecting the possibility that Overvaal's governing body can reasonably be accused of racism. This observation, in addition to a personal longstanding interest in race-relations, reinforced the decision to select opinion pieces on Overvaal as the case study for this chapter. However, similar analyses could also untangle complexities around other events where blame attribution might impede or cultivate media literacy. Although the details of this case study hinge on particularities from South Africa's historic, economic, social and political circumstances, the dominant trends of the results can still offer a guideline for comparative research in other (inter)national contexts.

Research Aims: Unpacking Warrants in Blame Attribution

The analysis reported below engages a purposely collected sample of opinion pieces, published by online news outlets in response to mounting racial antagonism during the crisis. It highlights the arguments authors used to accuse different blame-targets for escalating racial tensions. This aim is subdivided into three levels. First, the study identifies the most frequent blame-targets. Second, it unpacks the underlying argumentative premises, or warrants, that connect claims about who should be blamed, with supporting evidence (Toulmin, 2003). For the sake of brevity, the sections below report the most prevalent warrant, discussing the particular role of its *if-A-then-B* structure in the opinion pieces. Third, after reporting the most recurring warrant, attention is turned to assumptions about racism that accompany this warrant, especially the omission of attempts to link Overvaal with systemic obstacles to equity in post-1994 South Africa.

The prominence of racism in this analysis might require some explanation. Racism became a fulcrum of the investigation after observing the conflicting interpretations that were assigned to the exclusion of the fifty-five learners from Overvaal. Some journalists blamed the school's governing body of perpetuating racism and of concealing their prejudice under the guise of an outwardly neutral language policy (teaching in Afrikaans only). However, most of the opinion pieces under study blamed Panyaza Lesufi for levelling undeserved allegations against the school, in a self-serving ploy to cement his public persona as an advocate for social justice, rather than an altruistic concern for securing racial equity. Emulating Hansson (2018a), the analysis follows two procedures.

First, after a close reading of the sampled opinion pieces, all blame-relevant warrants were reconstructed. Doing this requires an awareness that warrants are, "rules of inference … tied more strongly to concepts than to words", with the implication that a single warrant, "can potentially be phrased in numerous ways" (Grue 2009, p. 309). Second, the role warrants played as assumptions that link an author's claims about who deserves blame for racial anger at Overvaal, with the evidence cited to buttress these claims was unpacked.

During the second stage, the degree to which authors' arguments contextualised the potential presence of racism at Overvaal within a systemic understanding of racism was interrogated. Systemic contextualisation calls for alertness to the present-day repercussions of historical arrangements, including some of the effects of apartheid that have survived its demise. This process of contextualising individual incidents within the consequences of historical factors remains crucial for enhancing critical awareness in South Africa (and elsewhere). Before accounting for the data collection methods, the next segment outlines the principles that anchored this chapter's approach to opinion pieces.

Discourse Analysis and Opinion Pieces

Like all categories of news media, opinion pieces are unstable, subject to evolution and can therefore be studied from numerous angles. This analysis prioritises two interrelated features.

First, authors generally write opinion pieces with a persuasive agenda. They assert a position and strategically explain its details to prompt audiences into sharing this position, partially if not completely. Second, they conduct arguments, whether implicit or explicit, whether grounded in cognitive or emotional appeals, or both. Criteria for persuasive arguments are also unstable, open to change and depend dramatically on an audience's preferences, which might prove challenging to predict (Hansson 2018a, 2018b).

The following section contextualises the persuasive and argumentative dimensions of opinion pieces in relation to a central concern in discourse analytic approaches to critical media studies.

Toulmin's Take on Argumentation and Blame Attribution in Media Discourses

Discourse analysts advocate alertness to the normalising effects that stem from treating certain assumptions and values as the common sense, taken-for-granted way of envisioning social relationships, identities and power relations. Analysing argumentation and blame attribution is one method of shedding light on the frames of reference within which newsworthy events, stakeholders and other elements are woven together (Boukala, 2016; Hansson, 2018a, 2018b). Toulmin's (2003) model is designed to examine the context-specific assumptions necessary for making arguments coherent. His framework refers to these assumptions as warrants, expressed in *if-A-then-B* structures that outline the conditions under which claims and evidence are connected.

The model summarised in Table 8.1 prioritises analyses of the strategies authors use to make statements about the issue at hand, how

Table 8.1 Toulmin's (2003) Model of Argumentation

Claims	Statements, opinions or conclusions that, in isolation, remain contestable and require corroboration.
Evidence	Reasons provided to substantiate a claim. The nature of acceptable evidence is defined and negotiated within the contextual parameters of the discourse setting and remain susceptible to evolutions in the communicative genre as well as authors' individual inclinations.
Warrants	Connections between claims and evidence that specify the *if-A-then-B* assumptions under which the connections valid, creating a coherent, logical infrastructure on which an argument turns. Warrants are generally rooted in views, norms and values that authors and addressees presumably share. Although they can be communicated openly, they are frequently implied.

they elaborate these statements along specific lines and how they supply (or omit) some kind of evidence as to why audiences should share their views. The relevance and suitability of evidence depends on context, genre and authors' ability to calculate their audiences' worldviews (Boukala, 2016; Hansson 2018a, 2018b). Generally, evidence can involve mainly cognitive data, such as statistical information, or comparatively less empirical appeals to outwardly agreed-upon norms, values and emotions (for research into cognition, affect and populism, see Breeze, 2019).

Taking these points as his premise, Hansson (2018a, p. 228) approaches blame attribution as "offensive and defensive symbolic performances," in which language is a potent symbolic resource. From this perspective, those parts of a text that function as claims perform three interconnected roles. First, claims often describe the events that instigated a search for culprits. More specifically, claims might confirm that the event was harmful enough to merit public outcry, prior to naming potential wrongdoers, or they could downplay the damage incurred in order to defend people who have already attracted blame. To illustrate, responses to Overvaal could claim that the fifty-five learners have the option of attending other schools, even if these are located farther away.

Second, claims can also expound the causes of a hurtful event and link these causes to human stakeholders who can feasibly be held accountable (see obligations and capacity below). Inversely, claims could suggest that no human actors bear causal responsibility.

Third, if an event was undoubtedly harmful, and if human actors were involved in its causes, claims can also affirm the intentionality of these actors. Audiences are more likely to blame an individual or a group if they have reason to believe that the actor/s caused damage intentionally. Claims about intentionality involves two other essential elements: obligations and capacity. Establishing intentionally requires that a blame-target was obligated to avoid damage and possessed the capacity to exercise her or his obligations. Government officials who are formally obliged to anticipate and mitigate social problems can be held liable for failing this duty when, for example, children's education has been disrupted. Capacity entails a stakeholders' ability to honour the obligations they are under and includes the necessary resources. The role that warrants play in relation to these three functions is outlined below.

Claims and evidence form part of the surface components of an argument, while warrants work at a deeper, often unwritten level. The *if-A-then-B* structures of warrants are generally communicated implicitly. Authors expect audiences to "fill in the gaps" necessary to link claims and evidence by drawing from presumably shared pools of general knowledge and values (Hansson 2018a, p. 232). In response to Overvaal, an author could claim that Lesufi's allegations of racism actually serve his own political career. To corroborate this claim, the author could cite earlier instances during which Lesufi manipulated accusations of racism to further his political aims (which audiences could view as factual or disputable evidence). The warrant under-pinning this claim-evidence chain can be articulated in the following *if-A-then-B* assumption: *if accusations of racism hinge on the blame-maker's self-serving goals, then the blame-taker/s should not be considered blameworthy.* To fill in the gaps necessary for deducing this warrant, audiences must possess some background knowledge about the possibility that voicing charges of racism can secure political gains. Put differently, placing this claim and evidence together presumes that audiences are familiar with the possibility that allegations of racism could potentially be misused for political advantage. The analysis be-low addresses this assumption.

Procedures for Collecting the Sample of Opinion Pieces

Over a three-month period starting in January 2018, regular Internet searches for all news items pertaining to Overvaal yielded an extensive initial corpus. Thereafter, the search was narrowed to all items explicitly marked as opinion pieces. Eventually, nineteen texts were collected (see the Appendix). All texts are available online without needing subscrip-tions to the hosting news website.

Toulmin's (2003) model was applied in three stages. An initial reading identified overall themes. During a second reading, blame-relevant argu-ments were identified based on Toulmin (2003) and Hansson (2018a). The next step ascertained claims that drove the argument of each piece, followed by an examination of the extent to which various types of sup-porting evidence was offered. Finally, the surface claim-evidence chains of each opinion piece was analysed to articulate the *if-A-then-B* war-rants on which these chains were predicated.

Since an adequately detailed account of all the warrants in all the articles oversteps the scope of this chapter, the next section concentrates on the most frequent warrant, prior to suggesting its implications for critical literacy.

Findings: Refuting Racism as Political Self-Interest

The Appendix summarises the warrants uncovered by an application of Toulmin's (2003) model. Panzaya Lesufi represents the primary blame-target. Some opinion pieces accused the incumbent government (led by the African National Congress) for failing to alleviate infrastruc-tural shortcomings across the Gauteng province in time to avoid the Overvaal debacle before it started.

Analysing the argumentative grounds on which the opinion pieces blamed Lesufi calls attention to the regular occurrence of a warrant that can be expressed as follows: *if a government official disregards existing policies or laws, that official is blameworthy* (abbreviated to a *warrant of legal procedure*).

Unpacking this warrant requires an analysis of the relevant claim-evidence chains in the opinion pieces. Most of the authors claim that Lesufi neglected constitutional protocols and take their evidence from his earlier actions during similarly race-sensitive cases in education, or from legal provisos that bear upon his official obligations and capacities. As an exemplar, consider the following extract:

> To some in the local media, Lesufi is a superstar – articulately and in dulcet tones slaying white, racist dragons in schools for violating the rights of their black victims. Except, this crusader often lights the racial fires or feeds the conflagration. … In the Koeitjies En Kalfies [Cows and Calves] pre-school debacle, his re-action was a knee-jerk allegation of racism deduced from a photo on social media. Lesufi tweeted that he was going there to "face-off with racists" [and] invited his 29 000 Twitter followers to join him in confronting the school. As if this wasn't bad enough, he re-tweeted photos of the toddlers, which enabled the public to identify them. Now he has tarred Hoërskool Overvaal with the brush of racism.
>
> (Gon, 2018)

The claim starts with a metaphor, insisting that Lesufi has cultivated an unearned reputation as a heroic crusader against racism. For evidence, the author summarises an earlier incident during which Lesufi unlaw-fully made minors identifiable by sharing a photograph of them at the Cows and Calves day-care centre in Gauteng. In brief, this earlier event started when a mother received a photograph from caretakers at the facility, showing her black child sitting alone and apart from the major-ity white children. Lesufi entered discussions after receiving the photo-graph from her. By framing Lesufi's reaction as an uncritical "knee-jerk" response, the author (Gon, 2018) proposes that his behaviour fuelled racial conflict rather than resolving it, in addition to the illegality of publicising the minors' faces. This proposition pivots on two points of evidence. First, Lesufi failed to safeguard the anonymity of the children involved, as required by law. Second, Lesufi condemned the staff of the day-care centre as racist without the benefit of a meticulous investiga-tion. Taken together, these points bolster the author's suggestion that Lesufi's conduct around Overvaal follows a similar pattern of disregard for constitutionally enshrined protocols. Put differently, the argument hinges on a warrant of legal procedure or the assumption that if a public official disrespects the codes of behaviour incumbent on her or his office, she or he should be held liable for (in this case) prioritising one's own reputations over public interests.

As might be evident from this example, in isolation the warrant of legal procedure is not inevitably related to racism. Like most warrants, it could conceivably connect a wide range of claims and evidence. However, most of the opinion articles rely on this warrant to animate a particular argumentative direction based on the premise that Lesufi's charges against the school can be discounted by counter-blaming him for breaching the obligatory protocols of his office. Doing so individualises and discredits him as the primary source of the allegations. Gradually, the opinion pieces developed the warrant of legal procedure into a keystone for defending Overvaal governing body. It was made into a rationalising pivot-point for the claim that Lesufi provoked racial aggression for personal, political gain despite his responsibility to selflessly oppose all forms of prejudice for the broader public good.

In terms of Hansson's (2018a) work on obligations, capacity and intentionality, the warrant takes its rationality from the understanding that government officials are obligated not only to abide by constitutional regulations but also to foster the welfare of the general public, rather than promoting sectarian interests or personal reputations. In principle, this obligation creates the justification for refuting an official's actions – provided that she or he clearly disregarded legal stipulations. In the exemplar cited above, these claim-warrant-evidence chains ultimately build up to the overall conclusion that if Lesufi had first undertaken a fair and painstaking investigation, he would have considered variables such as the fact that:

> Overvaal is an Afrikaans-medium school. Its refusal to accommodate the 55 was because the school was already at capacity, with pupils who accepted Afrikaans as the medium of instruction, including black children. A single-medium school cannot become a dual-medium school overnight. The Act [Gauteng Schools' Education Act 6 of 1995] sets out grounds for admission: Section 18 (A) provides that the governing body must determine the language policy of the school subject to the Constitution.
>
> (Gon, 2018)

Public officials are formally obligated to conduct rigorous investigations. Their capacity to meet this obligation is strengthened by the easy availability of existing laws and court rulings. Their awareness of this resource implies that dereliction of duty must involve intentionality. Holding office in the Executive Council is therefore taken to imply that Lesufi should have consulted earlier rulings, with the consequence that his oversight of due protocol indicates more than carelessness. Instead, it signals an active attempt to inflame racial turmoil. Intentionality is thus ascribed to Panyaza Lesufi, and, collectively, this combination yields the fulcrum of the claim-evidence chains that inculpate Lesufi and simultaneously absolve the school.

Other opinion pieces by different authors showed comparable patterns, using a warrant of legal procedure to discredit Lesufi's allegations. To reiterate, his accusations are invalidated by the twin claims that he acted on premature judgements and that he violated formal prescripts, despite a reasonable expectation that he should have grasped the illegality of his conduct. Factual evidence for these claims are sourced from earlier incidents and court rulings:

> The Rivonia Constitutional Court judgment summarises three similar cases. Lesufi should therefore have known he had no chance of telling a school to take in 55 learners speaking a different language at the last minute in December, without fair procedure. But he went ahead anyway. In short, what Lesufi has done is pure politicking, turning an issue of insufficient places at quality schools into a spectacle.
>
> (Child, 2018, para. 5)

> [School's governing bodies] are allowed to choose Afrikaans as their medium of instruction. They are also free to choose any other language, but in practice the only other language chosen is English. This is unlikely to change, despite what some ideologues might hope. Overvaal Hoërskool is full. This was confirmed by Judge Bill Prinsloo [in the Pretoria High Court]. Panyaza Lesufi ignored the Constitution when he turned the Hoërskool Overvaal wrangle into a racial drama with inflammatory statements like "there is no racist that can hide behind a broomstick."
>
> (Still, 2018, para. 3)

To understand the potential influence of subtly communicated warrants in extracts such as those cited earlier, it is worth recalling Toulmin (2003), Hansson (2018a) and Boukala's (2016) proposition that warrants can exert a persuasive influence precisely because they implicitly appeal to a particular audience's existing assumptions and worldviews. Discreetly relying on background assumptions allows those members of an audience who hold these views to interpret the opinion piece as supporting and legitimising their worldviews.

One further element is vital for a fuller understanding of how the warrant of legal procedure works in the analyses reported above. As mentioned earlier, the warrant is not automatically related to race-sensitive issues. Instead, warrants are made relevant in combination with background knowledge. In this case, audiences are expected to access the view that racially divisive moments in post-1994 South Africa are, at least potentially, open to exploitation for advancing political careers. This view accounts for the vehemence of the "crusader" metaphor cited in the first exemplar. Attaining a reputation as a committed anti-racist is politically valuable in South Africa, where racism continues to dog the process of democratisation and projects to instil unity after the violations of apartheid (Steyn, 2015). Politicians who are exposed for cultivating this reputation on invalid grounds can expect severe public outcry. Effectively, therefore, the warrant of legal procedure is entangled with a warrant of racism as a rhetorical resource: *if accusations of racism hinge on the blame-maker's self-serving goals, then the blame-taker/s should not be considered blameworthy.*

From a discourse analytic perspective on argumentation, one of the potential repercussions of incorporating this view of racism into the core of the opinion pieces under study is to redirect the conversation away from the plight of the fifty-five learners, away from the broader question of continued racial disadvantage and poor educational infrastructure across South Africa and towards the dangers inherent in launching politically expedient accusations of racism.

Uncomfortable though they might be, racially precarious moments provide opportunities for critical public conversations about the state of race relations and how historic inequities might survive into the present. Widely available, online opinion pieces exert a potent, albeit partial, screening effect, influencing the variables that enter conversations or get omitted. Shifting the conversational agenda in the manner suggested above increases the danger that a warrant of legal procedure will hinder the opportunity for contemplating the relationship between Overvaal and far wider, national concerns over equity and access to quality education among the most vulnerable members of society. Only two of the nineteen pieces collected for this analysis expanded their arguments to include critical readings of the incident within the historical context of South Africa's perilous transition to democracy. Combined with the rest of the analysis outlined above, and the overall discourse analytic precept that media discourses are always socially constituted and constitutive, the results suggest that most of the opinion pieces on Overvaal neglected at least one vital dimension of the debate that could have proven significant for promoting critical literacy. That is to say, although much of the evidence cited in the opinion pieces are arguably valid, inasmuch as they stem from verifiable documents, and although the claims are arguably viable, inasmuch as government officials are indeed constitutionally obligated to launch penetrating investigations, the presence of racial inequality in systemic forms did not draw methodical attention. Should this factor have been considered? Steyn (2015) has made a theoretically rigorous plea for cultivating citizens' aptitudes for carefully and critically evaluating the relevance of historical and structural dimensions.

The conclusion explores possible connections between her work and the above-mentioned results.

Conclusion

In closing, a warrant of legal procedure could conceivably bolster any number of different claim-evidence ties and could support an unpredictable host of overall conclusions. The analysis expounded in the previous section showcases how it was used in a very specific way. It illustrates how the warrant become entangled with a peculiar assumption about the nature of racism: its potential abuse for political gain at the expense of public harmony.

It is not suggested here that journalistic work of whatever genre should not engage with politicised exploitations of racism, or with public officials' failure to undertake painstaking investigations before issuing statements. However, this sample of opinion pieces highlights that although both angles were routinely foregrounded, very little space was spared for thorough considerations of the relationship between Overvaal and the persistence of poor access to quality education and its continued impact on the lives of rural South Africans along racial lines.

Since online news media are growing in popularity and affordability in South Africa (and elsewhere), and since these sources of knowledge are paramount to the intricate business of negotiating blame attribution, research into the assumptions that frame prominent events remains instructive (Steyn, 2015). Toulmin (2003) and Hansson (2018a) supply one method of driving this objective. Their work enables insight into some of the skills that critically literate audiences require. Specifically, in addition to exhorting audiences to scrutinise the evidence cited in journalistic work, Toulmin (2003) and Hansson (2018a) illustrate the necessity of widening attention to include the subtle assumptions, or warrants, that bridge evidence and claims.

Additionally, their approach to warrants adds another, more focused layer to Steyn's (2015) entreaty. Steyn (2015) calls for sensitivity to the interconnections between an individual media text, with all its internal argumentative manoeuvres, and broader historical, political and structural dynamics. She argues that an aptitude for reading these interconnections is indispensable for audiences' ability to notice, interpret and cumulatively develop informed views on possible relationships between media discourses and public reactions to polarising moments (Steyn, 2015). To identify warrants and reflect on their role, knowledge about wider social dimensions, including the variables at play during news production, is decisive. In the present case study, knowledge of systemic inequities in South Africa proved cardinal for questioning how a warrant of legal procedure operations in opinion pieces.

Appendix: Sample of Opinion Pieces

Title	Author	Publication
How can our schools ensure a more diverse and non-racial society?	Panyaza Lesufi	Eyewitness News
Hoërskool Overvaal: Lesufi's awful record.	Sara Gon	Politicsweb
Was the Hoërskool Overvaal crisis a plot by Gauteng's education department?	Anthony Still	BusinessLIVE
Lesufi ignored the constitution in Hoërskool Overvaal sage.	Katharine Child	Timeslive
Language: An emotive issue	Bert Olivier	Mail & Guardian
Language should not be the dominant factor.	Molefe Lengana	News24
Double medium schools ideal for racial integration.	Motsumi Ntsebo	News24
Every child will eventually need English.	Molula Musa	News24
EFF is protesting at the wrong place.	Anita Ferri	News24
Education problems: Are Afrikaans schools to blame?	Paul Colditz	News24
Time to get our priorities straight.	Matthew van Rensburg	News24
Overvaal: Where is the moral leadership?	Melanie Verwoerd	News24
Upgrade infrastructure and hire passionate teachers.	Craig Joseph	News24
A good teacher knows no race	Johann du Toit	News24
How to resolve the education challenges in South Africa?	Peter Nagel	News24
Mother tongue education in every child's interest.	Carla Rossouw	News24
Double shifts for schools?	Tobie Henning	News24
Hoërskool Overvaal: blame SA's wealth gap.	Sydney Majoko	The Citizen
Hoërskool Overvaal, where language is a proxy for race.	Prince Charles	ACTIVATE! Change Drivers

References

Boukala, S. (2016). Rethinking topos in the discourse historical approach: Endoxon seeking and argumentation in Greek media discourses on 'Islamist terrorism'. *Discourse Studies, 18*(3), 249–268.

Breeze, R. (2019). Emotion in politics: Affective-discursive practices in UKIP and Labour. *Discourse & Society, 30*(1), 24–43. https://doi.org/10.1177/0957926518801074

Child, K. (2018). Lesufi ignored the constitution in the Hoerskool Overvaal saga. TimesLive. Retrieved from https://www.timeslive.co.za/ideas/2018-01-19-gauteng-education-mec-panyaza-lesufi-ignored-the-constitution-in-horskool-overvaal-saga/.

Gon, S. (2018). Hoerskool Overvaal: Lesufi's awful record. Politics Web. Retrieved from https://www.politicsweb.co.za/opinion/horskool-overvaal-lesufis-awful-record.

Grue, J. (2009). Critical discourse analysis, topoi and mystification: Disability policy documents from a Norwegian NGO. *Discourse Studies, 11*(3), 305–328.

Hansson, S. (2018a). Analysing opposition-government blame games: Argument models and strategic manoeuvring. *Critical Discourse Studies, 15*(3), 228–246.

Hansson, S. (2018b). The discursive micro-politics of blame-avoidance: Unpacking the language of government blame games. *Policy Sciences, 51,* 545–564.

Hobbs, R. (2007). *Reading the media: Media literacy in high school English.* New York, NY: Teachers College Press.

Hobbs, R., & Frost, R. (2003). Measuring the acquisition of media literacy skills. *Reading Research Quarterly, 38*(3), 330–354.

Steyn, M. (2015). Critical diversity literature: Essentials for the twenty-first century. In S. Vertovec (Ed.), *Routledge International Handbook of Diversity Studies* (pp. 379–389). Abingdon: Routledge.

Still, A. (2018). Was the Hoerskool Overvaal crisis a plot by Gauteng's education department? BusinessLive. Retrieved from https://www.businesslive.co.za/bd/opinion/letters/2018-01-23-letter-was-the-overvaal-horskool-crisis-a-plot-by-gautengs-education-department/.

Toulmin, S. E. (2003). *The uses of argument.* Cambridge: Cambridge University Press.

9 Media Literacy and a Typology of Political Deceptions

Robert N. Spicer

Introduction

On May 24, 2019, Taegan Goddard's (2019) Political Wire blared the warning with a succinct headline: It's Going to Get Really Bad. The catalyst was a video of Nancy Pelosi circulating through social media platforms. According to the *Washington Post* the video was slowed to "about 75 percent of its original speed" and "altered to modify her pitch" in order to create the illusion that Pelosi was drunk (Harwell, 2019, para. 7). This was a day after Donald Trump tweeted (https://twitter. com/realDonaldTrump/status/1131728912835383300) out a video from the Fox News spinoff Fox Business that was a deceptively edited montage of clips of Pelosi misspeaking and stumbling on her words during a press conference (Manjoo, 2019, para. 4).

It appears Goddard is right. It is going to get really bad. The fake Pelosi "drunk" video appears to be the product of Internet hucksters. This is problematic because of the accessibility of the tools that make this kind of deception possible. The Fox News video is problematic for another reason: the presence of the word "news" in the channel's name. This video was created blatantly with the purpose of misleading the audience. If the person who created it has a degree in journalism, the institution where they earned it should consider disowning this alumnus. In *The Elements of Journalism*, Kovach and Rosenstiel (2014) remind us that "journalism's first obligation is to the truth" (p. 49). In this instance Fox and its host Gregg Jarrett jettisoned that obligation.

These two videos illustrate the impetus for this chapter. An important function of media literacy is helping people to better understand how political deception works. In one case, it's about how propagandists and social media con artists create fake content and how easily it circulates. In the other, it's about the obligation journalism has to the public and cultivating an understanding of how journalism does what it does; how content is created and to think critically about how we consume it.

This chapter explores the overlap of media literacy and political deception. It presents a typology of political deception practices. The analysis is broken into six subsections, one for each type of political deception: (1) the lie, (2) myth making, (3) spin, (4) true statements that allow/lead to false conclusions, (5) secrecy, and (6) pandering. The chapter will conclude with a brief discussion of the limitations and future directions for media literacy and political deception.

The Typology

Lies

One might think that lying would be the most easily explained concept here. Appropriately enough the concept is deceptive in its simplicity although the "clear-cut" lie, to use Sissela Bok's (1999) term, is often defined in simple terms (p. 16). The lie is a statement that is not only demonstrably *not true*, it is also a statement the sender makes knowing that it is false, with the intention of misleading the receiver of the message. Bok (1999) defines a lie as "an intentionally deceptive message in the form of a statement" (p. 15). F.G. Bailey (1991) critiques Bok's simplicity noting a few examples of what could be an infinite list of permutations where what might seem like a lie is not (pp. 7–9). For her part, Bok notes that not all deceptive messages are lies and that there can be self-deception involved in false statements. If a politician is deceiving himself in his own false statement, then, while he may be misleading his listeners, he is not lying to them.

For Mahon (2007), the distinction between lying and deceiving is the distinction between success and failure. If a politician makes a false statement, which she knows to be untrue, with the goal of leading her audience to believe (1) that she is sincere and (2) that the statement is true, then she has deceived. If the audience reacts with incredulity, then she lied but did not deceive. Martin Jay (2010) notes the long-standing public perception that lying is ubiquitous in politics (pp. 14–16). This is a problematic perception not just because cynicism is problematic but also because it misses the subtlety of the forms political deception can take, forms that will be explored in the remainder of this chapter.

It is difficult to label something a lie because supporting such an accusation requires the communique in question to be narrowly analyzed, to know something of the mindset of the sender, and in most cases, to have the benefit of hindsight. Even with all of that, it is still difficult. For example, there is a fine line between a lie and a broken campaign promise. During the 2008 presidential campaign, then candidate Barack Obama promised to close Guantanamo Bay prison in Cuba. He failed to do so. However, it would be difficult for an honest analysis to say that Obama lied about his intentions. As his presidency was drawing to a close, he was asked what he would have done differently, to which he responded, "I think I would have closed Guantánamo on the first day" (Bruck, 2016, para. 4). He proceeded to explain that he thought he would be able to get it done "in a more deliberate fashion" but political reality got in the way (Roth, 2016, para. 2). President Obama tried to do something but failed to accomplish it. Some might call his promise a lie, but to do so would require support that is not there.

Former Congressman Anthony Weiner, on the other hand, certainly lied about a lewd photo that he tweeted in May 2011. An image of Weiner's genitalia was tweeted at a female college student and was quickly deleted. What followed was a series of interviews in which Weiner claimed he could not say "with certitude" whether the image was actually of his body part (Tumulty & Sonmez, 2011, para. 1). Weiner told ABC News "I did not send that photo. My system was hacked. I was pranked" (Karl, 2011, para. 2). He even tweeted "Touché Prof Moriarity. More Weiner Jokes for all my guests! #Hacked!" (Weiner, 2011). With hindsight we can say Weiner was lying. He eventually admitted "that he had repeatedly lied to his constituents and the country in denying that he had sent a lewd picture" (Horowitz, 2011, para. 1). In this case we have a clear-cut example of a political lie.

More clearly, and narrowly, defining the concept of lying is useful for media literacy education if for no other reason than having that better understanding gives a person a better understanding of how political rhetoric works. One of the biggest problems facing media today is the hyper-partisan and tribal nature of the political culture. Teaching people to more narrowly define a lie will hopefully result in less inflammatory language in political debates by reducing the use of the accusation. It might also reduce cynicism when we recognize that research has found that "presidents make at least a 'good faith' effort to keep an average of about two-thirds of their campaign promises" (Hill, 2016, para. 4).

Myth-Making

The concept of political myth-making can be described as a general worldview, containing both truth and falsehood, which is collectively rationalized and accepted to varying degrees by members of a society at every level of the political hierarchy. There are many variations that have been used by philosophers and political thinkers to describe this. Some modify the concept, creating variations on the theme, but the basic premises remain the same. In Plato's (1987) *Republic* Socrates referred to a "noble lie." Walter Lippmann (1997) described a "pseudoenvironment." Raymond Williams (1978) uses the term "structures of feeling." It is important to understand that, despite the presence of the word "lie," what Plato describes is not really what we would think of as a lie as defined above.

Sir Desmond Lee, in his translation of Plato's *Republic*, argues that the use of the word "lie" is a mistranslation and an incorrect interpretation of what Plato was actually describing as a "foundation myth" (p. 177). With that clearer understanding, and linguistic adjustment, we better understand what has been called the "noble lie" as a myth. Philosopher Catalin Partenie (2009), writing for the *Stanford Encyclopedia of Philosophy*, defines the foundation myth as "a true story, a story that unveils the origin of the world and human beings" (para. 1). Partenie notes that while the term "myth" carries implications of falsity in its contemporary meaning, for Plato it meant a true story. Lee similarly argues that the foundation myth has been misconstrued to imply Plato "countenances manipulation by propaganda" (p. 177). However, Lee says, the foundation myth is not a top-down manipulation of the masses by political elites; it is "accepted by all three classes," the rulers, auxiliaries, and workers (p. 177).

A perfect example of a myth would be the notion of American exceptionalism, a concept that encompasses a variety of ideas, defined differently by various political commentators, that essentially boils down to the notion that there is something unique about the United States and its place in human history. The simplest explanation is in Hofstadter's (1962) oft-quoted comment: "It had been our fate as a nation to not have ideologies but to be one" (p. 43). In other words, America was not subject to the ideological divisions that plagued Europe but instead was based upon the notion that "hard work and common sense, were better and more practical than commitments to broad and divisive abstractions" (p. 43). The American political sociologist Seymour Martin Lipset (1996) defined the ideology of America in five words: "liberty, egalitarianism, individualism, populism, and laissez-faire" (p. 31). It does not matter if it is "true" that America is somehow special in the bigger picture of human history; the idea is not even something that can be called "true" or "false" because it is a political-philosophical concept used as an organizing, unifying principle of American political culture. To espouse a belief in American exceptionalism is more of a political statement, perhaps even a quasi-religious one, than a statement about anything that could even remotely be described as a fact.

American exceptionalism is a broad, all-encompassing myth about the nation within which is contained other myths about the character of its political culture. Lipset's five-word definition points especially to the ideals of individualism, as he describes an anti-statist position, the ability to live free of state intervention in personal decisions (pp. 31–32), and self-reliance, the ability of one to stand on their own without needing help from the state. These notions stand in contrast to collectivism and state-controlled economics. There is the high ideal of freedom of speech and the legal discourse that draws on free market (laissez-faire) economics to frame that concept of speech creating a marketplace for ideas. There is the notion of an objective press that acts as a "fourth estate" and a check on government power. Each of these "myths" contains at least a ring of truth, if not actual truth. However, there is plenty of empirical evidence, both anecdotal and in social science, to demonstrate that all of these ideas are open to questioning.

There is an element of deception in the concept of the big myth and each individual myth, even if a given myth contains some truth and is collectively co-accepted by the leaders and masses of a society. In Lee's translation, Plato uses the term "witchcraft" to describe the "involuntary" loss of belief in what is right. In other words, Lee argues in a footnote, what is being discussed here could loosely translate to propaganda (p. 179). Plato's hypothetical Republic would produce what in contemporary terms might be characterized as war propaganda by altering perceptions of the after-life in order to "produce a fighting spirit" (p. 140). In World War II era America, it was not so much feelings about the afterlife but rather feelings of patriotism that "produced a fighting spirit" through the images of Uncle Sam saying, "I want you" or Rosie the Riveter saying, "We can do it." The myth as part of propaganda is not about the specific acts being propagandized (e.g., enlisting in the military or working in a factory to help the war effort); it is about the underlying feelings about American greatness and the individual citizen's dedication to that greatness.

Where conflict between leaders and masses becomes a problem, and deception becomes part of the equation, is when the myth stands too starkly in contrast with the reality in front of the masses'/public's eyes. Again, this does not necessarily mean that political leaders cease to believe the myth, or they are purposefully lying to the masses. Political leaders can either continue to fully cling to a belief in the face of all evidence to the contrary or may break with the myth. This happened with former Federal Reserve chairman Alan Greenspan after the banking crisis at the beginning of the 21st century when he told the House Committee on Oversight and Government Reform (*Financial Crisis*, 2008) that he had found a "flaw" in his ideology (p. 46). In other words, his experience with his myth of market economics proved to be "the murder of a Beautiful Theory by a Gang of Brutal Facts" (Lippmann, 1997, p. 10). In the end, myth-making could probably be described as an act of collective self-deception.

Media literacy around myth-making is perhaps also understood as historical education. The examples discussed in this section illustrate the ways in which political communication strategies echo through the years, even centuries. This historical framework also draws the student's attention to the interplay of media platforms and messaging through that time. Even as technologies evolve, ways of thinking and ways of arguing reappear in the political culture. In order to understand contemporary political discourse in any medium, it is essential to understand the myths that are intertwined with that discourse.

Greg Grandin (2019) tells a story that perfectly illustrates this. In his book *The End of the Myth: From the Frontier to the Border Wall in the Mind of America*, Grandin establishes the mythology of America in the first sentence, writing that the "British colonies in America were conceived in expansion" (p. 11). Referencing the Mexican author Octavio

Paz, Grandin argues that the "American revolution is a permanent revolution … a nonstop expulsion of all 'elements foreign to the American essence'" (p. 13). The idea that constant expansion is part of the American mythos is seen in the writing of Benjamin Franklin (pp. 14–15), and Martin Luther King Jr. saw it feeding "racism, a violent masculinity, and moralism that celebrates the rich and punishes the poor" (p. 4).

Grandin makes an argument for understanding the 2016 election of Donald Trump to the presidency in relation to earlier racism in the presidency. The expansion of the United States into unsettled lands acted as a tool that "deflects domestic extremism" (p. 5). Trumpism, by contrast, is "extremism turned inward, all-consuming and self-devouring" (p. 7). If media literacy will teach us how to better understand media content, one example being the rhetoric of political campaigns, part of that should involve examining the earliest examples of political myths, the ways in which their mindsets are still with us, and how we can combat their corrosive effects.

Spin

You can put your best foot forward. You can offer "a glittery and partial side" (Altenhofen, 2010, p. 160) of an issue. You can alter the perspective from which an issue is viewed. This is what it means to "spin" something. Spin is the use of, sometimes manipulative, communication tactics to alter the way the receiver of a message thinks about an incident or issue in order to advance the immediate political goals of the sender of the message. Dale Hynd (2007) defines spin as "a collection of information control behaviours and techniques designed to lead the receiver away from the real intention of the communicator's message" (p. 77). It is when the communicator takes a problem and repositions it in relation to the audience or when the politician will "meticulously *massage* the facts, then *filter* them through letters, speeches, and *front groups* until even he could not say for sure what was truth and what was spin" (emphasis added, Tye, 2002, p. 75). With spin, the relative truth or falsity is rendered moot or meaningless in the face of the cleverness of spin or the power of the message. Whether something is true becomes secondary to its value to a political agenda. This is true for practitioners who are looking to advance their agendas. It is also true for audience members who are looking for validation of existing beliefs rather a challenge to them.

David Greenberg puts forth a compelling argument about spin that makes critiquing it a more complicated prospect. He also underlines the importance of media literacy as part of a citizen's political education. The term is often scornful, directed at those we see as dishonest, especially when they are political opponents. However, Greenberg (2016) argues, "spin is how leaders make their case to a sovereign public. It's a way to engage, persuade, and mobilize the public in whom power ultimately resides" (p. 3).

Greenberg devotes an excellent book to a history of presidential spin. In one chapter, he describes the Reagan campaign and administration's use of image and feeling as tools for maintaining political power. This is the perfect illustration of spin as the "glittery and partial side" of America. Reagan's presidency and 1984 campaign "drew from a wellspring of archetypes, cultural memories, and deeply-embedded national myths" (Greenberg, 2016, pp. 414–415). The Prouder, Stronger, Better ad is brimming with idealized imagery of the beauty of America. Of course, if you are a viewer watching this ad and you are living in poverty, and/ or are the target of racial discrimination, these images may ring hollow. This is the spin; the "glittery partial side."

In another chapter Greenberg recalls the 1988 presidential race, which *Time* dubbed the "Year of the Handlers," a year that saw a change of behavior from the so-called "spin doctors." Greenberg says that the men who coached Eisenhower and Nixon denied their roles in shaping the men and their messages. In 1988 the handlers of the day were all too happy to come out from behind the proverbial curtain where they were hiding, like the Wizard of Oz, and "boasted about their role in crafting message and ads and even candidates" (p. 416).

Possibly the greatest example of spin comes from pollster Frank Luntz. This last example has become legendary, being immortalized in countless articles, books, and even in dramatic portrayals in popular culture, including in one scene in Adam McKay's (2018) critically ac-claimed and award-winning film *Vice* (Pitt, 2018). The movie tells the story of former vice president Dick Cheney, his rise to power, and how that rise coincided with the evolution of the conservative movement in the United States. The film shows a scene of a very enthusiastic, dramatized version of Luntz testing out the phrase "death tax" with a focus group.

This is one of the most infamous acts of spinning in American politi-cal history. Luntz changed the estate tax to the death tax and with that altered public opinion of it. He explained this in an interview with PBS's *Frontline* (2009):

> Look, for years, political people and lawyers – who, by the way, are the worst communicators – used the phrase "estate tax." And for years they couldn't eliminate it. The public wouldn't support it because the word "estate" sounds wealthy. Someone like me comes around and realizes that it's not an estate tax, it's a death tax, be-cause you're taxed at death. And suddenly something that isn't via-ble achieves the support of 75 percent of the American people. It's the same tax, but nobody really knows what an estate is. But they certainly know what it means to be taxed when you die. I argue that is a clarification; that's not an obfuscation.

(para. 20)

Luntz's explanation here has to be quoted in its entirety to be fully appreciated. He, simply by changing the words used to describe something, found a way to change many opinions of that thing. The best part of the explanation, however, is the last sentence. Even as Luntz explains his spin, he spins.

Luntz also provides an illustration of why media literacy is important for helping us spot this sort of thing. He and George Lakoff (2006) have written extensively about wordsmithing and how it can be used to persuade the public. Across all forms of marketing, but especially in politics, words are chosen because they tap into, and are used to exploit, existing feelings. In his explanation, Luntz (2007) states that he wanted to replace "the elitist sounding 'estate tax,' with the "more emotional, more personal 'death tax'" (p. 164). In other words, Luntz is attempting to reframe thinking about the tax from something very wealthy people pay on their enormous inheritances to something people pay when they die. Media literacy can serve a linguistic function, helping people think about politicians' word choices and how they affect our thinking.

True Statements That Allow/Lead to False Conclusions

In his exploration of the definition of lying, Thomas Carson (2012) discusses how to use a true statement to mislead. He uses the example of a car salesman being asked if a car overheats. The salesman responds, "I drove this car across the Mojave desert [*sic*] on a very hot day and had no problems" (pp. 15–16). The salesman has made a true statement and, thus by definition, has not lied to the buyer, yet he has also presumably deceived the buyer. He has made a true statement that would allow for or lead to a false conclusion.

Political leaders can employ this tactic to attempt to encourage or allow the public to come to a false conclusion. Put another way, one might describe it as *giving the receiver license or at least the potential* to take away a false impression. This takes some, but not all, of the agency away from the sender of the message and places it in part on the receiver. It does not take away intent on the part of the sender; the salesman still intends for the buyer to have a false impression. It just allows for the fact that meaning is in the decoding as much as, maybe more than, in the encoding of a message. It also acknowledges the idea that the onus is at least in part on the receiver to think more critically about the message rather than accepting it at face value, to say, "wait, that salesman did not *really* answer my question."

On two occasions out-of-context quotes played a part in the 2012 presidential campaign. In both instances the questions surrounded the candidacy of a Republican candidate, former Massachusetts governor

Mitt Romney. In the first case, Romney's campaign produced an ad containing a quote from incumbent President Barack Obama in which Obama says, "If we keep talking about the economy, we're going to lose." Romney's campaign was criticized for using the quote "out of context" because in its original use, Obama was quoting a McCain campaign staffer talking about McCain's 2008 campaign strategy. Romney's use of the quote gave the appearance that Obama was saying this about his own campaign in 2012, which was deemed by critics to be misleading (Politifact, 2011; Shear, 2011).

In the second instance Romney became the target of this tactic. In early 2012, in a speech to the Nashua Chamber of Commerce in New Hampshire, Romney said, "I like being able to fire people." While this statement sounded bad on its face, when placed into the context of the entire speech, the statement shows that Romney was not revealing himself to be a heartless employer who gets pleasure from firing his employees. In context it is clear that Romney was talking about consumers purchasing health insurance and being able to drop their coverage and move to another provider if they are unhappy with the service they are receiving. (A video clip of the quote can be found in the *Washington Post* archives at this link: https://tinyurl.com/ybu9jcwa.)

Where this creates a problem in the political process, for both the public and the political figures, is when the out-of-context quote reinforces an established perception. If there is already a feeling about a politician in the public mind, a quote like Romney or Obama's, even if it was not actually said in the way the de-contextualization implies, can be believed and, even if it is corrected, can still have an impact. Brad Phillips (2012), president of the Phillips Media Relations firm, wrote about the incident on his blog, saying that mistakes like Romney's "reinforce an existing narrative about a candidate are almost always the most harmful ones" (para. 5). In other words, there was already bubbling in the public mind a perception of Mitt Romney as a heartless corporate raider. Even in context, that phrase "I like being able to fire people" reinforces and possibly strengthens such negative perceptions.

The essential point is that context matters in political speech, and an effective technique in political deception is to rip words from their contexts. Media literacy education can teach citizens a few useful things here. One is how to recognize edits. In the most extreme form, this can be a drastic cut where it is obvious that the speaker had more to say that might change the meaning of the phrase that is being cut. Another is how to find the full context in the form of a transcript of what was said. Finally, before all of that can be taught, people need to understand that this sort of thing happens in politics. It might be true that Mitt Romney said the words, "I like being able to fire people," but that doesn't necessarily mean that he's Ebenezer Scrooge.

Secrecy

Edward Shils (1956) begins his book *The Torment of Secrecy* by arguing, "A free society can only exist when public spirit is balanced by an equal inclination of men to mind their own business" (p. 21). Shils goes on to contrast the differences between the privacy of citizens with the "privacy" (or secrecy) of the government. He recounts the historic evolution from monarchy, which made governing a private process for a ruler and his advisors, to the development of "the modern liberal democratic movement" that considered "publicity regarding political and administrative affairs" to be one of its "fundamental aim[s]" (p. 23).

Shils presents a succinct definition of secrecy as "the compulsory withholding of knowledge, reinforced by the prospect of sanctions for disclosure" (p. 26). While the Shils definition is useful, secrecy is actually subtler than that. Political secrecy is more nuanced, taking on different qualities in different contexts. President Richard Nixon represents perfectly the problematic contrasts in the handling of government secrecy, the importance of balancing secrecy and transparency, and the problem of whether it is valid to deem something worthy of protection from public scrutiny. In June 1972 Nixon signed Executive Order 11652. In a March 1972 statement on this executive order Nixon (1972) said:

> Fundamental to our way of life is the belief that when information which properly belongs to the public is systematically withheld by those in power, the people soon become ignorant of their own affairs, distrustful of those who manage them, and – eventually incapable of determining their own destinies.
>
> (para. 6)

The statement takes on a strange character when considering the fact that the discussions heard on the "Nixon tapes," recordings that were made of discussions between the president and his advisors in the Oval Office, show a very different attitude about secrecy and government actions.

While Nixon demonstrates the problem of secrecy and its adverse effects on the rights of the public to be informed about government deeds and, more important, misdeeds, a report from a commission on government secrecy chaired by Senator Daniel Patrick Moynihan (D-NY) points to a greater complexity on the topic. Moynihan (1997) writes in the commission report, "some secrecy is vital to save lives, bring miscreants to justice, protect national security, and engage in effective diplomacy" (p. XXI). Eva Horn (2012) adds to this, arguing that secrecy cannot simply be contrasted with transparency as if the two were equal and opposite concepts. Instead secrecy and transparency should be thought of as complementary concepts, where secrecy paradoxically protects a democracy (e.g., as a necessary tool of national security) while also threatening democracy (e.g., through the potential for abuse and consolidation of power free from public scrutiny that might prevent it).

Alongside the paradox of secrecy as both a necessary protection of and a threat to democracy is the subtlety of the concept itself, which is something media literacy can help people understand. Horn argues that "the secret is not so much a piece of withheld knowledge as a 'secrecy effect' that structures social and political relations between those who 'are supposed to know' and those excluded from this knowledge" (p. 105). Media literacy should be a part of helping people understand secrecy, how it is wielded and by whom, and when it is appropriate to disrupt its power. Secrecy plays a "limited but necessary role" (Moynihan, p. xxi) in governance; the most important word there being "limited." When it runs rampant it allows for public deception through omission of information.

Pandering

One of the most famous campaign promises in modern political history came from then vice president George H.W. Bush during his speech at the 1988 Republican National Convention, where he officially became the Republican nominee for president of the United States. It was there where he uttered the aforementioned statement "Read my lips. No new taxes." This statement came back to bite him when, during a debate in the 1992 campaign, then-Arkansas governor Bill Clinton said, "The mistake that [Bush] made was making the 'read my lips' promise in the first place, just to get elected, knowing what the size of the deficit was" (Commission on Presidential Debates, 1992, para. 234). The implication of Clinton's statement there was that Bush knew full well he would need to raise taxes but told the electorate that he would not do so, just to get their votes.

For its part, the 1992 Bush campaign featured a TV ad called "Gray Dot" that displayed two candidates, side-by-side, both with their faces covered by a gray dot. The announcer went down a list of contradictory positions from the candidate on the left and the candidate on the right with the commercial ending with the gray dots disappearing to reveal that the two candidates were actually the same person – Governor Clinton (November Company, 1992). The obvious implication of the ad was that Clinton changes positions with the political winds.

The Clinton and Bush campaigns were accusing one another of pandering. Brandice Canes-Wrone (2004), in her analysis of presidents and public policy, defines policy pandering as when "presidents follow public opinion when they believe citizens are misinformed about their interests" (p. 104). She raises some important descriptive questions in a footnote citing other definitions of the term. For example, Canes-Wrone cites Jacobs and Shapiro (2000), who expand the definition of pandering to include not only situations where constituents are ill informed but also those times when constituents are well-informed. Their analysis of pandering argues that, despite popular perception, politicians actually do not pander to public opinion. Jacobs and Shapiro say that the "irony of contemporary politics" at least in the year 2000 was "that politicians both slavishly track[ed] public opinion and … studiously avoid[ed] simply conforming policy to what the public want[ed]" (pp. 7–8).

Pandering might simply be defined as those times when a politician tells constituents what they want to hear but *only because* of the fact that they want to hear it. In other words, a pandering politician does not necessarily believe what she is saying, but she is saying it because it is electorally advantageous to do so due to her constituents' beliefs. So, pandering's deceptive qualities are in its insincerity. It can also be deceptive because in some cases the politician is tapping into constituents' beliefs in order to manipulate the constituency. Lord (2003) notes that fears about such manipulation have been expressed in response to leaders from Hitler to Franklin Delano Roosevelt (pp. 13–14).

In a 2010 Rasmussen poll of likely voters, 81% of respondents said they believed that politicians do not keep the promises they make in campaigns. This public perception stands in contrast to Sulkin's (2009) findings that, in fact, most politicians after winning an election at least try to do what they promised during the campaign. This raises the question, why is there such a strong public perception that politicians are only liars and panderers? Why is there a perception that the political process itself is all charade and façade?

Conclusion

In his book *Uninformed*, Arthur Lupia (2016) writes that the "number of facts that can be relevant to the operation of government is infinite" (p. 2). Lupia argues that there are two groups of people. Those who know they don't (and can't) know everything there is to know in order to be fully informed and those who are delusional about how much they know, tricking themselves into thinking they are fully informed. "There is no third group," Lupia says (p. 3). This information overload contributes to political deception. If there is too much to know, it makes it much easier to hide things. It also becomes easier to lie about things because the heavy flow of information makes it harder to confirm claims.

danah boyd (2017) addresses this problem, asking the question, "Did media literacy backfire?" She writes:

> Addressing so-called fake news is going to require a lot more than labeling. It's going to require a cultural change about how we make sense of information, whom we trust, and how we understand our

own role in grappling with information. Quick and easy solutions may make the controversy go away, but they won't address the underlying problems.

(para. 24)

boyd sees media literacy having backfired in the Pizzagate incident. Pizzagate is a conspiracy theory that proposed that Hillary Clinton and other high-profile political figures were running an international ring of child sex slaves and that it was based out of a Washington, DC, pizza shop called Comet Ping Pong (Breiner, 2016). A man with a gun drove from his North Carolina home to the pizza shop to "rescue the children" (boyd, para. 12). boyd notes that this man, and many others like him, were doing "something that we've taught people to do – question the information they're receiving and find out the truth for themselves" (para. 11). What makes this especially unsettling is that there is little, perhaps nothing, that media literacy educators can do about this incident. The only solution at this level is for media practitioners to take more care with what they say and have greater concern for how their content might affect their audience.

This, perhaps, should be a source of worry for media literacy educators and advocates. There are massive cultural and political obstacles that have to be dealt with before we even get to the pedagogical ones. Media literacy must continue working to understand how political communicators communicate, especially how they communicate false information. It is also about the changing technological environment within which that information is communicated. Future work in media literacy is only going to be increasingly challenging. For example, it will need to address the rising problem of deepfakes, "highly realistic synthetic video or audio making it seem that real people said or did something they never said or did" (Chesney, Citron, & Jurecic, 2019, para. 3). This is just one of the more significant problems that new technologies will create for media literacy.

The main rationale behind this chapter is to demonstrate that political deception has a variety of faces and contexts; it takes on many forms and is a complicated concept. Even within each category there are subcategories. Each of the categories could likely be the subject of their own individual chapter. So, this chapter establishes a foundation for future research on how to think about and define various forms of political deception and how to think about each example on its own.

References

Altenhofen, B. (2010). Solace in symbols: Discovering cultural meanings in popular propaganda. *ETC: A Review of General Semantics, 67*(2), 156–163.

Bailey, F. G. (1991). *The prevalence of deceit.* Ithaca, NY: Cornell University Press.

Bok, S. (1999). *Lying: Moral choice in public and private life.* New York, NY: Vintage.

boyd, d. (2017, January 5). Did media literacy backfire? *Points.* Retrieved from https://points.datasociety.net/did-media-literacy-backfire-7418c084d88d

Breiner, A. (2016, December 10). Pizzagate, explained: Everything you want to know about the Comet Ping Pong pizzeria conspiracy theory but are too afraid to search for on Reddit. *Salon.* Retrieved from https://www.salon.com/2016/12/10/pizzagate-explained-everything-you-want-to-know-about-the-comet-ping-pong-pizzeria-conspiracy-theory-but-are-too-afraid-to-search-for-on-reddit/

Bruck, C. (2016, July 25). Why Obama has failed to close Guantanamo Bay. *The New Yorker.* Retrieved from https://www.newyorker.com/magazine/2016/08/01/why-obama-has-failed-to-close-guantanamo

Canes-Wrone, B. (2004). The public presidency, personal approval ratings, and policy making. *Presidential Studies Quarterly, 34*(3), 477–492.

Carson, T. (2012). *Lying and deception: Theory and practice.* Oxford: Oxford University Press.

Chesney, R., Citron, D, & Jurecic, Q. (2019, May 29). About that Pelosi Video: What to do about 'Cheapfakes' in 2020. *Lawfare.* Retrieved from https://www.lawfareblog.com/about-pelosi-video-what-do-about-cheapfakes-2020

Commission on Presidential Debates. (1992, October 19). October 19, 1992 debate transcript. CPD. Retrieved from http://www.debates.org/index.php?page=october-19-1992-debate-transcript

The Financial crisis and the role of federal regulators, Hearing before the Committee on Oversight and Government Reform, House of Representatives, 110th Cong. 11 (2008) (testimony of Alan Greenspan).

Frontline. (2009). Interview Frank Luntz. *PBS.* Retrieved from https://www.pbs.org/wgbh/pages/frontline/shows/persuaders/interviews/luntz.html

Goddard, T. (2019, May 24). It's going to get really bad. *Political Wire.* Retrieved from https://politicalwire.com/2019/05/24/its-going-to-get-really-bad/

Grandin, G. (2019). *The end of the myth: From the frontier to the border wall in the American mind.* New York, NY: Metropolitan Books.

Greenberg, D. (2016). *Republic of spin: An inside history of the American presidency.* New York, NY: W. W. Norton & Company.

Harwell, D. (2019, May 24). Faked Pelosi videos, slowed to make her appear drunk, spread across social media. *The Washington Post.* Retrieved from https://www.washingtonpost.com/technology/2019/05/23/faked-pelosi-videos-slowed-make-her-appear-drunk-spread-across-social-media/?utm_term=.fd41c209ce8c

Hill, T. (2016, April 21). Trust us: Politicians keep most of their promises. *FiveThirtyEight.* Retrieved from https://fivethirtyeight.com/features/trust-us-politicians-keep-most-of-their-promises/

Hofstadter, R. (1962). *Anti-intellectualism in American life.* New York, NY: Vintage Books.

Horn, E. (2012). Logics of political secrecy. *Theory, Culture, & Society, 28*(7–8), 103–122.

Horowitz, J. (2011, June 6). Rep. Weiner admits tweeting lewd photo of himself. *The Washington Post.* Retrieved from https://www.washingtonpost.com/lifestyle/style/rep-weiner-admits-tweeting-lewd-photo-of-himself/2011/06/06/AG7o1dKH_story.html

Hynd, D. (2007). The new spin: Effects of information control behaviours on source trustworthiness and persuasion (Unpublished thesis). Murdoch University, Perth, Australia.

Jacobs, L., & Shapiro, R. (2000). Politicians don't pander: Political manipulation and the loss of democratic responsiveness. Chicago: The University of Chicago Press.

Jay, M. (2010). *The virtues of mendacity: On lying in politics.* Charlottesville, VA: University of Virginia Press.

Karl, J. (2011, June 1). Rep. Anthony Weiner denies tweeting lewd photo, but won't comment on if it's him. ABC News. Retrieved from https://abcnews.go.com/Politics/rep-anthony-weiner-denies-tweeting-lewd-photo/story?id=13736214

Kovach, B., & Rosenstiel, T. (2014). *The elements of journalism.* New York, NY: Three Rivers Press.

Lakoff, G. (2006). *Thinking points: Communicating our American values and vision.* New York, NY: Farrar, Straus and Giroux.

Lippmann, W. (1997). *Public opinion.* New York, NY: Free Press.

Lipset, S. (1996). *American exceptionalism: A double-edged sword.* New York, NY: W. W. Norton & Company.

Lord, C. (2003). *The modern prince: What leaders need to know now.* New Haven, CT: Yale University Press.

Luntz, F. (2007). *Words that work: It's not what you say, it's what people hear.* New York, NY: Hyperion Books.

Lupia, A. (2016). *Uninformed: Why people know so little about politics and what we can do about it.* New York, NY: Oxford University Press.

Mahon, J. (2007). A definition of deceiving. *International Journal of Applied Philosophy, 21*(2), 181–194.

Manjoo, F. (2019, May 29). Worry about Facebook. Rip your hair out in screaming terror about Fox news. *The New York Times.* Retrieved from https://www.nytimes.com/2019/05/29/opinion/fox-news-facebook-pelosi.html

Moynihan, D. (1997). Secrecy: Report on the Commission on Protecting and Reducing Government Secrecy. Washington, DC.

Nixon, R. (1972, March 8). Statement on establishing a new system for classification and declassification of government documents relating to national security. *Public Papers of the Presidents of the United States: Richard M. Nixon, 1972.*

The November Company. (1992). Gray dot [television ad]. *The Museum of the Moving Image.* Retrieved from http://www.livingroomcandidate.org/commercials/1992/gray-dot

Partenie, C. (2009). Plato's myths. *Stanford Encyclopedia of Philosophy.* Retrieved from https://plato.stanford.edu/entries/plato-myths/

Phillips, B. (2012). Mitt Romney: "I like being able to fire people." *Mr. Media Training.* Retrieved from http://www.mrmediatraining.com/2012/01/09/mitt-romney-i-like-firing-people/

Pitt, B. (Producer), & McKay, A. (Director). (2018). *Vice.* [motion picture]. Los Angeles, CA: Plan B Entertainment.

Plato. (1987). *The Republic.* London: Penguin Classics.

Politifact. (2011, November 21). Mitt Romney ad charges Obama said, 'If we keep talking about the economy, we're going to lose'. *Tampa Bay Times.* Retrieved from http://www.politifact.com/truth-o-meter/statements/2011/nov/22/mitt-romney/mitt-romney-says-obama-said-if-we-keep-talking-abo/

Rasmussen. (2010). Voters believe overwhelmingly that politicians don't keep their promises, and most say it's deliberate. *Rasmussen Reports*. Retrieved from http://www.rasmussenreports.com/public_content/politics/general_politics/october_2010/voters_believe_overwhelmingly_that_politicians_don_t_keep_their_promises_and_most_say_it_s_deliberate

Roth, Z. (2016, February 23). Obama's lofty rhetoric on closing Gitmo has remained just that. MSNBC. Retrieved from http://www.msnbc.com/msnbc/obamas-lofty-rhetoric-closing-gitmo-has-remained-just

Shear, M. (2011, November 22). Democrats cry foul over new Romney ad. *New York Times*. Retrieved from http://www.nytimes.com/2011/11/23/us/politics/romney-ad-slams-obama-on-economy.html

Shils, E. (1956). *The torment of secrecy*. Chicago: The Free Press.

Sulkin, T. (2009). Promises made and promises kept. In L. Dodd & B. Oppenheimer (Eds.), *Congress reconsidered* (pp. 119–140). Washington, DC: CQ Press.

Tumulty, K., & Sonmez, F. (2011, June 1). Anthony Weiner's plan to cool Twitter photo furor backfires. *The Washington Post*. Retrieved from https://www.washingtonpost.com/politics/weiner-says-he-doesnt-know-with-certitude-whether-lewd-twitter-photo-is-of-him/2011/06/01/AGQcCkGH_story.html?utm_term=.bd8ec3f1ace3

Tye, L. (2002). *The father of spin: Edward Bernays and the birth of public relations*. New York, NY: Picador.

Weiner, A. [Anthony Weiner]. (2011, May 28). Touche Prof Moriarity. More Weiner jokes for all my guests! #Hacked! [tweet]. Retrieved from https://twitter.com/repweiner/status/74582925932376065

Williams, R. (1978). *Marxism and literature*. Oxford: Oxford University Press.

Part Three

Media Literacy and Education

10 Media Literacy and Professional Education

Oil and Water?

William G. Christ

Introduction

For those United States' scholars and teachers who are passionate about media literacy and higher education, an argument could be made that the last 15–20 years has been an especially vibrant and productive time. For example, to the list of journals like the National Telemedia Council's *Journal of Media Literacy* and the Association for Education in Journalism and Mass Communication's (AEJMC) *Journalism and Mass Communication Educator* have been added two more journals: the *Journal of Media Education*, which is an electronic, interactive reconceptualization of the Broadcast Education Association's (BEA) *Feedback* and was first published in 2010; and, the *Journal of Media Literacy Education*, which is the official journal of the National Association of Media Literacy Education (NAMLE), starting publication in 2009. (For more journals that relate to media literacy, see NAMLE's website: https://namle.net/grad-student/journals/.) Relatively recent publications include media literacy books and textbooks, articles discussing the definition, scope, measurement, and/or assessment of media literacy, and studies investigating how media literacy was being taught in higher education, including in journalism and mass communication classes and programs (for examples, see Table 10.1).

With all this scholarly activity, the question remains, "Does any of this media literacy scholarship have anything to do with what goes on in higher education professional media programs?" Or, said more broadly, "Does media literacy and professional media education overlap, or are they like oil and water?" One of the ways to answer this question is to first define media literacy and professional education and then analyze the student-learning outcomes of both.

Definitions

Media Literacy

Media literacy has been defined differently by different scholars, associations, citizen action groups, and government entities with the identification

Table 10.1 Examples of Recent U.S. Media Literacy Publications

Media Literacy Books and Textbooks	Articles Discussing the Definition, Scope, Measurement, and/or Assessment of Media Literacy	Studies Investigating How Media Literacy Was Being Taught in Higher Education, Including Journalism and Mass Communication Classes and Programs
De Abrea & Mihailidis, 2014	Anderson, 2008	Bordac, 2010
Cubbage, 2018	Bulger, & Davison, 2018	Butler, Fuentes-Bautista, & Scharrer, 2018 Byrd, 2018
Di Blas, Paolini, Rubegni, & Sabiescu, 2010	Arke & Primack, 2009	Casey & Brayton, 2018
	Burson, 2010	Christ & Potter, 1998
	Center for Media Literacy, n.d.	Clark, 2013
	Christ, 1997, 2004, 2006, 2014	Considine, 2004
	Christ & Blanchard, 1994	Considine & Considine, 2014
Hoechsmann & Poyntz, 2012	Christ & Henderson, 2014	Cubbage, 2016, 2018
	Christ & Hynes, 2006	Erp, 2012
Kellner & Share, 2019	Christ, McCall, Rakow, & Blanchard, 2006	Fry, 2018
	Cortoni, LoPresti, & Cervelli, 2015	Galacian, 2004
Macedo & Steinberg, 2007	Gutierrez & Tyner, 2012	Gutierrez & Tyner, 2012
	Hallaq, 2016	Jacobs, 2012
Moses, 2008	Henderson & Christ, 2014	Meehan, Brandi, Wells, Walker, & Schwarz, 2015
	Hobbs, 2010, 2011	Mihailidis, 2006, 2008, 2009a, 2009b
Potter, 2004, 2016a, 2016b	Hobbs & Frost, 2003	Mihailidis & Hiebert, 2005
	Hobbs & Jensen, 2009	Nam, 2010
Silverblatt, 2014	Jenkins, Clinton, Purushotma, Robison, & Weigel, 2006	Ramsey, 2017
	Kellner & Share, 2005, 2007	St. Onge, 2018
Silverblatt, Miller, Smith, & Brown, 2014	Jolls, Walkosz, & Morgenthaler, 2014	Schmidt, 2012a, 2012b, 2013a, 2013b, 2015
	Literat, 2014	Silverblatt, Baker, Tyner & Stuhlman, 2002;
	Martens, 2010	Stuhlman & Silverblatt, 2007
Tyner, 2010	Michael, 2014	Tisdell, 2008
White, 2016	Mihailidis, 2008	Woo, 2010
	Ostenson, 2012	
	Potter, 2010, 2011	
	RobbGrieco, 2014	
	Scharrer, 2003	
	Schilder, Lockee, & Saxon, 2016	
	Simons, Meeus, & T'Sas, 2017	
	UNESCO, 2013	
	Vraga, Tully, Kotcher, Smithson, Broeckelman-Post, 2015	
	Wenner, 2016	

of different skills, knowledge, behavioral, and attitudinal/affective elements (cf. Jenkins, Clinton, Purushotma, Robison, & Weigel, 2006; Potter, 2013; Wenner, 2016). Even the Aspen Institute's *Report of the National Leadership Conference on Media Literacy* (Aufderheide's 1993), a report used by many in the United States as a foundation for defining media literacy, indicates the complexity of trying to define the term. The *Foreword* of the report states:

> The groups' representatives settled on a basic definition of media literacy: **it is the ability of a citizen to access, analyze, and produce information for specific outcomes** [*sic*]. This definition could be expressed in many different ways. To some, analyzing was better expressed as decoding or evaluating, and producing was better explained as encoding or providing alternative expression. Information, too, had several meanings, from bare symbols to a continuum of media that extends from print to video, to the new digital world of computerized multi-media.
>
> (Firestone, 1993, p. v)

> More controversial was the extent to which "outcomes" should be a part of the definition of media literacy. Is media literacy important only to the extent that it enables one to be a better citizen in society? What is the role of ideology in the process? To what extent is an individual "media literate" if she just appreciates the aesthetics of a message without going further with it? Finally, by using the word "outcomes" we do not mean to confuse the reader between the common definition-viz., results or effects-and the specialized educational definition of "outcome assessment" …which refers to a specific kind of evaluation.
>
> (Firestone, 1993, p. vi)

A more recent definition is provided by the National Association of Media Literacy Education (NAMLE). Its basic definition adds the important words "evaluate, create, and act" and eliminates the word "produce." While making the wise political choice to link media literacy to traditional critical forms of literacy like reading and writing, NAMLE's definition reminds us that the job of media literacy is to empower people:

> Media literacy is the ability to ACCESS, ANALYZE, EVALUATE, CREATE, and ACT [*sic*] using all forms of communication. In its simplest terms, media literacy builds upon the foundation of traditional literacy and offers new forms of reading and writing. Media literacy empowers people to be critical thinkers and makers, effective communicators and active citizens.
>
> (NAMLE, n.d.)

Of course, the early definitions were created before the widespread development and use of the Internet and the rise of participatory culture. Jenkins et al. (2006) argue that the rise of a participatory culture requires a new set of knowledge and skills. Though Jenkins et al.'s argument is persuasive, it doesn't preclude the utility and fundamental nature of the NAMLE definition, which will be used in this chapter to define media literacy.

Professional Education

Professional education can be defined as:
a formalized approach to specialized training.... such an education also helps the participant acquire the competencies needed for proper practice and behavior. Some common goals of professional education include incorporating the knowledge and values basic to a professional discipline; understanding the central concepts, principles, and techniques applied in practice; attaining a level of competence necessary for responsible entry into professional practice; and accepting responsibility for the continued development of competence.

("Professional Education," 2007)

Though the Accrediting Council on Education in Journalism and Mass Communications (ACEJMC), the organization responsible for accrediting Journalism and Mass Communications (JMC) programs or educational units, does not define professional education per se; the council is clear about the mission of journalism and mass communication education:

Professional programs should prepare students with a body of knowledge and a system of inquiry, scholarship and training for careers in which they are accountable to: the public interest for their knowledge, ethics, competence and service; citizens, clients or consumers for their competencies and the quality of their work; and employers for their performance.

(ACEJMC, n.d.)

The media literacy and professional education definitions seem very different. Whereas media literacy emphasizes educating students to become informed, engaged, and empowered citizens, professional media education is geared toward preparing students for a career and seeing themselves as responsible, ethical, and competent practitioners. That being said, a question remains about outcomes and if or how the student-learning outcomes of each might overlap.

Student-Learning Outcomes

Media Literacy

Laying out all possible media literacy outcomes would not be helpful because the list would be too long. A more fruitful approach would be to narrow the scope of outcomes by starting with key constructs or concepts that drive media literacy education. We could use Masterman's (1989) 18 Basic Principles of media awareness education, where he argues, among other things, that media education is a serious and significant endeavor and that the central unifying concept of media education is that of representation. We could use the Duncan and the Association of Media Literacy's (AML) Eight Core Concepts that move from media literacy education to specific beliefs about media itself (cf. Jolls & Wilson, 2014). Or, when dealing with issues of representation, we could cite Thoman's (1993) Five Concepts. In this chapter, three related perspectives will be used to conceptualize media literacy student-learning outcomes.

First, the media literacy definition itself can be used to broadly think about and articulate outcomes: "Media literacy is the ability to ACCESS, ANALYZE, EVALUATE, CREATE, and ACT using all forms of communication" (NAMLE, n.d.). The definition suggests that central to media literacy are levels of thinking (analyze and evaluate communication) and acting (ability to access information/media; the ability to create different types of communication; and, the ability to act on what is learned). These levels of thinking and acting could be easily restated as student-learning outcomes. For example, a student-learning outcome might state: to be media literate, a student should demonstrate an ability to access different forms of communication, etc.

Second, since many media literacy core concepts are similar, this chapter will use the "shared beliefs" articulated in the Aspen Institute's *Report of the National Leadership Conference on Media Literacy* (Aufderheide, 1993). The report was based on a 1992 meeting of 30 top leaders in the field of media literacy. By articulating beliefs about the media, the report indirectly articulates student-learning outcomes: "understanding how reality is constructed through media means understanding three interacting elements: the *production process* (including technological, economic, bureaucratic and legal constraints), the *text*, and the *audience/receiver/end-user*" (Aufderheide, 1993, p. 2). [Of course, in the world of social media, there are "audiences" that are producing content for others with the lines between producer and receiver being blurred (cf. Delwiche & Henderson, 2013; Jenkins et al., 2006).] "In a slightly different formulation of the same understanding, they [people who are media literate] understand some basic precepts in common:

- Media are constructed, and construct reality.
- Media have commercial implications.
- Media have ideological and political implications.
- Form and content are related in each medium, each of which has a unique aesthetic, codes and conventions.
- Receivers negotiate meaning in media (Aufderheide, 1993, p. 2).

Stated as media literacy student-learning outcomes, we could write, for example, that to be considered media literate, a student must demonstrate an understanding about how media are constructed, and construct reality.

Finally, when looking at media texts, the Jolls and Wilson's (2014, p. 75) elaboration on the Center for Media Literacy's "Five Core Concepts and Key Questions" is useful in this discussion because it considers both consumers (this author would add citizens to consumers: consumer/citizens) *and* producers. For example, Jolls and Wilson suggest that in deconstructing *or* constructing a message, we need to determine authorship, format, audience, content, and purpose. In terms of authorship, a consumer would ask, "Who created the message?" A producer would ask, "What am I authoring?" In terms of format, a consumer might ask, "What creative techniques are used to attract my attention?" while a producer would ask, "Does my message reflect understanding of format, creativity and technology?" When analyzing an audience, a consumer asks, "How might different people understand this message differently?" A producer asks, "Is my message engaging and compelling for my target audience?" For content, a consumer asks, "What values, lifestyles and points of view are represented in or omitted from this message?" Producers should ask, "Have I clearly and consistently framed values, lifestyles and points of view in my content?" And, finally, for the purpose of a communication, a consumer might ask, "Why is this message being sent?" while a producer asks, "Have I communicated my purpose effectively?" (Jolls & Wilson, 2014, p. 75).

To turn the above statements into student-learning outcomes, we could write, for example, that to be media literate, a student must be able to deconstruct and construct messages based on their authorship, format, audience, content, and purpose. Again, the strength of the Center for Media Literacy's approach is that it considers both consumers and producers and therefore can be a helpful link between media literacy (emphasis on educating citizens and consumers) and professional media education (emphasis on educating producers).

Professional Media Education

In the United States, as stated earlier, the ACEJMC is the agency responsible for the evaluation of *professional* JMC programs in colleges and universities. Though there are regional and junior-college groups that accredit schools, colleges, and universities [e.g., Accrediting Commission for Community and Junior Colleges (ACCJC), Western Association of Schools and Colleges (WASC), Middle States Commission on Higher Education (MSCHE), and the Southern Association of Colleges and Schools Commission on Colleges (SACSCOC)], there are no other government-sanctioned accrediting bodies of professional Journalism and Mass Communications programs in the United States. There are groups like the Public Relations Society of America that accredits individual members (see: https://www.prsa.org/accreditation-in-public-relations-apr/), but no other group accredits programs or "units." For the Council for Higher Education Accreditation (CHEA), the group that monitors and accredits accreditation associations, the ACEJMC is the only professional accrediting body in communication, media, telecommunications, broadcasting and cablecasting, etc.

The ACEJMC (n.d.) proposes that "Irrespective of their particular specialization, all graduates should be aware of certain core values and competencies and be able to:

- understand and apply the principles and laws of freedom of speech and press for the country in which the institution that invites ACE-JMC is located, as well as receive instruction in and understand the range of systems of freedom of expression around the world, including the right to dissent, to monitor and criticize power, and to assemble and petition for redress of grievances;
- demonstrate an understanding of the history and role of professionals and institutions in shaping communications;
- demonstrate an understanding of gender, race, ethnicity, sexual orientation and, as appropriate, other forms of diversity in domestic society in relation to mass communications;
- demonstrate an understanding of the diversity of peoples and cultures and of the significance and impact of mass communications in a global society;
- understand concepts and apply theories in the use and presentation of images and information;
- demonstrate an understanding of professional ethical principles and work ethically in pursuit of truth, accuracy, fairness and diversity;
- think critically, creatively and independently;
- conduct research and evaluate information by methods appropriate to the communications professions in which they work;
- write correctly and clearly in forms and styles appropriate for the communications professions, audiences and purposes they serve;
- critically evaluate their own work and that of others for accuracy and fairness, clarity, appropriate style and grammatical correctness;
- apply basic numerical and statistical concepts;
- apply current tools and technologies appropriate for the communications professions in which they work, and to understand the digital world."

The student-learning outcomes for professional media programs are expected to be linked to these 12 professional values and competencies.

Other media values and competencies can be added, but these are the 12 required by the ACEJMC.

Media Literacy and Professional Education Outcomes

Journalism and Mass Communication (JMC) faculty might argue that they already teach media literacy. However, if the study by Schmidt (2015) is accurate, "Data indicate that many journalism students are developing only limited media literacy competencies" (p. 43). To see how much, if any, overlap there was between outcomes, media literacy "outcomes" (the definition, shared beliefs, and areas of analysis) were mapped against ACEJMC "outcomes" (professional values and competencies).

Outcomes/Curricular Map

Table 10.2 consists of three columns. The first column shows the 12 ACEJMC professional programmatic values and competencies (shortened to "competencies" for the rest of the chapter) and clusters them under (1) knowledge, (2) skills, and (3) knowledge/skills sections (these sections were created by the author and do not appear in the original list). Within each section each competence was labelled (again, by the author). For example, under the knowledge section, the first heading is called "History" because students are supposed to "demonstrate an understanding of *the history* and role of professionals and institutions in shaping communications" (emphasis added). The cluster could just as easily have been identified as the "Professional role" cluster. As a side note, though Christ and Henderson (2014) argue that most of the professional competencies contain multiple parts that increase their complexity, in this chapter, each competence will be presented as it is in the ACEJMC accreditation standards.

The second column in Table 10.2 contains the parts of the media literacy definition, shared beliefs, and/or textual analysis parts that apply to the ACEJMC competence. For example, for the "history" competence that emphasizes the importance of "understanding the history and role of professionals and institutions shaping communications," it can be argued that there would be overlap with the media literacy beliefs that students should "understand the *production process* (including technological, economic, bureaucratic, and legal constraints), and that "media have commercial, ideological and political implications." A closer look at this example suggests that the media literacy "outcomes" help elaborate or explicate the ACEJMC competence. That is, to understand history and the role of professionals and institutions in shaping communications, it would help to understand the production process as discussed in the media literacy literature. Of course, the overlap between the ACEJMC competences and the media literacy areas may not be 100% because the second column may cover more or less than what is in the professional competency. However, an overlap does exist.

Finally, the third column contains possible classes where the overlap between columns one and two might be taught and learned. Column three is not meant to be comprehensive of all possible classes; rather, it provides relevant, salient examples.

Table 10.2 Accrediting Council on Education in Journalism and Mass Communications (ACEJMC) Professional Values and Outcomes, Media Literacy Concepts/Skills/Objectives, and Possible Classes that Capture Both

ACEJMC Professional Values and Competencies	Media Literacy Concepts/ Skills/Objectives	Classes
Knowledge (Understanding)		
History[a]		
• Demonstrate an understanding of the history and role of professionals and institutions in shaping communications	• Understanding the *production process* (including technological, economic, bureaucratic, and legal constraints) • Media have commercial implications • Media have ideological and political implications	Introduction to Media Film History Media History
Diversity		
• Demonstrate an understanding of gender, race, ethnicity, sexual orientation, and, as appropriate, other forms of diversity in domestic society in relation to mass communications • Demonstrate an understanding of the diversity of peoples and cultures and of the significance and impact of mass communications in a global society	• Understanding the *text* • Understanding the *audience/receiver/ end-user* • Media are constructed, and construct reality • Media have commercial implications • Media have ideological and political implications	Introduction to Media Media Texts Media Audience Media and Diversity
Skill (Application)[b]		
Thinking		
• Think critically, creatively, and independently	• Media literacy is the ability to **ACCESS, ANALYZE, EVALUATE, CREATE,** and **ACT** using all forms of communication	All classes including Production classes Independent projects Capstone class

(Continued)

ACEJMC Professional Values and Competencies	Media Literacy Concepts/ Skills/Objectives	Classes
Research • Conduct research and evaluate information by methods appropriate to the communications professions in which they work	• Media literacy is the ability to **ACCESS, ANALYZE, EVALUATE, CREATE,** and **ACT** using all forms of communication • authorship, format, audience, content, and purpose	All classes Capstone class
Writing/Editing • Write correctly and clearly in forms and styles appropriate for the communications professions, audiences, and purposes they serve • Critically evaluate their own work and that of others for accuracy and fairness, clarity, appropriate style, and grammatical correctness	• Understanding the *text* and the *audience/ receiver/end-user* • Media are constructed, and construct reality • Form and content are related in each medium, each of which has a unique aesthetic, codes, and conventions • Receivers negotiate meaning in media • Media literacy is the ability to **ACCESS, ANALYZE, EVALUATE, CREATE,** and **ACT** using all forms of communication • Authorship, format, audience, content, and purpose	All classes including Reporting, Editing, Newspaper, Magazine Writing, Blogging, Scriptwriting classes Capstone class
Mathematics • Apply basic numerical and statistical concepts	• Media have commercial implications • Media literacy is the ability to **ACCESS, ANALYZE, EVALUATE, CREATE,** and **ACT** using all forms of communication	Introduction to Media Quantitative Methods Media Texts (content analysis) Media Audience class (ratings; readership) Production (budget)

ACEJMC Professional Values and Competencies	Media Literacy Concepts/ Skills/Objectives	Classes

Knowledge and Skills (Understanding and Application)

"First Amendment"

• Understand and apply the principles and laws of freedom of speech and press for the country in which the institution that invites ACEJMC is located, as well as receive instruction in and understand the range of systems of freedom of expression around the world, including the right to dissent, to monitor, and criticize power, and to assemble and petition for redress of grievances	• Understanding the *production process* (including technological, economic, bureaucratic, and legal constraints) • Media have commercial implications • Media have ideological and political implications	Introduction to Media Law and Regulation class

Visual Communication

• Understand concepts and apply theories in the use and presentation of images and information	• Understanding the *text* • Understanding the *audience/receiver/ end-user* • Media are constructed, and construct reality • Form and content are related in each medium, each of which has a unique aesthetic, codes, and conventions. • Receivers negotiate meaning in media. • Media literacy is the ability to ACCESS, ANALYZE, EVALUATE, CREATE, and ACT using all forms of communication. • Authorship, format, audience, content, and purpose	All classes Media Texts class Production classes

(Continued)

ACEJMC Professional Values and Competencies	Media Literacy Concepts/ Skills/Objectives	Classes
Ethics		
• Demonstrate an understanding of professional ethical principles and work ethically in pursuit of truth, accuracy, fairness and diversity	• Media are constructed, and construct reality • Media have commercial implications. • Media have ideological and political implications. • Form and content are related in each medium, each of which has a unique aesthetic, codes, and conventions. • Media literacy is the ability to **ACCESS, ANALYZE, EVALUATE, CREATE,** and **ACT** using all forms of communication.	Ethics class Writing classes Production Internships Workshops Laboratories
Digital World		
• Apply current tools and technologies appropriate for the communications professions in which they work, and to understand the digital world.	• All the above including play, simulation, appropriation, multitasking, distributed cognition, collective intelligence, judgment, transmedia navigation, networking, and negotiation. See Jenkins, Clinton, Purushotma, Robison, & Weigel, 2006, p. 4).	All the above

http://www2.ku.edu/~acejmc/PROGRAM/STANDARDS.SHTML. Retrieved November 15, 2018.
a   The titles for each competency are not part of the original document.
b   The judgement of whether a standard stresses knowledge, skills, or knowledge and skills is debatable.

Patterns?

An analysis of Table 10.2 indicates two major findings. The first is that media literacy concepts overlap with all the ACEJMC competencies and therefore could inform the total professional media education curriculum. The second finding is that three classes seem to capture many of the media literacy perspectives and the ACEJMC competencies. An Introduction to Media course appears to overlap with 10 of the 12 ACEJMC competencies at least at the level of "awareness." Awareness along with "understanding" and "application" are the three criteria the ACEJMC indicates should be used to "guide the assessment of student learning" (ACEJMC, n.d.). A course on Media Texts and a course on Media Audiences would each cover seven of the competencies.

A New Curriculum?

There are four parts to many higher education media curricula: a core, a scope of study or sequence of classes, a capstone class or internship, and experiential-learning experiences (e.g., internships, workshops, labs) (cf. Blanchard & Christ, 1985, 1993). The rest of this chapter will concentrate on core classes and experiential-learning (i.e., production) experiences and how a powerful, new media education curriculum would start with an intellectually robust core.

Core

In terms of developing a core, there are pedagogical, political, and financial factors to consider. Pedagogically, programs can use the core to give students a critical overview of the field. Here is where the past can be learned, the status quo can be challenged, and the future imagined. Here is where students can discuss their own experiences with media, including those literacies articulated by Jenkins et al. (2006) such as play, simulation, appropriation, multitasking, curating, etc. Here is where students get to see the "invisible" power relationships that form media systems and impact their own behaviors and attitudes. Politically, as part of a university's general education, core classes can be positioned as making intellectual contributions to the university. It is important that programs are perceived as active participants in universities. Being part of a university's general education is one way of saying our programs belong. Third, simply stated, cores that are linked to the major and general education can bring resources into and help financially stabilize a program. So, what should be in the core?

An analysis of Table 10.2 suggests that a nucleus of classes dealing with an Introduction to Media, Media Texts, and Media Audiences would make an excellent core because these three areas overlap with both media literacy outcomes and many of the ACEJMC competencies like history, diversity, critical thinking, visual communication, math, research, writing and editing, digital technologies, and freedom of the press. Interestingly, Introduction to Media, Media Texts, and Media Audiences classes could cover the three interrelated areas mentioned in the Aspen Institute's *Report of the National Leadership Conference on Media Literacy*: "the *production process* (including technological, economic, bureaucratic and legal constraints), the *text*, and the *audience/receiver/end-user*" (Aufderheide, 1993, p. 2).

Importantly, a media literacy core doesn't preclude creating or producing for clients; rather, it informs and empowers producers.

Experiential-Learning (Production)

The "doing" of media is important in many media literacy and professional media programs and appears in both the media literacy and ACE-JMC "outcomes." It is possible to add a production component within the three classes mentioned and/or offer media centers where all students can volunteer and learn to manage, create, and act. For example, within an Introduction to Media class, students can write blogs about their experiences with the media. In media texts class, students can create video mashups or develop advertising campaigns geared toward student concerns. In a Media Audience class, students can work on developing research questions for a class survey or in-depth interviews. If media laboratories are available (radio, newspaper, television centers), all students in the university should have the opportunity to work in them as part of an extracurricular activity.

Pedagogy

What Do We Study?

Saying a department should have an Introduction to Media class as a core class is not new. Having a Media Text or Media Audience class as part of the core is not as usual. The subject matter or emphasis within each of the proposed core classes would vary depending on the philosophy of the department, expertise of the faculty, the textbook selected, etc. (cf. RobbGrieco, 2014). The case being made here is that what is being identified as a media literacy approach would be best for both general students and future practitioners. For example: an Introduction to Media class that addresses the political economy and production of our media institutions would not only be appropriate for a media literacy core but for a professional core as well because it would provide a rich and deep context for understanding changes or lack of changes within the various media industries.

Table 10.3 suggests several questions that might be raised in the core classes from both a media literacy and a professional media education perspective. In all cases, an argument could be made that a media literacy orientation gives a deeper, richer understanding that would benefit both practitioners and general students.

Table 10.3 Questions about Different Emphases in Core Classes

---

I Introduction to Media: Media industries? Which ones (CBS, Facebook, Google)?

ML: Political economy and production? Who has power? How are media structured?

PE: Industry Overview? What are the current job structures and opportunities?

II Media texts: Which texts? Who and how are people represented? Valued communicated?
Authorship, format, audience, content, and purpose of communication?

ML: How are media used to inform, educate, and persuade us? Aesthetic, Feminist, Semiotic, Critical Theories.

PE: How we can use media to inform, educate, and persuade others? Aesthetic Theory?

III Media audiences: How are people who use media talked about by scholars and in the profession? How are they situated? How are media used by people? What are the media effects/impacts on people?

ML:How am I positioned as a consumer, citizen or producer? Effects; marketing; users; producers research.

PE: How can I position people as consumers, citizens or producers? Marketing and ratings.

IV Media production: What stories are or should be told? Through which media?

ML: How can I tell my own story? How can I use technology to communicate? Empowerment of people, groups, and communities.

PE: How can I execute what my clients/public need? How can I use technology to communicate? Public interest, ethics, competence and service.

How Is the Course Taught?

Of course, how classes are taught might be considered as important as the course itself. Pedagogical approaches to media literacy and professional education matter (cf. Buckingham, 2003; Hobbs, 2001; Kellner & Share, 2005; Masterman, 1985; Sholle & Denski,1994) with the National Association for Media Literacy Education (NAMLE) suggesting that over the last 25 years the move from what is taught to how it is taught is paramount: "MLE recognizes that HOW we teach matters as much as WHAT we teach. Classrooms should be places where student input is respected, valued and acted upon" (NAMLE, 2007, Core principle 4.8). The 1993 Aspen Institute's *Report of the National Leadership Conference on Media Literacy* argued that:

Media literacy educators in principle agree on a pedagogical approach. No matter what the setting or project, but particularly for formal learning, media educators insist that the process of learning embody the concepts being taught. Thus, media literacy learning is **hands-on and experiential, democratic** (the teacher is researcher and facilitator), and **process-driven**. Stressing as it does critical thinking, it is inquiry-based. Touching as it does on the welter of issues and experiences of daily life, it is interdisciplinary and cross-curricular.

(Aufderheide, 1993, p. 2)

This author agrees with those who call for an open, student-centered, experiential classroom.

Conclusion

An analysis that compared media literacy and professional media education student-learning outcomes revealed that media literacy education and professional media education are not like oil and water, but rather they can inform each other. Not only is media literacy and the ACE-JMC professional values and competencies overlapping and potentially symbiotic and not only can media literacy be an appropriate "added-value" to JMC education as has been persuasively argued by others (cf. Mihailidis & Hiebert, 2005) but, because the core classes suggested here can help *all* students become media literate, these classes should become the *foundation* of all media literacy and JMC programs.

In other words, a "media literacy core" that addresses the media production process, media texts, and media audiences while utilizing experiential-learning opportunities, and that challenges the status quo, provides a context that requires self-reflection and empowers students to think of themselves not only as practitioners but also as active citizens should be fundamental to all media literacy *and* professional media education programs.

References

Accrediting Council on Education in Journalism and Mass Communications (ACEJMC). (n.d.). Retrieved May 12, 2019 from http://www.acejmc.org/policies-process/principles/

Aufderheide, P. (1993). *Media literacy: A report of the national leadership conference on media literacy.* Washington, DC: The Aspen Institute.

Anderson, J. A. (2008). Media literacy, the first 100 years: A cultural analysis. In J. K. Asamen, M. L. Ellis, & G. L. Berry (Eds.) *Sage handbook of child development, multiculturalism, and media* (pp. 381–409). Thousand Oaks, CA: Sage.

Arke, E. T., & Primack, B. A. (2009). Quantifying media literacy: Development, reliability, and validity of a new measure. *Educational Media International, 46*(1), 53–65, doi:10.1080/09523980902780958

Blanchard, R. O., & Christ, W. G. (1985). In search of the unit core: Commonalties in curricula. *Journalism Educator, 40*(3), 28–33.

Blanchard, R. O., & Christ, W. G. (1993). *Media education and the liberal arts: A blueprint for the new professionalism.* Hillsdale, NJ: Lawrence Erlbaum Associates.

Bordac, S. (2010). Identifying undergraduate media literacy skills: An exploratory study of faculty perceptions. *Proceedings of the American Society for Information Science and Technology, 46*(1): 1–16.

Buckingham, D. (2003). *Media education: Literacy, learning, and contemporary culture.* Cambridge, UK: Polity Press.

Bulger, M., & Davison, P. (2018). The promises, challenges and futures of media literacy. *Journal of Media Literacy Education, 19*(1), 1–21.

Burson, J. K. (2010). Measuring media literacy among collegiate journalism students (Unpublished master's thesis). Oklahoma State University, Stillwater, Oklahoma. Retrieved from https://shareok.org/bitstream/handle/11244/9703/Burson_okstate_0664M_11022.pdf?sequence=1

Butler, A., Fuentes-Bautista, M., & Scharrer, E. (2018). Building media literacy in higher education: Department approaches, undergraduate certificate, and engaged scholarship. In J. Cubbage (Ed.), *Handbook of research on media literacy in higher education environments* (pp. 153–171). Hershey, PA: Information Science Reference, an imprint of IGI Global.

Byrd, L. S. (2018). Disrupting the media literacy learning process: Building a community media lab to transform digital journalism education. In J. Cubbage (Ed.), *Handbook of research on media literacy in higher education environments* (pp. 270–285). Hershey, PA: Information Science Reference, an imprint of IGI Global.

Casey, N., & Brayton, S. (2018). Media information and literacy in a higher education environment: An overview and case study. In J. Cubbage (Ed.), *Handbook of research on media literacy in higher education environments* (pp. 60–76). Hershey, PA: Information Science Reference, an imprint of IGI Global.

Center for Media Literacy. (n.d.). Assessment. Retrieved May 19, 2019 from www.medialit.org/assessment

Christ, W. G. (1997). Defining media education. In W. G. Christ (Ed.), *Media education assessment handbook* (pp. 3–21). Mahwah, NJ: Lawrence Erlbaum Associates; Annandale, VA: Speech Communication Association.

Christ, W. G. (2004). Assessment, media literacy standards, and higher education. *American Behavioral Scientist, 48*(1), 92–96.

Christ, W. G. (Ed.). (2006). *Assessing media education: A resource for educators and administrators.* Mahwah, NJ: Lawrence Erlbaum Associates.

Christ, W. G. (2014). So what is a model rubric? *Journal of Media Education, 5*(3), 5–8.

Christ, W. G., & Blanchard, R. O. (1994). Mission statements, outcomes, and the new liberal arts. In W. G. Christ (Ed.), *Assessing communication education: A handbook for media, speech, and theatre educators* (pp. 31–55). Hillsdale, NJ: Lawrence Erlbaum Associates.

Christ, W. G., & Henderson, J. J. (2014). Assessing ACEJMC professional values and competencies. *Journalism and Mass Communication Educator, 69*(3), 301–313.

Christ, W. G., & Hynes, T. (2006). Mission statements. In W. G. Christ, (Ed.), *Assessing media education: A resource for educators and administrators* (pp. 31–50), Mahwah, NJ: Lawrence Erlbaum Associates, Inc.

Christ, W. G., McCall, J., Rakow, L., & Blanchard, R. O. (1997). Assessing media education in an integrated communications program. In W. G. Christ (Ed.), *Media education assessment handbook* (pp. 23–56). Mahwah, NJ: Lawrence Erlbaum Associates; Annandale, VA: Speech Communication Association.

Christ, W. G., & Potter, W. J. (1998). Media literacy, media education, and the academy, *Journal of Communication, 48*(1), 5–15.

Clark, L. S. (2013). Cultivating the media activist: How critical media literacy and critical service learning can reform journalism education. *Journalism, 14*(7), 885–903.

Considine, D. M. (2004). "If you build it, they will come": Developing a graduate program in media literacy in a college of education. *American Behavioral Scientist, 48*(1), 97–107.

Considine, D. M., & Considine, M. M. (2014). Media literacy preparation in undergraduate teacher training: An American and Australian perspective. In B. S. De Abreu & P. Mihailidis (Eds.) *Media literacy education in action: Theoretical and pedagogical perspectives* (pp. 203–212). New York, NY: Routledge.

Cortoni, I., LoPresti, V., & Cervelli, P. (2015). Digital competence assessment: A proposal for operationalizing the critical dimension. *Journal of Media Literacy Education, 7*(1), 46–57.

Cubbage, J. (2016). Establishing a media literacy cognate at historically Black colleges and universities: A comparative analysis of existing courses and potential of implementation. In C. B. W. Prince, & R. Ford, (Eds.), *Administrative challenges and organizational leadership in HBCUs* (pp. 213–236). Hershey, PA: Information Science Reference, an imprint of IGI Global.

Cubbage, J. (Ed.). (2018). *Handbook of research on media literacy in higher education environments*. Hershey, PA: Information Science Reference, an imprint of IGI Global.

De Abreu, B. S., & Mihailidis, P. (Eds.) (2014). *Media literacy education in action (theoretical and pedagogical perspectives* (1st ed.). New York, NY: Routledge.

Delwiche, A., & Henderson, J. J. (2013). *The participatory cultures handbook.* New York, NY: Taylor & Francis Group.

Di Blas, N., Paolini, P., Rubegni, E., & Sabiescu, A. (2010). *Equipping higher education students with media literacy skills*. Published in the IEEE International Professional Communication Conference July 7–9, 2010. Retrieved from https://ieeexplore.ieee.org/xpl/mostRecentIssue.jsp?punumber=5510863

Erp, A. J. (2012). *Creating a foundation for media literacy education: A content analysis of higher education media literacy syllabi* (Unpublished master's thesis). Baylor University, Waco, TX.

Firestone, C. M. (1993). *Forward*. In P. Aufderheide, *Media literacy. A report of the national leadership conference on media literacy* (pp. v–vii). Washington, DC: The Aspen Institute.

Fry, K. G. (2018). Preparing to be digital: The paradigm shift for media studies and higher education. In J. Cubbage (Ed.), *Handbook of research on media literacy in higher education environments* (pp. 78–89). Hershey, PA: Information Science Reference, an imprint of IGI Global.

Galacian, M. (2004). Introduction: High time for "dis-illusioning" ourselves and our media: Media literacy in the 21st century, Part I: Strategies for schools (K-12 and higher education). *American Behavioral Scientist, 48*(1), 7–17.

Gutierrez, A., & Tyner, K. (2012). Media education, media literacy, and digital competence. *Scientific Journal of Media Education, 19*(38), 31–39.

Hallaq, T. (2016). Evaluating online media literacy in higher education: Validity and reliability of the digital online media literacy assessment (DOMLA). *Journal of Media Literacy Education, 8*(1), 62–84.

Henderson, J. J., & Christ, W. G. (2014). Benchmarking ACEJMC professional values and competencies. What does it mean for assessment? *Journalism and Mass Communication Educator, 69*(3), 229–242.

Hobbs, R. (2001). The great media literacy debates in 2001. *Community Media Review, 21,* 17–23.

Hobbs, R. (2010). Digital and media literacy: A plan of action. A white paper on the digital and media literacy. Recommendations of the Knight Commission on the Information Needs of Communities in a Democracy. *Communications and Society Program.* Washington, DC: The Aspen Institute.

Hobbs, R. (2011). The state of media literacy: A response to Potter. *Journal of Broadcasting and Electronic Media, 55*(3), 419–430.

Hobbs, R., & Frost, R. (2003). Measuring the acquisition of media-literacy skills. *Reading Research Quarterly, 38*(3), 330–355.

Hobbs, R., & Jensen, A. (2009). The past, present, and future of media literacy education. *Journal of Media Literacy Education, 1*(1), 1–11.

Hoechsmann, M., & Poyntz, S. R. (2012). *Media literacies: A critical introduction.* Malden, NJ: Wiley-Blackwell Publishing.

Jacobs, G. E. (2012). Developing multimodal academic literacies among college freshmen. *Journal of Media Literacy Education, 4*(3), 244–255.

Jenkins, H., Clinton, K., Purushotma, R., Robison, A. J., & Weigel, M. (2006). An occasional paper on digital media and learning. In *Confronting the Challenges of Participatory Culture: Media Education for the 21st Century.* The MacArthur Foundation. Retrieved January 3, 2019 from http://digitallearning.macfound.org

Jolls, T., & Wilson, C. (2014). The core concepts: Fundamental to media literacy yesterday, today and tomorrow. *Journal of Media Literacy Education, 6*(2), 68–78.

Jolls, T., Walkosz, B. J., & Morgenthaler, D. (2014). Voices of media literacy. In B. S. De Abreu & P. Mihailidis (Eds.). *Media literacy education in action: Theoretical and pedagogical perspectives* (pp. 11–20). New York, NY: Routledge.

Kellner, D. (1995). Cultural studies, multiculturalism, and media culture. In G. Dines & J. Humez (Eds.), *Gender, race and class in media* (pp. 5–17). Thousand Oaks, CA: Sage.

Kellner, D., & Share, J. (2005). Toward critical media literacy: Core concepts, debates, organizations, and policy. *Discourse: Studies in the Cultural Politics of Education, 26*(3), 369–386.

Kellner, D., & Share, J. (2007). Critical media literacy, democracy, and the reconstruction of education. In D. Macedo & S. R. Steinberg (Eds.), *Media literacy: A reader* (pp. 3–23). New York, NY: Peter Lang Publishing.

Kellner, D., & Share, J. (2019). *The critical media literacy guide: Engaging media and transforming education.* Leiden and Boston: Brill/Sense.

Literat, I. (2014). Measuring new media literacies: Towards the development of a comprehensive assessment tool. *Journal of Media Literacy Education, 6*(1), 15–27.

Macedo, D., & Steinberg, S. R. (Eds.). (2007). *Media literacy: A reader.* New York, NY: Peter Lang Publishing.

Martens, H. (2010). Evaluating media literacy education: Concepts, theories and future directions. *Journal of Media Literacy Education, 2*(1), 1–22.

Masterman, L. (1985). *Teaching the media.* London: Comedia.

Masterman, L. (1989). *Media awareness education: Eighteen basic principles.* Retrieved January 7, 2019 from https://www.medialit.org/reading-room/media-awareness-education-eighteen-basic-principles

Meehan, J., Brandi, R., Wells, S., Walker, A., & Schwarz, G. (2015). Media literacy in teacher education: A good fit across the curriculum. *Journal of Media Literacy Education, 7*(2), 81–86.

Michael, R. (2014). Why history matters for media literacy education. *Journal of Media Literacy Education, 6*(2), 3–22.

Mihailidis, P. (2006). Media literacy in journalism/mass communication education: Can the United States learn from Sweden? *Journalism & Mass Communication Educator, 60*(4), 416–428.

Mihailidis, P. (2008). Are we speaking the same language? Assessing the state of media literacy in U.S. education. *Studies in Media & Information Literacy Education, 8*(4), 1–14.

Mihailidis, P. (2009a). The first step is the hardest: Finding connections in media literacy education, *Journal of Media Literacy Education, 1*(1), 53–67.

Mihailidis, P. (2009b). Beyond cynicism: Media education and civic learning outcomes in the university. *International Journal of Learning and Media, 1*(3), 19–31.

Mihailidis, P., & Hiebert, R. (2005). Media literacy in journalism education curriculum. *Academic Exchange Quarterly, 9*(3), 162–166.

Moses, L. (2008). *An introduction to media literacy.* Dubuque, IA: Kendall/Hunt.

Nam, S. (2010). Critical media literacy as curricular praxis. *Javnost – The Public, 17*(4), 5–23. doi:10.1080/13183222.2010.11009038

National Association for Media Literacy Education (NAMLE). (2007). Core principles of media literacy education in the United States. Retrieved from https://namle.net/publications/core-principles/

National Association for Media Literacy Education (NAMLE). (n.d.). *Definitions.* Retrieved May 12, 2019 from https://namle.net/publications/media-literacy-definitions/

Ostenson, J. W. (2012). Connecting assessment and instruction to help students become more critical producers of multimedia. *Journal of Media Literacy Education, 4*(2), 167–178.

Professional Education. (n.d.). In Encyclopedia. Retrieved December 10, 2018 from https://www.encyclopedia.com/finance/finance-and-accounting-magazines/professional-education

Potter, W. J. (2004). *Theory of media literacy: A cognitive approach.* Thousand Oaks, CA: Sage.

Potter, W. J. (2010). State of media literacy. *Journal of Broadcasting and Electronic Media, 54*(4), 675–696.

Potter, W. J. (2011). Potter's response to Hobbs. *Journal of Broadcasting and Electronic Media, 55*(4), 596–600.

Potter, W. J. (2013). Review of literature on media literacy. *Sociology Compass, 7*(6), 417–435.

Potter, W. J. (2016a). *Introduction to media literacy.* Thousand Oaks, CA: Sage.

Potter, W. J. (2016b). *Media literacy* (8th ed.). Thousand Oaks, CA: Sage.

Professional Education. (2007). *Encyclopedia of Business and Finance* (2nd ed.). Retrieved from https://www.encyclopedia.com/finance/finance-and-accounting-magazines/professional-education

Ramsey, E. M. (2017). The basic course in communication, media literacy, and the college curriculum. *Journal of Media Literacy Education, 9*(1), 116–128.

RobbGrieco, M. (2014). Why history matters for media literacy education. *Journal of Media Literacy Education, 6*(2), 3–22.

Scharrer, E. (2003). Making a case for media literacy in the curriculum: Outcomes and assessment. *Journal of Adolescent and Adult Literacy, 46*(4), 354–361.

Schilder, E., Lockee, B., & Saxon, D. P. (2016). The challenges of assessing media literacy education. *Journal of Media Literacy Education, 8*(1), 32–48.

Schmidt, H. C. (2012a). Essential but problematic: Faculty perceptions of media literacy education at the university level. *Qualitative Research Reports in Communication, 13*(1), 10–20, doi:10.1080/17459435.2012.719204

Schmidt, H. (2012b). Media literacy education at the university level. *Journal of Effective Teaching, 12*(1), 64–77.

Schmidt, H. C. (2013a). Addressing media literacy within higher education: A comparison of faculty and student perceptions. *Northwest Journal of Communication, 41*(1), 133–159.

Schmidt, H. C. (2013b). Media literacy education from kindergarten to college: A comparison of how media literacy is addressed across the educational system. *Journal of Media Literacy Education, 5*(1), 295–309.

Schmidt, H. C. (2015). More than writing and reporting: Examining the overall media literacy of today's journalism students. *Teaching Journalism and Mass Communication, 5*(1), 43–56.

Sholle, D., & Denski, S. (1994). *Media education and the (re)production of culture.* Westport, CT: Bergin and Garvey.

Silverblatt, A. (Ed.) (2014). *The Praeger handbook of media literacy* [2 volumes]. Santa Barbara, CA: Praeger.

Silverblatt, A., Baker, F., Tyner, K., & Stuhlman, L. (2002). Media literacy in U.S. institutions of higher education. Webster university media literacy program survey. Retrieved January 20, 2019 from http://www.webster.edu/medialiteracy/survey/survey_Report.htm

Silverblatt, A., Miller, D., Smith, J., & Brown, N. (2014). *Media literacy: Keys to interpreting media messages* (4th ed.). Santa Barbara, CA: ABC-CLIO, LLC.

Simons, M., Meeus, W., & T'Sas, J. (2017). Measuring media literacy for media education: Development of a questionnaire for teachers' competencies. *Journal of Media Literacy Education, 9*(1), 99–115.

St. Onge, J. (2018). Teaching media literacy from a cultural studies perspective. In J. Cubbage (Ed.), *Handbook of research on media literacy in higher education environments* (pp. 136–152). Hershey, PA: Information Science Reference, an imprint of IGI Global.

Stuhlman, L., & Silverblatt, A. (2007). Media literacy in U.S. institutions of higher education: Survey to explore the depth and breadth of media literacy education. Retrieved January 20, 2019 from http://www.Webster.edu/medialiteracy/Media%20Literacy%20Presentation2.ppt

Thoman, E. (1993). Skills and strategies for media education. Retrieved January 7, 2019 from https://www.medialit.org/reading-room/skills-strategies-media-education

Tisdell, E. (2008). Critical media literacy and transformative learning: Drawing on pop culture and entertainment media in teaching for diversity in adult higher education. *Journal of Transformative Education, 6*(1), 48–67.

Tyner, K. (Ed.) (2010) *Media literacy: New agendas in communication.* New York, NY: Routledge.

Vraga, E., Tully, M., Kotcher, J. E., Smithson, A.-B., & Broeckerlman-Post, M. (2015). A multi-dimensional approach to measuring news media literacy. *Journal of Media Literacy Education, 7*(3), 41–53.

UNESCO. (2013). Global media and information literacy assessment framework: Country readiness and competencies. Paris: Author. Retrieved from http:/unesdoc.unesco.org./images/0022/002246/224655e.pdf

Wenner, R. M. (2016). Media literacy definitions (Master thesis), Communication/Theatre Arts, Old Dominion University. doi:10.25777/js5y-hk73. Retrieved from: https://digitalcommons.odu.edu/communication_etds/1

White, A. (2016). *Journalism Ethics: An inspiration for free expression and media literacy.* Retrieved January 2, 2019 from https://ethicaljournalismnetwork.org/resources/publications/ethical-journalism

Woo, Y. Y. J. (2010). Getting past our inner censor: Collective storytelling as pedagogy in a polarized media environment. *Journal of Media Literacy Education, 1*(2), 132–136.

11 News Media Literacy in the Digital Age

A Measure of Need and Usefulness of a University Curriculum in Egypt

Rasha Allam and Salma ElGhetany

Introduction

Imagining a life before a 24/7 digitally enhanced "switch on" mode has become impossible. Being in a constant state of distraction and disruption has become the norm. Results of a study conducted by UK's telecommunications regulatory body, OfCom (2018), revealed that on average people check their phones every 12 minutes, with 71% reporting they never switch off their phones and 40% claiming they even check their devices within five minutes of waking (Griffey, 2018).

Despite audiences, especially younger ones, spending more time using media, academics have reported a notable lack of media savviness in new university students. There is a tendency for students to have limited media literacy skills beyond simply being able to access content (Bergstrom, Flynn, & Craig, 2018). Furthermore, incorporating and assessing media literacy education is limited within college classrooms and receives limited scholarly attention. Media literacy education is argued to be an influential tool in reducing possible adverse effects of media messages on audiences exposed to misleading content (Bergstrom, Flynn, & Craig, 2018). Many scholars have discussed the importance of media literacy education; however, there is little published research on successful programs and interventions conducted (Arke & Primack, 2009; Garcia, Seglem, & Share, 2013), especially in higher education. The current need for more research was one of the main reasons for conducting this study: to attempt to measure the need for news literacy interventions at the university level for students of all majors at a prominent Egyptian-American university. Through surveys, the researchers gauged students' basic critical knowledge and digital skills in relation to their media consumption. They recommend a general introductory media literacy intervention course open as an elective to all students to better equip them with the skills and knowledge necessary for heightened awareness as well as smart use of media content they are exposed to on a daily basis.

Literature Review

Media Literacy and Distrust in the Media

In the early 2000s, new media – including social networking platforms – were considered spaces for lively discussion, open debate, and civic engagement. They have, however, come to overtake legacy media, taking control of the daily information and communication flow (Taplin, 2017). Whereas Disney, Viacom, Time Warner, Comcast, and CBS in the United States currently control the majority of mass media content, the "new monopolies" – Facebook, Google, and Amazon – now control the majority of media access and traffic online. Moreover, these new media platforms have increasingly shifted into spaces of conflict, where rhetoric of partisanship and polarization became encouraged over constructive engagement. Online users are increasingly exposed to algorithms for targeting and advertising, with their personal information exploited for targeted content designed for extracting more data and so on (Taplin, 2017). In their report on *Media and Manipulation*, Marwick and Lewis (2017) argue that these new media conglomerates provide a rich ground for Internet subcultures to propagate *spectacle*: more of a social intertwining among people that is mediated by sensational imagery (Debord, 1967). It can be said that due to the 24/7 information flow on fast-paced platforms whose content is designed for quick consumption or "skimming," an ecosystem of spectacle has emerged where audiences normalize the sensational and are desensitized toward the outrageous. Mihailidis (2018, p. 7) quoted Douglas Kellner's (2009) articulation of this phenomenon: "media constructs that are out of the ordinary and habitual daily routine which become special media spectacles…They are highly public social events, often taking a ritualistic form to celebrate society's highest values." The rise in sensational stories in the media, as well as the rise in people's acceptance of the phenomenon, has led to a crisis of legitimacy – sentiment of distrust in these media moguls. According to Edelman (2017), globally, trust in institutions, including media ones, is weakening. His findings are that an increase in trust in peer opinion has overtaken trust in what the media has to say; what one's peers share online mattered more than the source of the information. The distrust is worsened by the echo chambers created on social networking platforms and that reinforce personal beliefs while shunning differing viewpoints.

The "connectedness" people live in has come with a downside, including the fakeness of interactions and losing touch with reality that comes with this digital age. Academics and scholars have been racing to catch up with the latest digital communication trends that come and go in relation to people's relationships, businesses, political involvement, civic engagement, and the like. In 2017, for instance, "fake news" was listed as word of the year by the *Collins Dictionary* – partially thanks to Donald Trump's excessive use of the term. However, by the year 2018, the term had already gone out of style. Media figures, journalists, and academics alike have argued that the term has been broadly used, making it lose its meaning altogether. Moreover, its use can even have adverse or detrimental effects on democracies and the public's trust in media institutions, which is already decreasing. It has been claimed that the term has been used by politicians such as Trump in their attempt to demonize and discredit the media, especially. Some politicians have also used the term as a way to counter argue against those they disagree with.

In January 2017, Margaret Sullivan's *Washington Post* column was among the first to argue for the "retirement" of the term since it has been proven to lack accuracy in describing different types of media violations. Facebook later deserted the term "fake news," substituting it with "false news."

In their report at Harvard University's John F. Kennedy School of Government's online media literacy resource called *First Draft*, Claire Wardle and Hossein Derkhashan examined information disorder, defining three types of information that carry varying levels of inaccuracies or falseness:

> *Mis-information* is when false information is shared, but no harm is meant; *Dis-information* is when false information is knowingly shared to cause harm; *Mal-information* is when genuine information is shared to cause harm, often by moving private information into the public sphere.
>
> (Mulcahey, 2018, para. 8)

Given the growing distrust and people turning away from both legacy as well as new and social media platforms in terms of their information credibility, a reimagining of media literacy interventions becomes an inevitability: a civic responsibility. Media literacy can empower media users with a sense of being active in the world and able to induce active positive change. Constructs of agency, critical consciousness, and liberation place media literacy as a relevant player in the social and technological realities of modern life. In her research titled, *Did Media Literacy Backfire?*, Danah Boyd (2017, p. 83) explains one of the main challenges for media literacy today:

> Anxious about the widespread consumption and spread of propaganda and fake news during this year's [U.S.] election cycle, many progressives are calling for an increased commitment to media literacy programs. Others are clamoring for solutions that focus on expert fact-checking and labeling. Both of these approaches are likely to fail – not because they are bad ideas, but because they fail

to take into consideration the cultural context of information consumption that we've created over the last thirty years. The problem on our hands is a lot bigger than most folks appreciate.

The latter consideration is interesting for the Egyptian context, where the same concerns stand in relation to the media, both mainstream and new, and how they have contributed to the emergence of sentiments of distrust, polarization, and partisanship. A vocal culture like Egypt is one where rumors and inaccurate reports travel perhaps faster than "real" news. In 2017, the Egyptian Parliament's Committee of Communication and Information Technology conducted a study to investigate the amount and extent of rumors in Egypt. The study found that in only 60 days, 53,000 rumors had spread mainly on social media and that mainstream media cited 30% of these news items as true without fact checking first (*Egypt Today*, 2017).

Media literacy is not the only approach to regaining trust in the media. In fact, this particular approach has had its share of criticism recently given its assumption of virtual distance between the media consumer and the medium itself. This assumption posits that a news reader can actively and consciously step away from the written texts and the images, and critique them objectively. This contradicts theories such as confirmation bias, and selective exposure, that hypothesize that this critical detachment is more of an ideal rather than a realistic exercise (Mihailidis, 2018). Moreover, the approach of "learning" to become media literate can lead one to believe that once the knowledge and skills are acquired in critical media analysis, then media literacy has been reached. This, however, can in fact lead to an elevated sense of cynicism and distrust toward the media and not the opposite (Mihailidis, 2009). Mihailidis (2018) further explains that media literacy places individual responsibility at the forefront of the process. This notion, however, that people have a responsibility to be media literate, maintains what Boyd (2017) referred to as a "return to tribalism," where people destroy the social structure via polarization, distrust, and self-absorption.

Media Literacy and Civic Engagement

Media literacy, as a mindset, should place an emphasis on civic engagement and intentionality, meaning that the approach can help online consumers come together again in discussing key social problems constructively, and meaningfully through positive dialog. In his writings on reviving civic intentionality, Peter Levine (2015, p. 7) discusses how media institutions' role in embracing their societal functions needs "people [to] change the norms and structures of their own communities through deliberate civic action – something they are capable of doing quite well."

Latest elections in France, Turkey, and the United States presented windows for idea and ideology sharing, mostly aggressively debated in an online rhetoric of non-acceptance, and worse, endorsed by dangerous narratives of politicians and power groups reported through mainstream media. Moreover, the speed of communication online and on digital platforms far exceeds that of many institutions' abilities to respond in due time, resulting in some of the major social and civic challenges of our time having more in-depth dialogue online than on mainstream media. Topics such as migration and climate change are marked examples of such pressing issues that take up much more attention and space on digital platforms than on mainstream channels. In Egypt, the uprisings in January 2011 were later deemed by scholars a "Facebook Revolution" (Khamis, Gold, & Vaughn, 2012), given how fast and vast the mobilization took place on the social networks when mainstream media were still in the dark.

The mainstream view of social media is that they pose a force for negativity, that they are bad for us since they put us in a constant state of "detached connectedness" in lieu of "intimate relationships," and that the constant comparison of ourselves to others changes who we are. However, what some fail to acknowledge is that social media can also serve as a platform for empowerment and inducing positive social change. Examples are many, including the revolutionary hashtag movements such #MeToo and #BlackLivesMatter, which were started online and later picked up by the public sphere. Following the #MeToo campaign, the American NGO, Rape, Abuse and Incest National Network reported a 21% spike in calls made to anti-sexual-assault hotlines demonstrating how online conversations can help people seek the support they need offline. Civic engagement through social media provides an appealing venue for many reasons; it is easily accessible, gets constructive debates started, can sustain momentum, and empowers ordinary people and unheard voices (Leary, 2018).

Egypt: Media Literacy Education and Civic Engagement

The last decade has witnessed a surge in Internet and mobile phone penetration in the Arab world, which also reflected a rise in the use of social media platforms and other smart technologies (Howard, 2011). In Egypt, the rates of Internet users and mobile penetration have increased remarkably since 2011. In 2018, Internet penetration in Egypt reached up to 38 million and mobile broadband subscriptions reached 31%. Internet is accessed through mobile phones by 32 million subscribers. The percentage of families who have access to Internet at home counts for 46.5% of the population. Social media users (Facebook & Twitter) count for 30.5% of the population. The average time spent online per week in Egypt has increased from 18 hours in 2013, and 23 hours in 2015, to 26 hours in 2017 (Mideast Media, 2017).

Using smartphones to connect to the Internet is rising and computer use is declining. The usage of smartphones increased from 32% in 2015 to 47% in 2017, and computers went down from 34% in 2015 to 20% in 2017. Egyptians increasingly embrace social media as the use of Facebook increased by 8 points, WhatsApp by 12 points, YouTube by 13 points, and Instagram by 17 points (2017: 47% Facebook, 38% WhatsApp, 35% YouTube, 21% Instagram). Twitter is at only 11% in 2017 (Allam, n.d.).

There are no audience measurement organizations to provide accurate data about audience behavior, yet according to interviews with senior-level managers of public and private newspapers, social media networks come second after search engines for users to access content. Facebook is the most used social network. According to the Arab Social Media Report published in March 2017, about 30 million Egyptians are using Facebook, 1.7 million are using Twitter (second in the Arab World after Saudi Arabia), and around 800,000 users are on Instagram (third in the Arab world after Saudi Arabia and the United Arab Emirates) (Allam, n.d.).

This increased connectivity penetration allowed for wider diffusion of cultural and social content in the region, and in Egypt specifically, with user-generated content being spread via social media, such as Facebook and Twitter, video portals such as YouTube, and short message service (SMS) or conventional text messaging. Consumer-to-consumer communication has been enabled, allowing users to disseminate their ideas, opinions, and generated content to large groups of people. In today's connected world, it can be said that one of the most important platforms that shape public opinion and sphere in Arab societies is the Internet. In fact, social media act as a driver of societal change (Kamel, 2013).

In Egypt, current limitations make it difficult for average citizens to obtain an adequate understanding of the effects of news media on their daily lives; these limitations include but are not restricted to: firm state control on the media; a lack of the profession's ethical standards that result in wide spreading of rumors, false news, partisanship, and political bias; in addition to a lack of sufficient media awareness. Media consumers, therefore, need to be better prepared to overcome these obstacles by developing a sound grasp of the media landscape and be able to challenge flawed media practices, in addition to acquiring needed skills to screen provided information for reliability and accuracy. Furthermore, citizens should learn and appreciate the value of the media around them and the worth of freedom of expression and freedom of information. As mentioned earlier, the rich rumor environment on Egyptian media and social networking platforms has created a hub of false information; panic; and partisanship in areas of politics, religion, and even sports.

The merger between fact and opinion, the fast, wide spreading of memes and jokes with any local or international incident or major news, together with a culture of excessive sharing with little verification are all reasons why the Egyptian media and digital platforms are rich in untrusted news content. Despite all that, Egyptians have been using their newly acquired voice through online connectivity to also advocate humanitarian and civic causes and initiatives. There are many examples that stand out. A recent example was when users of social media waged a heavy campaign against popular television show presenter Reham Saeed, for airing photos of a survivor of a street sexual harassment incident, slandered her, and engaged in victim-blaming during her show's special episode dedicated to the incident airing in October 2015. The hashtag condemning the episode translated into #Riham_has_died (#ريهام_ماتت) trended on Twitter. The public anger fueled by social media eventually resulted in the suspension of her television show, as well as charging Saeed with a misdemeanor and one year in prison in addition to a LE15,000 fine for violating the victim's privacy. Furthermore, Saeed was charged with six-month imprisonment together with a LE10,000 fine for libel (Sorour & Dey, 2014).

Youth in Egypt face many of the same challenges found in other Arab countries, and perhaps globally, mainly in the area of unemployment. Failing to land in proper job opportunities hinders the young generation's abilities to acquire new skills or make good use of their education, resulting in feelings of detachment from their country or its plans for growth and prosperity. Not only that, but lack of youth engagement in social and civic affairs prevents this young generation from having the experience, skills, and mature confidence needed to build effective political and positive social change (Innovations in Civic Participation: Egypt, 2014). On the other hand, in his report titled *Studies on Youth Policies in the Mediterranean Partner Countries*, Ahmed Abdelhay (2005) argues that Egypt has seen a surge in civic participation by its youth over the past decade, including bigger use of community-based organizations of social media platforms for civic engagement (Abdelhay, 2005).

Media Literacy Education

The high dependence on social media and other forms of digital communication comprised mainly of audience-generated content has expanded how people actively engage with media rather than merely receiving content. These new forms of engagement include bigger influence and power from the platforms and the content creators, raising concerns of responsibility and control.

Studies conducted to examine the effects of media literacy education reveal advances in critical thinking skills that may also result in positive behavior change. In their meta-analysis of media literacy interventions,

Jeong, Cho, and Hwang (2012) argue that critical analysis of media messages, including an awareness of the message purpose and biased representation, was more likely than action outcomes (change in accustomed practice). They attributed this to the fact that media literacy interventions typically focus on critical skills rather than behavior change. Another study of more than 2,000 middle-school students in Los Angeles schools claimed that media literacy education increases critical attitudes toward media, together with an educated appreciation of media (Webb & Martin, 2012).

Moreover, media literacy has been linked to smarter usage of digital platforms for positive change and empowerment. According to Maksl, Craft, Ashley, and Miller (2016, P. 3), "research addressing educational interventions that put definitions into action in a variety of settings demonstrates that they are often successful and have had positive effects on outcomes such as media knowledge, criticism, perceived realism, influence, behavioral beliefs, attitudes, self-efficacy, and behavior." So what can be done at the university level? One solution is a basic media literacy elective course for university students that will provide students with an overview of the industry and its mechanisms to be better trained to consume media with more critical understanding. Furthermore, the course will cultivate an appreciation of the power and influence of media channels for both constructive and destructive content. A media literacy course will include topics explaining why audiences seek news; how audiences and/or editors decide what constitutes news; differences between facts and opinion; how to detect bias and subjectivity; how information can be controlled – historically as well as currently; how to find reliable information; and how to critically deconstruct media content, including evaluation of sources and verification of provided information (Center for News Literacy, n.d.). For the purposes of this study, a survey was conducted to gauge the level of knowledge/literacy among university students, serving as a baseline of student media literacy. Communication and non-communication majors were included in the sample, with some interesting findings that support the need for such introductory course for all majors alike. More in-depth research can attempt to measure whether varying media literacy courses should be offered to communication majors apart from non-communication majors based on perceived and measured differences in media literacy. While the researchers build an argument for a need for such elective course based on the subject matter's salience, this survey serves as a starting point to measure the areas where the course can begin.

Theoretical Framework

This research is inspired by Potter's news literacy model. In his book titled, *Theory of Media Literacy: A Cognitive Approach*, Potter (2004) addresses a range of concepts pertaining to the media literacy research literature and creates a cognitive model based on four constituents: "knowledge structures, personal locus, competencies and skills, and information processing" (p. 68). The knowledge structure aspect includes knowledge about the media field, content, and its effects. The personal locus comprises of needs and abilities that the individual brings to this knowledge to process the information accessed. Contrasting with other theorizations of media literacy, this model addresses media literacy as an approach that requires "conscious processing of information" and "preparation for exposures" to media messages (Potter, 2004, p. 68). In other words, it is when audiences understand the message and the motivations behind its production that they can better understand the extent of the influence. When people understand that the effects will positively influence them, they can actively increase these effects. Potter's model is one of the media literacy frameworks that academics and educators apply to the emerging fields of "news media literacy" and "public relations literacy" (Hobbs, 2010; Mihailidis, 2011). More recently, scholars have made efforts to adapt Potter's model to news media literacy (Maksl, Ashley, & Craft, 2016), postulating that individuals who are news media literate think deeply about their media exposure and have basic knowledge about content, the industry running it, and its effect. They also have higher control on the media's influence. Maksl, Ashley, and Craft (2015) tested the Potter's scale with teenagers and revealed that it was able to distinguish between levels of news media literacy, whereas teens with higher news literacy exhibited greater motivation to consume news, were more cynical of news, and were more knowledgeable about current affairs than their counterparts with lower news literacy.

Methodology

This study relied on surveys using a purposive (convenient) random sampling of undergraduate students enrolled at the American University in Cairo (AUC), one of Egypt's leading private American-accredited English language universities established in 1919. (A copy of the survey questions is presented in the Appendix.) Students targeted to take the survey were of different majors and class standing (freshman, sophomores, juniors, and seniors). AUC students were selected as a sample for this survey since this is where a university-level media literacy course may be introduced by the Department of Journalism and Mass Communication and offered as an open elective. The purpose of the survey was to measure what basic media literacy skills and knowledge students possess that are essential for positive civic engagement and responsible content sharing in the digital world. In addition to two screening questions at the beginning (major and class), the survey was comprised of 27 closed-ended multiple choice or Likert Scale questions. Some of the survey questions were referenced in the study by Maksl, Craft, Ashley, and Miller (2016). The survey was administered both electronically via emails and WhatsApp, as well as in hard copies distributed on campus. Institutional Review Board (IRB) approval was obtained to conduct the survey. A total of $N = 184$ AUC students took the survey in fall 2018 and spring 2019 semesters. While students exhibited a measurable amount of media-literacy-related knowledge, a dedicated class on media literacy constituencies would cater more toward building the mindset and the character of a media-savvy generation. This generation of active and engaged citizens become less prone to the adverse effects of media consumption nowadays (fake content, rumors, polarization, hate speech… etc., just to name a few), and have more to offer in terms of content production that is knowledgeable, creative, and civically responsible at the same time.

RQ1 – Do undergraduate students at AUC have basic critical knowledge and digital skills of media literacy?

The variables on which the survey questions were built are basic critical knowledge and basic digital skills; both are typically employed by media users who have received media literacy education or who can be considered "media literate" to an extent. Basic critical knowledge includes but is not exclusive to differentiating between an advertisement and a news item; differentiating between fact and opinion in the news; spotting potentially false information as well as having the knowledge of how to verify it; having basic information about media ownership, advertisement influence, media roles within an institution, issues of objectivity and bias in the news, how the media set the public agenda, and how critical thinking and mindfulness need to be employed when consuming news items online or via legacy media.

Basic digital skills include knowing how to conduct a Google reverse image search to check for photo manipulation or photos used out of context to protect oneself online by having a strong password for example; know about one's digital footprint and its implications in real life; have information about big data; and, understand how one's personal information can be used in aggregate levels.

Results

The majority of the respondents were seniors (63%) and mostly from non-communication majors (84%), including mechanical and construction engineering, political science, and business majors. Although we differentiated between communication and non-communication majors in the analysis, for this chapter, we will emphasize more on presenting results of combined/all majors since the course we envision and propose is intended for all students. Gender was not factored in the survey since a university-level elective course would be offered to eligible and interested students regardless of considerations such as gender, race, or ethnicity.

Although communication major students did better compared to non-communication majors, results showed that communication majors still lack some fundamental media-related information, which reveals that the proposed course is important to enrich students' knowledge regardless of their major.

The first set of questions measured the mindfulness of the respondents, or in other words, if they practice any critical analysis during their general news/media consumption. The majority of the respondent answers varied between neutral and agree in that they do not like to do much thinking while they are consuming news on social media. This can perhaps be attributed to the fact that being mindful requires certain dispositions, including when, where, and how a person is consuming content at a given time. Furthermore, around 54% of all majors said that spending longer times on deep or mindful thinking gives them little satisfaction (strongly agree and agree with the statement). The majority of communication major students, however, (57%) reported being neutral to that statement.

Of all majors, around 67.4% believed that they can differentiate between facts and opinions; 90% said that they can identify advertisements, 86% are aware that social media platforms use their demographics and other personal information to sell advertisements, and 92% are aware of the fact that they have digital footprints for their online usage habits.

When asked about their ability to exert control over how news that comes from either legacy or social media may affect them, the answers were distributed among agree (39%), neutral (22%), and disagree (33%) for all majors combined. However, the majority (85% strongly agree or agree from all majors) believed that if they checked different sources, they can avoid being misinformed. Although 52% believed that they should not blame themselves when they are misinformed (strongly disagree and disagree with the statement), around 85% believed that if they exert efforts and paid attention to different sources, they can avoid this misinformation.

A majority of all majors were aware of the impact of media exposure on audiences. One of the questions measured the theoretical perspective of third person effect, where 63% of respondents selected the correct answer: "*A greater effect on other people than themselves.*"

However, knowledge of concepts like agenda setting and determining the importance of the topic compared to the time it is spent covered in the media was confirmed, with 89% of all majors getting the right answer that they believed that the topic is important if it gets a lot of coverage in the news.

Communication major students as well as those from other majors selected the correct answer when asked what being biased or not objective in the news means; 57% of all majors combined selected *"The reporter puts his or her opinion in the story."* However, interestingly, 29% of communication majors also selected *"The reporter's story relies too much on the opinions of people who are neutral,"* while only 2.6% of non-communication majors selected that wrong answer.

Another question that showed discrepancy between communication students' knowledge and that of their non-communication counterparts was the question about whom the responsibility of writing a press release falls on, with 43% of communication students selecting *"a spokesperson,"* which is the correct answer, and 44% of non-communication students selecting the wrong answer, *"a reporter."*

Of the 10 multiple choice questions posed to the respondents in this survey, students were incorrect on 20% of them. Of the 17 questions on Likert scale (strongly agree to strongly disagree), students responded incorrectly on 20% of them. While the percentage seems small, given that the questions address basic media literacy skills and knowledge, an apparent gap presents itself where an introductory-level course becomes useful. Summary of the results for Likert scale questions is in Table 11.1.

Table 11.1 Summary of questions with percentage of "strongly agree + agree" combined

Statements	Communication Major (%)	Other Majors (%)	Majors Combined (%)
Q3-1: I do not like to have to do a lot of thinking when consuming news on social media.	71.4	33.3	39.1
Q3-2: I try to avoid social media posts that require thinking in depth about something.	0	15.3	13.0
Q3-3: I prefer to do something that challenges my thinking abilities rather than something that requires little thought.	57.1	79.4	76.0
Q3-4: I prefer complex to simple problems.	0	66.6	56.5
Q3-5: Thinking hard and for a long time about something gives me little satisfaction.	28.5	58.9	54.3
Q4-6: If I am misinformed by the news media, it is my own behavior that determines how soon I will learn credible information.	71.4	71.7	71.7
Q4-7: I am in control of the information I get from the news media, whether via social networks or legacy media.	57.1	43.5	45.6

Statements	Communication Major (%)	Other Majors (%)	Majors Combined (%)
Q4-8: When I am misinformed by the news media, I am to blame.	28.5	25.6	26.0
Q4-9: If I pay attention to different sources of news, I can avoid being misinformed.	85.7	84.6	84.7
Q6-21: I believe I can differentiate between fact and opinion in a news article I read.	71.4	66.6	67.3
Q6-22: I can identify an advertisement when I see one.	85.7	92.3	91.3
Q6-23: I am aware that a news piece I can come across in a trustworthy newspaper might not be true.	57.1	71.7	69.5
Q6-24: I am aware that social media platforms use my demographic data to sell advertisements to different companies.	57.1	92.3	86.9
Q6-25: I am aware that there is a digital footprint for my online usage habits	83.3	92.3	91.1
Q6-26: I know how to come up with a strong password for my online use.	42.8	61.5	58.6
Q6-27: I know how to use Google reverse image search.	28.5	51.2	47.8

Conclusion and Discussion

The lack of basic news media literacy of students, especially non-communication majors, is an interesting finding given its implications for conceiving and developing curricula in the news literacy discipline. The authors recommend introducing basic news media literacy education through a general introductory-level communication course at the university level. This can be in the form of a core course to help them expand on their media-related critical skills and attitudes to be more responsible media consumers as well as content producers. This intervention does not depend on students' educational majors as it provides skills and knowledge utilized by individuals in their daily lives. Having media literacy education can help younger generations regain trust in the media since they will feel more empowered, less exploited, and less susceptible to adverse media effects. In addition, an important initial stage for any news literacy intervention is to help students to mindfully understand and become aware when, where, and how the news is delivered to them, encouraging more thoughtful attention when processing news (Sivek, 2018). Furthermore, students can have a more constructive role in their communities when they are better able to voice their opinions and instill positive change. Since media literacy entails a "production" component, civic intentionality and engagement can be one major takeaway when youth possess the right tools for expression and critical handling of the media they consume every day.

Limitations and Directions for Future Research – One limitation of this study is that it does not have a control variable. This means that students' knowledge about and attitudes towards the media were assessed to determine whether a media news literacy educational program will be of benefit. It needs, however, to measure the same against a control group of students after taking a proposed media literacy course to be able to reduce confounding variables. Furthermore, this study may serve as a pre-test for media literacy intervention at the collegiate level. Additional studies are required after the course has been introduced to gauge pre- and post-intervention statistical differences and reevaluate the course. Those who take the course can then act as a control group against other students who have not taken it.

Appendix: Survey Questions

"By clicking next, you agree that you have read and understood the information included in this form and agree to participate in this study." Thank you for your cooperation.

If you are an undergraduate student in AUC, please take 10 minutes of your time to complete this survey on news media literacy. This survey will attempt to gauge your basic knowledge about and attitude towards news media you consume via traditional or digital channels. *Social media referred to in this survey include Facebook and Twitter.*

What is your major?

What is your class standing?

- Freshman
- Sophomore
- Junior
- Senior

Please rate the following statements on a scale of 1 to 5, where 1 is Strongly Agree and 5 is Strongly Disagree.

1 I do not like to have to do a lot of thinking when consuming news on social media.
2 I try to avoid social media posts that require thinking in depth about something.
3 I prefer to do something that challenges my thinking abilities rather than something that requires little thought.

4 I prefer complex to simple problems.

5 Thinking hard and for a long time about something gives me little satisfaction.

On a scale of 1 to 5, where 1 is Strongly Agree and 5 is Strongly Disagree, please indicate how much you agree or disagree with these statements.

6 If I am misinformed by the news media, it is my own behavior that determines how soon I will learn credible information.

7 I am in control of the information I get from the news media, whether via social networks or legacy media.

8 When I am misinformed by the news media, I am to blame.

9 If I pay attention to different sources of news, I can avoid being misinformed.

Please select the option that best represents the answer to the following:

10 National media outlets in Egypt are:

   • For-profit businesses
   • Owned by the government (correct answer)
   • Non-profit businesses
   • I do not know

11 If you wanted to get a job as a journalist in Egypt, you would need to become a member in...

   • The Supreme Council for Media Regulations
   • The Federal Trade Commission
   • The Journalists' Syndicate (correct answer)
   • I do not know

12 Which of the following news outlets relies on government subsidy for financial support?

   • ON Sport
   • Channel 1 (correct answer)
   • Al Masry Al Youm
   • MBC
   • I don't know

13 When it comes to reporting the news, the main difference between a website like Google News and a website like Al Masry Al Youm. com is that:

   • Google does not have reporters who gather information, while Al Masry Al Youm does (correct answer)
   • Google focuses on national news, while Al Masry Al Ayoum focuses on local news

- Google has more editors than Al Masry Al Youm does
- Google charges more money for news than Al Masry Al Youm does
- I do not know

14 Who has the most influence on what gets aired on local TV news?

- Individual reporters
- The anchor, the person reading the news
- The cameraman
- The producer/editor (correct answer)
- I do not know

15 One common criticism of the news is that it is not objective. What do people who make that criticism typically mean by it?

- The reporter gives only the facts about the story
- The reporter puts his or her opinion in the story (correct answer)
- The reporter's story relies too much on the opinions of people who are neutral
- The reporter does not make the purpose of the story clear
- I do not know

16 Writing a press release is typically the job of:

- A reporter
- A spokesperson (correct answer)
- A lawyer
- A producer
- I do not know

17 Most people think the news has:

- A greater effect on themselves than other people
- A greater effect on other people than themselves (correct answer)
- The same effect on themselves as others
- Does not have any effects on anyone
- I do not know

18 People who watch a lot of television news often tend to think the world is:

- More violent and dangerous than it actually is (correct answer)
- Less violent and dangerous than it actually is
- Just as violent and dangerous as it actually is
- I do not know

19 If a topic gets a lot of coverage in the news, people who pay attention to the news are:

- More likely to think the topic is important (correct answer)
- Less likely to think the topic is important

- Neither more nor less likely to think the topic is important
- I don't know

20 Most news outlets depend on advertising to make money. What is a possible effect of this?

- News could encourage people to buy things they do not need
- News could emphasize things that are not really important
- All of the above (correct answer)
- None of the above. There are no effects
- I do not know

On a scale of 1 to 5 where 1 is Strongly Agree and 5 is Strongly Disagree, please indicate how much you agree or disagree with these statements.

21 I believe I can differentiate between fact and opinion in a news article I read.
22 I can identify an advertisement when I see one.
23 I am aware that a news piece I can come across in a trustworthy newspaper might not be true.
24 I am aware that social media platforms (ex. Facebook) use my demographic data to sell advertisements to different companies.
25 I am aware that there is a digital footprint for my online usage habits (search history, sharing habits, posting information…etc.).
26 I know how to come up with a strong password for my online use.
27 I know how to use Google reverse image search.

References

Abdelhay, A. T. (2005). Studies on youth policies in the Mediterranean partner countries. *MarlyleRoi: EUROMED.*

Allam, R. (n.d.). Egypt. Retrieved from https://medialandscapes.org/country/egypt

Arke, E. T., & Primack. B. A. (2009). Quantifying media literacy: Development, reliability, and validity of a new measure. *Educational Media International, 46*(1):53–65. doi:10.1080/09523980902780958

Bergstrom, A., Flynn, M., & Craig, C. (2018). Deconstructing media in the college classroom: A longitudinal critical media literacy intervention. *Journal of Media Literacy Education, 10*(3), 113–131. doi:10.23860/jmle-2018-10-03-07

Boyd, D. (2017). Did media literacy backfire? *Journal of Applied Youth Studies, 1*(4), 83.

Center for News Literacy. (n.d.). Model syllabus. Retrieved from http://www.centerfornewsliteracy.org/wp-content/uploads/2012/04/Model-Syllabus-JRN101.pdf

Country Profile: Egypt. (2014, August 19). Innovations in civic participation. Retrieved from http://www.icicp.org/resource-library/icp-publications/global-youth-service-database/africa-2/north-africa/egypt/

Debord, G. (1967). *The society of the spectacle*. New York, NY: Zone Books.

Edelman. (2017). Trust barometer – 2017 annual global study. Retrieved from http://www.edelman.com/executive-summary/

Egypt Today. (2017, November 13). 53K rumors spread in Egypt in only 60 days, study reveals. Retrieved from http://www.egypttoday.com/Article/1/32378/53K-rumors-spread-in-Egypt-in-only-60-days-study

First Draft News. (n.d.). Retrieved from https://firstdraftnews.org/

Garcia, A., Seglem, R., & Share, J. (2013). Transforming teaching and learning through critical media literacy pedagogy. *LEARNing Landscapes, 6*(2) 109–124.

Griffey, H. (2018, October 14). The lost art of concentration: Being distracted in a digital world. *The Guardian*. Retrieved from https://www.theguardian.com/lifeandstyle/2018/oct/14/the-lost-art-of-concentration-being-distracted-in-a-digital-world

Hobbs, R. (2010). *Digital and media literacy: A plan of action*. Washington, DC: The Aspen Institute.

Howard, P. N. (2011). The digital origins of dictatorship and democracy: Information technology and political Islam. Oxford: Oxford University Press.

Jeong, S., Cho, J., & Hwang, Y. (2012). Media literacy interventions: A meta-analytic review. *Journal of Communication, 62*(3), 454–472.

Kamel, S. H. (2013). Egypt's ongoing uprising and the role of social media: Is there development? *Information Technology for Development, 20*(1), 78–91. doi:10.1080/02681102.2013.840948

Kellner, D. (2009). Media spectacle and media events: Some critical reflections. Retrieved from https://pages.gseis.ucla.edu/faculty/kellner/essays/2009_Kellner_MediaEventsJulyFINAL.pdf

Khamis, S., Gold, P. B., & Vaughn, K. (2012). Beyond Egypt's "Facebook revolution" and Syria's "YouTube uprising": Comparing political contexts, actors and communication strategies. *Arab Media & Society, 15*, 1–30.

Leary, A. (2018, January 28). Social media has its pitfalls but you can use it for positive change [Web log post]. Retrieved from https://theestablishment.co/social-media-has-its-pitfalls-but-you-can-use-it-for-positive-change-c4f4c71dd5e2/

Levine, P. (2015). *We are the ones we have been waiting for: The promise of civic renewal in America*. Oxford: Oxford University Press.

Maksl, A., Craft, S., Ashley, S., & Miller, D. (2016). The usefulness of a news media literacy measure in evaluating a news literacy curriculum. *Journalism & Mass Communication Educator, 72*(2), 228–241. doi:10.1177/1077695816651970

Maksl, A., Ashley, S., & Craft, S. (2015). Measuring news media literacy. *Journal of Media Literacy Education, 6*(3), 29–45.

Marwick, A., and Lewis, R., (2017). Media manipulation and disinformation online. *Data & Society*. Retrieved from https://datasociety.net/output/media-manipulation-and-disinfo-online/

Media Use in the Middle East. (2017). A seven-nation survey. Northwestern University in Qatar. Retrieved from Mediastmedia.org

Mihailidis, P. (2009b). Beyond cynicism: Media education and civic learning outcomes in the university. *International Journal of Learning and Media, 1*(3), 19–31.

Mihailidis, P. (2011). New civic voices and the emerging media literacy landscape. *Journal of Media Literacy Education, 3*(1), 4–5.

Mihailidis, P. (2018). Civic media literacies: Re-imagining engagement for civic intentionality. *Learning, Media and Technology, 43*(2), 152–164, doi:10.1080/17439884.2018.14286

Mulcahey, T. (2018, October 26). As misinformation crisis deepens, 'fake news' becomes less accurate. Retrieved from https://ijnet.org

Potter, W. J. (2004). *Theory of media literacy: A cognitive approach.* Thousand Oaks, CA: Sage.

Sivek, S. (2018). Both facts and feelings: Emotion and news literacy. *Journal of Media Literacy Education, 10*(2), 123–138. Retrieved from https://digitalcommons.uri.edu/cgi/viewcontent.cgi?article=1355&context=jmle

Sorour, K., & Dey, B. (2014). Energizing the political movements in developing countries: On the role of social media. *Capital and Class.* 38. doi:10.1177/0309816814550390

Taplin, J. (2017). *Move fast and break things: How Facebook, Google, and Amazon cornered culture and undermined democracy.* New York, NY: Little Brown.

Webb, T., & Martin, K. (2012). Evaluation of a US school-based media literacy violence prevention curriculum on changes in knowledge and critical thinking among adolescents. *Journal of Children and Media, 6*(4), 430–449.

12 The MOOC for Media Literacy

Examining Media Literacy Practices in a Massive Open Online Course

Kristy Roschke

Introduction

The run-up to and aftermath of the contentious 2016 U.S. presidential election epitomized the complicated state of digital information consumption, with the term "fake news" evolving from a way to describe the proliferation of misinformation online into a catch-all phrase to include factual news people do not like (Lazer et al., 2018). A survey conducted after the 2016 presidential election by Ipsos Public Affairs and BuzzFeed News found that American adults believe fake news headlines about 75% of the time and that those who cite Facebook as a major source of news are more likely to believe fake news headlines than those who do not (Silverman & Singer-Vine, 2016). Facebook users over the age of 65 were nearly seven times more likely to share fake news stories ahead of the 2016 election than the youngest users (Guess, Nagler, & Tucker, 2019). Several years later, the confusion surrounding how to identify credible news sources continues to be high, with Americans ranking made-up news as a bigger problem than violent crime, climate change, and terrorism (Pew Research Center, 2019).

But falling for fake news tells only part of the story. One of the most profound ways in which media consumption changed in the 21st century is through the social sharing of information online. As news consumers take a more active role in producing, critiquing, and sharing information (or misinformation), it complicates two of the critical components of media literacy: the ability to analyze and evaluate media messages (Aufderheide, 1997; Aufderheide & Firestone, 1993). Common media literacy practices for evaluation might include verifying the source of a news story; recognizing if a story is intended to inform or persuade; and identifying the process that legitimate, ethical journalists follow to report information.

In today's digital media ecosystem, the information stream is no longer one-way, nor are the means for producing and disseminating news controlled by the mass media. Making sense of all there is to see, hear, and watch requires a specialized set of competencies, what many scholars would refer to as digital literacies (Lankshear & Knobel, 2008). Kellner and Share (2007) discuss the importance of developing an array of media literacy competencies related to consuming and interacting with emerging forms of digital, multimedia, and entertainment communication (2007).

Scholars in such diverse fields as linguistics, literacy studies, information studies, political science, education, and psychology have been developing a broader picture of what it means to be literate in today's world. The concept of a singular literacy has developed into multiple literacies that are developed over a lifetime (Koltay, 2011). In contrast to a functional view of literacy, which suggests that literacy – as narrowly defined by the ability to read and write – is a skill that a person either has or does not have, the field of New Literacy Studies views literacy as a sociocultural process that is inextricably linked to the values, norms, and cultures in which they are used (Street, 2003). In this view, digital media literacy comprises a set of social practices "that are marked by an ethos characterized by deep interactivity, openness to feedback, sharing of resources and expertise, and a will to collaborate and provide support" (Knobel & Lankshear, 2016, p. 98).

Interest in media literacy research has grown as a means to address the complexities of digital media use. In addition to focusing on how people are acted upon by media, today mass communication and media studies has largely shifted its focus to the examination of how the digital landscape impacts how people use, consume, share, participate in, and make sense of media (Hobbs, 2011; Martens, 2010).

In the digital realm, media users participate in practices such as creating and remixing content, commenting, sharing, and liking. Media users regularly contribute to and share control of the flow of information. And though digital news users have become more technologically savvy about how to create and share media, it does not necessarily mean they have received formal training on how to engage with media and news texts of any sort. This raises the question: as citizens who are not formally trained as media creators take a more active role in creating and amplifying information in a digital environment, what media literacy practices to access, analyze, evaluate, and create media messages are informing their decisions?

This study examines the media literacy practices that may inform news use among adult participants in a digital media literacy Massive Open Online Course (MOOC). The chosen population for study is significant because it comprises two underrepresented areas in the media literacy literature that offer opportunities to expand media literacy research: adult learners outside of formal educational spaces and the effectiveness of the MOOC as a platform for teaching media literacy.

Literature Review

As news consumers and technology platforms drive more of what content receives attention within social networks through acts of content selection and sharing, questions of authenticity, credibility, and bias become increasingly important.

Today's news users have a sense of feeling "bought-in" because in addition to consuming, they share, comment, and rework information as it relates to professional, social, or civic needs (Robinson, 2011, p. 174). Oeldorf-Hirsch and Sundar (2015) found that when Facebook users share a news story, they are more likely to stay involved in the story one week after they posted it. Receiving valuable comments on an item shared on Facebook was found to be "psychologically powerful" (Oeldorf-Hirsch & Sundar, 2015, p. 247). The global rise of Facebook-owned platforms Instagram and messaging app WhatsApp has started to shift information sharing into private groups, where concern for spreading false misinformation is high (Reuters Institute, 2019).

Metzger (2007) found that people reported spending very little time verifying information they encounter online, opting mostly for verification strategies that take the least time and effort. Without sufficient time or desire to ascertain the credibility of every news item, social media users may share false or misleading information – unwittingly or purposefully. Thus, it is necessary to consider the literacy practices that are informing individuals' media use in the context of their contribution to larger information ecosystems.

Defining Media Literacy

A widely cited definition of media literacy is the "ability to access, analyze, evaluate, and communicate messages in a wide variety of forms" (Aufderheide & Firestone, 1993). Hobbs' (2011) definition adds creation, reflection, and action to the list of ways in which people interact with media. Some media literacy research situates media literacy within or alongside other literacies, most notably information literacy. However, few mass communication scholars have grounded their research in the sociocultural perspective of New Literacy Studies, which is "characterized by researchers documenting in detail literacy-in-use within people's everyday lives" (Knobel & Lankshear, 2016, p. 151).

Coiro, Knobel, Lankshear, and Leu (2008) argue that the Internet's impact is the central question in literacy education research and that the Internet is the defining technology for literacy. The New Literacy Studies' shift from the singular literacy to plural literacies represents moving away from thinking of literacy as reading and writing and instead acknowledging literacies as a set of social practices (Street, 2003).

Martin (2008) describes digital literacies in a three-phase model that comprises a range of increasingly complex competencies. Phase 1 is the functional phase, which includes the skills and concepts required for "digital competence"; Phase 2 is sociocultural, or effective digital usage in a variety of applications including personal, professional, and within certain interest groups; and Phase 3 is the digital transformation that enables innovation and creativity (p. 167). The second and third phase in Martin's model emphasize media literacy as a practice rooted in its context.

Studying media literacy within a sociocultural digital literacies framework puts the focus on the way people use media in the context of people's sense of reality and moves beyond the "production-content-reception" premise of media (Deuze, 2011, p. 143).

Media Literacy Education and Assessment

Media literacy is commonly conceived of as a set of competencies or skills, creating a close connection between media literacy and education (Kellner & Share, 2005). Hobbs (2011) argues for an approach to teaching media literacy that emphasizes how digital tools can be used to foster critical thinking, creation, and collaboration skills. Mihailidis and Viotty (2017) caution against approaches that position traditional media literacy practices such as critiquing media messages as a "panacea for the spread of misinformation" and instead advocate for the development of media literacy research and practices "directed at the critique and creation of media in support of a common good" that can address a social news sharing culture (p. 451). Building media literacy curricula on a sociocultural framework both incorporates knowledge and skills for assessing media and considers contextual factors like the "social, political, and economic environments" in which media are created (Ashley, Maksl, & Craft, 2013).

Assessing educational outcomes is difficult, but not impossible. However, there is a lack of substantial research on this topic (Mihailidis, 2009). Hobbs and Jensen (2009) have argued for more support for the work of those who are developing and testing curriculum and instructional methods that connect students' mass media experience to developing deeper critical thinking skills. Quantitative measures such as experimental and nonexperimental group designs are central to research measuring the effects of educational interventions (Hobbs & Frost, 2003; Tully & Vraga, 2019). Livingstone (2004) argues that quantitative findings alone cannot address the "textuality and technology that mediates communication" (p. 8). Jones (2013) argues that the research goal is not to determine if people are "learning" something "but rather to *find out* what they are *doing* as they engage in their everyday practices [*emphasis original*]" (Jones, 2013, p. 844). By examining media literacy practices – including how students use and engage with media in order to verify information, assess credibility, and make meaning – in a particular space, researchers gain understanding of both the tactical skills and the contextual factors that impact media literacy as a social practice.

Despite the fact that critical media consumption remains important throughout one's life, Dennis (2004) finds that media literacy education "for the most part ignores adults" (p. 205). Livingstone, Van Couvering, and Thumim (2005) also note that the effectiveness of media literacy has rarely been tested in relation to informal or lifelong learning. The need to address this hole in the research is heightened in a digital media environment, as successful navigation requires a "sophisticated ability" in terms of both technical and critical thinking skills (Dennis, 2004, p. 205). An increase in informal learning opportunities brought about by the Internet, in particular the increasing popularity of MOOCs, has the potential to meet this need.

Massive Open Online Courses (MOOCs)

Massive Open Online Courses, or MOOCs, have been touted as a next wave in 21st-century learning because they offer a low- or no-cost opportunity for global, online learning (Stephens & Jones, 2014). People choose to participate in MOOCs for myriad reasons, from professional development to lifelong learning pursuits (Stephens & Jones, 2014). Research is mixed on the effectiveness of the MOOC model (Bartolome & Steffens, 2015; Stephens & Jones, 2014), with much attention being paid to low completion rates that hover at or below the low teens (Jordan, 2013). Course Central reported the number of students who signed up for their first MOOC in 2018 was 20 million, bringing the total number of MOOC learners to 101 million (Shah, 2019), so the popularity of the MOOC as a learning platform is evident (Siemens, 2012b).

MOOCs generally fit into two categories: xMOOCs and cMOOCs (Stephens & Jones, 2014). By emphasizing instructor lectures, xMOOCs take a form more akin to traditional instructor-driven education (Stephens & Jones, 2014). cMOOCs take a constructivist approach to learning by focusing on creating a community of learners fostered by the open online environment (Siemens, 2012a; Stephens & Jones, 2014). Stewart (2013) argues that the MOOC model has the potential to foster digital literacies. Courses set up in the cMOOC model, in particular, emphasize a participatory approach.

Scholars agree that in order to successfully navigate the 21st-century media landscape, citizens must possess a collection of skills and competencies, from the functional and technical to the critical (Buckingham, 2015; Coiro et al., 2008; Hobbs, 2011). As people negotiate media in a variety of contexts, from the individual to the collaborative, they practice a diverse set of literacies throughout this continuum (Gee & Hayes,

2011; Jenkins, 2006; Lankshear & Knobel, 2008; Lave & Wenger, 1991; Street, 2011).

Using a sociocultural framework of digital media literacy that emphasizes social practice that include "socially developed and patterned activities" (Knobel & Lankshear, 2015, p. 152), this research takes a qualitative grounded theory approach to answer the following research questions.

RQ1: What literacy practices were identified in the MediaLIT MOOC and how were they defined?

RQ2: What, if any, media literacy themes emerged from media literacy discussions in the MediaLIT MOOC?

RQ3: Is the MOOC an effective platform for teaching media literacy?

Method

Much of the media literacy research in the field of mass communication employs quantitative methods, such as experimental design, to test how media literacy intervention can impact the effects of some media message (Pinkleton et al., 2008; Scharrer, 2006). However, researchers within and outside of mass communication have also utilized a variety of qualitative methods. In the field of media literacy education, qualitative methods can be useful because they have largely spawned from constructivist philosophy (Caelli, Ray, & Mill, 2003), which aligns well with the teaching of philosophy in many classrooms.

The author conducted a qualitative constant comparative analysis of participant discussion and blog posts from a seven-week digital media literacy MOOC offered in summer 2015 through a partnership with a large U.S. public university and an international MOOC platform provider.

Constant comparative analysis is a widely used process for developing grounded theory (Corbin & Strauss, 1990; Glaser & Strauss, 1967), which allows for themes to emerge from the data (Lincoln & Guba, 1985). It is a systematic method for "constructing a theoretical analysis from data, with explicit analytic strategies and implicit guidelines for data collection" (Charmaz & Belgrave, 2012, p. 347; see also Glaser & Straus, 1967; Strauss & Corbin, 1997). Charmaz (2006) describes grounded theory as "inductive, comparative, iterative, and interactive" (as cited in Charmaz & Belgrave, 2012). Through each iteration, data are comparatively analyzed until conceptual themes begin to emerge that help inform new theoretical understanding.

As part of the course design and instructional team for the MediaLIT digital media literacy MOOC that serves as the basis for this study, the author was involved in the process of determining course objectives, developing course content, and monitoring participant discussion and progress. Participants were informed at the beginning of the course that content from the course may be anonymized and used for media literacy research purposes. (For a list of MediaLIT course objectives and topics, see the Appendix.)

The MediaLIT MOOC explored topics and issues related to media use in a complex digital environment characterized by an overabundance of information. Instructors used the definition adopted by the National Association for Media Literacy Education: "Media literacy is the ability to access, analyze, evaluate, create and act using all forms of communication" (NAMLE). A core objective of the course was to empower media users to become active and ethical media creators; the course activities analyzed in this study were designed to enable participants to put what they were learning into practice via content creation and discussion.

Discussion among participants in the MOOC happened in two places within the course: the weekly discussion board and weekly blog assignment, in which participants were tasked with becoming expert media critics on a subject for which they already had a lot of knowledge and were passionate. For both assignments course instructors provided suggested prompts related to course concepts, though participants were encouraged to also choose their own relevant topics. Analyzing the two writing assignments offered insight into the media literacy practices used in the context of the norms and routines established by participants in the MOOC.

Original discussion board posts and blog posts and their ensuing comments were treated the same as units of analysis during the coding process, because each new entry contributed to the conversation and application of course topics. An initial round of in vivo descriptive coding of nearly 1,200 discussion and blog posts in the MOOC revealed several recurring concepts. Common themes emerged even when participants disagreed on discussion topics. In vivo coding is a process that derives codes from terms that are used by the participants themselves (Saldaña, 2015).

Qualitative field researchers can use both *etic* and *emic* perspectives when coding data (Babbie, 2013). Deriving from anthropology, in an etic approach the research takes a more distant and objective approach to the data, whereas in an emic approach, the researcher takes on the point of view of those being studied, drawing connections between the words and phrases used by the participants themselves (Babbie, 2013). During the first round of coding, I used both objective etic and emic approaches, as my close relationship to the course experience informed my position as a researcher. This research process is inherently reflexive, as it stems from personal and professional experience. I introduced myself both as a member of the course team and as a researcher, and I believe my role to be someplace in between neutral observer and participant observer. However, I cannot state definitively that my presence as course teaching assistant and researcher did not have an impact on participants. The course designers' intent of the discussion was that it was "for participants, by participants," and my observations indicate that this is, in fact, the way it took shape.

As with any educational intervention, the MediaLIT MOOC discussion activities were designed to measure the retention and application of course objectives set by instructors – including me. My dual role of educator and researcher afforded me a connection with the material that resulted in a deep reading of the discussion situated in its context.

Following the initial coding, two subsequent rounds of axial coding were completed to reorganize similar codes into larger categories (Charmaz, 2014). In the final round of coding, the categories were sorted into two overarching categories that reflected a dominant theme of responsibility: categories for which the media have responsibility and categories for which individual media users should take responsibility.

Approximately 4,000 participants from 149 countries enrolled in the MedaLIT MOOC. The median age of participants was 34. In keeping with common findings in the MOOC literature (Jordan, 2013), the number of active users within the digital media literacy MOOC constituted about 10% of the total enrollees. However, the corpus of conversation paints a rich and robust picture of key themes that resonate from the course material.

Findings

Discussions in the MediaLIT MOOC can be described as media literacy practices because they reveal the ways in which participants navigate, interact with, and negotiate meaning in the media they consume. Because media literacy practices are situated in the learning environment, the bulk of the ideas shared in the discussion forums stemmed from course materials.

Participants engaged in three main literacy practices during the MOOC. In the most common type of post found within the course, participants synthesized and reacted to what they had learned during the week, using hyperlinks and other supporting material. Other popular types of posts involved participants sharing personal experiences related to course concepts and participants asking questions of the group to seek understanding or additional points of view.

Nine thematic categories emerged from the course discussion, which were further separated into two main categories related to ownership over media literacy practices: the practices the media have responsibility for, and the practices for which individual media users have responsibility.

Media Responsibility

In the main category of "media responsibility," participants discussed media literacy concepts that relate to the obligation media organizations have to keep the public informed. Much discussion examined the norms, routines, and processes of the professional media that contribute to aspects of individual information overload and confusion. Categories presented in discussion that emphasized a responsibility on the media's part include: the public's need for information that is accurate and transparent; the role profit plays in the agenda of commercial media; and the affordances of digital technology in gathering, displaying, and disseminating information. In discussions about media responsibility, participants recognize that there are a number of external forces that impact the news process, but they also called attention to journalistic practices – both good and bad – that contribute to the current confusion and media overload.

Media User Responsibility

The second major category to emerge from the themes present in MediaLIT MOOC discussion is that of "media user responsibility." In these discussions, participants recognize that users are ultimately in control of the media they consume but that the deluge of information that abounds in the digital sphere can make it difficult to manage. Being a discerning media user includes being able to evaluate the parts of a news story, from the credibility of the sources to the potential biases of the journalist and/or news organization. Participants acknowledge that even trusted news sources with reputations for producing quality journalism can make mistakes, so the individual news consumer must develop a personal "crap detector" (Rheingold, 2010, p. 24) that can help balance "skepticism and judgment."

Common tools in participants' crap detection tool kit include triangulation of multiple sources on the same topic; reading past the headline so as not to allow clickbait headlines to perpetrate misleading information; following hyperlinks that provide context in stories; and paying particular attention to the data, statistics, and visuals shared in a news story. Participants acknowledge that the biggest deterrent to crap detection is a lack of time, but that critical issues require in-depth analysis, and research at the individual level is necessary, as one participant put it, because "it's our judgement and urge to gain knowledge which helps in decoding which information is genuine and which is just a hoax."

Participants' Learning Lessons

In the final week of the MOOC, participants were asked to reflect on the course experience and what they found to be the most compelling

takeaways. This discussion was not included in the constant comparative analysis because of its culminating and reflexive purpose; however,
the researcher did review the posts for common responses in an effort to
encapsulate what pieces of the media literacy curriculum most resonated
with participants.

Participants expressed greater confidence in their ability to take control of their media use, to recognize and challenge their own biases,
and the desire to expand their sources of news for a more well-rounded
information "diet." An example:

> [T]here is in fact no information overload. There is no more infor-
> mation overload than there is calorie overload at a buffet. You don't
> need to eat everything you see. But perhaps you need some guidance,
> discipline & [sic] strategies for making healthy choices. Learning to
> consume news in balance is a discipline we never needed before this
> era of information abundance. And now we are figuring it out.

Discussion

In a media landscape ruled by digital and social technology, the "people
formerly known as the audience" (Rosen, 2006, n.p.) are active users,
even if they are not themselves creating media. Increasingly, through the
acts of reacting, commenting, and sharing news information through social media, users are participating in the practice of news dissemination,
once exclusively the domain of professional journalists.

The purpose of this research was to examine how individual media
users inform their personal media decisions through media literacy practices. The dearth of studies related to adult media literacy has left a
hole in our understanding of how adults apply media literacy principles outside of the traditional classroom. This line of research is critical,
as adults are participating in the news distribution process and their
actions can negatively affect the health of the information ecosystem.
The research also examines the Massive Open Online Course (MOOC)
platform as an egalitarian tool for engaging in media literacy practices.

The dominant theme that arose from the discussion within the digital media literacy MOOC was that of responsibility: the responsibility
for media organizations to provide accurate, trustworthy information,
and the responsibility for individuals to educate themselves on the media
literacy competencies needed to be a conscientious and reliable media
user. In many cases, participants wrote with a sense of urgency about
the timeliness of course topics in relation to the news landscape, under-
scoring the importance of informal educational opportunities for adults
to practice media literacy. By emphasizing important course concepts
but still allowing for conversation to take shape organically, discussion
prompts often led participants down a path of self-realization relating
to their media use.

The act of participating in a course on media literacy is an intentional one; individual reasons vary, but those who participated in MediaLIT were moved to enroll because of a desire to learn, test, and refine how they go about interacting with media. Several participants reflected that connecting with a community of people who have an interest in media literacy was an important part of the course experience. One participant commented,

> Long term, I think it's MOST helpful to know that there's a whole COMMUNITY of concerned digital citizens who want the quality of information to remain high, and the people who read it to remain knowledgeable/skillful. That means that answers to questions really are just a well-constructed search away, and that you CAN have a good online experience with a low troll to citizen ratio [*emphasis original*].

Discussion of this type is instructive for building similar models in other educational or affinity spaces. If the positive behaviors can be modeled in other contexts, there may be positive implications for the spread and subsequent application of media literacy practices.

The MOOC as a Tool for Teaching Media Literacy

MOOC participants' discussion posts and reflections indicate that using a cMOOC model that emphasizes and encourages participation was a good fit for teaching media literacy principles. The low barrier to entry in MOOC learning mirrors the low barrier to entry to digital media creation, which created a parallel between course learning and post-course application.

One international MOOC participant reflected on how important the open access MOOCs provide is to people in smaller countries around the world:

> But the truth is that you have no idea the tremendous support that courses like this mean in a small country with a long gap in education and technology. I've been in the world of communication ten years and I'm about to finish my college career and I've never heard concepts that have been discussed here.

Conclusions and Future Study

There are limitations to this study. The population studied self-selected to participate in a MOOC about media literacy. The motivation to enroll in such a class indicates a pre-existing interest in the subject; thus, the knowledge, level of engagement, willingness to adopt competencies taught in the course, and satisfaction with the course are inherently higher than one would find in a random sample of the population. Findings cannot be extrapolated to apply to other online or educational situations.

It is also worth noting that the researcher's dual role as an instructor and a researcher may have had an impact on discussion. The researcher was not active in the discussion, but it is possible that participants took more care in their writing because they knew the content may be used for research purposes.

This study also offers several opportunities for possible future research to revise the course for ongoing study and to test some of the conclusions drawn from the analysis.

Though nearly 150 countries were represented in the enrollment, the course was very U.S.-centric, to the disappointment of the international participants. Future iterations of this course and others like it should reflect a more global view of the complexities of media and media literacy to encourage further participation and deeper understanding.

The commitment to enrolling in a MOOC may be a deterrent for many. Fortunately, the web provides myriad opportunities for people to learn and to engage with others. The collegial engagement that took place in the MediaLIT MOOC aligns with Mihailidis and Viotty's (2017) recommendations for repositioning media literacy practice in connecting humans, facilitating caring, emphasizing participation, and fostering civic impact. To put these recommendations to test, one suggested area for future research would be to apply a media literacy curriculum to other informal learning spaces that appeal to some shared humanity, and subsequently analyze the media literacy practices within that space.

Discussion and feedback from digital media literacy MOOC participants throughout the experience illuminate the lasting positive effects of media literacy education developed in a cMOOC model for a mass audience. Providing space for learners to discuss course concepts with others reinforced the learning objectives and enhanced the learning as participants connected it to their own experience. Given the lack of media literacy education opportunities for adults beyond the typical college years, this research indicates that MOOC courses could fill the gap and provide a widely available, easily accessible forum in which to learn and practice media literacy.

That the dominant themes in the discussion relate to responsibility emphasizes a need for action with regard to media literacy education: action in the teaching, action in the learning, action in the process of journalism, and action outside of traditional learning environments.

Media literacy cannot simply be viewed as a way for individuals to change their own isolated interaction with media; it is now a fully social construct. The findings in this research come at a critical time in the evolution of our complex digital information ecosystems, as the viral spread of mis- and disinformation has led to a credibility crisis. The responsibility theme indicates a clear need to develop solutions from a sociocultural perspective that emphasize media literacy as a social practice and equip stakeholders to actively contribute to improving the public's media literacy. In the current hyper-partisan and polarizing media climate, it is imperative to find ways to embed media literacy education within people's regular online use to improve the collective intelligence of our democratic society.

Appendix: List of Medialit Course Objectives and Topics

Course objectives from the MediaLIT syllabus: At the completion of this course, you will be able to:

- Describe the changes that have transformed the way we create and consume media
- Understand essential principles for being an active media consumer
- Utilize tactics to tame the information deluge and be better informed
- Analyze how media are used to persuade
- Evaluate the tools and techniques of media creation
- Employ a "slow news" approach, especially as a consumer of news
- Put media in an ethical and legal context

Course topics from the MediaLIT syllabus:

- Week 1: How media have changed; key principles for becoming an active user of media; and why media/news literacy is so important in a data-saturated environment. What it means to be a critical thinker.
- Week 2: Be skeptical of everything, but not equally skeptical of everything. Why judgment is so important. More on why we all need a personal credibility scale. We'll look at the two-sides fallacy, understanding risk (statistical), social media, and the velocity of information.
- Week 3: Where to find credible information, and spot bad information ("crap detection"). Slant vs. opinion; astroturfing and native advertising.
- Week 4: Opening our minds: escaping echo chambers and filter bubbles. Recognizing "confirmation bias" in ourselves, not just others. Seeking out opposing views and other cultural worldviews.
- Week 5: Literacy is also creation: principles of creating media with integrity: ownership of media, tools for creating media, legal and ethical issues in media creation, integrity in creating media.
- Week 6: Trust and reputation in a saturated media landscape. How media providers engender trust (or mistrust), fact-checking, transparency, community. How we in the audience can help our

information providers be more trustworthy. Why we audiences and information providers alike need to adopt a "slow news" approach.
- Week 7: Next steps: How you can put all of this into long-term action; why you should be a media literacy advocate (and how to do it). Plus: resources for parents and teachers.

References

Ashley, S., Maksl, A., & Craft, S. (2013). Developing a news media literacy scale. *Journalism & Mass Communication Educator, 68*(1): 7–21.

Aufderheide, P. (1997). Media literacy: From a report of the National Leadership Conference on Media Literacy. In R. Kubey (Ed.), *Media literacy in the information age* (pp. 79–80). New Brunswick, NJ: Transaction Publishers.

Aufderheide, P., & Firestone, C. (1993). *Media literacy: A report of the national leadership conference on media literacy.* Queenstown, MD: The Aspen Institute.

Babbie, E. R. (2013). *The basics of social research.* Boston, MA: Cengage Learning.

Buckingham, D. (2015). Defining digital literacy – What do young people need to know about digital media? *Nordic Journal of Digital Literacy, 10*(Jubileumsnummer), 21–35.

Caelli, K., Ray, L., & Mill, J. (2003). 'Clear as Mud': Toward greater clarity in generic qualitative research. *International Journal of Qualitative Research, 2*(2), 1–23.

Charmaz, K. (2014). *Constructing grounded theory.* Thousand Oaks, CA: Sage.

Charmaz, K., & Belgrave, L. L. (2012). Qualitative interviewing and grounded theory analysis. In J. F. Gubrium, J. Holstein, A. B. Marvasti, & D. McKinney (Eds.), *The SAGE handbook of interview research: The complexity of the craft* (pp. 347–366). Thousand Oaks, CA: Sage.

Coiro, J., Knobel, M., Lankshear, C., & Leu, D. J. (2008). Central issues in new literacies and new literacies research. In J. Coiro, M. Knobel, C. Lankshear, & D. J. Leu (Eds.), *Handbook of research on new literacies* (pp. 1–21). New York, NY: Taylor & Francis Group.

Corbin, J. M., & Strauss, A. (1990). Grounded theory research: Procedures, canons, and evaluative criteria. *Qualitative Sociology, 13*(1), 3–21.

Dennis, E. E. (2004). Out of sight and out of mind: The media literacy needs of grown-ups. *The American Behavioral Scientist, 48*(2), 202–211.

Deuze, M. (2011). Media life. *Media, Culture & Society, 33*(1), 137–148.

Glaser, B., & Strauss, A. (1967). *The discovery grounded theory: Strategies for qualitative inquiry.* London: Wiedenfeld and Nicholson.

Gee, J. P., & Hayes, E. R. (2011). *Language and learning in the digital age.* New York, NY: Routledge.

Guess, A., Nagler, J., & Tucker, J. (2019). Less than you think: Prevalence and predictors of fake news dissemination on Facebook. *Science advances, 5*(1), eaau4586.

Hobbs, R. (2011). The state of media literacy: A response to Potter. *Journal of Broadcasting & Electronic Media, 55*(3), 419–430.

Hobbs, R., & Frost, R. (2003). Measuring the acquisition of media-literacy skills. *Reading Research Quarterly, 38*(3), 330–355.

Hobbs, R., & Jensen, A. (2009). The past, present, and future of media literacy education. *The Journal of Media Literacy Education, 1*(1), 1–11.

Jenkins, H. (2006). *Convergence culture: Where old and new media collide.* New York, NY: New York University Press.

Jones, R. H. (2013). Research methods in TESOL and digital literacies. *TESOL Quarterly, 47*(4), 843–848.

Jordan, K. (2013). (2013, February 13). Synthesising MOOC completion rates [Web log post]. Retrieved from https://moocmoocher.wordpress. com/2013/02/13/synthesising-mooc-completion-rates/

Kellner, D., & Share, J. (2005). Toward critical media literacy: Core concepts, debates, organizations, and policy. *Discourse: Studies in the Cultural Politics of Education, 26*(3), 369–386.

Kellner, D., & Share, J. (2007). Critical media literacy, democracy, and the reconstruction of education. In D. Macedo & S. R. Steinberg (Eds.), *Media literacy: A reader* (pp. 3–23). New York, NY: Peter Lang Publishing.

Knobel, M., & Lankshear, C. (2015). *Language, creativity, and remix culture. The Routledge handbook of language and creativity.* London, England: Routledge.

Knobel, M., & Lankshear, C. (2016). Digital media and literacy development. In A. Georgakopoulou & T. Spilioti (Eds.), *The Routledge handbook of language and digital communication* (pp. 151–165). New York, NY: Routledge.

Koltay, T. (2011). The media and the literacies: Media literacy, information literacy, digital literacy. *Media, Culture & Society, 33*(2), 211–221.

Lankshear, C., & Knobel, M. (Eds.). (2008). *Digital literacies: Concepts, policies and practices* (Vol. 30). New York, NY: Peter Lang Publishing.

Lave, J., & Wenger, E. (1991). *Situated learning: Legitimate peripheral participation.* Cambridge, UK: Cambridge University Press.

Lazer, D. M. J., Baum, M. A., Benkler, Y., Berinsky, A. J., Greenhill, K. M., Menczer, F., … Zittrain, J. L. (2018). The science of fake news: Addressing fake news requires a multidisciplinary effort. *Science, 359*(6380), 1094–1096. doi:10.1126/science.aao2998

Lincoln, Y. S., & Guba, E. G. (1985). *Naturalistic inquiry* (Vol. 75). Thousand Oaks, CA: Sage.

Livingstone, S. (2004). Media literacy and the challenge of new information and communication technologies. *The Communication Review, 7*(1), 3–14.

Livingstone, S., Van Couvering, E., & Thumim, N. (2005). *Adult media literacy: A review of the research literature.* London: Department of Media and Communications, London School of Economics and Political Science.

Martens, H. (2010). Evaluating media literacy education: Concepts, theories and future directions. *The Journal of Media Literacy Education, 2*(1), 1–22. Retrieved from http://altechconsultants.netfirms.com/jmle1/index.php/JMLE/article/view/71

Martin, A. (2008). Digital literacy and the "digital society". In C. Lankshear & M. Knobel (Eds.), *Digital literacies: Concepts, policies and practices* (pp. 151–176). New York, NY: Peter Lang Publishing.

Metzger, M. J. (2007). Making sense of credibility on the Web: Models for evaluating online information and recommendations for future research. *Journal* of the American Society for Information Science and Technology, 58(13), 2078–2091.

Mihailidis, P. (2009). The first step is the hardest: Finding connections in media literacy education. *Journal of Media Literacy Education, 1*(1). 53–67.

Mihailidis, P., & Viotty, S. (2017). Spreadable spectacle in digital culture: Civic expression, fake news, and the role of media literacies in "post-fact" society. *American Behavioral Scientist, 61*(4), 441–454.

National Association for Media Literacy Education. (2019). Media literacy defined. Retrieved July 1, 2019 from https://namle.net/publications/media-literacy-definitions/

Oeldorf-Hirsch, A., & Sundar, S. S. (2015). Posting, commenting, and tagging: Effects of sharing on Facebook. *Computers in Human Behavior, 44*, 240–249.

Pew Research Center. (2019, June) Many Americans say made-up news is a critical problem that needs to be fixed. Retrieved from https://www.journalism.org/2019/06/05/many-americans-say-made-up-news-is-a-critical-problem-that-needs-to-be-fixed/

Pinkleton, B. E., Austin, E. W., Cohen, M., Chen, Y. C., & Fitzgerald, E. (2008). The effects of a peer-led media literacy curriculum on adolescents' knowledge and attitudes toward sexual behavior and media portrayals of sex. *Health Communication, 23*(5), 462–472.

Reuters Institute (2019). Digital news report. Retrieved from http://www.digitalnewsreport.org/

Rheingold, H. (2010). Attention, and other 21st-century social media literacies. *Educause Review, 45*(5), 14–24.

Robinson, S. (2011). "Journalism as process": The organizational implications of participatory online news. *Journalism & Communication Monographs, 13*(3), 137–210.

Rosen, J. (2006). The people formerly known as the audience. Retrieved from http://archive.pressthink.org/2006/06/27/ppl_frmr.html

Saldaña, J. (2015). *The coding manual for qualitative researchers.* Thousand Oaks, CA: Sage.

Scharrer, E. (2006). "I noticed more violence:" The effects of a media literacy program on critical attitudes toward media violence. *Journal of Mass Media Ethics, 21*(1), 69–86.

Shah, D. (2019, January 6). Year of MOOC-based degrees: A review of MOOC stats and trends in 2018. Retrieved from https://www.class-central.com/report/moocs-stats-and-trends-2018/

Siemens, G. (2012a). Designing, developing, and running (massive) open online courses. (PowerPoint slides). Retrieved from http://www.slideshare.net/gsiemens/designing-and-running-a-mooc

Siemens, G. (2012b). MOOCs are really a platform. *Elearnspace* [Web log post]. Retrieved from http://www.elearnspace.org/blog/2012/07/25/moocs-are-really-a-platform/

Silverman, C., & Singer-Vine, J. (2016). Most Americans who see fake news believe it, new survey says. *BuzzFeed News (www.buzzfeed.com).* Retrieved from https://www. buzzfeed.com/craigsilverman/fake-newssurvey

Stephens, M., & Jones, K. M. (2014). MOOCs as LIS professional development platforms: Evaluating and refining SJSU's first not-for-credit MOOC. *Journal of Education for Library and Information Science, 55*(4), 345–361.

Stewart, B. (2013). Massiveness + openness = new literacies of participation? *Journal of Online Learning and Teaching, 9*(2), 228–238. Retrieved from http://jolt.merlot.org/vol9no2/stewart_bonnie_0613.htm

Strauss, A., & Corbin, J. M. (Eds.). (1997). *Grounded theory in practice*. Los Angeles, CA: Sage.

Street, B. (2003). What's "new" in New Literacy Studies? Critical approaches to literacy in theory and practice. *Current Issues in Comparative Education, 5*(2), 77–91.

Street, B. V. (2011). Literacy inequalities in theory and practice: The power to name and define. *International Journal of Educational Development, 31*(6), 580–586.

Tully, M., & Vraga, E. K. (2018). Who experiences growth in news media literacy and why does it matter? Examining education, individual differences, and democratic outcomes. *Journalism & Mass Communication Educator, 73*(2), 167–181.

13 A Model for Media Literacy Across a Lifespan
Wisdom from Pedagogical Pilots

George L. Daniels

Introduction

Imagine yourself around the dinner table at Thanksgiving, a holiday that tends to bring families together across generations. The most senior dinner attendees may be from the so-called "Silent" generation, born before 1945, while a few seats over or across the table are family members born in the 1990s, described as millennials. Those millennials' parents came of age as Generation Xers in a way much different from their parents described as baby boomers. All these family members have consumed media messages. But, their consumption habits differ, largely based on the technological advances of their time. Now, at the end of the second decade of the 21st century, increasing the media literacy of this inter-generational crowd will require different tools and techniques. While media literacy has most often been associated with K-12 students, new attention is being given to media literacy interventions for individuals of different ages (Lantela, 2019; Oliver & Williams-Duncan, 2019; Rasi, Vuojarvi, & Ruokamo, 2019).

Understanding that media literacy is a process rather than a thing, this chapter introduces a Model for Media Literacy Across a Lifespan (MLAL) with emphasis at three key points in that process of one becoming media literate: elementary school, college age, and seniors (65+). The author is an award-winning community-engaged researcher with a professional background as a broadcast journalist. Seeking to conceptualize much of his community work in the larger arena of mass media education, he developed the MLAL to argue for various "interventions" in which he was involved. Additionally, the model could serve to help attract external support for many media projects and programs, especially those outside of the traditional college classroom.

Grounded in the rich literature on media literacy, the model was put to the test in a series of pedagogical pilots. An elementary school re-branded itself to be a "School for Global Communicators and Leaders." The re-branding in 2018 coincided with classroom-learning activities and teacher training that included media literacy education. On the other end of the lifespan, a seven-week media literacy class was offered in 2018 for students in the University's Osher Lifelong Learning Institute (OLLI). "The Mass Media and Me" afforded about 20 seasoned adults a unique opportunity to explore the role of the mass media in their lives as seniors, most of whom were 65 and over. Wisdom from designing and teaching the class and insight from a reunion breakfast with some class members seven months later inform the MLAL Model. A third key point in the MLAL happens between the elementary school stage and the seniors' stage: College age. Taking an "integrative approach," media literacy exercises in 2018 and 2019 were employed in two college instructional settings. One course was primarily skills-based instruction on news reporting while the other setting engaged students in exercises that were introduced in diversity-centric conceptual courses.

The discussions in the media literacy arena continue to be robust, with more and more scholarship from a sub-field known as news or news media literacy (Maksl, Ashley, & Craft, 2014). Even after three journals – *Journal of Communication, American Behavioral Scientist* and *Journal of Broadcasting & Electronic Media* – offered special issues or point-counterpoint discussions about media literacy things remain somewhat unsettled. Many writers have pointed to the diversity or lack of consensus on what the term "media literacy" means. In this chapter, after reviewing the relevant literature on media literacy, a discussion of the pedagogical pilots follows with an emphasis on takeaways.

Review of the Literature

Defining Media Literacy

The movement known as media literacy gained much of its fuel a quarter-century ago when the Aspen Institute Communication and Society Program convened 25 educators and activists for a National Leadership Conference on Media Literacy (Aufderheide, 1997). A definition, vision, and framework for developing media literacy programs in the United States were developed. From that conference, we know a media-literate person is someone who can decode, evaluate, analyze, and produce both print and electronic media (p. 79). As Hobbs (1996) puts it, media literacy includes the skills of literacy extended to all message forms, encompassing reading and writing, speaking and listening, critical viewing and the ability to make your own messages using a wide range of technologies including audio technology, billboard, cameras, camcorders, and computers (p. 105).

The National Association for Media Literacy Education (NAMLE), which publishes the *Journal of Media Literacy Education*, defined media literacy as a "series of communication competencies, including the ability to access, analyze, evaluate and communicate information in a variety of forms, including print and on-print messages" (National Association for Media Literacy Education, 2012).

The concept may be presented differently for college students where scholars such as Lind (2019), in her fourth update of the widely used text *Race/Gender/Class/Media* in aiming to get students to be critical thinkers, employs the tactic of the Center for Media Literacy, which says media literacy is a "21st century approach to education – a framework to analyze, evaluate, create and participate with messages in a variety of forms" (p. 7). Now in its ninth edition, Potter's (2019) media literacy text defined media literacy as "a set of perspectives that we actively use to expose ourselves to the mass media to interpret the meaning of the messages we encounter" (p. 19).

Because it's built on a very sophisticated framework, Potter's (2019) definition is the one that guides our effort here to speak to media literacy across a lifespan. The foundation for his definition is comprised of three building blocks: skills, knowledge structures, and personal locus. He lists seven skills – analysis, evaluation, grouping, induction, deduction, synthesis, abstracting – before explaining media literacy is about getting better at using the skills when one encounters media messages. Beyond the skills, knowledge structures or sets of organized information in our memory, help us to make sense of the social and factual information we are exposed in the media every day. Potter (2019) argues that to be media literate, one needs knowledge structures in four areas: media industries, media audiences, media content, and media effects. The final building block of media literacy is one's personal locus, which includes an individual's goals and drives. In this chapter, we'll talk about media literacy referring back to Potter's (2019) definition and these building blocks as they appear across one's lifetime.

Lifetime Learning

While media literacy has been widely written about, debated, and theorized by scholars (Christ & Potter, 1998; Hundley, 2004; Kubey, 2004; Lewis & Jhally, 1998; Meyrowitz, 1998; Potter, 2004), scholars are now examining the concept as it plays out across one's lifespan.

In introducing their special issue on *Journal of Media Literacy Education* on media literacy across a lifespan, Rasi, Vuojarvi, and Ruokamo (2019) noted that adopting a life course perspective allows for media literacy competencies unfolding over time in response to changing historical conditions, social institutions, and policies. Their special issue included articles on adolescents' media literacy along with studies on developing adults' media literacy in university context. Additionally, one article discussed the media literacy of older adults in technology-supported home care services.

More than a decade ago, Poynton (2005) organized computer literacy into four developmental domains: childhood, young adulthood, middle adulthood, and older adulthood. Recently, Orzech, Moncur, Duran, and Trujillo-Pisanty (2018) investigated the digital personhood among UK citizens in one's online activity at three life transitions: leaving secondary school, becoming a parent, and retiring from work. Their study examined opportunities and challenges of navigating one's digital lifespan. Both of these studies focused on digital or computer literacy.

Oliver and Williams-Duncan (2019) spotlighted digital literacy across career stages. Their analysis of "ages and stages" in theological education was based on three dozen interviews with those involved in a Digital Media for Ministry course. The primary outcomes of the study were findings suggesting the importance redirecting instructor and student attention away from operational details of technology and toward the context of digital literacy practice and experience (rather than age).

One book-length project comes close to examining media literacy across a lifespan. Bolin's (2017) *Media Generations: Experience, Identity and Mediatised Social Change* used both quantitative and qualitative comparative research to analyze the role of the media in the formation of generational experience. The opening chapter unpacks generational theory while also explaining that one's generational media experience is an "intimate relationship that develops with media personalities and content from one's formative youth period" (p. 10). Bolin (2017) acknowledges that in terms of research on generations, many studies have focused on specific, single cohorts or generations such as the baby boomers of the 1960s, but few that have with cross-generational and cross-national comparisons of generations.

In the field of education, Heydon, McKee, and Daly (2017) produced an exploratory case study on how integrated digital media was used in an intergenerational art class. The participants in the ethnographic study were 15 elders and 9 preschool children (ages 4–5). The study revealed how uses of digital media in conjunction with other media allowed the class for a full spectrum of multimodality in making text. The digital media acted as a mediator to bring people physically together and virtually together through the sharing of accomplishments with loved ones. Sociability and opportunities for relationship were created by referencing texts together and created new opportunities for design (p. 370).

Elementary School

Potter (2019) says media literacy is comprised of skills, knowledge structures, and personal locus. The skills of which he speaks are developed in the earliest stages of life. For example, Hobbs (2017) presented a portrait of the Norrback Avenue School in Worcester, Massachusetts that since 1999 has operated with six communication themes: public speaking, dramatics, publishing, media analysis, media production and telecommunication. Being able to read to write using symbol systems of visual and electronic media is deeply connected to the traditional literacy skills of reading, writing, speaking and listening. In Hobbs' (2017) words "Media literacy is literacy for an information age" (p. 518). Starting at the elementary-school level increases the chances of achieving the end result, which Hobbs and Frost (2003) argue can occur by the time a child reaches high school. Students who received media-literacy instruction were more likely to recognize the complex blurring of information, entertainment, economics that are present in contemporary nonfiction media.

Also, those students who received media literacy instruction appeared to have a more nuanced understanding of interpreting textual evidence of different media formats (p. 351).

Based on Hundley's (2004) experience, fourth graders can be taught persuasive techniques in television commercials. And, Kubey (2004) argued for the critical importance of media education to the teaching of civics and social studies.

College Level

At the college level, Ashley (2015) found that introductory media studies courses most often address media ethics, media industries, and media history, with media literacy ranking fourth in the list of responses to the question "What do you cover in your course?" But when asked what they say is the primary focus – media literacy was tops. It was suggested that more emphasis should be placed on political economy, critical/cultural studies, and comparative media systems, topics associated with those in the field of critical media literacy (Ashley, 2015) In other words, introductory media studies courses should cover not just the content of the media but the political and economic contexts for that media content. Additionally, when it comes to assessment of the learning about media studies, few instructors used group projects or presentations or blogs. As tools associated with active learning and engagement, group projects, presentations, or blogs can facilitate the important outcome of media literacy (p. 171). Active learning and engagement can reflect student development of those knowledge structures that Potter (2019) notes is a component of media literacy.

Also at the college level, Lewis and Jhally (1998) in their essay on "The Struggle over Media Literacy" suggested that media literacy should integrate a textual analysis with questions of production and reception. In their view, media literacy is a way of "extending democracy to the place where democracy is increasingly scripted and defined" (p. 109).

Examining news media literacy, Vraga, Tully, Akin, and Rojas (2012) used a web-based experiment with biofuels-related interest groups and college students to determine if hostile interpretations of media content can be reduced through news media literacy training. They found strong support for the notion that media literacy affects individuals' perceptions of media credibility. Tully and Vraga (2018) published results of their latest study, a two-wave panel survey of college undergraduates enrolled in a basic communication course designed to assess students' growth of news media literacy (NML) over the course of the semester. They found course performance had no impact on gains in NML over the course of a semester (Tully & Vraga, 2018). The content of basic communication courses that does not explicitly address news media literacy does not directly encourage growth in NML measures (p. 169).

In the development of a media literacy college-level intervention, these perspectives on how to introduce it at the level of the introductory media course (Ashley, 2015) coupled with conveying the link to extending democracy (Lewis & Jhally, 1998) are especially important. For instance, if the group projects and class presentations are important, the size of the course is a consideration in structuring the optimum learning experience. If extending democracy is a goal, a service learning or civic engagement experience would facilitate that kind of learning.

Senior Citizens

When it comes to the media literacy of seniors, much of the writing and research on this segment of the population appears to have been done outside the United States. As Sargant (2004) reported in *Adults Learning* magazine, a publication from the United Kingdom, it is important to place the needs and interests of the entire adult population on the media literacy learning agenda. Media literacy exists when the user not only has access to full range of electronic media but also is able to comprehend the choices available and evaluate them. Providing some context for this discussion in the UK is Ofcom, UK's communications regulator, which says the government has the duty to promote media literacy under that country's Communications Act 2003 (Sargant, 2004).

Meanwhile in Spain, concerns about the aging population prompted Abad (2014) to study media literacy for older people facing the digital divide. Data showed that there is a generational digital divide to be overcome, which has triggered public policies that include a number of media literacy and e-learning projects that have been less than successful. Abad (2014) proposed a number of approaches to tackle the design of digital literacy programs for older people based on their degree of autonomy and the possibilities of enjoying everyday life.

Also from Spain, Del-Moral and Oviedo (2013) focused on seniors in the so-called "silent generation" to understand their level of media literacy through critical awareness, participation, and responsibility of seniors in the Austurias, a region on the northern edge of that country.

They surveyed a sample of elderly women of the so-called "silent generation" who were part of the Asturian Housewives Association. Their findings show the women surveyed believed that advertising lacks credibility and most don't consider themselves to be among the 86% of the population reportedly vulnerable to advertising's persuasive messages (Del-Moral & Oviedo, 2013).

In Canada, Schreurs, Quan-Haase, and Martin (2017) conducted face-to-face interviews and administered surveys to older adults to investigate how this population views its own digital skills, barriers to digital literacy, and support systems for help with technology. Their face-to-face interviews and surveys of older adults ranging in age from 60 to 84 in southwestern Ontario showed while many of the participants were adopters of technology, they sometimes lacked confidence in using technology even after they acquired it. The takeaway from this research is that media literacy efforts targeting this population should not assume lack of exposure to the technology but rather stress the importance of employing ways to build confidence in using it. A media literacy instructional model might include activating that allows those in this age group to use social media or mobile devices with which they have had less practice.

The most recent of these articles comes from Finnish Lapland, where 20 municipalities in 2017–2018 were involved in a trial of home technology solutions for seniors. Lantela (2019) interviewed 16 older adults with a mean of age 84 who used tablets and a so-called "smart flower stand," which sends alerts to a family member in the case of any disruption in daily life, such as staying in bed all day or leaving the house and not returning. Results showed that sensemaking among the older adults in this population or use or rejection of technologies is not an individual endeavor but intertwined with wider social issues (Lantela, 2019). Thus, media literacy education initiatives aimed toward older population should focus on access to technologies and the understanding of the digital environment (p. 160).

A Model for Media Literacy across a Lifespan (MLAL)

Based on the idea that media literacy operates on a continuum based on our overall perspective on the media (Potter, 2019) and that it is a perspective that we actively use to interpret meaning of messages we encounter, this chapter proposes a model that represents how one's literacy is constantly in a state of development from birth to death (see Figure 13.1). At every point of one's life, he or she is potentially in a position to build or improve on the knowledge structures, which Potter (2019) says are necessary to increase one's media literacy.

It is important to explain that this model was not pre-set or predetermined and then tested based on a set of pre-planned activities. Rather,

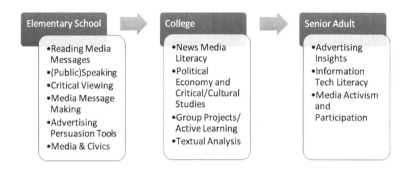

MODEL: Media Literacy Across a Lifespan

Figure 13.1 Media Literacy Across a Lifespan.

the author was engaged in settings where media literacy activities were already underway. The author attempted to take a "wider view" of the work of media scholars and media teachers through their interactions with different populations – pre-college, college, and post-college. All three populations reflect different points in one's life. The Model for Media Literacy Across a Lifespan (MLAL) suggests that rather than focusing on one stage of life, one should see the potential of impact on one's knowledge structure early in life (elementary school), at a key point in development into adulthood (college), and maturity later in the lifespan (seniors).

On the Model for Media Literacy Across Lifespan (Figure 13.1), at the elementary-school level, the elements of reading media messages, critical viewing of media messages, and media message making (Hobbs, 1996) are included. Also, we've added *Advertising Persuasion Techniques* (Hundley, 2004) as well as the topic of *Media and Civics/Social Studies* (Kubey, 2004).

At the college students phase, on the Model for Media Literacy Across a Lifespan (MLAL), we place *news media literacy* as an explicit topic that must be directly addressed (Tully & Vraga, 2018), *political economy and critical cultural studies* (Ashley, 2015), *group projects and active learning assignments* (Ashley, 2015), and *textual analysis to understand production and reception* (Lewis & Jhally, 1998).

And, finally at the Senior Adults Phase, we place three areas of emphasis or priority at the Senior Citizen moment on the Model for Media Literacy Across a Lifespan: **Advertising Insights** (Del-Moral & Oviedo, 2013), *Information Technology Literacy* (Schreurs, Quan-Haase, & Martin, 2017), *Media Activism and Participation* (Abad, 2014; Del-Moral & Oviedo, 2013).

At each moment on the Model for Media Literacy Across a Lifespan, there are key points that inform the approach to literacy at that stage, based on what's known from the literature. The inclusion of a particular activity does not preclude its importance in other stages. Rather, the activities might change as one gets older or may be introduced (rather than emphasized) at a younger stage. For example, critical viewing is emphasized at the elementary-school phase in this Model for this chapter, but one should be a critical viewer as a senior adult too. By the same token, information tech literacy has been a focus of research on seniors. However, we know that students are developing information tech literacy at younger ages. To further investigate the aspect of change over time would require a more sophisticated longitudinal study, which is beyond the scope of this chapter. Nonetheless, what follows are the specific areas addressed at the three points on the lifespan.

Since they existed before this investigation was conducted, the activities described here essentially became what the chapter refers to as "pedagogical pilots," or places for teaching that potentially could help students achieve media literacy learning outcomes. Within these three pilots, students would complete activities or exercises that strengthen the seven skills that Potter (2019) outlined as building blocks for media literacy. Likewise, the knowledge structures of media literacy could also be established or strengthened. Within each of the three pedagogical pilots, there were multiple assignments with different learning outcomes that were media literacy-related.

Popsicles, Public Speaking, Publications, and Podcasting

The first phase of the Model for Lifelong Media Literacy would take place in the early stages of formal schooling – pre-Kindergarten to fifth grade. In this pedagogical pilot, a schoolwide focus on communication includes "media literacy" as one of nine focus areas designed to engage the more than 300 students enrolled. While the school, which is situated in a predominantly African American, low-income community in the Southeastern United States, where most of the students are on free and reduced lunch, re-opened in Fall 2018 in renovated facilities that included a studio for broadcast television production and public-speaking consultations, the specific assignments began even earlier. Four noteworthy media literacy activities at the newly branded "School for Global Communicators and Leaders" reflect components on the MLAL.

Activity One

In Spring 2018, college student mentors from a university service-learning class guided fifth graders in doing online research about a particular country and then assisted them in developing a popsicle flavor, which reflected the culture and traditions of that country. In a poster presentation to their fellow fifth graders, they explained how they would advertise the popsicle. The popsicle project exercise integrated advertising insights and media activism components of the Media Literacy Across a Lifespan model. The fifth graders were engaged indirectly in the "doing" and "making" components of media literacy. Not only did the students meet and exceed expectations for learning about other cultures while understanding how the advertising industry works, they also successfully engaged in some "media making" in the development of their posters. A year after this activity was conducted, the Popsicle Project won the Top award in the 2019 International Communication Division Teaching Contest sponsored by the Association for Education in Journalism and Mass Communication (AEJMC).

Activity Two

In Summer 2018, a group of third and fourth graders were challenged to use the technologies of the Internet to research different facts and details about an assigned country. They took those facts and details and used them to prepare one-minute speeches. They presented their "Global Communication" speeches at the local university in a speak-off, which involved university students as judges. The judges recognized the top speeches for this public-speaking activity demonstrating the "participation" component of the MLAL. This activity was replicated with a group that included at least four participants from 2018. While the media and civics learning outcome (associated with media literacy) was not as strong in 2019, the achievement of public-speaking learning outcome was equally as dynamic as the prior year.

Activity Three

Third, fourth, and fifth graders worked collaboratively with a university journalism class to re-design the elementary school's seven-year-old newsletter. The elementary school students wrote and researched articles for the newsletter and by the end of the March 2019 had produced three editions of the re-designed publication. The third edition was themed to coincide with a statewide bicentennial celebration. The newsletter exemplified media activism and participation. The "media making" aspect of media literacy was demonstrated in a strong fashion in the production of the three newsletters.

Activity Four

A fourth example of a pedagogical pilot for the elementary media literacy phase took place in February and March of 2019 as a team of fifth graders was introduced to the medium of podcasting. By drafting questions, conducting interviews, and building the podcast, this activity emphasized the public-speaking, media-making, and persuasion aspects of media literacy. After visiting a college student radio station for guidance on how to conduct interviews, the students used the Vocaroo app on their Chromebooks to record conversations with special guests who visited the school. With some assistance from students and faculty from a local university, the students selected audio interview clips and produced what turned out to be one of nearly 6,000 entries for the Student Podcast Challenge, which was issued by National Public Radio. In their participation on the podcast team, the fifth graders developed information technology literacy, which is not featured until the senior adult phase of the model. As partners in learning about media, college students were integrated into each of the activities. But, the activities were not necessarily ones at the core of the second phase of the Media Literacy Across a Lifespan model.

Newscast Analysis and a Power Exercise

Activity One

At the college level, media literacy instruction can be embedded in skills courses where students are learning about professional media operations. In one activity, students in an Introduction to Electronic Reporting class, a core requirement for all majors in journalism/news media, prepared a newscast analysis. The assignment is primarily designed to force undergraduate students, many of whom are not accustomed to watching local television news, to consume at least one 30-minute show to detect what's happening behind the scenes. Emphasizing the active learning component at the college phase of the MLAL, the newscast analysis assignment also promotes news literacy instruction as students applied their knowledge of the news values and sharpened their ability to detect why some stories were chosen and others were not. The learning outcome is to get students to develop a critical eye when watching a news program, focusing less on their opinions about the stories and more on the media strategies employed by the developers of the message.

Activity Two

A second activity in the college students' pedagogical pilot focused on the political economy and critical cultural studies aspects of the Media Literacy Across a Lifetime model. After participating in multiple discussions about films, documentaries, and news reports in a course on Race, Gender, and Media, students in 2019 completed a "I've Got the Power" exercise. In the exercise, the college juniors and seniors were asked to identify individuals who could be influential in taking action in a number of areas. The areas included changing the way women are portrayed, changing the number of women in leadership roles, changing how seriously the feminist agenda is taken, and changing the way masculinity is performed. For each area – which person has the power? After naming these individuals, then they asked what they would do if they were given $5,000 to devise a plan for creating change in one of those areas in the questions. The last part of the exercise required students to plan an agenda for a lunch meeting with one of the power-players they identified could create change. Besides applying the concept of political economy and the media activism component of media literacy, this pedagogical pilot for college students set up the possibility for some intense classroom discussions. Among the power-players named were Actress Taraji P. Henson, Actor and Producer Dwayne "the Roc" Johnson, Former First Lady Michelle Obama, and Gloria Steinem. The results of these exercises with college students generally reflect success in achieving the intended learning outcomes. The "I've Got the Power" exercise has the potential to be expanded to a point where the college students would meet virtually with real players who can make change in the media.

Mass Media and Me

Targeted at those in the Senior Adults phase of the Media Literacy Across a Lifetime Model, the final pedagogical pilot was a seven-week continuing education course that targets senior citizens interested in expanding their horizons. Since 2001, Bernard Osher has made grants available to launch what are known as Osher Lifelong Learning Institutes (OLLI), which offer noncredit courses with no assignments or grades to "seasoned" adults. Most are retired. The course incorporating media literacy titled "The Mass Media and Me" notes in its course description: "This course is focused on how you as an individual are impacted by some non-news and non-political aspects of mass media. It focused on six areas where mass media play a key role in our lives: weather, sports, health, children, food and religion." It is worth noting that news media literacy was excluded from this course, since there are separate courses at the institute that focus on news and politics.

Roughly 20 senior adults enrolled in the course that began in September 2018. On the first day, the author administered an eight-question "Media Habits Check-up." It was designed to see if the findings in the research on seniors and information technology habits as reported by Schreurs, Quan-Haase, and Martin (2017) in Southwestern Ontario and Abad (2014) in Spain were the same among the retirees in this OLLI class taught in the Southeastern United States. While the surveys were not collected for analysis (as the purpose of the class was not data collection for research), in sharing their responses in class, the seniors reported that most spent several hours per day online and all had smartphones.

One member of the class was 90 years old and had his smartphone out during class each week. Most of the students began the class by talking about their social media experiences, and by the time of the unit on media and food, these senior adults demonstrated their skill at using digital coupons for their grocery and other shopping needs.

While the seven-week course ended in October 2018, the author invited students to share their insights in an informal follow-up discussion over breakfast in May 2019. Five of the 20 adults showed up (along with many of their spouses) for a "reunion" to talk about what they had learned from the OLLI course. It should be noted that four of the five had taken another course with the author called "The News about the News" in 2016. So, their recollections from both classes surfaced. The topics ranged from discussions about their decisions to stop subscribing to the local newspaper, the use of anonymous sources to the ethical dilemmas that they were asked to be involved in the class, and use of algorithms by some Internet websites. One class member readily admitted he did not remember specific things he learned from the OLLI class but took away "something that made him think in a different direction." Recalling our unit about advertising, one woman in the group noted, "Those hidden persuaders are subtle and effective." This informal discussion was not the only post-course feedback received. After the course ended, two students took time to send information in the mail to the author about a topic from the course, while the 90-year-old (mentioned earlier) called to leave a voicemail exclaiming how much he enjoyed the experience.

What Does It All Mean?

The evidence of experience in the three pedagogical pilots helps support the ideals of the Media Literacy Across a Lifespan (MLAL) Model. From the reflections of the seniors from the OLLI course to the insights the fifth-grade students gained from participating in the NPR Podcast Challenge or the college students who were required to analyze local newscasts, media literacy is indeed happening across one's lifespan. In the future, media literacy scholars would be well-served to employ a method of intentionally examining this "process" across a lifespan using a cohort of students. That cohort would be monitored over several years. For example, a seniors group composed of recent retirees could be monitored for a five or ten-year period to see how media literacy interventions might impact their experiences over that time period. Even more ambitious and a challenge, a group of elementary-school students could be followed through the point that they are attending college. A third way of increasing our knowledge about media literacy across the lifespan would be to study inter-generational groups within the same setting (i.e., extended family household including those at all three points on the MLAL or members of the same church or community group) to see how those in this inter-generational group benefit from media literacy activities.

Of course, no model is without its imperfections. One such imperfection in the MLAL is the long gap between a person reaching college age and a person who might classify himself or herself as a senior citizen. Rasi, Vuojarvi, and Ruokamo (2019) point out that a life course perspective means understanding that there is diversity both between and within the age groups. Additionally, looking at media literacy needs as purely a product of one's birth cohort is problematic. Terms such as "digital native" and "digital immigrant" fail to account for the diversity within a generation.

Further research might identify an intermediate point in one's working adult life span (i.e., second full-time job, geographic relocation, birth of first child). Studies should employ a design that enables the researcher to look within a generation to account for generational diversity. Wisdom from the lifespan research in the special issue of *Journal of Media literacy Education* could inform an "update" of the pedagogical pilots described in this chapter, which could be more formally evaluated with some type of summative assessment, the results of which could be used to clarify moments on the Media Literacy Across a Lifespan Model.

References

Abad, L. (2014). Media literacy for older people facing the digital divide: The e-inclusion programmes design. *Comunicar, 21*(42), 173–180.

Ashley, S. (2015). Media literacy in action? What are we teaching in introductory college media studies courses? *Journalism & Mass Communication Educator, 70*(2), 161–173.

Aufderheide, P. (1997). Media literacy: From a report of the National Leadership Conference on Media Literacy. In R. Kubey (Ed.), *Media literacy in the information age: Current perspectives* (pp. 79–86). New Brunswick, NJ: Transaction Publishers.

Bolin, G. (2017). *Media generations: Experience, identity and mediatized social change*. New York, NY: Routledge.

Christ, W. G., & Potter, W. J. (1998). Media literacy, media education and the academy. *Journal of Communication, 48*(1), 5–15.

Del-Moral, M. E., & Oviedo, L. V. (2013). Media literacy, participation and accountability for the media of generation of silence. *Comunicar, 20*(40), 173–181.

Heydon, R., McKee, L., & Daly, B. (2017). iPads and paintbrushes: Integrating digital media into an intergenerational art class. *Language and Education, 31*(4), 351–373.

Hobbs, R. (1996). Teaching media literacy—Yo! Are you hip to this? In E. E. Dennis & E. C. Pease (Eds.) *Children and the Media*. (pp. 103–111) New Brunswick, NJ: Transaction Publishers.

Hobbs, R. (2017). Media literacy, general semantics, and K-12 education. *ETC: A Review of General Semantics, 74*(3/4), 517–521.

Hobbs, R., & Frost, R. (2003). Measuring the acquisition of media-literacy skills. *Reading Research Quarterly, 38*(3), 330–355.

Hundley, H. L. (2004). A college professor teaches a fourth-grade media literacy unit on television commercials. *American Behavioral Scientist, 48*(1), 84–91.

Kubey, R. (2004). Media literacy and the teaching of civics and social studies at the dawn of the 21st century. *American Behavioral Scientist, 48*(1), 69–77.

Lantela, P. (2019) "So, tell me what kind of a thing it really is"—Finnish older adults making sense of home technology. *Journal of Media Literacy Education, 11*(2),146–166.

Lewis, J., & Jhally, S. (1998). The struggle over media literacy. *Journal of Communication, 48*(1), 109–120.

Lind, R. (2019). Laying a foundation for studying race, gender, class and the media. In R. A. Lind (Ed.) *Race/Gender/Class/Media: Considering diversity across audiences, content and producers* (4th ed., pp. 1–9). New York, NY: Routledge.

Maksl, A., Ashley, S. & Craft, S. (2014). Measuring news media eiteracy. *Journal of Media Literacy Education, 6*(3), 29–45.

Meyrowitz, J. (1998). Multiple media literacies. *Journal of Communication, 48*(1), 96–108.

National Association for Media Literacy Education. (2012). Media literacy defined. Retrieved from https://namle.net/publications/media-literacy-definitions/

Oliver, K. M., & Williams-Duncan, S. (2019) Faith leaders developing digital literacies: Demands and resources across career stages according to theological educators. *Journal of Media Literacy Education, 11*(2), 122–145.

Orzech, K. M., Moncur, W., Durrant, A., & Trujillo-Pisanty, D. (2018). Opportunities and challenges of the digital lifespan: Views of service providers and citizens in the U.K. *Information, Communication & Society, 21*(1), 14–29.

Potter, W. J. (2004). *Theory of media literacy: A cognitive approach.* Thousand Oaks, CA: Sage.

Potter, W. J. (2019). *Media literacy* (9th ed.). Thousand Oaks, CA: Sage.

Poynton, T. A. (2005). Computer literacy across the lifespan: A review with implications for educators. *Computers in Human Behavior, 21*(6), 861–872.

Rasi, P., Vuojarvi, H., & Ruokamo, H. (2019). Media literacy education for all ages. *Journal of Media Literacy Education, 11*(2), 1–19.

Sargant, N. (2004, December). Why does media literacy matter? *Adults Learning, 16*(4), 28–30.

Schreurs, K., Quan-Haase, A., & Martin, K. (2017). Problematizing the digital literacy paradox in the context of older adults' ICT use: Aging, media discourse, and self-determination. *Canadian Journal of Communication, 42*(2), 359–377.

Tully, M., & Vraga, E. K. (2018). Who experiences growth in news media literacy and why does it matter?: Examining education, individual differences, and democratic outcomes. *Journalism & Mass Communication Educator, 73*(2), 167–181.

Vraga, E. K., Tully, M., Akin, H., & Rojas, H. (2012). Modifying perceptions of hostility and credibility of news coverage of an environmental controversy through media literacy. *Journalism: Theory, Practice & Criticism, 13*(7), 942–959.

Part Four

Media Literacy and Social Action

14 Civic Standpoint and the Pursuit of Media Literacies

Paul Mihailidis, Moses Shumow[t], and Christopher Harris

Introduction: The problem of Media Pedagogies and Civic Outcomes

In a recent article titled "Elementary Education Has Gone Terribly Wrong," *Atlantic* reporter Natalie Wexler uncovers what she argues is a potentially detrimental evolution in the teaching of reading to young people. Wexler believes that a focus on skills, namely comprehension, inference, and the ability to draw conclusions, is doing serious harm to their ability to understand and process knowledge about the world and apply that knowledge to what they are reading and experiencing beyond the book. Writes Wexler (2019):

> American elementary education has been shaped by a theory that goes like this: Reading – a term used to mean not just matching letters to sounds but also comprehension – can be taught in a manner completely disconnected from content. Use simple texts to teach children how to find the main idea, make inferences, draw conclusions, and so on, and eventually they'll be able to apply those skills to grasp the meaning of anything put in front of them.
>
> (para. 28)

The argument that this approach is potentially disastrous emerges from data that shows that since the focus has been on "critical thinking" and "learning to learn," youth's actual knowledge retention and reading trajectories have been in decline (Wexler, 2019). But what Wexler finds particularly troubling is that this approach has created even greater inequalities between middle-to-upper-class communities and lower socio-economic communities. At the conclusion of her reporting, Wexler points to a few examples where teachers are inspiring interest and curiosity and using such engagement to build reading skills and knowledge base. The examples shared in the article detail stories of children who, initially evaluated as low-tier readers, become curious and passionate about subjects in class, and their reading improves dramatically.

This example resonates with contemporary debates around media literacy approaches to preparing young people for lives of active engagement in the world. In recent years there has been an increase in the call for, and question of, media literacy's relationship to civic participation and social change. A debate was initiated in 2010 when James Potter penned an essay titled "The State of Media Literacy," in which he argued that, despite the growth of research and practice around the term "media literacy," little cohesion, direction, or application has shown precisely how or what the outcomes of media literacy pedagogies or interventions are. While Potter praised the abundance of interest in the space of study, and attention that media literacy was receiving, his review of the field found definitional diffusion, and lack of cohesion with respect to what media literacy is intended to achieve and the actual outcomes of what scholars say media literacy produces. Most focus of the research and teaching was around "the design of specific interventions that can successfully train people to avoid negative media effects" (Potter, 2010, p. 690).

In a spirited response to Potter's essay, Renee Hobbs pushed back on what she believes is a conservative and outdated review of the media literacy space: "Holding on to outdated views will not enable communication researchers to contribute productively to the robust and transdisciplinary dialogue about media literacy now occurring in schools, colleges, and nonprofit community centers across the nation" (Hobbs, 2011, p. 428). Hobbs is particularly concerned with the lack of complexity or willingness to embrace a more expansive idea of the type of research that is pushing media literacy in new directions. While this debate was confined to the pages of the *Journal of Broadcast and Electronic Media* (JoBEM), with an additional response by Potter and a rejoinder published by Hobbs, it resonated with a larger narrative around the intentions of media literacy interventions, and how we understand their impacts, whether as providing skills to cope with negative media effects or how they connect to citizenship outcomes writ large.

In 2017, danah boyd published a controversial essay in which she critiques media literacy's efficacy in general: "Did Media Literacy Backfire?" Boyd (2017) stoked controversy by questioning the basic premises of the media literacy movement, where she writes:

> In the United States, we're moving towards tribalism, and we're undoing the social fabric of our country through polarization, distrust, and self-segregation. And whether we like it or not, our culture of doubt and critique, experience over expertise, and personal responsibility is pushing us further down this path.
>
> (para. 27)

Boyd argues that in contemporary digital culture, contemporary approaches to media literacy are perhaps perpetuating some of the fractures that exist in how young people are using and misusing media for personal and public use. Boyd (2017) argues that "media literacy asks people to raise questions and be wary of information that they're receiving. People are. Unfortunately, that's exactly why we're talking past one another." While this argument received significant pushback, it led to needed questioning about what media literacy approaches today are prioritizing. In the wake of 2016 U.S. presidential elections and the fake news phenomenon, media literacy is being called upon to serve as a solution to these problems. Boyd is right to say that this focus is misguided, largely because media literacy efforts are constrained by what she articulates as a "failure to take into consideration the cultural context of information consumption that we've created over the last thirty years" (Boyd, 2017, p. 83). While Boyd's argument perhaps generalizes a complex space of research and practice, her instincts to question the value of media literacy bring important questions to light about media literacy's outcomes.

In a recent book by one of the authors of this chapter titled *Civic Media Literacies: Re-Imagining Human Connection in an Age of Digital Abundance*, Mihailidis (2018) picks up on boyd's argument to present structural constraints that are hampering contemporary media literacy initiatives. Mihailidis identifies five constraints – critical distance, transactionality, deficit focus, content-orientation, and individual responsibility – that are constraining media literacy initiatives as they relate to contemporary digital culture. Media literacy, Mihailidis argues, continues to prioritize skill development, comprehension, and drawing conclusions over the types of knowledge and interests that can spur using media to find interests and engagement with the world.

Returning to the opening example of the American elementary education system, we find similar challenges in contemporary approaches to media literacy initiatives. In the call for teaching more people how to deconstruct media, make smart media choices, analyze, evaluate, compare, and create information, we run the risk of providing a set of detached skills that are not connected to any of the individual or collective knowledge bases or content structures that motivate a sense of accountability to communities and societies. We also run the risk of assuming that teaching such skills equates to a moral good. Danah Boyd (2018) warns us that "developing media making skills doesn't guarantee that someone will use them for good. This is the hard part" (para. 41). Boyd (2018) continues:

> Most of my peers think that if more people are skilled and more people are asking hard questions, goodness will see the light. In talking about misunderstandings of the First Amendment, Nabiha Syed of Buzzfeed highlights that the frame of the "marketplace of ideas" sounds great, but is extremely naive. Doubling down on investing in individuals as a solution to a systemic abuse of power is very

American. But the best ideas don't always surface to the top. Nervously, many of us tracking manipulation of media are starting to think that adversarial messages are far more likely to surface than well-intended ones.

(para. 42)

There are significant risks associated with focusing on skills detached from the social and civic contexts within which media are situated. Studies have shown that this may breed heightened cynicism and refusal to engage (Mihailidis, 2009) or simply expand the inequalities that exist in young learners (Kahne, Nam-Jin, & Feezell, 2012).

If a heightened sense of civic engagement and participation are the true goals of media literacy, then we need to find ways to re-prioritize what media literacy interventions look like when they focus on explicit civic outcomes. In other words, we may ask the question, what is a media literacy intervention that embraces social justice and civic identity? And what are the attributes of media literacy initiatives that, as Ito, Soep, Kligler-Vilenchik, Shresthova, Gamber-Thompson, and Zimmerman (2015) write "mobiliz[es] young people's deeply felt interests and identities in the service of achieving the kind of civic voice and influence that is characteristic of participatory politics" (p. 17). In this chapter we argue for the need for media literacy initiatives, across all levels of formal and informal education, to revisit, and reprioritize, their connection to civic and social life. As we have argued in the past, we believe that media literacy must be more intentional in its connection to civic realities of young people:

> Media literacies…must be more intentional in how they connect to stated claims of empowering people to better engage and participate in civic life. In its growth over the last decades, and even half a century, media literacies have emphasized skills and assumed positive outcomes of not only more critical media viewers but also citizens who are better equipped to engage.

(Mihailidis, 2018, p. 101)

We place this emphasis within the context of an American culture enveloped in neoliberal realities, where giant tech companies and platforms are driven by the pursuit of market gain and revenue accrual over that of civic responsibility.

In the following sections, we will define the current state of neoliberal society that media literacies exist within and argue for this to be the departure point for media literacy initiatives in formal and informal spaces of learning. We then reintroduce the work of three seminal scholars that emerged from the activist pedagogy tradition. bell hooks, W.E.B. DuBois, and Paolo Freire have much to teach us about pedagogies that support a more inclusive and just world and that resist knowledge as transaction and skill attainment alone. While these three scholars are well known to the media literacy field and often evoked as thinkers who helped set a foundation for media literacy interventions, we place them together to show how we may consider refocusing the design and deployment of media literacy initiatives to have an explicit civic mindedness. Our intention is to draw from the radical tradition to start robust conversations about the assumptions that we carry into our media literacy work on a daily basis.

Media Literacy's Civic Identity in Neoliberal Times

The neoliberal era in which we find ourselves is characterized by a market-driven and hyper-individualistic morality that exalts self-interest, promotes indifference toward others, devalues imagination, and acts to pervert notions of the public/common good (see Giroux, 2014; Hedges, 2015; McNally, 2011). These realities are complemented by the growth of platforms that prioritize transaction over relation, profit over responsibility, and control over reciprocity. Large media companies regularly manipulate their information architectures to be evermore extractive. We have seen the likes of Amazon, Google, Facebook, Snapchat, and YouTube completely disrupt information flows and the ways in which we access and assess information online. Regulators continue to struggle to harness these companies as they evolve their technologies and algorithms beyond what any policy can respond to in a timely manner.

The result is a media ecosystem beset by a culture of distrust: brought about by the fracturing of societies as they identify more with peer online groups than with the public institutions designed to serve the common good. Studies have highlighted the growing distrust of public institutions, and specifically media institutions (Edelman, 2017). At the same time, social networks have increased the levels of perceived bias and inaccuracy of the press by readers (Knight, 2018). The dismantling of old media archetypes and the emergence of new platforms have fueled users' distrust in media to the extent that some platforms are attempting to build in measures of trust, quality, and reliability into systems never designed to evaluate such elements. The fragile and error-prone nature of these changes has eroded user confidence and may finally be slowing user adoption for some social media sites (Newman, 2018). Message apps are now replacing social media sites as sources for news for much of the world, according to the Reuters and Oxford 2018 Digital News Report, which found "WhatsApp is now used for news by around half of our sample of online users in Malaysia (54%) and Brazil (48%) and by around third in Spain (36%) and Turkey (30%)" (Newman, 2018). As old ecosystems crumble, the impetus on sharing reliable and factual information is shifting to the publisher or platform instead of with the individual reporter or journalist. The same study found "most respondents believe that publishers (75%) and platforms (71%) have the biggest responsibility to fix problems of fake and unreliable news" (Newman, 2018). Where government intervention in media was once akin to censorship or authoritarian control, calls for citizens are government intervention on behalf of stopping fake news from proliferating are increasingly common (Applebaum, 2019).

Confronted with these new realities, media literacy interventions are being called upon to produce learning experiences and outcomes that serve to combat unbound and unregulated technological expansion and market forces that continue to destabilize the public mission of news and media. Media literacies, in short, are being asked to contribute to the creation of emergent publics that possess the capacity and motivation to address the conditions of the day (Glaude, 2008).

Publics are forged when, through dialogue, a group of people develop a sense of purpose and decide to collaboratively and systematically care for the consequences of the problems they collectively face (Dewey, 1954). To this end, today's media literacy interventions must be concerned with fostering dialogue. They must work to bridge gaps between their interventions and the communities in which people work and live, marshaling their experiences, passions, and positions in efforts to facilitate the "authentic, trusting, and mutually beneficial" exchange of ideas (Koirala-Azad & Fuentes, 2009). Such dialogue pushes participants to achieve the civic-minded standpoint – an individual-orienting philosophy born from the realization of a structurally enforced shared social location, defined by empathy for others, and achieved through collective struggle – requisite for mounting meaningful challenges to the atomizing, exploitative, and hard-hearted discourses that underpin the neoliberal project (Giroux, 2011; Wood, 2005). As technologies increasingly fracture our civic infrastructures, and mediate public discourse, it has become increasingly difficult to navigate what strong publics look and feel like online and how media literacy can support such publics.

DuBois Freire and hooks: Revisiting Media Literacy's Civic-Minded Roots

To reflect on how media literacies may best support publics to face the challenges of the day, we may benefit by exploring the declarations of activist scholars that have come before us. W.E.B. DuBois, Paolo Freire, and bell hooks, although writing against varying historical backdrops and in response to distinct socio-political exigencies (informed by differences in race, class, gender, and nationality), share an approach to education defined by a deep commitment to humanistic and democratic ideals. Their work reveals the pivotal importance of critical pedagogy to the process of a civic-minded standpoint and the construction of emergent publics. And, they unanimously contend that education should be action-oriented, responsive, and help learners navigate the tension between individual pursuits and community purpose.

DuBois, Freire, and hooks wrote with passion and urgency, embracing education as an ameliorative force for the bettering of society through aiding the development of self-reliant and socially responsible citizens – individuals able and motivated to intelligently intervene in the world around them. For education to be successful in this endeavor, they argued, it must move beyond a narrow instrumentalism and emphasize empathy, self-reflection, and social interaction. To this end, they echoed the earlier work of John Dewey, who wrote in 1897, "education is the fundamental method of social progress and reform" and should guide students in the process of "coming to share in the social consciousness; and that the adjustment of individual activity on the basis of this social consciousness is the only sure method for social reconstruction" (pp. 77–78).

An abiding commitment to humanism and democracy animates DuBois, Freire, and hooks's perspective on civic-mindedness. And owing to their membership in and work with oppressed social groups, they explicitly addressed standpoint formation and placed great emphasis on the politicizing effects of activist pedagogy. As an African American scholar working in a period plagued by a socially, economically, and legally enforced racial caste system, DuBois's primary pedagogical concern was what he termed the problem of Negro education. For DuBois, Negro education needed to have as its focus the training of talented persons of broad vision who could, through a method of organized intelligence, effectively press for social change and racial uplift. Speaking in 1933, on the responsibilities of black colleges at Fisk University (his alma mater), DuBois claimed, "If the college can pour into the coming age an American Negro who knows himself and his plight and how to protect himself and fight race prejudice, then the world of our dreams will come and not otherwise" (Provenzo, 2002).

DuBois emphasized the need for education to challenge the inherent racism of institutional structures. Education, to DuBois, was a form of emancipation from the status quo that empowered the few and kept many in poverty and excluded from the types of privilege that societies offered. DuBois' focus on education for leadership in the black community meant a necessary struggle against the ideas that kept oppression and segregation in daily life. DuBois prioritized making explicit the connections between ideas and practices that support democracy. He advocated for a standpoint formation, where by black people understood their social position and education was just one way in which *social reconstruction* could begin. To achieve this reconstruction, education "always will have, an element of danger and revolution, of dissatisfaction and discontent" (DuBois, 1903, p. 8). It is this activism and tension that pushes the pursuit of education into an emancipatory lens and context. DuBois advocated for these positions as core to the goal of building a more equitable future for black people, and democracy.

Freire (1921–1997) developed his philosophies on education through teaching literacy to Brazil's rural poor during the early days of the neoliberal project. Committed to dialogue and convinced of the transformative power of education, Freire promoted a pedagogy aimed at the creation of critically conscious individuals – radically curious, politically aware, and empowered to intervene. He advocated an approach to education that sought to politicize through problematizing the future, explaining that "it is necessary to reinvent the future" and that "education is indispensable for this reinvention" (Freire & Macedo, 1998, p. 268). Freire believed that genuine education grounded in democratic praxis could provide conditions that would allow even the most downtrodden learners to re-create themselves into self-aware, self-determined, and community-minded shapers of their own destiny. Freire (1970) pushed against what he considered a "banker model" of education, where he suggests:

> The teacher talks about reality as if it were motionless, static, compartmentalized, and predictable. Or else he expounds on a topic completely alien to the existential experience of the students. His task is to "fill" the students with the contents of his narration – contents which are detached from reality, disconnected from the totality that engendered them and could give them significance. Words are emptied of their concreteness and become a hollow alienated and alienating verbosity. The outstanding characteristic of this narrative education, then, is the sonority of words, not their transforming power.
>
> (p. 72)

In this model of teaching, skills and information dissemination are prioritized over situating learning in the struggles of contemporary times. Freire acknowledges this type of education as a form of depositing information to those who are "on the inside" of society, supported by structures and systems designed to assist them. Education in this context signifies domination by those who learn the skills and norms of the systems but not the pursuit of liberation, which to Freire (1970) means "adopting instead a concept of woman and man as conscious beings, and consciousness as consciousness intent upon the world" (p. 6).

Freire's termed *conscientização* – or "critical consciousness" – are pedagogies that help people see the world "not as a closed world from which there is no exit, but as a limiting situation which they can transform" (Freire, 1970, p. 49). In a Freirean model of media literacy, young people begin their learning experiences eager to participate in civic life, to challenge injustices, to advocate for change they believe in, and to support marginalized populations around the world. This eagerness emerges from inquiries that reside within their personal and lived experiences, and that they are familiar and engaged with. Their lofty ideals are often constrained by structural barriers that orient knowledge around usefulness and career and sees digital and social media as primarily antithetical to the teaching and learning in the classroom. Freirean approaches work to destabilize such constraints and bring the pursuit of media pedagogies into the realm of consciousness and liberation of publics oppressed by current structures.

Bell hooks (1952–present) employs a radical interpretation of feminist theory to expand upon and deepen the activist pedagogies advanced by DuBois and Freire. She agrees wholeheartedly with her predecessors' claims that educating change agents must involve fostering standpoint formation and takes an even more oppositional stance advocating an approach to teaching that embraces transgression – challenging and moving beyond socially imposed boundaries/limits on identity and behavior that seek to reproduce the status quo – as a principal building block (hooks, 1994). Having attended segregated primary schools in the rural south, coming of age in the twilight of the Black Power movement, and entering the academia at the dawn of the Reagan revolution, hooks also argues for a critical pedagogy that seeks to illuminate the ways that racism, sexism, and wealth-worship intersect and act to devalue and dispossess vulnerable groups. hooks asserts that education as it should be is a practice of freedom. hooks (1994) calls for a manner of teaching that "respects and cares for the souls" of students and for her: "[T]he classroom remains the most radical space of possibility in the academy" (pp. 12–13).

This radical formation of the classroom is, to hooks, a space that is empowered by relation and a sense of commitment to each other. She writes, "as a classroom community, our capacity to generate excitement is deeply affected by our interest in one another, in hearing one another's voices, in recognizing one another's presence" (hooks, 1994, p. 10). What does a learning space that is empowered by interest in one another look like? To hooks it's a space that is not marked by knowledge as information, that is not about obedience and the retention of information, or by the learning of skills. Rather, it's about collective engagement in ideas, in others, and in the resources that can lead to a disruption of systems. hooks articulates this as the process of freedom, whereby learners are challenged by and challenge status quos and transgress together to new ideas and provocations against the structures that work to oppress.

Why place Dubois, Freire, and hooks in dialog with one another? And why now? In a moment where media literacies are being asked to be evermore present in formal and informal spaces of learning, we believe that their core mission and value to civic life must be reinforced. The risk is that we continue to prioritize teaching skills that are disconnected from interests and that we unwillfully prioritize drawing conclusions about media structures and systems over the need to connect such learning experiences to people's pursuit of liberation, emancipation, and freedom from that which oppresses.

This is especially prescient; in a time marked by stark systemic inequalities – brought on and exacerbated by predatory economic policies, divisive political rhetoric, and the misguided worship of technology – collaborative efforts of sustained resistance are imperative (see Eubanks, 2012; Sassen, 2014). To this end, DuBois, Freire, and hooks, through their emphasis on pedagogy that supports standpoint formation and collective struggle to empower those at the margins of society, take on a vital role in this grim set of circumstances. Revisiting their core ideas allows us to reclaim the urgency, democratic commitment, and optimism of their words and actions. It also allows us to advocate for media literacy interventions to continue to teach skills and competencies but to do so within the contexts set by these scholar-activists.

The structural systems of injustice and inequality, as well as attacks on the role of education, with which scholars such as hooks, Freire, and DuBois were concerned are as relevant, if not more so, today: one can argue that in the current moment the ideological underpinnings justifying harmful social disjunctures have become even more deeply entrenched and go widely unquestioned. Media literacy, we believe, must start here, to meet the lofty goals it asks of itself.

Media Literacies: Re-Prioritizing Civic-Mindedness

In this chapter we have evoked the work of scholar activists bell hooks, W.E.B. DuBois, and Paolo Freire to call for a re-prioritization of the civic-minded pursuit of media literacy. In a sense, we are calling for a commitment of educators, activists, and practitioners at all levels and in all spaces of work to articulate and assert the civic value and purpose of their work. Is it to simply make young people better able to discern facts from fiction? Is it to help teach how advertising works? Or is it to help them understand how these skill sets can be used to empower communities? To find ways to support those in need? To liberate societies from the oppressive structures that exacerbate and sustain inequities?

In his *Team Human* initiative Rushkoff highlights the need for human connection in our mediated realities:

> Eye contact is what forges solidarity, that's when the mirror neurons are going off, when you build rapport, when you see someone's pupils getting bigger because they're agreeing with you, or smaller because they're confused, or they nod: they breathe with you. That's when the conspiracy begins. Literally, conspire means to breathe together. When people are breathing together is when they're dangerous.
>
> (Pasternak, n.d.)

In a time where humans exist in less physically connected spaces, we may ask how media literacies can bring people together not to share information alone but to be present, conscious, and invested in each other. We believe that media literacy initiatives need to re-prioritize the human element in our mediated realities.

Media literacies that combat the current crises of trust and engagement necessitate a type of soulful engagement: a commitment to be in relation with others, to experience co-liberation and focus on a civic standpoint. If our media pedagogies are to focus not only on giving more resources for learning but also on providing more spaces for the type of engagement needed to persist towards a civic standpoint, then they necessitate the type of presence and commitment to learning that is not just a signal of affiliation or a way to show that we care about an idea, or have learned a set of skills. They must transcend transaction-mindset, where learners succeed in mastering a skill or competency, and towards building as a form of co-liberation, where learners, educators, and communities transform and are transformed by the pedagogical process itself.

Where can this begin? hooks, DuBois, and Freire focus on the need for education to transgress, to lead to a critical consciousness: the ability for people to envision themselves as able to transform situations within which oppression exists. Such visioning may start with a focus on care. What do we care for, why, and how? This focus may help learners to engage in media literacy experiences that develop what education scholar Nel Noddings (2003) called a *caring ethic*. Caring ethics embrace relation; they ask people to engross themselves in sympathy for others and in energy devoted to the natural human urge to combat injustices. As Noddings advocated for a feminist approach to a caring ethic, she asked her readers not only to *care about* – signal their affiliation for a cause or issue – but to strive to *care for* to commit time and energy to the social pursuits that matter in the world.

Media literacy today, if it is to meet the lofty standards placed upon it in a time when our digital infrastructures are causing significant stress on our social systems, must focus on a civic standpoint and the pursuit of liberation, transgression, and critical consciousness. Otherwise, it runs the risk of teaching skills to combat technologies that will always outpace their educational responses and that will prepare people to draw conclusions to issues and ideas that they find little value in pursuing, personally or publicly.

References

Applebaum, A. (2019, February 1). Regulate social media now. The future of democracy is at stake. *The Washington Post*. Retrieved from https://www.washingtonpost.com/opinions/global-opinions/regulate-social-media-now-the-future-of-democracy-is-at-stake/2019/02/01/781db48c-2636-11e9-90cd-dedb0c92dc17_story.html?noredirect=on boyd, D. (2017). Did media literacy backfire?. Data + Society. Retrieved from https://points.datasociety.net/did-media-literacy-backfire-7418c084d88d

boyd, D. (2018, March 9). You think you want media literacy, do you? *Data + Society*. Retrieved from https://points.datasociety.net/you-think-you-want-media-literacy-do-you-7cad6af18ec2

Dewey, J. (1954). *The public and its problems.* Athens, GA: Swallow Press/Ohio University Press.

Dewey, J. (1897). My pedagogical creed. *The School Journal, LIV*(3), 77–78.

DuBois, W. E. B. (1903). *The souls of black folk.* Chicago, IL: A.C. McClurg & Co.

Edelman. (2017). *Edelman trust barometer.* Retrieved from https://www.edelman.com/research/2017-edelman-trust-barometer

Eubanks, V. (2012). *Digital dead end: Fighting for social justice in the information age.* Cambridge, MA: MIT Press.

Freire, P. (1970). Pedagogy of the oppressed (revised). New York, NY: Continuum.

Freire, A. M. A., & Macedo, D. (1998). The Paulo Freire reader. New York, NY: Cassell and Continuum.

Giroux, H. A. (2011). The crisis of public values in the age of the new media. *Critical Studies in Media Communication, 28*(1), 8–29.

Giroux, H. A. (2014). *Neoliberalism's war on higher education.* Chicago, IL: Haymarket Books.

Glaude, E. S. (2008). *In a shade of blue: Pragmatism and the politics of Black America.* Chicago, IL: University of Chicago Press.

Hedges, C. (2015). *Wages of rebellion: The moral imperative of revolt.* New York, NY: Nation Books.

Hobbs, R. (2011). The state of media literacy: A response to Potter. *Journal of Broadcasting & Electronic Media, 55*(3), 419–430.

hooks, bell. (1994). *Teaching to transgress: Education as the practice of freedom.* New York, NY: Routledge.

Ito, M., Soep, E., Kligler-Vilenchik, N., Shresthova, S., Gamber-Thompson, L., & Zimmerman, A. (2015). Learning connected civics: Narratives, practices, infrastructures. *Curriculum Inquiry, 45*(1), 10–29.

Kahne, J., Lee, N. J., & Feezell, J. T. (2012). Digital media literacy education and online civic and political participation. *International Journal of Communication, 6,* 24. Retrieved from https://ijoc.org/index.php/ijoc/article/view/999

Knight Foundation. (2018, June 30). Perceived accuracy and bias in the news media. A report by the Knight Foundation. Retrieved from https://knightfoundation.org/reports/perceived-accuracy-and-bias-in-the-news-media

Koirala-Azad, S., & Fuentes, E. (2009). Introduction: Activist scholarship-possibilities and constraints of participatory action research. *Social Justice, 36*(4), 1.

McNally, D. (2011). *Global slump: The economics and politics of crisis and resistance.* Oakland, CA: PM Press.

Mihailidis, P. (2009). Beyond cynicism: Media education and civic learning outcomes in the university. *International Journal of Media and Learning, 1*(3), 1–13.

Mihailidis, P. (2018). *Civic media literacies: Re-imagining human connection in an age of digital abundance.* New York, NY: Routledge.

Newman, N. (2018). Reuters Institute digital news report. England: Oxford University. Retrieved from http://www.digitalnewsreport.org/survey/2018/overview-key-findings-2018/

Noddings, N. (2003). *Caring: A feminine approach to ethics and moral education.* Berkley, CA: University of California Press.

Pasternak, A. (n.d.). The economy needs to be more human: A chat with Douglas Rushkoff. *Motherboard.* Retrieved from https://motherboard.vice.com/en_us/article/qkjwa3/douglas-rushkoff-team-human-podcast

Potter, W. J. (2010). The state of media literacy. *Journal of Broadcasting & Electronic Media, 54*(4), 675–696.

Provenzo, E. F. Jr, (Ed.). (2002). *Du Bois on education* (p. 248). New York, NY: Altamira Press.

Sassen, S. (2014). *Expulsions.* Cambridge, MA: Harvard University Press.

Wexler, N. (2019, August). Elementary education has gone terribly wrong. *The Atlantic.* Retrieved from https://www.theatlantic.com/magazine/archive/2019/08/the-radical-case-for-teaching-kids-stuff/592765/

Wood, J. T. (2005). Feminist standpoint theory and muted group theory: Commonalities and divergences. *Women and Language, 28*(2), 61.

15 The Colombian Freedom of Information Act

Using Media Literacy to Understand and Implement the Law

Paula Pérez, Jairo Becerra, and Julián Rodríguez

Introduction

The Law of Transparency and Right to Access Public Information in Colombia (hereinafter "Transparency Law"), equivalent to the Freedom of Information Act (FOIA) of the United States, was developed within the framework of a set of policies, laws, and decrees issued in the last 15 years (Becerra et al., 2015, p. 179). This Colombian Act seeks to guarantee the right to access public information and defines the procedures for its exercise, encouraging, in this way, the use of information and communication technologies (ICT) (Law 1712, 2014, Art. 1). Although the exercise of these rights allows communication between citizens and the administration, the report prepared by the Colombian Ombudsman concluded that the law is little known and, therefore, little used by citizens (Defensoría del Pueblo, 2016).

The findings by the Colombian Ombudsman's report presented an opportunity to develop a media and information literacy (MIL) project. The literacy project adopted the definition of MIL developed by the UNESCO's Communication and Information Sector: "Skills that allow citizens to understand the role and functions of the media in democratic societies, recognize the need for information, locate and access relevant information" and participate with the media, including the Internet, in democracy (Grizzle et al., 2013, p. 13).

In this context, the *Universidad Católica de Colombia* and The University of Texas at Arlington worked on the research project on the Colombian Transparency Law and later on the research project on Law and Big Data. As a result, these universities developed software for the implementation of the Law on Transparency that seeks to facilitate citizen-administration communication through the use of the Internet. In the application phase of these projects, a software called *Transparenci@* was used in two communities located in the metropolitan area of Bogotá, Colombia, for the purpose of creating a Transparency Law training protocol, and, therefore, increasing awareness of the right to access public information.

Normative Framework

Importance of the Transparency Law

The Transparency Law is the result of an interdisciplinary effort in search of the guarantee of the right to access to public information, transparency, and improvement of the citizen-administration relationship (Pérez Gómez, 2017, p. 143). The importance of Law 1712 (2014) lies in the recognition of the right to access public information as a fundamental right and in the promotion of the use of ICT in favor of its guarantee. The right to access public information has been defined as a "universal human right, so that every person is entitled to this right without further limitations than those stipulated by law"(Hernández Chávez & Álvarez Enríquez, 2015, p. 6). Thus, the American Convention on Human Rights (1969) and the International Covenant on Civil and Political Rights (1966), which are part of the Colombian constitutionality block, highlight the right to access information in their Articles 19 and 13, respectively.

The guarantee of the right to access public information strengthens the function of the government administration by recovering legitimacy for state institutions; facilitating the exercise of social control of public management; and contributing to the development of the constitutional principles of transparency, responsibility, effectiveness, efficiency, impartiality, and citizen participation in the management of public resources (Ministry of Education, 2018). It is important to highlight that the right to access public information not only includes the duty of the subjects bound by the Transparency Law to disclose public information but also the right of those administered to request public information enshrined in Articles 24, 25, and 26 of Law 1712 (2014).

This norm allows individuals and groups "to have access to the policies through which the government makes decisions regarding health, education, housing and infrastructure projects, and the reasons that support such decisions" (Neuman, 2002, p. 5). In this way, citizens and the media and information industries acquire roles enabling them to exert their rights and exercise supervision and control over public management. "These pro-social and democratic behaviors depend, to a large extent, on the information provided through the media" (Gil de Zúñiga, Diehl, & Ardévol-Abreu, 2017, p. 574).

Even though the law guarantees the right to access public information, when the researchers presented the first version of the digital tool Transparenci@ to the municipality of San Francisco (Colombia), they found that the city preferred not to promote the tool among the community because information and public data requests would greatly increase and negatively affect personnel demands and operational budgets. Although San Francisco's government showed lack of interest, a local radio station (106.6 FM) recognized the potential benefits of the digital tool to request and obtain public information for the purpose of monitoring city budgets and officials.

Law 743 of 2002 Referring to Community Action Agencies

In order to teach Transparency Law and its application, we determined that the Communal Action Boards (JAC, acronym in Spanish) would be ideal entities. JACs are civic groups of neighbors that work for the benefit of their community, and, as a consequence, JACs constitute "democratic mechanisms of representation in the different instances of participation, that are established for the coordination, control, and monitoring of public management" (Political Constitution of Colombia, 1991, Art. 103).These entities have played a prominent role in the promotion of economic development and in the performance of small and medium public works and improvement and decoration activities (Constitutional Court. C520, 2007).

JACs were chosen for the implementation phase of the Transparency Law literacy project because of the important role they play in a participatory democracy and their main objective of "getting the community permanently informed about the development of the facts, policies, programs, and services of the State and of the entities that affect their welfare and development" (Law 743, 2002, Art. 19 literal j).

The research has the following normative support framework:

Colombian Legislation

---

1 Law 1712 (2014): Law of Transparency and the Right to access public information. Partially regulated by National Decree 103 of 2015 and by decree 1081 of 2015.
2 Law 743 (2002), by which article 38 of the Political Constitution of Colombia is developed in relation to the organisms of communal action.
3 Law 1581 (2012), by which general provisions are issued for the protection of personal data.

Law and Media Literacy Approach

The Transparency Law is a recently enacted law, so it is little known by the community, and this ignorance prevents its proper application. According to provisions of the *Guardianship and Access to Public*

Information Report prepared by the Ombudsman Office of Colombia, and consistent with our findings during training sessions, there is a "generalized ignorance about the right to access public information in the country and the law that regulates the procedures for its exercise and guarantee, that is, on the content and scope of Law 1712 of 2014" (Defensoría del Pueblo, 2016, p. 31).

Considering the need for literacy about the law and the means of communication that allows its exercise, specifically the Internet, training activities were organized in two communities that are part of the metropolitan area of Bogotá, Colombia, which were attended by members of different JACs, for the purpose of developing a teaching methodology for the Transparency Law with the aid of the Transparenci@ software implementation.

The Fontibón and Yomasa communities were chosen for the Transparenci@ training; they were selected taking into consideration the socioeconomic diversity of these metropolitan zones, therefore, providing us with experience that will help us develop a sensitive training protocol accessible to most Colombians and useful to the news information industry in need of digital tools to request and receive public information.

Socioeconomic zones are important because Colombian cities are zoned, classified into strata 1 to 6, where stratum 1 corresponds to the population with the lowest socioeconomic level (income, education, etc.). According to the National Department of Statistics (DANE, acronym in Spanish), "socioeconomic stratification is the mechanism that allows classifying the population into different strata or groups of people with similar social and economic characteristics" (District Planning Secretariat, 2016).

Strata 1 and 2 reflect communities living in poverty or extreme poverty, which translates into limited educational opportunities (DANE, 2005, p. 83). Stratum 3 is considered a medium-low socioeconomic level where there is a greater possibility of access to formal education. Taking this into consideration, the researchers visited the communities, compiled information, and developed a digital booklet for the training sessions.

Description of the Training Program

We trained in the community of *Fontibón Centro* (Locality of Fontibón, Bogotá) and in the community of Yomasa (Locality of Usme, Bogotá) using the Transparenci@ online digital tool. The Transparenci@ training targeted multiple community leaders of different ages and socioeconomic backgrounds living in these two communities; the details of the training are listed below (see Table 15.1).

246 *Paula Pérez et al.*

Table 15.1 General Description of the Training

Training recipients	• Dignitaries of the Communal Action Boards (JACs). • Social leaders. • Young leaders and multipliers. Note: Young people are included so that they can train and support those who find it difficult to use digital tools (multipliers). The foregoing considering that "a democracy is not sustainable unless it succeeds in continuously fostering norms, cognitions, and behavioral patterns of citizenship in new generations of citizens" (Moeller, Kühne, & De Vreese, 2018, p. 3).
Requirements for recipients	1 Be interested in the purpose of training and the vocation to teach what they learn to the community. 2 Know how to read and write. This requirement is necessary for the recipient to be a training multiplier. 3 Have a personal email address, since it is one of the minimum requirements of the Transparenci@ tool. Note: Bearing in mind that not all community and social leaders have emails, if the leader met the requirements of numerals 1 and 2, an email was created for them to be able to participate in the training.
Territories	• Community of Yomasa (Locality of Usme, Bogotá). • Locality of Fontibón, Bogotá.
Challenges	Existence of the digital divide in some sectors of the community. • The digital divide is determined by several factors: Impossibility to pay for access to the Internet, lack of digital culture in the population (welfare generated by access and use of the Internet,) and the generational gap (Digital Ecosystem Consortium, 2016). • Lack of understanding of legal language. • The challenge of approaching the JAC and social leaders.
Length of training	Eight (8) hours: It was evidenced in the fieldwork that this is the time required to carry out proper training. It was also identified that carrying out the training in one day guarantees continuity and attendance.
Number of participants	Approximately ten leaders and ten young multipliers. Small groups allow for more one-on-one interaction and training.
Multiplication strategy	In order to cover the largest number of people, it is expected that in the future the multiplication strategy can be applied, which implies that the training participants will disseminate the knowledge acquired to at least ten (10) people in the community.

Number of trained leaders per neighborhood (eight hours/initial training)	20
Number of people trained by each leader (Leaders have two months after the initial training)	10
Total number of people trained per neighborhood in two months	200

	It is proposed to execute this strategy in a second stage of field work.
Training/ teaching methodology	Service-learning methodology. This methodology "is not limited to the diagnosis and analysis of reality, but integrates learning in the development of a transformative action, in which the recipients must have an active participation" (CLAYSS, 2016, p. 8).

Software: Transparenci@ Tool and Use of Digital Applications

With the help of the concepts developed by the fourth technological revolution, the state should focus its strategy towards flexible institutions that seek the efficient solution of social, political, and economic problems (Becerra et al., 2018a, p. 30). The Transparenci@ tool is an open source software that facilitates and mediates the request of public information on behalf of a requester in an easy and secure way using the World Wide Web (Becerra et al., 2018b). This software was used as a teaching tool during the Transparency Law training; the tool requires the use of the Internet for its operation as well as the use of an email address per user through which the follow-up of the petitions filed are communicated. Once the user is registered in the tool (*Register* interface), the user can download the Transparency Law learning booklet (*About Us* Interface), track the requests, and download the requested information (*Citizen Consultation* interface).

Prior to the Transparency Law training, the researchers visited the communities and, in order to facilitate the assimilation of knowledge, organized recreational activities requiring trainees to use digital tools. In these previous visits it was found that the old participants had difficulties using digital tools, so it was decided to include young leaders in the training to support them.

During these and on training day, participants were taught to access some official Colombian government websites, including, but not limited to, the Colombian National Archives (AGN, acronym in Spanish). Trainers also reinforced knowledge acquisition by means of digital games, such as online Hangman and word games.

Results

The findings of this media and law literacy study result in a list of recommendations to effectively educate and train Colombian communities on Transparency Law and the use of the Transparenci@ digital tool to request access to public data (see the Appendix for full list of recommendations).

Involvement of the JACs in Transparency Law trainings

When researchers approached community members without JAC dignitaries as mediators, community members showed little interest in participating in the trainings. Once JAC dignitaries were included in the recruitment process, community members came together and participated in the training. As a consequence, researchers recommend involving in the training the participation of community leaders.

i   Secure the participation of the dignitaries of the JACs to facilitate the convening of other community leaders.

According to Bucheli (2006), "the vision of change of the leaders and the community is based on the economic, political, social, and ideological point of view that a community has" (p. 28). Bucheli resonated in our media and law literacy project; we found that the effectiveness of involving the JACs depends on the JAC's point of view and their capacity to put aside their political ideologies to focus on projects benefiting the community. For instance, in the community of Fontibón, where leaders left aside their political ideologies, the organization and execution of the training were efficient and effective.

When carrying out the fieldwork, particularly during visits prior to the Transparency Law training day, we found great political ideology divisions among JAC dignitaries of the community of Yomasa (Usme Locality). It should be noted that the training phase coincided with the congressional and presidential elections in Colombia in 2018, a situation that increased friction among social organizations, the community, and social leaders. As a consequence, Yomasa had a low number of JAC dignitaries participating in the Transparency Law training. For instance, of 16 Yomasa trainees, only 3 were JAC dignitaries, 8 were social leaders performing social, cultural, and recreational work with the community, and 5 were students who participated as young multipliers in the training. Regardless of political tensions, the training session was enriched by having five young multipliers as they improved the effectiveness of the training by assisting JAC dignitaries and social leaders with Internet use, the Transpareci@ tool, and, in some cases, creating email addresses for those who did not have one.

In the community of Yomasa, the researchers observed the existence of a clear ideological division. This division hinders the development of projects promoted for the community; hence it would be interesting to look more deeply into what types of political influences affect the development of projects and divides the leaders of the community. The experience was different with Fontibón JAC dignitaries. In the Fontibón case, the dignitaries were cooperative and unified by common interests and a solid track record of teamwork. Even with existing opposite political principles, Fontibón JAC dignitaries came together and participated in the training. Of 11 Fontibón trainees, 7 were JAC dignitaries, 2 social leaders, and 2 young multipliers.

Given the previous observations, researchers recommend:

ii Procure to organize Transparency Law training sessions during off-elections periods to avoid divisive political animosity.

In sum, the media and law literacy project found that including JACs in the training process is convenient, especially when we consider their power of convocation. But in the fieldwork, it was evident that in some JACs, there are disagreements because of political ideologies that impede the good development of projects such as the one we executed. However, the fact that our literacy project coincided with presidential and congressional elections, affected the call and projection of trainings.

Teaching Challenges

According to the Economic Commission for Latin America and the Caribbean of the United Nations (ECLAC), "the digital divide is the line or distance that separates the group that can access ICT, from that which cannot do it" (Peña Gil, Cuartas Castro, & Tarazona Bermúdez, 2017, p. 60). According to the article *The Digital Divide in Colombia: An Analysis of Governmental Policies for Its Decrease*, "Internet penetration in developing countries is at 35%, but in less developed countries it does not reach 10%" (Peña Gil et al., 2017, p. 62). This article also evidences the existence of a regional digital divide in Colombia.

Despite the existing digital divide in Colombia, "technology can be a powerful tool to transform learning" (Office of Educational Technology, 2017). In this sense, teaching Transparency Law with the Transparenci@ tool was difficult in the low-income communities, and especially challenging for older generations; however, the strategy of young leaders and the use of digital spaces helped overcome this difficulty.

In response to these needs, the following actions were defined and taken:

iii   Foster the use of spaces designed to promote access, use, and appropriation of ICT in Colombia, such as the spaces offered in Colombia through the *Vive Digital* (Live Digital) program.

According to the first ICT National Survey of the Ministry of Information and Communication Technologies of Colombia (MinTIC, acronym in Spanish) (2017), only 11% of the Colombian population has used *Vive Digital* centers. Taking into consideration MinTIC's survey findings, the researchers used a *Vive Digital* center with computers, Internet access, and dry-erase boards to train in the community of Fontibón and promote the use of such dedicated spaces. Some of the participants in the training were not aware of the existence of the *Vive Digital* center in their neighborhood. Furthermore, there is not a *Vive Digital* center in Yomasa, a fact that goes against the interests of MinTIC and the "positive relationship between income and access to ICT" (El Tiempo, 2016). Given the lack of a *Vive Digital* center, the researchers secured an appropriate training space at a public high school in Yomasa.

To increase awareness and adoption of existing online public re-sources, the researchers recommend to:

iv   Promote the use of official websites containing public information by using short informative videos (interactive information segments) disseminated in multimedia platforms.

It was evidenced in the course of the training that few trainees have had experience interacting and using important public websites. Only three (3) people from the two trained groups had previously accessed the official websites of the Electronic System for Public Procurement (SECOP, acronym in Spanish), and only one (1) knew about the Public Employment Information and Management System (SIGEP, acronym in Spanish). This situation demonstrates the need to promote digital literacy and use of websites containing public information. Furthermore, intergenerational age gaps show different levels of technological understanding and proficiency; as a consequence, the researchers also recommend to:

v   Promote projects that use intergenerational relationship strategies, where young people support digital literacy (use of digital tools and the Internet) and recognize the importance of access to public information.

According to the results of the First Great ICT Survey of 2017, in Colombia "8% of the population consulted does not have Internet coverage" (MinTIC, 2017, p. 8). On the other hand, it was identified that the population over 55 believes that the Internet is not important in their lives. Furthermore, the DANE's statistics show the Colombian population at approximately 43 million in 2018, and 18.5% of that population (7.7 million) will be 55 years of age or older. Considering that the guarantee of the right to access public information allows the exercise of fundamental rights and that senior citizens enjoy special protection under Article 46 of the Political Constitution of Colombia, the need for digital inclusion of this part of the population is evident. Considering DANE's population projections and in favor of guaranteeing the right to access public information as a human right, it is important to promote intergenerational support in Internet literacy and digital tools.

Feasibility of Teaching Transparency Law with the Help of the Transparenci@ tool

The book titled *Application of the Law of Transparency and Access to Public Information* of the Universidad Católica de Colombia pro-poses the creation of an adequate mechanism that contributes to the implementation of the Transparency Law. Considering the importance of e-governance, this book emphasizes the importance of using ICT as tools that promote and guarantee the right to access public information (Becerra et al., 2018b, p. 7).

Currently, the community can access and consult public information in the official websites of each subject required by law. The development of the Transparenci@ tool seeks to facilitate the awareness of the rights and duties assigned by the Transparency Law with respect to the exercise of the right that every person has to request and receive public information from the parties bound by law (Becerra et al., 2018b, p. 156).

In the same way, the tool allows access to public information to more than one compelled subject. In accordance with the above, it was possible to corroborate through training that the Transparenci@ tool served as a viable vehicle for Transparency Law education and application. This software allows learning by means of exemplification and practice of exercising the right to request public information.

However, on the other hand, this study found the need to make improvements in the User Interface (UI) of the tool to make it more effective and accessible, not only to the community but to journalists working in mainstream news. Among UI pending improvements is the use of simple terminology, a need prompting researchers to recommend to:

vi   Use more accessible terminology, less technical language, in the Transparenci@ tool UI.

During the training sessions, researchers had to constantly repeat information that was already provided, which brings us to the second Transparenci@ tool UI recommendation:

vii Develop and include information capsules (e.g., videos, graphics) to instruct users and facilitate access to multimedia trainings providing flexibility to the learning pace of each user.

Researchers also found the need to provide a platform allowing the exchange of documents to add clarification to requests and secure prompt request processing. Obligated subjects might, for instance, request media credentials as proof of membership of a news organization and, therefore, possible preferential processing. In this case, the recommendation is:

viii The Transparenci@ tool must develop and offer a system that allows users to attach supporting documents to their public information requests.

The Transparenci@ tool began Beta testing with a limited number of public entities listed in its database. Without question, adding and updating these entities must be a priority to future UI improvements. Researchers recommend to:

ix   Expand and maintain the database of public entities that can be reached with the Transparenci@ tool.

Finally, researchers must be sensitive to the realities of a connected society; the First Great ICT Survey found that Colombian "access to the Internet has been democratized in all regions of the country; smartphones have been the key to this transformation" (MinTIC, 2017, p. 7). This survey highlighted that 72% of Colombian homes have access to smartphones, devices that serve as main Internet access points for Colombian homes. Researchers noted this deficiency in the tool and recommended the:

x   Development and deployment of a Transparenci@ application (app) allowing access to the tool from mobile devices with different operating systems (e.g., iOS, Android).

According to Statcounter (2019), 87% of mobile operating systems in Colombia use Android platforms. Given the market share and potential impact, researchers focused heavily on the development and beta test of an Android-based Transparenci@ app that is expected to go live – at no cost – by the end of 2019, followed by an iOS app version release in 2020.

Conclusion

In order to contribute to the reduction of ignorance about the Transparency Law, the law was taught in two communities of Bogotá with different socioeconomic characteristics and with the help of the Transparenci@ tool. It was found that the Transparenci@ digital tool is a viable vehicle for Transparency Law education, media literacy, and for requesting public information (with User interface improvements pending).

This study showed that the forces of political corruption present considerable obstacles to the embracement of an open government (even if required by law.) This was evidenced by the difficulties faced by researchers while approaching and training community leaders divided by their political ideologies and the rejection of the Transparenci@ tool by San Francisco local authorities. City officials mainly feared the ease of use of the Transparenci@ tool and what the use of such interface would mean to their ability to govern and the effect that these open records requests would have on City budgets and personnel. City officials' fear is only amplified by the prospect of an effective and efficient Transparenci@ tool as part of Colombian journalists' toolbox to hold public officials accountable.

It was also found that the need for digital and media literacy is much greater among low-income communities and older generations. To address these needs, researchers created alliances with an Internet access center (Vive Digital) and a local high school and recruited and trained young community members for the purpose of intergenerational support. Young community members were given the responsibility of aiding older generations with the use of the Transparenci@ tool during training sessions. The involvement of younger people facilitated learning and secured access to a digital and media literate local community member.

Digital and media literacy is essential for democracy; it facilitates the understanding and application of Colombia's Transparency Law. Access to public data is an indispensable watchdog instrument, one that, if applied properly by citizens and media companies, has the power to secure positive and lasting changes in Colombia. Effective and efficient requests and accesses to public information steer nations away from wasteful practices and in favor of functioning public administrations; access to public data reduces institutional corruption and invites citizens to take an active part in nation building by aligning themselves with the principle of transparency.

Appendix

Recommendations to Effectively Educate and Train Communities on Transparency Law and the Use of the Transparenci@ Digital Tool

i   Secure the participation of the dignitaries of the JACs to facilitate the convening of other community leaders.

ii Procure to organize Transparency Law training sessions during off-elections periods to avoid divisive political animosity.

iii Foster the use of spaces designed to promote access, use, and appropriation of ICT in Colombia, such as the spaces offered in Colombia through the *Vive Digital* (Live Digital) program.

iv Promote the use of official websites containing public information by using short informative videos (interactive information segments) disseminated in multimedia platforms.

v   Promote projects that use intergenerational relationship strategies, where young people support digital literacy (use of digital tools and the Internet) and recognize the importance of access to public information.

vi Use more accessible terminology, less technical language, in the Transparenci@ tool UI.

vii Develop and include information capsules (e.g. videos, graphics) to instruct users and facilitate access to multimedia trainings providing flexibility to the learning pace of each user.

viii The Transparenci@ tool must develop and offer a system that allows users to attach supporting documents to their public information requests.

ix Expand and maintain the database of public entities that can be reached with the Transparenci@ tool.

x Development and deployment of a Transparenci@ application (app) allowing access to the tool from mobile devices with different operating systems (e.g., iOS, Android).

References

Becerra, J., Cotino Hueso, L., Garcia Vargas, C., Sanchez, M., Torres Avila, J. (2015). *La responsabilidad del Estado por la utilización de las tecnologías de la información y la comunicación (TIC)*. Bogotá, Colombia: Editorial Universidad Católica de Colombia.

Becerra, J., Cotino Hueso, L., Leon, I. P., Sanchez Acevedo, M., Torres Avila, J., & Velandia, J. (2018a). *Derecho y Big Data*. Bogotá, Colombia: Editorial Universidad Católica de Colombia.

Becerra, J., Torres, J., Sánchez, M., Cotino, L., Rodríguez, J., Velandia, J., & Pérez, P. (2018b). *Aplicación de la ley de transparencia y el acceso a la información pública*. Valencia, España: Tirant Lo Blanch.

Bucheli, M. (2006). *Curas, campesinos y laicos como gerentes del desarrollo*. Sangil: Edisocial.

Congreso de Colombia. (6 de marzo de 2014). *Ley de Transparencia y del Derecho de Acceso a la Información Pública Nacional*. [Ley 1712 de 2014]. Diario Oficial 49084.

Congreso de Colombia. (5 de junio de 2002). *Por la cual se desarrolla el artículo 38 Constitución Política de Colombia en lo referente a los organismos de acción comunal*. [Ley 743 de 2002]. Diario Oficial 44.826.

Congreso de Colombia. (25 de noviembre de 1958). *Sobre reforma administrativa* [Ley 19 de 1958]. Diario Oficial 29835. 9.

Congreso de Colombia. (17 de octubre de 2012). *Por la cual se dictan disposiciones generales para la protección de datos personales*. [Ley 1581 de 2012]. Diario oficial 48.587.

Consorcio Ecosistema Digital. (2017). *Ecosistema digital y economía digital para Bogotá D.C. documento base o diagnóstico contrato no. 1210200-423 de 2.016*, Recuperado de http://ticbogota.gov.co/sites/default/files/documentos/documentobase_estudioeconomia.pdf

Constitución política de Colombia (1991) 2da Ed. Legis

Convención Americana sobre derechos Humanos. OEA. (7 al 22 de noviembre de 1969).

Corte Constitucional De Colombia (11 de julio de 2007) Sentencia C520 De 2007. (M.P. Nilson Pinilla Pinilla)

CLAYSS. (2016). Manual para Docentes y Estudiantes Solidarios. Buenos Aires: Clayss. Disponible en http://www.clayss.org.ar/04_publicaciones/manual_docentes_LATAM.pdf

Defensoría del Pueblo. (2016). Informe tutela y acceso a información-2016. Recuperado de http://desarrollos.defensoria.gov.co/desarrollo1/ABCD/bases/marc/documentos/textos/Informe_tutela_2016_final_Defensoria.pdf.

Departamento Nacional de Planeación – DANE. (2005). Hacia una Colombia equitativa e incluyente. Informe de Colombia objetivos de desarrollo del milenio. Bogotá: DNP

Departamento Nacional de Planeación – DANE. (2018). Estructura de la población por edad y sexo Censo 2018Recuperado de https://sitios.dane.gov.co/cnpv-presentacion/src/#cuantos00

El Tiempo. (7 de septiembre de 2016). Brecha digital es amplia entre estratos altos y bajos en Bogotá. El Tiempo.

Gil de Zúñiga, H., Diehl, T., & Ardévol-Abreu, A. (2017) Internal, external, and government political efficacy: Effects on news use, discussion, and political participation. *Journal of Broadcasting & Electronic Media, 61*(3), 574–596, doi:10.1080/08838151.2017.1344672

Grizzle, A., Moore, P., Dezuanni, M., Asthana, S. Wilson, C., Banda, F., & Onumah, C. (2013). *Media and information literacy: Policy and strategy guidelines.* Paris: UNESCO. Retrieved from https://unesdoc.unesco.org/ark:/48223/pf0000225606

Hernández Chávez, M. A., & Álvarez Enríquez, J. P. (2015). *La transparencia y el derecho al acceso a la información en México.* México D.F.: Tirant lo Blanch.

Ministerio de educación de Colombia. (2018). *Rendición de cuentas.* Recuperado de https://www.mineducacion.gov.co/1759/w3-article-195770.html (Consultado el 18 de diciembre de 2017)

Ministerio de las Tecnologías de la Información y la Comunicación. (2017). Primera gran encuesta TIC/2017. Recuperado de https://colombiatic.mintic.gov.co/679/articles-74002_cartilla_resumen.pdf

Moeller, J., Kühne, R., & De Vreese, C. (2018). Mobilizing youth in the 21st century: How digital media use fosters civic duty, information efficacy, and political participation. *Journal of Broadcasting & Electronic Media, 62*(3), 445–460, doi:10.1080/08838151.2018.1451866

Neuman, L. (Ed.). (2002). *Access to information: A key to democracy.* Atlanta, GA: The Carter Center.

Office of Educational Technology. (2017). Reimagining the role of technology in education: 2017 national education technology plan update. Recuperado de https://tech.ed.gov/files/2017/01/NETP17.pdf

Pacto Internacional de derechos Civiles y Políticos. Naciones Unidas. (16 de diciembre de 1966).

Peña Gil, H. A., Cuartas Castro, K. A., &Tarazona Bermúdez, G. M. (2017). The digital divide in colombia: An analysis of governmental policies for its decrease. *Redes de Ingeniería,* 59–71. doi:10.14483/issn.2248-762X

Pérez Gómez, P. A. (2017) Alignment of information systems with online government strategy. *Revista Novum Jus, 11*(1), 143–173.

Presidencia de la República de Colombia. (20 de enero de 2002). *Por el cual se reglamenta parcialmente la ley 1712 de 2014 y se dictan otras disposiciones.* [Decreto Nacional 103 de 2015]. Diario Oficial 49400.

Presidencia de la República de Colombia. (26 de mayo de 2015). *Por medio del cual se expide el decreto reglamentario único del sector presidencia de la república*. [Decreto 1081 de 2015]. Diario Oficial 49523.

Secretaria Distrital de Planeación. (2016). Estratificación socioeconómica recuperado de. Retrieved from http://www.sdp.gov.co/gestion-estudios-estrategicos/estratificacion/generalidades

Secretaria Distrital de Planeación. (2017). Estratificación socioeconómica por localidades [Grafica]. Retrieved from http://www.sdp.gov.co/gestion-estudios-estrategicos/estratificacion/estratificacion-por-localidad.

Statcounter. (2019). Mobile operating system market share Colombia. Retrieved from https://gs.statcounter.com/os-market-share/mobile/colombia/#monthly-201807-201907

16 The Literacies of Participatory Cultures

Jennifer J. Henderson

Introduction

Christopher M. Kelty (2013), an anthropologist from UCLA's Institute for Society and Genetics, points out that one of the true challenges of understanding participatory cultures, and therefore what literacies are needed, is that each discipline has defined the same basic activity with a different term. For example, groups of people who come together, often through the use of digital technologies, are called "smart mobs" (Rheingold, 2002), "convergence cultures" (Jenkins, 2006a), "assemblies" (Mulgan, 2017, "fandoms" (Jenkins, 1992), "knowledge cultures" (Jenkins, 2006b), the "cosmopedia" (Lévy), and "networked publics" (Varnellis, 2008). What they do together has been labeled "collective intelligence" (Lévy, 1994), "swarm intelligence" (Foss, 2017; Seeley, 2010), "the wisdom of crowds" (Surowiecki, 2004), and "crowdsourcing" (Brabham, 2013; Estellés-Arolas & González-Ladrón-de-Guevara, 2012) as well as many other things. Are unique literacies needed for each conceptualization of participatory cultures? Or, do the same literacies transcend them all?

The identification and implementation of these literacies by scholars and teachers, then, has been underway for more than a decade, but no single set of literacies needed to navigate participatory cultures has been established. Agreeing that a one-size-fits-all approach does not make sense for these many and varied communities, this chapter applies to a subset of participatory cultures – those working toward an articulated goal. This subset of participatory cultures constitutes what can be termed "consensus cultures," ones that are "agreement-based" and "frequently reside in the realm of 'work' where there is a goal or outcome to be met" (Delwiche & Henderson, 2013). Pearce and Venters (2013) explain just such a consensus culture among particle physicists. Members of the European Organization for Nuclear Research (CERN) work in facilities around the globe but choose one project to focus on at a time. "Because of the scale of the particle physics experiments now, no one can afford to work alone: we have to collaborate, and our individual goals rely on the whole endeavor working" (p. 131). Distributed, focused, intelligence. A participatory culture with a goal.

To best identify the literacies necessary to build a successful consensus culture, the author reflected on a spring 2019 course on Collective Intelligence. The first half of the course was based on understanding the concept of collective intelligence from multiple disciplinary perspectives and included talks with researchers of the subject, such as Philosopher Pierre Lévy, who literally wrote the book *Collective Intelligence*; Anita Woolley from Carnegie Mellon University, who studies the composition of teams with high levels of collective intelligence; and Geoff Mulgan, who had just published the bestselling book *Big Mind: How Collective Intelligence Can Change the World.*

The second half of the course was focused on carrying out those theories in practice. As Mulgan (2018) suggested, we took on a big issue in the class, one many may even call gigantic: Comprehensive Immigration Reform in the United States. For the final project, students completed a white paper that was delivered to our U.S. congressional representatives and mayor. This class experiment not only introduced students to new theories but also required them to think outside of traditional boundaries and expected them to participate in new ways. As with all experiments, there were days of success and failure. Both kinds of days taught lessons.

Looking back, the literacies necessary for these consensus cultures to thrive turned out to be more than media literacies, though many certainly could be classified this way. Most of them were literacies surrounding human interaction rather than the technologies that extended (and often complicated) those interactions. Teaching this course revealed that there are five key literacies to learn and, maybe even more importantly, three literacies to unlearn in order to successfully find a creative solution to a complex problem.

Five Literacies to Learn

Collecting

The first essential literacy students needed to master a successful consensus culture was the ability to collect. Collecting is the process of both searching for and sifting through information. While a decade ago, these two processes could be divided into discrete steps, today, because much of the world's knowledge is accessible immediately, the literacy of collecting is essential. Marr (2018) estimates that there are "2.5 quintillion bytes of data created each day at our current pace" and that "[o]ver the last two years alone 90 percent of the data in the world was generated" (para. 1). Because it is so easy to collect information, especially information unrelated to the concern at hand, picking and choosing the tiny bits of relevant information from the vast sea of online "knowledge" collected during a search moves the group significantly closer to its objective. In addition, by all individually searching and combining content, what may be one person's bias could be adjusted or corrected by another's search approach.

This literacy is a combination of what Henry Jenkins and his colleague in the 2006 MacArthur Foundation report, *Confronting the Challenges of Participatory Cultures*, call the skills of "transmedia navigation" and "networking," defined as "the ability to follow the flow of stories and information across multiple modalities" and "the ability to search for, synthesize, and disseminate information" (Jenkins, Clinton, Purushotma, Robinson, & Weigel, 2006, p. 4).

Teaching students how to gather information may seem extraneous in a classroom of digital natives. It is not the technology part of collecting that stumps students, however. It is the process of collecting, especially in the initial stages of problem identification and keyword selection, that slows them down. In fact, many high-school librarians have noted that students lack basic information searching skills. For example, Gregory (February 2018) explained that "many information literacy skills are lacking, most notably the vocabulary for formulating and effective information search" (p. 29). She concluded that "students are not being given enough time or opportunity to develop these search strategies" (p. 33). Kenney (2004) notes that Bell recommends:

[we] must help our students understand that taking the results of a poorly thought-out, simplistic search that yields far too much irrelevant and questionable content and then wrapping it in a professional-looking clear plastic binder is no way to access the path that will lead to lifelong learning and success.

(p. 46)

If done well, the act of collecting finds new ways of looking at the problem and seeds new ideas for solutions. The information collected at this stage is not simply the primary and secondary sources of traditional research papers. Collecting also involves the gathering of what Lévy calls "collective memory," the sum of all the group members' knowledge, background, and history – sifted and saved to draw upon as a collective. Remember that participatory cultures often involve thousands of members, distributed worldwide, who are connected through the Internet. Bringing together their collective memory can be challenging, but it is a crucial element of success.

A successful consensus culture, then, requires the collection of diverse and often opposing data points. Applying this approach, the Collective Intelligence class combined Internet and database searches with original surveys distributed around the globe in multiple languages and used both digital tools and face-to-face collection methods. Students began the project portion of the class – the creation of a white paper suggesting solutions for comprehensive immigration reform – by creating a collaborative Google Doc of words that were associated with immigration in the United States. By individually collecting information and then combining content, one person's biases could be adjusted or corrected by a classmate's collection efforts.

They broadened their perspective by working with students at the Sorbonne Université in Paris to determine global issues of immigration. Together they built a list of issues, possible survey questions, and ways of distributing surveys that would best reach diverse populations. For example, they determined that the survey needed to be distributed globally, online and in face-to-face interactions with people directly affected by forced migration and purposeful immigration, including refugee camps and detention centers worldwide.

A mastery of collecting also requires thoughtful deliberation, where the weighing of information takes place. All of the foundational thinkers acknowledge the importance of information that has been vetted. Lévy (2015) says we must cross-check contributions; Jenkins et al. (2006) call this "Judgement" – to "evaluate the reliability and credibility of different information sources" (p. 4). This ability to determine, through individual and collective analysis, the value of the "found" information or people's contributions is at the heart of good collecting. In the Collective Intelligence course, multiple students were asked to determine the value of the collected sources. Not surprisingly, many discussions and disagreements regarding source credibility and information usefulness consumed our early efforts.

Finally, in this class, the literacy of collecting was an iterative process. Students returned to the collection process multiple times, especially when they realized they did not have enough or the right kind of information needed to develop an argument in the paper. Where one would see value in a governmental report, another would see ideological bias.

Curating

Curating is the ability to put information (and people) into the most effective categories within the context of the project. This literacy is vital in a world where, as Lankshear and Knobel (2006) argue, the focus of intelligence has shifted from a quality of possession by an individual to intelligence held online by a collective. Curating asks a participatory culture to collectively choose not just what information to search and sift but how to organize that information for use. As Mulgan (2018) notes: "The first vital infrastructure is a set of agreed-upon rules and standards… These are a necessary condition for knowledge commons of any kind, and greatly reduce the transaction costs of thought and coordination" (p. 10).

Curating involves the ability to organize collected information and ideas into useful, usable categories. The more effective the arrangement of the information, the more likely the project will be built upon a solid foundation. Lévy (2011) notes that it is essential to have a classification system for gathered information "whether this system is implicit and unconscious or explicit and deliberately constructed" (p. 94). In groups with an intentional purpose, the latter is clearly preferable. Woolley and Fuchs (2011) explain the need for curating in field-organizing activities as "defining" which involves "the clarifying of definitions and identification of subtypes of a construct" (p. 1361).

Students in the Collective Intelligence class were asked to develop their own organization system without assistance from the instructor. As with collecting, curating was not a one-time event for the class. In fact, the organization system changed substantially over the course of the semester and looked very different for the first half of the class, which focused on the theories of collective intelligence, than it did the second half of the semester when applying the theories to the problem of immigration reform.

Students began with Google Folders for individual class periods and speakers at the start of the semester, making the system appear more like a binder of class notes than a thoughtful curation of content. By midterm, the class's original day-by-day structure was replaced with thematic folders that combined content from class readings, speakers, discussions, and their own thoughts. By the end of the semester, the organizational structure had morphed even further, with folders renamed to reflect the sections of the white paper. In these final few weeks, students were more likely to move content out of folders than into them. It was a winnowing system that kept only the most important, most compelling evidence in place.

Listening

The Collective Intelligence class showed that one of the core literacies of participatory collaboration is listening. Anyone who has worked on a team project knows this is not easy, however. The give-and-take of compromise only works when every member of the team is willing to do so. The Collective Intelligence class was comprised of 15 students, from majors as varied as pre-med, philosophy, urban studies, and communication. They all had strong opinions. On any given day, five of them had both strong and *vocal* opinions. On most days, this was fine. The vocal five changed regularly depending on the day's topic. However, there were days when this participatory experiment was simply a mess. Those were the days when people stopped listening.

Participatory cultures thrive best when people listen as well as contribute. In fact, contributing is the easiest part of collective activities.

Listening may be the most difficult. The ability to listen means not just being quiet (although that is critical); it also means focusing real attention on what is being said. Most of us actually do the opposite when people talk – we either think about what we are going to say in reply (this is why so many people interrupt others; we are anxious to add our two cents) or think about something else entirely (when can I get that paper written? Or, what do I need to get from the grocery store on the way home?). Derek McCracken, an expert on narrative medicine from Columbia University, pinpointed this problem while visiting class one day. He began by asking: "what are you thinking about other than this discussion right now?" The answers were as profound as they were simple: "my exam next period," "my brother's surgery," "that I'm going to the beach this weekend." So many thoughts occupy each mind that only by drawing attention to the distractions were members of the group able to really listen.

Listening is also an equalizer of power imbalances. If listening is valued and reinforced in a participatory culture, all voices, and thus all ideas, can be considered. To listen to the voices of others, students in the class met with representatives of several immigration, refugee, and asylum organizations, including the Center for Refugee Services, Catholic Charities, and the City of San Antonio's Immigration Office. They conducted face-to-face interviews with approximately 50 students, faculty, and staff at the university seeking input on creative solutions. Significantly, they also implemented the two online surveys mentioned previously, one targeting individuals currently living in the United States, and one targeting those living in other countries. The goal of the former was to better understand the current perceptions of the U.S. immigration system and provide suggestions for change specifically related to that system. The latter was solely interested in finding original solutions to the many obstacles of immigration reform, specifically targeting the areas of (1) entry, (2) visas, (3) legal processes, and (4) services. In all, the two U.S.-based surveys (one distributed in English and one in Spanish) yielded a combined 478 responses, and the international survey asking for creative solutions yielded 50 responses from 17 countries.

Students found that listening by reading survey responses was much easier than listening in real time. The students tried many tactics to improve listening in their class sessions: computers were closed, phones excluded, and rules about speaking and for how long were implemented. These tactics helped, but only for short periods. In truth, only about one-third of the students were actively listening at any one time, and rarely the same third. Depending on how interesting the topic of the day was to the students – the validity of collected research, the content to be included in the white paper, the arguments to be made supporting their position, or the writing styles – greatly influenced how many and who was listening.

Some students in the class were hesitant to speak; others would rarely be silent even when requested by others to do so. One of the students with the most to contribute including experiences of an immigrant background always listened but spoke only when she was extremely frustrated. This uneven listening directly impacted the success of individual tasks, some of which would take days longer than needed.

The importance of their face-to-face listening was reinforced by Anita William Woolley's research, discussed when she visited class. She and her colleagues found that "socially perceptive people," women, and "the distribution of speaking turns" were more likely to increase collective intelligence in a group than the IQ of individual members (Woolley, Aggarwal, & Malone, 2015, p. 421). A second study found that "groups that communicated more were more collectively intelligent, but groups in which one or two people dominated the discussion and activity were less collectively intelligent, whether the groups were online or face-to-face" (Engel, Woolley, Jing, Chabris, & Malone, 2014, p. 10).

Feeling

In the late 1970s, Architect Christopher Alexander (1979) proposed a new way of approaching complex building problems. The "walk about" asked regular people who use the facilities to walk around the space telling him how they "feel" when they consider options for design. After conducting many "walk about" sessions, he concluded:

> It is easy to dismiss feelings as "subjective" and "unreliable," and therefore not a reasonable basis for any form of scientific agreement.... However, in the domain of patterns, where people seem to agree 90, 95, even 99 percent of the time, we may treat this agreement as an extraordinary, almost shattering, discovery, about the solidity of human feelings, and we may certainly use it as scientific. (Alexander, 1979, p. 294)

This "emotional" literacy is essential in the realm of media as well as architecture. Potter (2005) identified it as one of the four domains of media literacy (pp. 24–25). We rarely require students to learn this literacy, however. Members of a group are almost never asked how they "feel" about the challenge, the data, the solutions, or the other members of the group.

Teaching students in the collective intelligence course to trust their feelings about an issue or a proposed solution was challenging. This was an upper-division course at an academically rigorous university. Students had been repeatedly taught to only make claims supported by evidence. Now, they were facing an issue – immigration – that carried great emotional weight. They had to re-learn a literacy taught in kindergarten, that their feelings and those of others carried value.

While logic played an important role in collecting and curating information, feeling was fundamental to finding novel outcomes to issues that meant a great deal to the students. Attending college in South Texas, students in the course were exposed daily to the realities of a broken immigration system. They all had friends and family members impacted by government policies, limited resources, economic sanctions, and delays at the border. Some had Deferred Action Childhood Arrivals (DACA) siblings, others aunts and uncles trying to immigrate. This was not just an abstract, logical exercise. To students in the class, this was reality.

Creating Through Doing

How to approach creativity, how to instill it, and whether or not creativity can be a literacy are all contested ideas. The need for creating new ways to solve problems, however, is not. The act of creating in the Collective Intelligence class happened in multiple phases throughout the second half of the course. This involved tasks such as selecting a name for the proposed legislation (a highly contentious and lengthy process), determining the actual policy recommendations, and articulating those recommendations in writing. These creative projects were approached at different stages by small teams, large groups, and individual contributors. Usually many times. For example, a large group would think about categories for the survey, individuals would propose questions, and then small teams would revise the survey questions in each section, retaining and editing out those that applied most to the concerns at hand. A different small team would then reread the proposed questions, suggest revisions and additions, and individuals would go back to the questions once again for edits. The entire group then agreed on the order and flow of survey questions, and individuals translated the questions into multiple languages.

Ensuring an equitable division of intellectual labor was essential to the success of these creative tasks. While everyone was required to have a hand in getting things done, some did more than others, and some did little-to-nothing. These varying levels of student contribution fell in line with the diverse views of contributions made by scholars during the first half of the semester. For example, Brabham argued new ways of solving problems most often arise when significant contributions are made by all stakeholders in a participatory culture (Brabham, 2019). Mathematician Nikos Salingaros argued the opposite – that participants should not feel as if their contributions are so significant that others are relying on their input. It is only through the freedom of thought that comes from feeling as if one has no responsibility that creativity can actually take hold. Salingaros believes participants should feel that their ideas are just one of many. This frees them up to provide more "out of the box" suggestions and more creative solutions (Salingaros, 2019).

No matter how much or in what ways students contribute to a consensus culture project, they need to do something with it once it is completed. As educators, we often forget to teach students about this important last step. For example, students in this class often felt like an assignment was done when they uploaded their "part," even if that assignment contains action items, suggestions for improvement, or recommended solutions. This, though, was only the beginning.

Along with creating, it is imperative that we begin to teach students the literacy of *doing* – implementing their ideas and putting them into practice. There is a substantial amount of research in higher education to support the literacy of doing – and many universities have made "experiential learning," "service learning," or the theory/practice model a part of their curricula. This is not a new idea, however. Almost a century ago, Alfred North Whitehead (1929) described the problem of "inert knowledge" – that which is learned but never used. More recent researchers note that learners often (1) don't see the relevance of the information they learn and (2) cannot access what they know when confronted with an opportunity for application of that knowledge (Bransford, Brown, & Cocking, 2000). It is by teaching the ability to *do* in participatory cultures, not just the ability to think about doing, that change takes place.

Three Literacies to Unlearn

One of the biggest challenges in the Collective Intelligence course was trying to get students to undo old literacies, engrained over time until they were habitual. To think in new ways and seek out new perspectives, they all had to unlearn almost as much as they had to learn.

The first, and most important, literacy they needed to abandon was the value of traditional leadership.

Traditional, Top-Down Leadership

Every class has its leaders. Most are happy to announce their self-appointed status to the group. But, traditional, top-down management decisions rarely make participatory cultures possible because they do not allow enough space for contributions from enough people.

For students to engage in effective participatory cultures, they must throw out their tendencies to act like bureaucrats, abandoning traits like dominating the conversation and making immediate decisive decisions (all of the things they've been taught for years they need to do to be successful). They need to learn to replace those behaviors with the literacies described before – listening and feeling and creating – all literacies that traditional leaders often undervalue, literacies that in the past have been deemed too "feminine" to succeed. Woolley et al.'s (2010) research on the composition of teams, though, tells us that work groups with the highest levels of collective intelligence are comprised of a majority of women. Bear and Woolley (2011) suggest that when it comes to STEM teams,

> it is not enough to simply examine the number of women in a particular institution or role. In order to reap the rewards of gender diversity, it would be most beneficial to ensure that women are represented in collaborative scientific teams at parity to men.
>
> (p. 151)

We could also learn something from honey bees. Seeley (2010) found that swarms make intelligent decisions precisely because of their decentralization of power. He wrote in *Honey Bee Democracy*: "If a leader shows partiality at the outset of the deliberations, or expresses displeasure if the discussion is not going in a certain direction, then he or she is likely to subvert good group decision making" (p. 222). Human groups may also take on the characteristics of other animal collectives as well. Muchnik, Aral, and Taylor (2013) found that Reddit groups exhibited a social "herding effect." When a person of authority (in this case the group administrator) voted a comment "up," their action "created a positive social influence bias that persisted over increased comments' final mean ratings by 25% relative to the final mean ratings of control group comments" (p. 648).

Abandoning traditional leadership as our insect and animal colleagues do is difficult, though. Many of our students behave as dominant participants, even when asked not to do so, expressing what Gen Zers would call "unearned confidence" regarding a topic. Unearned confidence is a student telling you how to use an app on your phone even though you use it every day or why their favorite band clearly makes a stronger political statement than yours ever did. One student in the Collective Intelligence course pointed to this kind of unearned confidence, a trait often found among traditional leaders, as a stumbling block:

> The point is that we are all supposed to contribute different things and view things differently, so even if we don't know much about a topic that doesn't mean our ideas are invalid, but I sometimes felt like I wasn't smart enough to contribute or like I didn't know enough to speak confidently since I'm not an expert on the subject (because others in the class act like know-it-alls).

Competition

Competition is a well-established American value, and some would argue, an inherently human trait. There is no arguing that the ability to compete is a literacy taught and reinforced in our earliest classrooms.

But competition is of little use when consensus must be reached or when a single solution must be found among members of a participatory culture. Collaboration, rather than competition, is the foundation of participatory knowledge cultures. To have the most successful teams, Gloor (2017) says, "Our goal should be to channel our competitive energies into better collaboration" (p. 138). He explains that there are two kinds of people in teams: "collaborative competitors" and "competitive collaborators." "Collaborative competitors are egoists, and they collaborate for their own benefit; competitive collaborators are altruists, and they compete to collaborate for the benefit of their group" (p. 138). The latter type of team member, of course, is preferred, in participatory knowledge groups.

Unlearning competition is much more difficult than it may seem, however. People raised in cultures that do not value collaboration often find it very difficult to move to this model of action. In the Collective Intelligence class, this was clear from the very start. On Fridays, students would undertake collective intelligence puzzles. Whether word puzzles or engineering puzzles, they inevitably resorted to a model of competition – who finished first, who had the largest quantity, who was the cleverest. But, "Friday Puzzle" day was never described as a competition. Students just automatically made it one. While it would be great to report otherwise, honestly, the Friday puzzles sessions remained a site of rivalry, leading to the conclusion that dismantling the literacy of competition may be the single biggest hurdle to a successful consensus culture.

The competitive model of "in" and "out" groups makes little sense in participatory cultures, which are often large, widely distributed, and diverse. They simply are not about competition. Woolley, Aggarwal, and Malone (2015) note that "Collective intelligence includes a group's capability to collaborate and coordinate effectively, and this is often much more important to the group's performance than individual ability alone" (p. 143). We all know, as Mulgan (2018) states, that "crowds, whether online or off-line, can also be foolish and biased, or overconfident echo chambers" and are often "a site for competition, deception, and manipulation" (p. 3).

No wonder we think that individuals often think they know what is best. But individual thinking only offers one of literally billions of perspectives on a problem. If members of consensus cultures are to even come close to solving the most important issues – poverty, climate change, violence against women – they must do it together. Educators everywhere must begin teaching students that the ability to ask others for their input is one of the most important literacies of the 21st century. We cannot productively go forth in the world alone anymore.

Specialization

One of the challenges of the Collective Intelligence course was getting students to think beyond their departmental majors to find original solutions. Students are taught how to think (research methodologies) and what to think about (subjects of inquiry) through disciplinary prisms. In the Collective Intelligence class, students with majors in sociology wanted to conduct ethnographies to discover how immigrant communities functioned, while business students wanted to look at purchasing data. A pre-med student had a hard time thinking past the health concerns of the population, while an urban studies major was convinced we could solve most immigration issues with job training and transportation in the city center. All of these students' perspectives were important to our project, but all of them needed to become generalists about immigration policy – to think both holistically about this issue and from disciplinary perspectives they were unaccustomed to using.

About half way through our semester, one of the Collective Intelligence students sent me detailed instructions for an in-class activity. She wanted to see if we could get people to think about, and possibly change, their perspective and their roles in the class. To do this, she set up a prompt. Upon entering the classroom, students were asked to sit anywhere in the room other than their usual seat. (I don't assign seats in classes, but students quickly pick a seat and stick to it throughout the semester.) Her goal was to see "what, if any, coalitions have formed," "whether people would break the norms and sit on top of desks or on the floor," and "what explanations were given for the selection of new seats – was it purposeful?" She wanted to use this exercise as an onramp for the class to "propose solutions that defy regular conventions or that seem naïve and idealistic."

The student's exercise, like many in the classroom, did not go exactly as planned. Her classmates didn't look up from their phones to see the new instructions when they entered the room. When prompted to read the instructions, they just moved to other chairs in the room rather than tables or floors. They did, though, seriously consider the space from new perspectives. During our debriefing session, students immediately pointed out their discomfort in the new space – it was "so cold over here," "it's hard to see everyone from this seat," or "I can't hear what anyone is saying from the back of the room." While these were not creative breakthroughs regarding immigration policy, the exercise did get students thinking about perspectives – theirs and others – an important first step beyond specialization.

This movement outside of their comfort zone was in line with what many collective intelligence researchers have also learned is essential to successful, creative solutions. For example, Pretz, Naples, & Sternberg (2003) found that "the development of a highly specialized body of knowledge can lead to an impairment in the ability of experts to incorporate new rules in their thinking or modify old ones" (p. 15). Woolley, Arggarwal, and Malone (2015) concluded that "a diverse team with a relatively broad range of task-related knowledge, skills, and abilities has a larger pool of resources for dealing non-routine problems" (p. 158). Noriega-Campero et al. (2018) supported this finding, noting "that dynamic influence networks can adapt to biased and non-stationary environments, inducing individual and collective beliefs even far more accurately than the independent beliefs of the best-performing individual" (p. 13).

Many researchers have noted that it's not our field of expertise, but one closely related, to which we are most effectively able to contribute. Their rationale is this: every discipline is talented at teaching students to learn within its framework of acceptable methods. It takes students trained outside of particular disciplines to see the problem in new ways or the possibility of a solution that lies just outside the boundaries. Much of this new research on problem solving tells us that students who find the most creative solutions to complex problems are in fields tangential to, but not actually, the field in which the problem is located.

But, here's the problem: our current education system forces students to think narrowly about the topics they address. Many universities require faculty to support a narrow research agenda throughout our careers, even if we are working on that topic in a team. But who is thinking broadly? Or over the boundary lines of disciplines? What solutions could be found if all professors abandoned expertise, even for a day?

There is no doubt that the ability to think beyond narrow subject areas will become a central literacy of future participatory cultures, so we must all unlearn our tendencies to lean toward specialization. Instead, students must learn the value of both depth and breadth in knowledge acquisition. They should be able to enter into a consensus culture with a deep understanding of at least one subject, but a willingness to learn many others.

Conclusion

If students of the future are to make stronger participatory consensus cultures – ones that engage actively with the big problems of the world in search of solutions – they must learn and unlearn many literacies. If our students are to rise to the challenge of tackling the big problems of the day – climate change, hunger, resource limitations, human suffering – they must be flexible thinkers who embrace the collaborative efforts of consensus cultures.

Participatory cultures are like May poles. They are delicate dances with many members, which often involve complicated interactions and multiple misunderstandings. The outcome is more often a beautiful, tangled mess than a picturesque pole. But, when members get the dance right and there is collection, curation, listening, feeling, and creating, when they abandon traditional leadership structures, competition, and specialization, the outcome is breathtaking.

References

Alexander, C. (1979). *The timeless way of building.* London: Oxford University Press.

Bear, J., & Woolley, A. (2011). The role of gender in team collaboration and performance. *Interdisciplinary Science Reviews, 36*(2): 146–153.

Brabham, D. C. (2013). *Crowdsourcing.* Cambridge, MA: MIT Press.

Brabham, D. C. (2019). Unpublished lecture. San Antonio, TX: Trinity University.

Bransford, J., Brown, A., & Cocking, R. (Eds.) (2000). *How people learn: Brain, mind, experience, and school* (2nd ed.). (p. 43). Washington, DC: National Academy Press.

Delwiche, A., & Henderson, J. J. (2013, 6 May). What do we know about participatory cultures: An interview with Aaron Delwiche and Jennifer Jacobs Henderson (Part One). *Confessions of an Aca-Fan.* Retrieved from http://henryjenkins.org/blog/2013/05/what-do-we-now-know-about-participatory-cultures-an-interview-with-aaron-delwiche-and-jennifer-jacobs-henderson-part-one.html

Engel, D., Woolley, A. W., Jing, L. X., Chabris, C. F., & Malone, T. (2014). Reading the mind in the eyes or reading between the lines? Theory of mind predicts collective intelligence equally well online and face-to-face. *PLOS One, 9*(12). Retrieved from https://www.ncbi.nlm.nih.gov/pmc/articles/PMC4267836/

Estellés-Arolas, E., & González-Ladrón-de-Guevara, F. (2012). Towards an integrated crowdsourcing definition. *Journal of Information Science. 38*(2): 189–200.

Foss, R. A. (2017). Major mechanisms contributing to swarm intelligence. *Systems Research and Behavioral Science, 34*: 746–758.

Gloor, P. A. (2017). *Swarm leadership and the collective mind: Using collaborative innovation networks to build a better business.* Bingley: Emerald Publishing Limited.

Jenkins, H. (2006a). *Convergence culture.* New York, NY: New York University Press.

Jenkins, H. (2006b). *Fans, bloggers, and gamers.* New York, NY: New York University Press.

Jenkins, H. (1992). *Textual poachers: Television fans and participatory culture.* New York, NY: Routledge Books.

Jenkins, H., Clinton, K., Purushotma, R., Robinson, A., & Weigel, M. (2006). *Confronting the challenges of participatory culture: Media education for the 21st century.* New York, NY: MacArthur Foundation.

Kenney, B. (2004, December). Googlizers v. resistors: Library leaders debate our relationship with search engines. *Library Journal, 129*(20), 44–46.

Kelty, C. M. (2013). From participation to power. In A. A. Delwiche & J. J. Henderson (Eds.). *The participatory cultures handbook* (pp. 22–31). New York, NY: Routledge.

Lankshear, C., & Knobel, M. (2006). *New literacies: Everyday practices and classroom learning* (2nd ed.). Maidenhead, UK: Open University Press.

Lévy, P. (1994). *Collective intelligence: Mankind's emerging world in cyberspace.* Cambridge, MA: Perseus Books.

Lévy, P. (2011). *The semantic sphere1: Computation, cognition, and the information economy.* Hoboken, NJ: Wiley-Iste.

Lévy, P. (14 April 2015). Collective intelligence for educators. *Pierre Lévy's Blog.* https://pierrelevyblog.com/2015/04/14/collective-intelligence-for-educators/

Marr, B. (2018, May 21). How much data do we create every day? *Forbes.* Retrieved from https://www.forbes.com/sites/bernardmarr/2018/05/21/how-much-data-do-we-create-every-day-the-mind-blowing-stats-everyone-should-read/#2512719760ba

Muchnik, L., Aral, S., & Taylor, S. J. (2013). Social influence bias: A randomized experiment. *Science, 341*(6146), 647–651.

Mulgan, G. (2017). *Big mind: How collective intelligence can change our world.* Princeton, NJ: Princeton University Press.

Noriega-Campero, A., Almaatouq, A., Krafft, P., Alotaibi, A., Moussaid, M., & Pentland, A. (2018). The wisdom of the network: How adaptive networks promote collective intelligence. arXiv.org, https://arxiv.org/abs/1805.04766" https://arxiv.org/abs/1805.04766

Pearce, C., &Venters, W. (2013). How particle physicists constructed the world's largest grid: A case study in participatory cultures. In A. A. Delwiche & J. J. Henderson (Eds.). *The participatory cultures handbook* (pp. 130–140). New York, NY: Routledge.

Potter, J. W. (2005). *Media literacy* (3rd ed.). Thousand Oaks, CA: Sage.

Pretz, N., & Sternberg (2003). In J. E. Davidson & J. Sternberg (Eds.), *The psychology of problem solving* (pp. 3–30). Cambridge, UK: Cambridge University Press.

Rheingold, H. (2002). *Smart mobs.* New York, NY: Basic Books.

Salingaros, N. (2019). Unpublished lecture. San Antonio, TX: Trinity University.

Seeley, T. D. (2010). *Honey bee democracy.* Princeton, NJ: Princeton University Press.

Surowiecki, J. (2004). *The wisdom of crowds.* New York, NY: Anchor Books.

Woolley, A. W., Aggarwal, I., & Malone, T. W. (2015). Collective intelligence in teams and organizations. In M. Bernstein & T. W. Malone (Eds.), *Handbook of collective intelligence*, Cambridge, MA: MIT Press.

Woolley, A. W., Chabris, C. F., Pentland, A., Hashmi, N., & Malone, T. W. (2010). Evidence for a collective intelligence factor in the performance of human groups. *Science, 330*, 686–688.

Woolley, A. W., & Fuchs, E. (2011). Collective intelligence in the organization of science. *Organization Science,22*(5): 1359–1367.

Varnellis, K. (2008). *Networked publics.* Cambridge, MA: MIT Press.

17 Civic Engagement, Social Justice, and Media Literacy

Srividya "Srivi" Ramasubramanian and Ramin Chaboki Darzabi

Introduction

With mainstream media perpetuating partisan politics and populist rhetoric, there is an increase in vitriolic hate online, spread of sensationalism, and easy dissemination of misinformation in what has been referred to as an era of "spreadable spectacle" in "post-fact" societies (Mihailidis & Viotty, 2017; Silverman, 2015). In this chapter, we argue that there is an urgent need to counter these divisive forces and toxicity by refocusing media literacy pedagogy and praxis toward social justice and civic empowerment. Going beyond traditional definitions of media literacy as the ability to access, evaluate, and produce media, we expand the notion of media literacy to incorporate social responsibility, critical civic consciousness, and anti-oppression pedagogy. We argue that without a critical media literacy approach that is explicitly aimed at dismantling social injustices and structural inequalities through civic engagement, the participatory power of digital media could be left untouched, or worse, used for furthering fascism, imperialism, patriarchy, and other systems of domination. We end the chapter with some recommendations and guidelines for consideration by media literacy scholars and practitioners.

Critical Pedagogies, Engaged Citizenship, and Participatory Media Cultures

Contemporary educational paradigms have moved toward active experiential learning through collaboration and mutual respect, using the resources available to them. Critical approaches to literacy place emphasis on legitimizing the cultural and social capital that learners bring to their learning spaces. Instead of passively consuming dominant texts that reproduce mainstream ideologies, this approach focuses less on comprehension and analysis and more on the potential for social transformation and socio-political change (Freire & Macedo, 1987).

Expanding the concept of literacy, digital and media literacies offer opportunities in both formal and informal ways to contribute to fostering the competencies, skills, and knowledge needed for civic engagement. Critical pedagogy helps us reimagine the relationships among media, popular culture, education, and power. Media culture can serve as a learning space for fostering critical awareness, civic consciousness, and identity development. Media literate people are able to identify different agendas, including personal, corporate, and political ones, and also use media as a tool for civic actions.

In identifying the core competencies of media literacy, beyond the traditional definition of media literacy as the ability to access, analyze, evaluate, and create messages (Aufderheide, 1993), Hobbs (2010) includes the ability to engage in reflection and being active in community. *Reflection* is defined as "applying social responsibility and ethical principles to one's own identity and lived experience, communication behavior and conduct," while *action* is defined as "working individually and collaboratively to share knowledge and solve problems in the family, the workplace and the community, and participating as a member of a community at local, regional, national and international levels" (Hobbs, 2010, p. 19). These last two aspects of media literacy – *reflection* and *action* – emphasize that media literacy should include social responsibility, collaborative work, and ethical considerations in the service of one's family, workplace, and community at various levels beyond simply for the sake of gratifying individual needs and personal growth. Similarly, Mihailidis (2014) presents the 5A's framework incorporating access, awareness, assessment, appreciation, and action, where civic engagement is emphasized especially in the "action" aspect of the framework.

The notion of *engaged citizenship* is central to civic participation. Traditionally, citizenship has been conceptualized as legal members of a nation-state (see Choi, 2016, for a detailed analysis). However, citizenship is much more than just a legal or administrative definition in terms of an individual's relationship to a nation or state. It is about identity and a sense of community. It is a certain mindset and approach to life where one acts in ethical and socially responsible ways toward social justice. Gozálvez and Contreras-Pulido (2014) discuss various types of citizenship: *political citizenship* as active participation in public affairs, *social citizenship* as working toward social welfare of all in a society, *economic citizenship* as responsible consumption and business activities, *ecological citizenship* as fostering civic values of environmental sustainability, and *global/cosmopolitan citizenship* as appreciation for cultural diversity.

In today's ubiquitous mediated contexts, to be a fully active citizen, one should also incorporate *media citizenship*, where citizens not only have access to media technologies but are provided the skillsets and means to process information and produce content effectively. *Digital citizenship* has been conceptualized as the ability to use digital media technologies to their full potential through creative expression, economic attainment, political participation, and civic engagement, especially in the context of older adults (Mossberger, Tolbert & Stansbury, 2007).

More recently, Choi (2016) has conducted content analysis about the concept of digital citizenship to uncover the various elements associated with this concept within participatory spreadable convergence media cultures. They delineate four different ways in which digital citizenship is understood and practiced: *ethics, media and information literacy, participation/engagement,* and *critical resistance.* Ethical approaches to digital citizenship emphasize how to use digital media in safe, ethical, and responsible ways. The media and information literacy perspective focuses on critical competencies needed to access, analyze, evaluate, and produce media in online contexts. The participation/engagement aspects of digital citizenship includes political participation, such as on-line petitions, deliberations on public policies, and e-voting, but also non-traditional micro-forms of civic engagement in everyday activities. Finally, digital citizenship as resistance takes a more critical and radical perspective that challenges existing power structures in online spaces.

Within the context of the proliferation of new media technologies in the participatory convergence culture, contemporary critical literacy scholars have to contend with the fact that how individuals learn from media has changed dramatically. Digital citizens today are reading, pro-ducing, curating, archiving, repurposing, and recirculating media con-tent, often doing all of these several times a day (Jenkins, 2006; Jenkins, Ford, & Green, 2013). This *participatory media culture* within digital contexts is shaping identities, social relationships, collaboration, and community building. Social media platforms have created what is re-ferred to as *networked publics* (Castells, 2012) that have both facilitated large-scale socio-political movements, such as Arab Spring and #MeToo, but also created a sense of more personal agency in everyday engagement with social causes. Beyond access to digital technologies, media literacy education focuses on overcoming the *participation gap* (Jenkins, 2006) so that digital citizens can participate fully and engage freely the various aspects of media and technology.

As we work to promote active citizenship within the shifting digital environments, we need to use a critical lens to examine how power, privilege, and social capital continue to be renegotiated in these digital spaces. One of the concerns has been the rapid homogenization of main-stream content and a focus on neoliberal capitalism where transmedia digital storytelling has focused much more on global brands rather than on promoting civic empowerment for social justice (Ramasubramanian, 2016). Another issue is the focus on self-promotion and branding at the individual level without using the transformative power of digital new media technologies to foster social change. Media literacy education without a clear civic focus has often facilitated what has been referred to as *mecosystem* (Interbrand, n.d.), which focuses on the individual level of creative expression, self-branding, and self-discovery through media rather than on social justice, political participation, and civic engagement. We argue that from a critical digital media literacy perspective, media and technology should be used as tools to create safe spaces for meaningful dialogue, for re-negotiating and affirming the identities of stigmatized groups, and fostering social transformation.

Civic Engagement, Political Participation, and Community-Building

Mere active engagement on the Internet does not lead to civic engagement. However, digital new media technologies can serve as excellent avenues for learning about civic participation and community-building. Civic engagement includes both informal and formal political participation as well as community participation. Traditionally, civic engagement has focused on political actions such as voting in elections, contacting elected officials, attending town hall meetings, and knowledge about political parties, which has arguably decreased among youth today, who are active in digital spaces (Bennett, 2008; Putnam, 2000). However, when we take a broader definition of civic engagement to go beyond political engagement to also include community-building and service activities, such as fundraising, volunteering, petitioning for a cause, then we see that active digital participation online, especially among youth, enables such civic actions (Martens & Hobbs, 2015).

In terms of *political participation*, traditional definitions focus on civic duties, such as voting and party affiliation at the local, state, and national levels, but more recent definitions emphasize the civic, social, and economic aspects of being part of a community (Choi, 2016). Rather than enacting *dutiful citizenship*, which is driven by a sense of civic responsibility to vote, attend town hall meetings, and engage in traditional political activities, digital natives of today envision citizenship as *engaged citizenship*; that is a more expanded notion of political participation that involves informal networks and online communities (Bennett, 2008). Banaji and Buckingham (2013) remind us that civic engagement in digital environments is more fluid than how it has been conventionally conceptualized and tends to happen at irregular intervals, emerging from within specific contexts in organic ways. That is, rather than civic engagement for the sake of civic duty, digital citizens today express engaged citizenship through more dynamic notions of participatory politics, such as blogging, online petitions, charity fundraisers, and so on. It is highly likely that those who are active politically and engaged civically online are also doing so offline. Therefore, isolating the unique effects of media literacy education is a challenging task. Nevertheless, exploratory survey research by Martens and Hobbs (2015) demonstrates that after controlling for demographic variables such as age, income, and education, digital media literacy is positively correlated with intention toward civic engagement.

What this dynamic, more informal, and broader conceptualization of engaged digital citizenship online looks like could range from organizing flash mobs, creating online campaigns for social awareness, playing mobile phone games that could raise awareness about environmental issues, and creating memes to use humor to challenge cultural stereotypes (Banaji & Buckingham, 2013; Jenkins et al., 2013). These activities could at times combine fun and play with more serious conversations and could cover a range of socio-cultural and political issues beyond traditional notions of political participation.

Media literacy is an important competency needed for civic agency and citizen engagement. Active participation online can help forge social bonds and friendships, which could lay the foundation for civic engagement and political participation. A solid foundation in media literacy education teaches how to ask good questions, seek relevant information, assess the quality and credibility of the information, discuss issues with others, express your views effectively, and collaborate with others to take collective action. All of these competencies relating to critical thinking, active reasoning, collaboration learning, information seeking, and respect for difference are essential for active participation in the public sphere on socio-political issues as part of civic engagement.

Mihailidis and Thevenin (2013) suggest three critical media literacy outcomes that make media literacy necessary for civic engagement: *critical thinkers, creators and communicators*, and *agents of social change*. They believe that in the 21st century, all citizens should be critical thinkers to be capable of analyzing and evaluating information on which to build their civic engagement. Through critical thinking, people are able to collect accurate facts about their community and also challenge the power. From this perspective, civic media literacy makes people ready to participate in community effectively "by helping them analyze mediated representations of their communities, as well as address issues within their communities" (p. 1615). Critical media literate citizens are able to express their unique perspectives on different issues in their communities and develop new ways for circulating their ideas. Encouraging citizens to act as agents of social change is a crucial outcome that critical media literacy approaches focus on. These scholars argue that media literacy helps people "to make significant contributions to civic life – the organization of political movements, the creation of new political practices and processes, and the institution of new legislative policies – when citizens see themselves as agents of social change" (p. 1616).

Building on these contemporary notions of engaged digital citizenship for civic participation, McDougall and colleagues (2015) propose a three-step research methodology for incorporating civic engagement into media literacy curriculum that incorporates Mihailidis's 5A's framework

(2014). In Step 1, which focuses on access and appreciation, participants use survey methods to complete an online profiling map of media engagement. In the next step, which emphasizes awareness and assessment, participants conducted fieldwork based on interviews about their media usage and critical use of media texts. In the final stage, which corresponds with the "Action" aspect of the 5A's framework, participants engaged in an online creative political task. Here participants had to complete a creative task with the explicit purpose of civic engagement where the media products had to be shared with a broader audience who were then engaged in conversations within a three-week period.

One of the limitations of using such a framework for teaching how to incorporate civic engagement in media literacy is that in the real world, such civic engagement typically happens in organic ways. Forcing learners to deliberately make their creative work public and encouraging them to engage with an audience might not be a natural way in which such civic actions typically take place in voluntary ways within specific contexts of online communities. Another related concern is that it is difficult to isolate the unique effects of media literacy education in serving as a catalyst to promote civic engagement, making the research aspects of examining the relationship between media literacy interventions and civic engagement a challenging one for media scholars.

Social Justice, Anti-Oppression Pedagogy, and Media Activism

Participation and active engagement alone are not sufficient when it comes to media literacy. With the political re-emergence of populism, fascism, and alt-right around the world, media literacy stands at a critical juncture. Online communities are often self-segregated echo chambers that serve as homophilous networks where dissent is vehemently silenced. As more community members contribute to the sharing and recirculation of rumors and false information, it can quickly work to delegitimize news outlets, strengthen conspiracy theories, and lead to confusion about what is fact and what is reality (Mihailidis & Viotty, 2017; Silverman, 2015). The increase in hateful rhetoric online by white supremacists, nationalists, and neo-Nazis points to how the spreadability and anonymity of media can be misused for virulent hate, bigotry, and terror (Ramasubramanian & Miles, 2018). Unless we explicitly link media literacy education to the decolonial project of emancipation and dismantling of social inequalities, the participatory power of spreadable media ecosystem could easily be used to create, perpetuate, and spread misinformation, false rumors, gossip, and hearsay. They can lead to reinforcing rather than questioning status quo power relations.

Anti-oppression pedagogy is an important part of fostering social justice orientation into media literacy education. Social justice scholarship

278 Srividya "Srivi" Ramasubramanian and Ramin Chaboki Darzabi

and pedagogy challenges the status quo, questions power imbalances, and works to reduce social inequalities. It is explicitly critical in its approach and works toward dismantling structural inequities and questions hierarchical ideologies. Ranieri and Fabbro (2016) argue that media literacy can provide the opportunity for individuals to develop their participatory abilities especially by challenging various ways in which existing systems might lead to discriminatory practices and social inequalities. Media literate citizens are motivated to share their ideas about and question discrimination in their community. This critical consciousness about addressing power differences and achieving equity is an important aspect of civic engagement.

Scholars make a distinction between critical scholarship from a "first-person perspective" of being directly involved in political action, social movements, and social causes versus "third-person perspectives," where the scholar describes and studies groups and individuals doing social justice work without being directly involved with it (Frey & Carragee, 2007). Critical media scholarship has been influenced by many different bodies of scholarship, including feminist, critical race, Marxism, queer, postmodernist, and poststructural perspectives. Media literacy education with a social justice orientation challenges various intersecting systems of domination such as patriarchy, white supremacy, imperialism, colonization, ableism, heteronormativity, and capitalism.

While critical consciousness and a social justice orientation are essential to civic engagement using media, there are other factors that help to move beyond individual ethics to the realm of social responsibility, community orientation, and collective action. Mihailidis (2018) recognizes some limitations to current media literacy practices that constrain the civic potential of media literacy. They suggest that media literacies have to prioritize a civic intentionality and recommend five constructs: *agency, caring, critical consciousness, persistence,* and *emancipation* that concentrate in civic renewal and develop media literacy pedagogies that encourage citizens to support everyday activism. In this model, *agency* enables people to have an overall assessment of their social position and a constant self-reflection on the power and authority they have individually or collectively. In their opinion, civic media literacies also encourage people to *care for* one another. Mihailidis (2018) argues:

> media literacies that embrace caring ethics establish the need to focus on bringing communities together in receptivity, relatedness, and where we care for and care with. Civic media literacies, in this sense, support relation, interdependence, and engrossment, and do not dictate the grounds upon which they emerge

(p. 161)

Critical consciousness is another dimension in this framework that refers to developing a capability in citizens that leads to the "possibility of response" in the real life. Civic media literacies embrace transgression and all of the competencies in media literacy, such as analysis, evaluation, production, reflection, and action, and try to undermine institutional authority and challenge systemic power. *Persistence* as another aspect develops "stamina in young people to persist in their media pursuits" (p. 162). *Emancipation* as the last factor in this model refers to this idea that civic media literate people are able to challenge the power and existing authority that limit them in their pursuit. This framework is helpful as we re-envision media literacy through the lens of social justice because it incorporates aspects such as an ethics of care, emancipation, and persistence, which are not competencies that are typically included in media literacy education.

What Now? The Future of Media Literacy in the Context of Social Justice and Civic Engagement

Here, we outline some specific recommendations as we move forward, as we reframe and reposition it within the larger context of the digital ecosystem of spreadability but also in this new emerging socio-political context of the re-emergence of political partisanship, right-wing authoritarianism, online hate, fake news, and delegitimization of journalists and media as a whole. In order to work toward media literacy that is explicitly oriented toward emancipation, anti-oppression, social justice, and civic engagement, we need to re-envision media literacy pedagogy, practice, research, and scholarship.

Digital media are public goods that serve community members. The market-based logic of neoliberal capitalism has led to broadcast reregulation, which have led to lesser content and source diversity. An important aspect of social justice in media contexts continues to be media access and participation, which are tied to media industries and monopolization by a handful of corporations. If we have to incorporate social justice and civic engagement within media literacy, we have to continue to advocate for greater access to media in affordable ways to the public.

Going beyond individual level of emphasizing the role of media literacy as a tool for self-actualization and self-expression, we believe that media literacy education should move toward teaching individual learners what it means to be an active engaged citizen who uses the tools of digital media literacy for furthering community goals.

Simply encouraging the creation of online communities and participation is not sufficient. Collaboration and community-building should be tied clearly with a critical emancipatory approach that incorporates social justice and anti-oppression pedagogy. Otherwise, the participatory power of spreadable media culture could reinforce rather than challenge social inequalities. This social justice orientation will have to use participation, engagement, and community-building to lead to social transformation in ways that lead to decreased power imbalances and greater equity.

From a critical pedagogy perspective, it is crucial that the learning space itself is not hierarchical but allows for collaboration, co-learning, and critical assessment. It is crucial, then, that beyond examining media's role in our societies, media literacy education should prepare learners to be active digital citizens who are agents of transformative socio-political change.

An essential aspect of media literacy education has to be diversity literacy that teaches learners about difference, power, bias, and privilege. Media literacy itself has to be culturally inclusive and sensitive to the socio-cultural contexts in which it is situated. Diversity literacy is essential not just to understand who we are as individuals within a larger social context but also to understand how to build coalitions across diverse groups in furthering social justice goals. It is important to recognize Eurocentric white hegemonic aspects of literacy studies, including media literacy. Currently it continues to be rooted in ideas of digital democracy and participatory culture, which might be centered in Western notions of individualism, neoliberal capitalism, and colonialism, which need to be re-examined and dismantled.

In order to further media literacy through the lens of social justice and civic engagement, we would also need greater institutional and disciplinary support for media literacy research and activist/engaged scholarship. It might also be beneficial to have a network of hyperlocal, ethnically inclusive, and alternative citizens' media that could help amplify efforts to bring light to social issues. Such networks could also provide support for leadership training, micro-financing, organizing, and mentoring.

In adapting and repositioning media literacy education for social justice in the digital hypermedia landscape, we should be open to taking multi-method, multi-perspectival approaches to tackling difficult social issues. This could mean learning about critical big data analysis, data visualization, data curation, and meme analysis, which might not be considered traditional media research or methods.

We need to make a concerted effort to incorporate social justice into media literacy from all perspectives such as pedagogy, research, and community involvement. That requires educators, activists, community leaders, scholars, and administrators to commit to being proactive in their approach by providing the required tools and competencies instead of as a reactive response to crises. It also requires coordinated organizational efforts and coalition-building across various media literacy organizations and networks, which are sometimes diffused, distinct, and even divided.

In conclusion, as engaged global citizens, there are crucial social inequalities that continue to remain challenges that need to be overcome: forced migrations, human trafficking, mass incarceration, wage gap, climate change, natural disasters, food insecurity, unequal access to basic rights such as education and healthcare, and increased hate crimes on religious minorities, people of color, and LBGTQ+ individuals. Although this description presents us with a bleak picture of the future of the world, the hope that keeps us grounded in our work as educators and scholars is that community members from various backgrounds are also coming together in powerful ways to collaborate, organize, protest, and challenge social inequalities. Media are important venues that can facilitate, foster, and strengthen these efforts toward community building, participatory democracy, and social justice initiatives. Through intentional and persistent efforts to reposition media literacy as anti-oppression pedagogy that uses critical approaches to civic engagement for social change, we can make media literacy scholarship more meaningful, relevant, transformative, and even healing within a larger global context of hate, bigotry, inequalities, and injustices.

References

Aufderheide, P. (1993). *Media literacy: A report of the national leadership conference on media literacy.* Washington, DC: The Aspen Institute.

Banaji, S., & Buckingham, D. (2013). *The civic web: Young people, the Internet and civic participation.* Cambridge: MIT Press.

Bennett, W. L. (2008). Changing citizenship in the digital age. In W. L. Bennett (Ed.), *Civic life online: Learning how digital media can engage youth* (pp. 1–24). Cambridge, MA: MIT Press.

Castells, M. (2012). *Networks of outrage and hope: Social movements in the Internet age.* Malden, MA: Polity Press.

Choi, M. (2016). A concept analysis of digital citizenship for democratic citizenship education in the Internet age. *Theory & Research in Social Education, 44*(4), 565–607.

Freire, P., & Macedo, D. (1987). *Literacy: Reading the word and the world.* New York, NY: Continuum.

Frey, L. R., & Carragee, K. M. (2007). *Communication activism: Communication for social change.* New York, NY: Hampton Press.

Gozálvez, V., & Contreras-Pulido, P. (2014). Empowering media citizenship through educommunication. *Comunicar, 21*(42), 129–136.

Hobbs, R. (2010). *Digital and media literacy: A plan of action.* Washington, DC: The Aspen Institute.

Interbrand (n.d.). *The definition of mecosystem.* Retrieved May 17, 2019 from https://www.interbrand.com/views/the-definition-of-mecosystem/

Jenkins, H. (2006). *Convergence culture: Where old and new media collide.* New York, NY: NYU Press.

Jenkins, H., Ford, S., & Green, J. (2013). *Spreadable media: Creating value and meaning in a networked culture.* New York, NY: New York University Press.

Martens, H., & Hobbs, R. (2015). How media literacy supports civic engagement in a digital age. *Atlantic Journal of Communication, 23*(2), 120–137.

McDougall, J., Berger, R., Fraser, P., & Zezulkova, M. (2015). Media literacy, education & (civic) capability: A transferable methodology. *Journal of Media Literacy Education, 7*(1), 4–17.

Mihailidis, P. (2014). *Media literacy and the emerging citizen: Youth, engagement and participation in digital culture.* New York, NY: Peter Lang Publishing.

Mihailidis, P., & Thevenin, B. (2013). Media literacy as a core competency for engaged citizenship in participatory democracy. *American Behavioral Scientist, 57*(11), 1611–1622.

Mihailidis, P., & Viotty, S. (2017). Spreadable spectacle in digital culture: Civic expression, fake news, and the role of media literacies in "post-fact" society. *American Behavioral Scientist, 61*(4), 441–454.

Mihailidis, P. (2018). Civic media literacies: Re-Imagining engagement for civic intentionality, *Learning, Media and Technology, 43*(2), 152–164.

Mossberger, K., Tolbert, C. J., & McNeal, R. S. (2007). *Digital citizenship.* Cambridge, MA: MIT Press.

Putnam, R. (2000). *Bowling alone: The collapse and revival of American community.* New York, NY: Simon & Schuster.

Ramasubramanian, S. (2016). Racial/ethnic identity, community-oriented media initiatives, and transmedia storytelling. *The Information Society, 32*(5), 333–342. doi:10.1080/01972243.2016.1212618

Ramasubramanian, S., & Miles, C. (2018). White nationalist rhetoric, neoliberal multiculturalism and colour blind racism: Decolonial critique of Richard Spencer's campus visit. *Javnost: The Public, 25*(4), 426–440.

Ranieri, M., & Fabbro, F. (2016). Questioning discrimination through critical media literacy. Findings from seven European countries. *European Educational Research Journal, 15*(4), 462–479.

Silverman, C. (2015). *Lies, damn lies, and viral content: How news websites spread (and debunk) online rumors, unverified claims, and misinformation.* Retrieved from http://tow-center.org/wp-content/uploads/2015/02/LiesDamnLies_Silverman_TowCenter.pdf

18 Critical Media Literacy and Environmental Justice

Jeff Share

Introduction

Advancements in information communication technologies are occurring at exponential rates, connecting the world in ways never imagined possible, while at the same time, we are breaking all records for the amount of CO_2 in the atmosphere, the severity of extreme weather events, the acidification of oceans, and the melting of glaciers and permafrost. In 2019, NASA released a report declaring, "The past five years are, collectively, the warmest years in the modern record." Scientists are also reporting on the warming of the oceans and the thawing of ice from the Himalayas to the Antarctic. At the same time as temperatures increase in our global village, more than half of the world's population are now online, creating new opportunities for media and technology to become powerful tools for understanding our environmental crisis and for taking actions to confront the problems.

Human-caused climate change is the most decisive crisis to affect life on this planet, and we are seeing corporations and politicians spinning facts and emotions to create doubt about the science and reframe the discourse. Neoliberal ideology, unregulated capitalism, rampant consumerism, sensationalized journalism, and the extraction and burning of fossil fuels are combining to create an environmental catastrophe that is changing everything (Klein, 2014). The media messages about these issues are an ideal space for students to critically analyze and challenge the assumptions, actions, and inactions. Using an inquiry-based framework of critical media literacy (CML), educators can guide students to question and create their own media messages about environmental justice and sustainability.

What media post, publish, and broadcast, or choose not to report, has significant consequences; and when they do decide to tell the story, how they frame it and explain it matters greatly. Antonio López (2014) asserts, "Crucially, mass media play an instructional role by defining the status quo, setting the agenda for our socio-economic system, defining what to think about, and recursively reinforcing non-sustainable cultural beliefs" (p. 72).

To encourage students to use their critical capacity, imagination, and creativity to explore and respond to climate change, educators need to break from the confines of the printed page. By incorporating ideas from CML, we can enhance students' reading and writing skills with all types of texts (movies, music, videogames, photographs, social media, books, etc.), deepen their understanding about the power of literacy, and stoke their creative spirits to learn about, as well as challenge, dominant narratives regarding our interdependence with the natural world.

With the popularity and accessibility of cell phones and new mobile devices, youth are communicating and socializing every day in numerous ways, such as texting, tweeting, tagging, blogging, posting, pinning, instant messaging, photographing, podcasting, and sharing all types of texts. It is significant that the introduction to the Common Core State Standards specifically mentions the need for students to read and write with digital texts and "use technology and digital media strategically and capably" (Common Core State Standards, 2015, p. 7). According to a report by The National Environmental Education and Training Foundation (2005), "children get more environmental information (83%) from the media than from any other source" (Coyle, p. x). Since social media, smartphones, and the Internet have become the dominant conveyors of information as well as students' preferred option for communication and entertainment, teachers should be integrating these tools and practices into the classroom with theory and pedagogy that support critical thinking.

Critical Media Literacy Framework

In *Greening Media Education: Bridging Media Literacy with Green Cultural Citizenship*, López (2014) explains that there are many people in environmental education who think "media and technology are anti-nature" and that "the general practice of media literacy marginalizes ecological perspectives" (p. 1). However, it does not have to be this way. Critical media literacy that has evolved from cultural studies and critical pedagogy can provide an important framework for uniting information communication technologies (ICTs) with environmental justice. Even though media education has not always supported sustainable practices and environmental perspectives, critical media literacy provides the potential to make education more transformative because it promotes social and environmental justice through critiquing dominant ideologies. The six conceptual understandings and questions of critical media literacy offer a framework for exploring and questioning all media representations:

1   *Social Constructivism:* all information is co-constructed by individuals and/or groups of people who make choices within social

contexts (WHO are all the possible people who made choices that helped create this text?),

2 *Languages/Semiotics:* each medium has its own language with specific grammar and semantics (HOW was this text constructed and delivered/accessed?),

3 *Audience/Positionality:* individuals and groups understand media messages similarly and/or differently, depending on multiple contextual factors (HOW could this text be understood differently?),

4 *Politics of Representation:* media messages and the medium through which they travel always have a bias and support and/or challenge dominant hierarchies of power, privilege, and pleasure (WHAT values, points of view, and ideologies are represented or missing from this text or influenced by the medium?),

5 *Production/Institutions:* all media texts have a purpose (often commercial or governmental) that is shaped by the creators and/or systems within which they operate (WHY was this text created and/or shared?)

6 *Social and Environmental Justice:* media culture is a terrain of struggle that perpetuates or challenges positive and/or negative ideas about people, groups, and issues; it is never neutral (WHOM does this text advantage and/or disadvantage?) (Kellner & Share, 2019, p. 8).

For decades, informal science education has worked with a deficit perspective and failed to promote critical thinking. A one-way transmission model, known as the Public Understanding of Science approach (PUS), has not been effective at educating the public about the seriousness of climate change (Cooper, 2011). The PUS approach is giving way to the Public Engagement in Science (PES) model of education, which is more in line with CML because it supports critical thinking and an inquiry model of questioning. Caren Cooper (2011) argues, "In order to be climate change literate, the public must first be media literate" (p. 235). She writes:

> Science education efforts must be strategic and must expand courageously to provide the public with the critical thinking and media literacy skills that will help people recognize the barrage of media messages constructed to mislead, confuse, or predispose individuals to apathy or denial when engaging in dialogues about climate change.
>
> (p. 235)

While the PES model is an improvement over the more traditional "banking" approach, it does not prepare people to interrogate messages, to question dominant ideologies that shape assumptions, to recognize the influence of the medium through which information passes, and to see through the false notions of objectivity to identify the economic structures that support commercial media. By using the CML framework of conceptual understandings and questions, educators can guide students to analyze media messages along with the structures and systems that support and influence them.

The commercial media accessed on TV, radio, cell phones, and the Internet may seem free, yet it is important to recognize that they are economically dependent on advertising, which, in turn, needs endless consumption. Our consumerist ideology requires what Lewis and Boyce (2009) state is a "need to acknowledge the role that advertising plays in *creating a set of cultural conditions* that makes us less inclined to deal with climate change" (p. 8). Naomi Klein (2014) argues that we must change the consumption economic system through "de-growth" reductions. Klein (2014) asserts that social justice and environmental justice are profoundly interdependent:

> the climate moment offers an overarching narrative in which everything from the fight for good jobs to justice for migrants to reparations for historical wrongs like slavery and colonialism can all become part of the grand project of building a nontoxic, shockproof economy before it's too late.
>
> (p. 154)

Klein encourages us to understand climate change less as a single issue and more as a frame for seeing how all the problems that colonialism, imperialism, capitalism, and neoliberalism have been causing around the world are only going to become worse as temperatures rise.

The Inequality of Climate Effects and Responsibilities

For years, environmental problems in the United States have been represented in mainstream media as if everyone were affected equally by environmental dangers. This hid the fact that low-income neighborhoods, especially communities of color, have been impacted with far worse consequences of environmental hazards than middle- and upper-class areas. Kate Aronoff (2018) writes,

> People of color in the United States are far more likely to live near coal-fired power plants and suffer the associated health effects, and live in places where heavy weather hits hardest, thanks to years of targeted disinvestment in things like housing and infrastructure.

When one takes into consideration issues of age, along with class and race, it becomes very apparent that the inequality of the effects of climate change put poor children of color on the front line. Frederica Perera (2016) reports,

While air pollution and the adverse health impacts of climate change affect us all, they are most damaging to children, especially the developing fetus and young child and particularly those of low socioeconomic status, who often have the greatest exposures and least amount of protection.

The effects of climate change are also worse for people living on islands like the Maldives, where rising sea levels are causing increasing flooding and putting the entire nation at risk (Berge, Cohen, & Shenk, 2011). Students need to understand that climate change is a problem that affects everyone, but not equally.

Another often repeated myth in commercial media is the idea that we are all equally responsible for the environmental damages. While it is important that everyone feel a sense of responsibility and desire to improve the environment, it is also essential that corporations, governments, non-sustainable economic practices, and unjust ideologies be held accountable for the majority of the harm they have caused and are currently causing to the environment. In the August 1, 2018, issue of the *New York Times Magazine,* the entire magazine is dedicated to Nathaniel Rich's article, "Losing Earth: The Decade We Almost Stopped Climate Change." This in-depth analysis of climate change, public debate, and action provides an excellent narrative of growing critical awareness about the accelerating dangers of climate change but assigns blame and ascribes agency largely to individuals rather than seeing the complex interplay of individuals, corporations, the media, government, and social movements. Rich fails to address the idea that not everyone is equally responsible for the crisis we are now facing. Aronoff (2018) points out that Rich's article does not hold the fossil fuel companies or the largest carbon emitters to task.

> Just 100 companies have been responsible for 71 percent of emissions since 1988. According to a 2015 study from Oxfam, the poorest half of the world's population accounts for just 10 percent of emissions; around half stem from the richest 10 percent.

The nations in the northern hemisphere have emitted far more CO_2 into the atmosphere than the countries currently experiencing the worst effects of global warming.

News Reporting on Environmental Problems

News reporting on environmental issues is often hampered by conventions of commercial journalism. While many journalists produce excellent investigative reporting, the economic structures of commercial journalism unfortunately create systems that tend to prioritize profit over journalistic integrity (McChesney, 2015, 2004). The practice of publishing and broadcasting corporate-created press releases and video press releases without attribution has been increasing as media corporations merge and cost-saving measures cut the funding and personnel necessary for original reporting. Another problem with commercial media's economic model is the culture of spectacle that favors sensationalism over in-depth analysis (Kellner, 2003).

A challenge with media representations of environmental issues is what Rob Nixon (2013) describes as the problem of "slow violence." Much of news media and movies appeal to audiences through sensationalizing momentary visual spectacles as dramatic entertainment. However, what is rarely portrayed is the slow violence:

> that is neither spectacular nor instantaneous but instead incremental, whose calamitous repercussions are postponed for years or decades or centuries... Stories of toxic buildup, massing greenhouse gases, and accelerated species loss because of ravaged habitats may all be cataclysmic, but they are scientifically convoluted cataclysms in which casualties are postponed, often for generations.
>
> (Nixon, 2011)

As a result, climate change gets inadequate coverage, as evident in an analysis of CNN's coverage during a week in 2015 that experienced record-breaking temperatures when they aired five times more oil industry advertising than coverage of climate change (Kalhoefer, 2016). During 2016, the hottest year on record at the time, the major TV networks spent 66% less time covering climate change than they did in 2015 (Kalhoefer, 2017). According to research by *Media Matters*,

> There was a 45 percent drop in climate change coverage on the broadcast networks' nightly news and Sunday morning political shows from 2017 to 2018 – from a total of 260 minutes in 2017 down to just 142 minutes in 2018.
>
> (MacDonald & Hymas, 2019)

In 2019, when the United Nations released a landmark study on the drastic decline of biodiversity due to climate change and other human causes, "Out of 25 total prime-time news programs on the networks, only three reported on the U.N. assessment" (MacDonald, 2019). Nixon (2013) notes the lack of media representation of "slow violence" is particularly evident in poor Southern Hemisphere countries, such as Ecuador, where there are few, if any, regulations on oil drilling, or the building of a dam in Brazil that displaced 40,000 mostly indigenous people and flooded 200 square miles of forests – furthering deforestation of Brazil.

Media stories about climate change are too often under-reported, and when they are represented in mainstream media, they tend to be sensational and controversial. Seldom are commercial media messages helpful to understanding the complexity of climate change in a way that motivates people to care and act. Most of the reporting creates a false balance related to framing the issue as debatable or controversial. Finis Dunaway (2015) writes, "Yet, even as media images have made the environmental crisis visible to a mass public, they often have masked systemic causes and ignored structural inequalities" (p. 2). Educators should encourage students to do their own investigations about current media coverage. They can conduct quantitative research by counting the number of articles and news broadcasts on climate change and also qualitative research by evaluating the bias and construction of the reporting. *Fairness & Accuracy in Reporting* (FAIR) (*http://fair.org*) is a non-profit organization that provides regular critiques of media coverage in articles and in their podcast *CounterSpin* that can be useful for students to study specific examples of news reporting through a critical lens.

It is important for students to understand that critical engagement does not mean only analyzing negative problems; it also involves appreciating positive representations and constructive actions. One example of journalism that is working to ethically inform the public can be seen in the way *The Guardian* newspaper has changed its house style guide to more accurately report on the climate crisis. Instead of using the terms "climate change" and "global warming," they now refer to the problem as "climate emergency," "climate crisis," and "global heating." According to the editor-in-chief, Katharine Viner, "We want to ensure that we are being scientifically precise, while also communicating clearly with readers on this very important issue" (Carrington, 2019). Along with changing their words, they are also providing a daily record of the global carbon dioxide levels in their weather pages.

These changes by *The Guardian* are steps in the right direction, yet the fact that some news media and politicians still question the science of climate change makes the need for a media literate populace more important than ever. While the debate in the scientific community ended decades ago, the popular discourse in commercial media is heavily influenced by public relations companies receiving large amounts of money from the fossil fuel industry (Oreskes & Conway, 2010). For students swayed by this deception, there are many resources available to critique climate deniers and triangulate the vast amount of scientific evidence. It is essential that students adopt a critical stance, given the history of the fossil fuel industry's covering up of information. Beginning in the 1970s, the fossil fuel industry launched a public relations campaign to silence or censor even the companies' own scientists warning about emissions effects, as well as provided support for scientists who voiced denials regarding human causes of climate change (Oreskes & Conway, 2010).

Attempts to deny the facts of climate change have also been supported by the Heartland Institute, a conservative think tank. In 2017, they sent 300,000 unsolicited copies of a book full of misinformation about climate change to science teachers throughout the United States. The 135-page book, *Why Scientists Disagree About Global Warming,* and the accompanying DVD, is full of misleading claims, logical fallacies, and cherry-picked data based mostly on citations from their own people (Kelly, 2017). Curt Stager (April 27, 2017), professor of natural sciences, explains, "The book is unscientific propaganda from authors with connections to the disinformation-machinery of the Heartland Institute." Strategic propaganda campaigns like this, focused on schoolteachers and funded by conservative think tanks with ties to the fossil fuel industry, require CML skills so students and teachers can deconstruct media messages and make sense of the facts. A powerful CML activity could involve students using the CML framework to compare and contrast the Heartland Institute publication with *The Teacher-Friendly Guide to Climate Change* published at the same time by the Paleontological Research Institute (Zabel, Duggan-Haas, & Ross, 2017). This activity can help students learn about the importance of climate change and also develop their critical thinking skills to analyze information. It is important that this inquiry delves beyond the idea that there are simply two different opinions on the topic and instead investigates how propaganda functions by selecting and framing the facts, language, and sources that position the audience about what to think and believe.

Fake News and Climate Change

Recent interest in "fake news" can be an opportunity for students to think critically about media, or it can be a dangerous ploy to confuse the public into thinking that there is just "fake news" contrasted to "real news." This false dichotomy tends to suggest that "fake news" is bad and "real news" is something we don't need to question because it is factual and objective. In between those two extremes lies much complexity and a need for critical engagement with all information, communication, and entertainment.

The term "fake news" became popular during the 2016 election, when it was used to describe hoaxes that went viral. These were reports people created and disseminated for the intended purpose of fooling the public for political and/or economic gains, such as the fictitious Pizzagate and the false Papal endorsement of candidate Trump. The *New York Times* has called fake news "a neologism to describe stories that are just not true," which they suggest has since been "co-opted to characterize unfavorable news" (Ember, 2017). Neal Gabler (2016) provides a more critical analysis, arguing that fake news is an attack on truth that is intended "to destroy truth altogether, to set us adrift in a world of belief without facts, a world in which there is no defense against lies." It is important to consider who would benefit from a post-truth era in which science and facts are free for any interpretation. In the absence of accountability for facts or evidence, it is highly likely that those who control the airwaves and algorithms will define reality and truth as best fits their interests.

"Fake news" and "alternative facts" can be devastating to issues in which understanding observable facts and knowing scientific evidence is essential, such as anthropocentric climate change. For decades scientists have reported the data, facts, and evidence that human-caused CO_2 emissions are increasing the temperature of our planet. And yet, a small powerful group of individuals have managed to create doubt in public perceptions with unfounded claims that ignore the scientific evidence. This false notion of a controversy and uncertainty, as Naomi Oreskes and Erik Conway (2010) describe in their book, *Merchants of Doubt*, is not simply misinformation; it is actually a well-organized campaign of disinformation. When the president of the United States makes claims that are obviously false and completely unsubstantiated (such as crowd sizes, illegal voting, and climate change denials), he challenges the power of truth and honesty that the rule of law is based on. When media outlets repeat and disseminate these lies, they contribute to undermining a key foundation of democracy. These are actions that if unchecked, and allowed to continue, can only benefit those in power by allowing them to choose the versions of reality that best meet their political and financial interests.

The most dangerous "fake news" being repeated in commercial media, social media, and now government-sponsored media is the denial of human-caused climate change. Transnational corporations have already spent billions buying rights to extract fossil fuels all over the world, something that will be devastating to our planet if it is allowed to continue. These multibillion-dollar companies stand to lose large amounts of money if they do not adapt their practices as countries shift to renewable energy. Even though extracting and burning fossil fuels has been proven to be the primary cause of global warming, these corporations are spending less of their fortunes on switching to cleaner renewable energy and more on trying to convince people that climate change is fake. This challenge to the truth could not be more important at this point to determine the fate of human civilization.

Therefore, an educational commitment to critical media literacy is essential for empowering students to critically question media and dominant ideologies, such as unregulated capitalism, overconsumption, fossil fuel dependency, and human exploitation of nature. Students at all grade levels can learn to search for truth through accessing multiple sources, triangulating different data, critically questioning the messages and the medium through which they travel, and then making informed decisions based on facts, evidence, and research. Critical media literacy can help educators and students see through the smoke screen of "fake news" and "alternative facts" to learn the truth about climate change and take action before it is too late.

Creating Media to Challenge the Problems

While social media and new technologies are often contributing to the problem, it is important to remember that they can also be tools we can use to create solutions. Employing humor and political satire to challenge the problematic way commercial media have framed climate change as an equal debate between two opposing positions, John Oliver (2014) challenges the imbalance in reporting by providing his own "mathematically representative climate change debate" (https://tinyurl. com/k5uslqx). During this episode of *Last Week Tonight*, Oliver invites three climate change deniers to debate 97 scientists and visually demonstrates the trouble with disproportionate reporting. This problem of "false balance," when reporting on climate change, was addressed by the *British Broadcasting Corporation* (*BBC*) in 2018, when they sent their journalists guidelines for how to report on climate change. The *BBC* policy states, "To achieve impartiality, you do not need to include outright deniers of climate change in BBC coverage, in the same way you would not have someone denying that Manchester United won 2-0 last Saturday. The referee has spoken" (Rosane, 2018).

During the 2016 Summer Olympics in Rio de Janeiro, *ExxonMobil* aired a deceptive television commercial that portrayed an environmentally conscious company "powering the world responsibly" (https:// tinyurl.com/j5lmm2x). In response to this attempt at greenwashing *Exxon*'s image, ClimateTruth.org created a parody video that exposes the hypocrisy of *Exxon*'s claims by remixing the same music and style of the original commercial with additional text that challenges their assertions of environmental responsibility (https://tinyurl.com/yd92h3no). Sharing these two short videos with students can be a powerful way to engage youth in critically analyzing media messages about the environment and the role of fossil fuel companies in contributing to the problems of climate change. The Climatetruth video can also be an excellent example of how students can become adbusters themselves and create their own media to challenge misleading attempts by industry and government to greenwash reality and deny the science about anthropomorphic climate change.

Using Digital Media to Participate in Civic Society

While adults may be accessing information about climate change through print or TV news, young people are more likely to obtain their news through online social media outlets, such as Twitter, Instagram, and YouTube (Anderson & Jiang, 2018; Newman et al., 2016). Given the popularity of social media for sharing information and ideas, students can use social media platforms to communicate their perspectives on climate change. Through the use of Twitter, Facebook, Instagram, TikTok, Snapchat, Pinterest, and other platforms, students can share narratives and videos with hashtags describing their specific actions for fostering sustainability.

Adolescents are increasingly turning to digital media to voice their perspectives on issues, as documented in the book *By Any Media Necessary: The New Youth Activism* (Jenkins et al., 2016) and the book by Parkland, Florida, students David Hogg and Lauren Hogg (2018) *#Never Again: A New Generation Draws the Line.* The skills students are learning by using social media in their participatory culture are potential resources and strategies for their participation in political actions and collective activism (Jenkins et al., 2016). Information communication technologies provide opportunities for youth and adults to connect, organize, and carry out actions to counter commercial media and politicians who are ignoring and/or denying the realities of climate science. Educators can be key players in this work, teaching students how to use literacy and technology to read and write the word and the world (Freire & Macedo, 1987).

Using a critical media literacy framework of conceptual understandings and questions, educators can encourage their students to ask critical questions about the messages they are hearing and seeing in media all around them. CML is an inquiry process that applies to all aspects of our lives because we live in such mediated societies in which public discourse always reflects ideological values and perspectives. We must help students question and respond to the messages, systems, and structures that are supported by ideologies of over-consumption, toxic patriarchy, and savage capitalism that are putting our survivability at risk.

Teachers in all subjects can make their content more meaningful and relevant by engaging with popular culture and current events. Incorporating movies, TV, music, social media, news reports, video games, photographs, and all types of media can make classrooms more engaging for students growing up in this media-saturated environment. However, simply using more media is not sufficient. As the public is becoming more accustomed to the media spectacle with infotainment and "alternative facts," educators need to guide their students to think critically about information and entertainment, analyze its construction, and evaluate its effects. Critical media literacy can be an ideal pedagogy to support teachers and students in their struggle to make sense of the messages and to create their own alternative media that can challenge the myths and support the facts.

References

Anderson, M., & Jiang, J. (2018). Teens, social media & technology 2018. *Pew Research Center.*

Aronoff, K. (2018, August 2). What the "New York Times" climate blockbuster got wrong. *The Nation.* Retrieved from https://www.thenation.com/article/new-york-times-climate-blockbuster-misses/

Berge, R., Cohen, B. (Producers), & Shenk, J. (Director). (2011). *The island president.* [Motion picture].New York, NY: Samuel Goldwyn Films.

Carrington, D. (2019, May 17). Why the Guardian is changing the language it uses about the environment. *The Guardian.* Retrieved from https://www.theguardian.com/environment/2019/may/17/why-the-guardian-is-changing-the-language-it-uses-about-the-environment

Common Core State Standards. (2015). *Common core state standards for English language arts & literacy in history/social studies, science, and technical subjects.* Common Core State Standards Initiative. Retrieved from http://tinyurl.com/kjgs8a5

Cooper, C. B. (2011). Media literacy as a key strategy toward improving public acceptance of climate change science. *BioScience, 61*(3), 231–237.

Coyle, K. (2005). Environmental literacy in America: What ten years of NEETF/Roper research studies say about environmental literacy in the U.S. *National Environmental Education and Training Foundation.* Retrieved from http://tinyurl.com/jk3jfkj

Dunaway, F. (2015). *Seeing green: The use and abuse of American environmental images.* Chicago, IL: The University of Chicago Press.

Ember, S. (2017, April 3). This is not fake news (but don't go by the headline). *New York Times, Education Life, EDTALK.* Retrieved from https://www.nytimes.com/2017/04/03/education/edlife/fake-news-and-media-literacy.html

Freire, P., & Macedo, D. (1987). *Literacy: Reading the word and the world.* Westport, CT: Bergin & Garvey.

Gabler, N. (2016, November 30). Who's really to blame for fake news? Look in the mirror, America. *Common Dreams.* Retrieved from http://www.commondreams.org/views/2016/11/30/whos-really-blame-fake-news-look-mirror-america

Hogg, D., & Hogg, L. (2018). *#Never again: A new generation draws the line.* New York, NY: Random House.

Jenkins, H., Shresthova, S., Gamber-Thompson, C., Kligler-Vilenchi, N., & Zimmerman, A. M. (2016). *By any media necessary: The new youth activism.* New York, NY: New York University Press.

Kalhoefer, K. (2016, April 25). Study: CNN viewers see far more fossil fuel advertising than climate change reporting. [Bog post]. Retrieved from http://tinyw.in/SZcr

Kalhoefer, K. (2017, March 23). How broadcast networks covered climate change in 2016. [Web log post]. Retrieved from https://tinyurl.com/yb4kyfcs

Kellner, D. (2003). *Media spectacle.* New York, NY: Routledge.

Kellner, D., & Share, J. (2019). *The critical media literacy guide: Engaging media and transforming education.* Leiden, The Netherlands: Brill/Sense Publishers.

Kelly, S. (2017, June 17). US senators deem Heartland Institute mailings to grade school science teachers "possibly fraudulent." *Truthout.org.* Retrieved from https://truthout.org/articles/us-senators-heartland-institute-mailings-to-grade-school-science-teachers-possibly-fraudulent/

Klein, N. (2014). *This changes everything: Capitalism vs. the climate.* New York, NY: Simon & Schuster.

López, A. (2014). *Greening media education: Bridging media literacy with green cultural citizenship.* New York, NY: Peter Lang Publishing.

Lewis, J., & Boyce, T. (2009). Climate change and the media: The scale of the challenge. In T. Boyce & J. Lewis (Eds.), *Climate change and the media* (pp. 1–16). New York, NY: Peter Lang Publishing.

McChesney, R. W. (2004). *The problem of the media: U.S. communication politics in the twenty-first century.* New York, NY: Monthly Review Press.

McChesney, R. W. (2015). *Rich media, poor democracy: Communication politics in dubious times.* New York, NY: The New Press.

MacDonald, T. (2019, May 8). ABC, NBC, and MSNBC prime-time shows ignored landmark UN report on biodiversity. *Media Matters for America.* [Blog]. Retrieved from https://www.mediamatters.org/blog/2019/05/08/ABC-NBC-and-MSNBC-prime-time-shows-ignored-landmark-UN-report-on-biodiversity/223644

MacDonald, T., & Hymans, L. (2019, March 11). How broadcast TV networks covered climate change in 2018. *Media Matters for America.* Retrieved from https://www.mediamatters.org/research/2019/03/11/How-broadcast-TV-networks-covered-climate-change-in-2018/223076

NASA (2019, February 6). 2018 fourth warmest year in continued warming trend, according to NASA, NOAA. Release 19-002. Retrieved from https://www.nasa.gov/press-release/2018-fourth-warmest-year-in-continued-warming-trend-according-to-nasa-noaa

Newman, N., Fletcher, R., Levy D. A. L., & Nielsen, R. K. (2016). *Reuters institute digital news report 2016.* New York, NY: Reuters. Retrieved from http://tinyw.in/AaiB

Nixon, R. (2011, June 26). Slow violence. [Blog post]. Retrieved from http://tinyw.in/zEt5

Nixon, R. (2013). *Slow violence and the environmentalism of the poor.* Cambridge, MA: Harvard University Press.

Oliver, J. (2014). Climate change debate. *Last Week Tonight with John Oliver* (HBO). [Video]. Retrieved from https://tinyurl.com/k5uslqx

Oreskes, N., & Conway, E. (2010). *Merchants of doubt: How a handful of scientists obscured the truth on issues from tobacco smoke to global warming.* New York, NY: Bloomsbury Press.

Perera, F. (2016, June 21). The case for a child-centered energy and climate policy. *Environmental Health News.* Retrieved from http://www.environmentalhealthnews.org/ehs/news/2016/june/opinion-the-case-for-a-child-centered-energy-and-climate-policy

Rich, N. (2018, August 1). Losing Earth: The decade we almost stopped climate change. *New York Times Magazine.* Retrieved from https://tinyurl.com/y8dojc43

Rosane, O. (2018, September 11). BBC issues first climate change reporting guidelines. *EcoWatch.* Retrieved from https://www.ecowatch.com/bbc-climate-change-reporting-guidelines-2603944755.html

Stager, C. (2017, April 27). Sowing climate doubt among schoolteachers. *New York Times,* Op-Ed. Retrieved from https://www.nytimes.com/2017/04/27/opinion/sowing-climate-doubt-among-schoolteachers.html?emc=eta1&_r=o

Zabel, I. H. H., Duggan-Haas, D., & Ross, R. M. (Eds.). (2017). *The teacher-friendly guide to climate change.* Ithaca, NY: Paleontological Research Institute. Retrieved from https://tinyurl.com/y7jmg3mq

Index

302   *Index*

knowledge interventions 67–71; domains of knowledge 70–71; facts *vs.* beliefs 67–68; information-based interventions 69; information *vs.* knowledge 68, **68**; knowledge-based interventions 69–70; *see also* media literacy

Korzenny, B. A. 114

Korzenny, F. 114

Kovach, B. 135

Kubey, R. 215

Lakoff, George 142

language: and Latino media 112–114; and Latino population in the U.S. 112–114

Lankshear, C. 42, 196, 260

Lantela, P. 217

Last Week Tonight 292

Latino-oriented media (LOM): and demographics 110–112; language 112–114; and news literacy 109–117; overview 114–116; radio stations 115; social media 116; Telemundo 115; television networks 115; Univision 115

Latino population (United States): democracy 116–117; demographics 110–112; governance 116–117; language 112–114

LATV 115

Law of Transparency and Right to Access Public Information in Colombia *see* Transparency Law

Lay, Carol 95

Lee, Sir Desmond 137–139

Lesufi, Panyaza 122–123, 124, 127–130

Leu, D. J. 196

Levine, Peter 178–179

Lévy, Pierre 258, 259, 261

Lewis, J. 215, 286

Lewis, R. 176

lies: *vs.* deception 136; defined 136; political deceptions 136–137

Lind, R. 213

Linvill, Darren 99

Lippmann, Walter 137

Lipset, Seymour Martin 138

listening (literacies): face-to-face 263; and participatory culture 262

literacies: collecting 258–260; for "consensus cultures" 257–258; creating through doing 264–265;

curating 260–261; feeling 263–264; listening 261–263; of participatory cultures 257–269; to unlearn 265–269

Livingstone, S. 30, 197, 198

López, Antonio 283

Lord, C. 146

Los Angeles Times 81

"Losing Earth: The Decade We Almost Stopped Climate Change" 287

Lotan, Gilad 97

Luntz, Frank 141–142

Lupia, Arthur 146

Maksl, A. 81, 182–183, 184

mal-information 177

Malone, T. W. 267, 268

Marr, B. 258

Martens, H. 275

Martin, A. 197

Martin, K. 217, 222

Marwick, A. 176

Massive Open Online Course (MOOC): described 198–199; as tool for teaching media literacy 204

Massive Open Online Course (MOOC) for media literacy 194–207; definition of media literacy 196–197; and grounded theory 199; media literacy education and assessment 197–198; "media responsibility" 202; "media user responsibility" 202; MOOCs, described 198–199; overview 194–195; participants' learning lessons 202–203; research findings 201–203; research method 199–201

"The Mass Media and Me" course 212, 222–223

Masterman, L. 11, 41, 157

Mattis, James 99

Mayer-Schönberger, Viktor 37

McCracken, Derek 262

McKay, Adam 141

McLuhan, Marshall 14, 17, 39

mecosystem 274–275

media activism 277–279

media and information literacy (MIL) 39, 42; and Transparency Law 242

Media and Manipulation (Marwick and Lewis) 176

media citizenship 273

/>